P9-CMA-221

NORTH AMERICA

Country Inns
and Back Roads

"Why should not the New Englander be in search of new adventures?"
THOREAU: *Walden*

NORTH AMERICA
Country Inns and Back Roads

23rd Year—Revised Annually
1988–89

New England, West Coast,
Canada, Middle Atlantic, South, Midwest,
Rocky Mountains

Norman T. Simpson

The Berkshire Traveller

PERENNIAL LIBRARY

HARPER & ROW, PUBLISHERS, New York
Cambridge, Philadelphia, San Francisco, Washington
London, Mexico City, São Paulo, Singapore, Sydney

TRAVEL BOOKS BY NORMAN T. SIMPSON

Country Inns and Back Roads, North America
Country Inns and Back Roads, Britain and Ireland
Country Inns and Back Roads, Continental Europe
Bed and Breakfast, American Style

COVER PAINTING: Beaumont Inn, Harrodsburg, Kentucky, by Wooster Bard Field
DRAWINGS: Janice Lindstrom

COUNTRY INNS AND BACK ROADS, NORTH AMERICA: 1988–89 (*23rd Edition*). Copyright ©
1988 by Harper & Row, Publishers, Inc. All rights reserved. Printed in the United States of
America. No part of this book may be used or reproduced in any manner whatsoever without
written permission except in the case of brief quotations embodied in critical articles and
reviews. For information address Harper & Row, Publishers, Inc., 10 East 53rd Street, New
York, N.Y. 10022. Published simultaneously in Canada by Fitzhenry & Whiteside Limited,
Toronto.

ISSN: 70-615664
ISBN: 0-06-096272-0

88 89 90 91 92 RRD 10 9 8 7 6 5 4 3 2 1

Contents

CANADA

WEST INDIES

Preface

Before this book went to press I was browsing through some of the earlier editions, particularly those in the late 1960s and the early 1970s. I enjoyed rereading the accounts of my first visits to many inns that are still included in the book. In those days it was necessary to define what a country inn was. The great value of the book lay in the fact that it told everyone where they were. Country inns were just not well known in those days.

Today that is all turned around. There has been a significant proliferation of inns, whether they are full-service, offering both lodgings and meals, or bed-and-breakfast inns. As a result, the governing standards of this book have naturally become highly selective, and only inns of mature experience and proven capabilities have been included.

Almost from the very beginning, in 1966, each inn in this book became a member of an informal innkeeping association through which each was vigorously encouraged to maintain the highest standards.

This small association of innkeepers that I formed many years ago has become a full-fledged, hard-working group, now named the Country Inns and Back Roads Innkeepers' Association. (Most of the inns in this book are dues-paying members.) The association has been incorporated and has a "hands-on" board of directors whose enthusiasm and involvement ensure the ideals and objectives for which we are all striving.

Association members are encouraged to attend regional meetings held twelve to fifteen times a year throughout North America. In addition, an international meeting is held each year, to which inns (hotels) in Great Britain and Europe are invited.

Work-study seminars are arranged in England and Europe as well as seminars in the West Indies or a similar location.

The association has successfully established a "twin inn" program, which pairs North American inns with British, Irish, and European inns (hotels). This program has met with excellent response, and owners on both sides of the Atlantic are adding their own touches.

In my evaluation of the important qualities that I am delighted to find in an inn, I look for a distinct personal involvement with guests on the part of the innkeepers and their staffs; the rudiments of good innkeeping, which include clean, comfortable guest rooms furnished with individuality; an imaginative menu with good, well-prepared food; and an atmosphere that encourages guests to become acquainted with each other.

In the decision as to which of the many applicants to include, one of the determining factors is enthusiasm for holding to the high ideals and standards which the inns themselves have set for the past twenty-two years.

Twenty-two, or even 122, years have not seen any changes in the fundamentals of good innkeeping, although most of today's innkeepers are families who have sought out innkeeping as a second career. In many cases they moved their own family heirlooms and personal furniture into the inn and are sharing them with their guests. Each inn is a highly individual enterprise reflecting the philosophies, tastes, and enthusiasms of the innkeepers and their families. That's one of the great reasons why inns continue to grow in popularity each year.

In much the same way that staying at inns is a different experience from staying at commercial, impersonal hotels or motels, so is the attitude of the inn guest different from that of the motel traveler. The ideal inn guest is someone who values the qualities offered by a country inn, and who contributes to that ambience with his or her own consideration and friendliness. When visiting an inn, think of yourself as a guest in the home of a good friend—in the smaller, more intimate inns becoming friends with the innkeepers and their family is a distinct possibility. And there is always the opportunity to make friends with other inn guests.

So that the reader can see just how long each inn has been a part of *Country Inns and Back Roads,* after the heading of each write-up we have inserted the date the inn was first included in the book. As you will see, quite a few inns go back to the early years.

I am most fortunate to have the services of my colleague, Virginia Rowe, to assist in the task of editing the accounts of visits to inns. As some of you may already know, we also have *Country Inns and Back Roads, Britain and Ireland* and *Country Inns and Back Roads, Continental Europe.* These are revised every other year. A fourth book, *Bed & Breakfast, American Style,* contains at least 400 recommendations for B&B establishments in North America. This is revised yearly.

With this edition, we are including a listing of rates in the Index. Space limitations preclude a more than general range of rates for each inn, and these should not be considered firm quotations. Please check with the inn for their various rates and special packages.

Here are some basic guidelines for reservations and cancellations at most of the inns listed in this book:

A deposit is required for a confirmed reservation. Guests are requested to please note arrival and departure dates carefully. The deposit will be forfeited if the guest arrives after date specified or departs before final date of reservation. Refund will be made only if cancelled from 7 to 14 days (depending upon the policy of the individual inn) in advance of arrival date and a service charge will be deducted from the deposit.

It must be understood that a deposit ensures that your accommodations will be available as confirmed and also assures the inn that the accommodations are sold as confirmed. Therefore, when situations arise necessitating your cancellation in fewer than the allowed number of days in advance, your deposit will not be refunded.

Stockbridge, Massachusetts
February 15, 1988

To our readers in Great Britain and other countries in Europe:

Welcome to North America! Many of you are making your first visit and we're delighted that you'll be experiencing some of the *real* United States and Canada by visiting these country inns. Incidentally, all of them will be very happy to help you make arrangements and reservations at other inns in the book.

Romantik Hotels

Many readers have undoubtedly noticed that during the past few years I have occasionally put the words "Romantik Hotels" in parenthesis in the paragraph containing the basic information about an inn. Romantik Hotels is a voluntary association of well-known historical hotels, each under personal management of the owner. There are Romantik Hotels located in ten European countries as well as those in North America. They are chosen for individuality as well as on the basis of high quality of the lodgings and excellence of the food. There has always been a great deal of comradeship between the *CIBR* inns and those Romantik Hotels in Europe.

A number of inns have nearby airports where private planes may land, and further information may be obtained directly from each inn. We have indicated those inns near such airports by putting the following symbol at the end of each inn's directions.

MONTREAL

Inn on the Common,
● Craftsbury Common

■ BURLINGTON

Philbrook Farm, Shelburne●
Spalding Inn,
ST. JOHNSBURY ■   ● Whitefield

V E R M O N T

Lovett's, Franconia   NORTH CONWAY
●
Rockhouse Mountain Farm, Eaton Cent●
Darby Field Inn, Conway ●
Stafford's-In-The-Field, Chocorua ●

Blueberry Hill Farm,
Goshen   Shire Inn, Chelsea ● Lyme Inn, Lyme
Brookside Farms, ● ●
Orwell ● Mountain Top Inn, Chittenden   ● Moose Mountain Lodge, Etna
RUTLAND ■   ■ HANOVER
Middletown Springs● Inn,   ● Hickory Stick
Middletown Springs   The Corner House Inn, Farm, Laconia
The Governor's Inn, Ludlow ●   Center Sandwich
                ● Inn at Weathersfield, Weathersfield
        Village Inn, Landgrove
            ● Rowell's Inn, Simonsville ● Dexter's Inn, Sunapee
        ● Birch Hill Inn, Manchester   N E W   ■ CONCORD
West ●   ● Three Mountain Inn,
Mountain Inn,   Jamaica H A M P S H I R E
Arlington   ● ● Colby Hill Inn, Henniker
Old Newfane Inn, Newfane
        Inn at Crotched Mt., Francestown
Inn at Sawmill Farm,   ●
West Dover ●   John Hancock Inn, Hancock

        ● Birchwood Inn, Temple

Northern New England

Eastern Time Zone

MAINE

CALAIS

● Country Club Inn, *Rangeley*

■ BANGOR

● Waterford Inne,
  E. Waterford

The Crocker House Country Inn, *Hancock Point*

The Pentagoet Inn, *Castine* Grey Rock Inn,
Northeast Harbor

Whitehall Inn, *Camden*

Claremont Inn,
Southwest Harbor

Squire Tarbox,
Westport Island

Goose Cove Lodge,
Pilgrim's Inn, *Deer Isle*

Homewood Inn,
Yarmouth

Bradley Inn, *New Harbor*

Charmwoods, *Naples*

PORTLAND ■

Black Point Inn, *Prouts Neck*

Captain Lord, Old Fort Inn, *Kennebunkport*

Hartwell House, *Ogunquit*

Dockside Guest Quarters, *York*

BIRCH HILL INN
Manchester, Vermont (1982)

Life takes some interesting twists and turns, doesn't it? For many, many years I used to drive north from Stockbridge on Route 7 to Manchester, Vermont, and then turn left at the Johnny Appleseed Bookstore, taking a shortcut around Manchester Center to reach Route 30 and continue on west to Dorset, and up the valley of the Mettowee through Pawlet on up to Lake St. Catherine.

I'm sure that almost every time I took this Manchester shortcut I was attracted to a very large, handsome white house that sat on a rise in a grove of trees. In the winter the snow would be shoveled out and piled high around the entrance, which was reached by a circular driveway. I used to imagine what kind of people lived in that house and what the interior was like.

In 1981 I learned that my lovely white house had indeed become an intimate inn. In the course of events I visited it and met Pat and Jim Lee, who were then new innkeepers, and I subsequently included it in the 1982 edition of this book. Pat's family has lived in that house since 1917, so the chances are I may have seen various members of the family outside as I passed to and from en route.

The interior is every bit as attractive as the exterior. For example, there are windows on three sides of the living room, which has a wonderful warm feeling, aided by a low ceiling, a sizeable fireplace, a spinet piano, the ongoing, never-ending jigsaw puzzle, and innumerable books and magazines. Over the big fireplace is a print of George Washington's triumphal entry into New York City after the Revolutionary War.

For 190 years Birch Hill was a family home and today it has retained that same homelike feeling. It's obvious that the Lee family has a great deal of interest in art, music and history.

Accommodations are in five comfortable and cheerful guest rooms in the main house, all of which have views toward the mountains, farm, and pond. They are well decorated with paintings and furniture from the family home. A nearby cottage on the grounds has been converted into an ideal family-style accommodation as well.

Dinner is offered only to houseguests every night except Wednesday and Sunday, and I was most interested in what Pat Lee had to say about the "Beefalo" that she often serves. "Beefalo," she explained, "is a breed of cattle originally developed by the introduction of American bison (buffalo) genes into domestic cattle. Beefalo meat contains less than 15% of the fat of supermarket beef, and only 3% of the cholesterol.

"We have small steers and heifers here in the fields around the inn. They are always a great source of conversation among our guests."

One of the things that I enjoy at Birch Hill Inn is the custom of having the guests sit down around the big table together and really get acquainted By the way, Pat serves a full breakfast every morning.

The well-groomed cross-country ski trails start out right from the inn's property and continue over hill and through the woods. These become excellent jogging or running trails at other times of the year.

In summertime there's good swimming and a trout pond, where the fish are reproducing at such a rate that guests can bring them back to the inn to be cooked for breakfast.

I think it's wonderful that my beautiful white house has become an inn that I can share.

BIRCH HILL INN, Box 346, West Rd., Manchester, VT 05254; 802-362-2761. A 5-guestroom (all private baths) extremely comfortable country-home inn, with a family cottage, 5 min. from downtown Manchester Center. Modified American plan includes dinner and breakfast. B&B plan available. Dinners offered to houseguests only, every night except Wed. and Sun. Open after Christmas to mid-April, and May to late Oct.; 2-night minimum preferred (be sure to make reservations). Swimming pool, xc skiing, trout fishing, and walking trails on grounds. Alpine skiing at major areas nearby as well as tennis and golf facilities; great biking. Children over 6 welcome. No pets. No credit cards. Pat and Jim Lee, Innkeepers. (See Index for rates.)

Directions: From Manchester Center, where Rtes. 7, 7A, and 30 meet, take Rte. 30 north 2 mi. to Manchester West Rd. Turn left on West Rd. and continue ¾ mi. to Birch Hill Inn. 🛶

The date in parenthesis in the heading represents the first year the inn appeared in the pages of Country Inns and Back Roads.

BLUEBERRY HILL
Goshen, Vermont (1973)

I first visited Tony Clark at Blueberry Hill in midsummer of 1972, when the idea of opening up an inn exclusively for cross-country skiers was just taking shape in his mind. It became a reality the following year, and, as I guess all of New England knows, Tony was an innovator in what has become a very popular winter pastime. Today, most inns in New England, or in fact anywhere in the mountains, have some kind of cross-country skiing facilities on the premises or nearby.

In the meantime, Tony has continued to look for new paths to follow. Let me put it in his words:

"As you know, we are open for skiing from December through March. But, May through October, and especially summertime here in the Green Mountains is just fabulous. We're very popular with summer and fall backpackers and walkers. Many, many of our cross-country trails are used for walking and hiking, and it's possible to use the inn as a central point for such activities or to include it on an itinerary. We use our ski trails as nature and educational paths, providing all kinds of guides to help our guests learn the names of the trees and birds."

"Actually," he said, pronouncing it as only a native-born Britisher can, "we have a lot of other summertime activities here, including a kite flying weekend during the second week in September. There are all kinds of kite contests, and with this wonderful open field immediately across from the inn, it's ideal for such activity. We also have a Mozart festival and a chamber music festival in the offing.

"I think the biggest attraction in summer is the peace, quiet, and fresh air. These are some luxuries that we sometimes take for granted—the luxury of fresh air, clean water, and no noise pollution—which are pretty special to people who live in cities."

Blueberry Hill is very definitely family style. Everyone sits around the big dining room table, and there is one main dish for each meal, cooked in the farmhouse kitchen. This main dish is likely to be something quite unusual, depending upon the cook's gourmet proclivities.

Bedrooms are plain and simple with hot water bottles on the backs of doors and handsome patchwork quilts on the beds. It is truly like visiting a Vermont farm.

In late July, to continue the summer saga, there has been an annual cross-country footrace and Blueberry Festival. The course covers ten kilometers on the paved and gravel roads, leading the runner down through the cool, shaded heart of Goshen, up a series of hills, and back through the woods and pastures, with beautiful views of the Green Mountains. Following the race, the Blueberry Festival, open to competitors and spectators alike, features a chicken barbecue with salads, homemade breads, and blueberry baked goods. An old-time square dance wraps up the festivities.

In June, Blueberry Hill hosts the annual Vermont croquet competition, and all competitors are asked to wear whites.

"As far as the cross-country skiing season is concerned, there is a ski touring center right across the road from the inn, which has a waxing area, repair shop, and an expert staff. There are seventy-five kilometers of trails with both challenging and moderate terrain."

Blueberry Hill is an unforgettable experience, whether it's early-morning coffee in the greenhouse, a day-long ski tour, or a romantic evening of relaxation in front of a roaring fire. There is great fishing, hiking, biking, and tennis nearby and always a refreshing dip in the pond.

Reservations for winter accommodations should be made as early as possible, as the inn is often booked solid for weeks at a time in winter.

BLUEBERRY HILL, Goshen, VT 05733; 802-247-6735. An 8-guestroom (private baths) mountain inn passionately devoted to xc skiing, 8 mi. from Brandon. Modified American plan for overnight guests. Open from May thru Oct and Dec. to March. Public dining by reservation only. Closed Christmas. Wheelchair access. Swimming, fishing, hiking, nature walks, and xc skiing on grounds. Much other recreation nearby. Tony Clark, Innkeeper. (See Index for rates.)

Directions: At Brandon, travel east on Rte. 73 through Forest Dale. Then follow signs to Blueberry Hill.

BROOKSIDE FARMS
Orwell, Vermont (1987)

I cannot begin to tell you how many times in the last twenty years my imagination has been inspired when I've driven by the shimmering white Ionic columns and the neo-classic Greek revival buildings of Brookside Farms. Each time I've reflected on what a beautiful country inn it would make.

Then I discovered that Brookside indeed has now become just that. I immediately made an unannounced visit, and innkeepers Joan and Murray Korda couldn't have been more gracious. Joan is a very attractive woman, and her penchant for music and art is noticeable, not only in the interior decorations of the inn but also in her conversation. Not incidentally, she is also the cook. Murray Korda is an internationally known concert violinist, and when he's not sharing the innkeeping duties with Joan, he's giving concerts throughout the world, as evidenced by numerous posters and photographs that have publicized his many appearances.

Naturally, our conversation turned to the house. "There are nineteen Ionic columns, twenty-seven feet high around the front of the house," Murray told me. "Actually, there are two houses. The first house was built in 1789, and a second was built in 1843. You can see where the two of them were joined."

Elegantly furnished guest rooms are located in the main house. The restored 1810 guest house has a guest suite on the first floor, along with its own Keeping Room and parlor, and is an excellent example of a Federal farmhouse. On the second floor are four guest rooms of assorted sizes with authentic country wallpaper and appropriate country furniture.

"When our guests arrive we welcome them with a board of cheese and crackers and fresh fruit," Joan said. "We have a single entrée every night, and our main dishes include chicken grenadine, beef Stroganoff, prime roast beef, and various Hungarian dishes because Murray is Hungarian. As far as breakfast is concerned, we'll prepare whatever our guests desire."

The talk drifted to things to do in the Orwell area, which is not far from Lake Champlain. "We have our own cross-country ski trails on 300 acres here," Murray said. "Some of our guests like to ski early in the morning, so Joan keeps a great big iron kettle with hefty soups in it all winter long. We also have hot cider and hot chocolate, and there's always a fire roaring in the fireplaces."

"Much time is spent right here in the dining room, because what Murray and I enjoy the most about innkeeping is getting acquainted with our guests," Joan told me. "Murray speaks seven languages fluently, and with his knowledge of Europe and his involvement in many things, including antiques, archeology, and history, along with our extensive travels, we have a variety of things to talk about."

There are wonderful old trees, some with nine-foot diameters; Hampshire sheep and Hereford cattle graze in the pasture, and two blue herons and many Canada geese sojourn on the 26-acre pond behind the 1810 barns.

There is so much more to tell about Brookside Farms; however, my main message is that this truly elegant, artistically oriented environment offers a really memorable country-inn experience.

BROOKSIDE FARMS, Hwy. 22A, Orwell, VT 05760; 802-948-2727. A 6-guestroom (some shared baths) country estate in western Vermont near Lake Champlain. Breakfast included in room rate. Dinner available to houseguests only. Open year-round. Wheelchair access. Ski trails and antique shop on grounds. The Shelburne Museum, Morgan Horse Farm, Frog Hollow Crafts Center, Sheldon Museum, and Fort Ticonderoga nearby. Children welcome. No credit cards. Joan and Murray Korda, Innkeepers. (See Index for rates.)

Directions: Rte. 22A is the relatively undiscovered highway that starts near New York City. Near Granville, New York, 22A continues in Vermont on the east side of Lake Champlain.

THE GOVERNOR'S INN
Ludlow, Vermont (1987)

What a perfectly splendid mid-September day for me to visit the Governor's Inn! The roads weren't crowded, and there were sudden bursts of orange, yellow, and red amid the backdrop of greenery covering the hills and valleys.

Deedy Marble met me at the front door of the inn, and as she showed me to my guest room on the second floor, she pointed out five generations of family photographs along the staircase. My bedroom had a beautiful brass head and footboard that had been in Deedy's family for over 100 years. The furnishings and decorations were pure Victorian, with the exception of two watercolors by artist Virginia Ann Holt, whose work is also found throughout the inn.

Some of the amenities include the option of a morning tray of coffee and sparkling Mimosa delivered to your room, some special Governor's Inn chocolates, and in the hallway a "butler's basket" of necessities for guests who forgot toothbrushes, toothpaste, and the like. By the way, my bed was turned down at night and my towels had been changed.

"You've missed our complimentary three o'clock tea for our house-guests," Deedy scolded me, laughingly. "But that's your own fault. It is served on our beautiful Victorian silver service. We actually have second- and third-time guests who try to get here in time for tea. It's a wonderful way to begin a country visit. It gives you a chance to meet the other guests."

Although I missed tea, I was still in ample time to join the other guests in the "front room." Deedy introduced all of us and we were soon chatting away about what a wonderful time of year it was to be in upper New England. We were then individually escorted to our tables in the candlelit dining room by one of the turn-of-the-century-clad waitresses. Deedy, who is an artist-cum-chef, described the six-course dinner. As each course was served, the dish was again described, in much the same way it is done at the Old Rittenhouse Inn in upper Wisconsin.

Whether there are five courses or six, dinner always begins with cream cheese and the Governor's sauce (the only recipe, incidentally, not included in the inn's delightfully refreshing cookbook). I don't see how any guest could leave the inn without a jar of this sauce, which is available for purchase.

Here are a few brief hints on the menu: Appetizers include mushroom strudel or marinated fish l'orange or steak strips with horseradish cream. Some of the main dishes are Lamb Gourmet, bluefish flambé, and Village Inn Steak Diane. These are augmented by intriguing side dishes. Desserts include chocolate walnut pie and peach ice with raspberry melba sauce.

If all of these seem to be a bit unusual it's because both Deedy and

Charlie (he does the wonderful breakfasts) are passionately devoted to cookery. They have attended cooking schools in France, and their skills are evident in the menu.

Another of their innovations is the gourmet picnic hampers, for which the Governor's Inn has now become rather well known.

This brief account of the Governor's Inn has not done justice to this handsomely restored and preserved Victorian mansion, built by a governor of Vermont in 1890. It is beautifully furnished with family antiques and all the appointments and decorations are done with impeccable taste. However, I did want to leave sufficient room to say that there are many qualities about the Governor's Inn that will delight both confirmed and novice inn-goers. Among these are devoted attention to detail, dedication to making certain that guests' needs are met, and, perhaps best of all, a sincere, deep-rooted desire to bring loving care to everyone.

THE GOVERNOR'S INN, 86 Main St., Ludlow, VT 05149; 802-228-8830. An 8-guestroom (private baths) village inn in central Vermont. Modified American plan includes dinner, breakfast, and afternoon tea. Open all year. Downhill skiing at Okemo Mountain and cross-country skiing nearby. Conveniently located to enjoy all of the rich recreational, cultural, and historical attractions in central Vermont. No facilities for small children or pets. Charlie and Deedy Marble, Innkeepers. (See Index for rates.)

Directions: Ludlow is conveniently reached from all of the north-south roads in Vermont. It is located just off the village green, where Rte. 100 crosses Rte. 103.

INN AT SAWMILL FARM
West Dover, Vermont (1970)

It was mid-November. The southern Vermont sky was lowering, and all around me were signs and portents of snow. I was driving north from Dalton, Massachusetts, on Route 8A to the Mount Snow area in Wilmington, Vermont. This road goes through some most interesting northern Massachusetts and southern Vermont country with many villages. I was headed toward Sawmill Farm in West Dover, Vermont, and the reports on the radio indicated that snow was, indeed, on the way. Just imagine being snowbound at Sawmill Farm! Boy, oh boy!

With Wilmington behind me, I could now see the buildings of Sawmill Farm on my left. My last turn was over the bridge, which had been reconstructed since a previous visit.

I asked Rod Williams what he would do if all the guests were snowbound. "We would try to amuse them by getting everyone out to cross-country ski," he said. "If you can walk, you can cross-country ski. It's not like downhill. We can even start off with people who have never been on skis. Then we would organize picnics on the trails. We'd keep the fire in the fireplace going bigger and better than ever, and normally we would do tea at four o'clock, but on a snowbound day we start around one."

When Rod and Ione Williams made the "big break" from the pressures of urban life, they brought their own particular talents and sensitivities to this handsome location, and it is indeed a pleasing experience. There was plenty of work to do — a dilapidated barn, a wagon shed, and other outbuildings all had to be converted into lodgings and living rooms. However, over the years, the transition has been exceptional. The textures of the barn siding, the beams, the ceilings, the floors, and the picture windows combine to create a feeling of rural elegance.

Guest rooms have been both added and redecorated, and again I was smitten with the beautiful quilted bedspreads, the bright wallpaper and white ceilings, the profusion of plants in the rooms, and all of the many books and magazines that add to their guests' enjoyment. Lodgings are also found in outbuildings, including the Cider House Studio, which has a bedroom, dressing room, bath, and living room. The king-sized bed is in an alcove facing a fireplace.

In the living room of the inn there is a superb conversation piece that perhaps symbolizes the entire inn—a handsome brass telescope mounted on a tripod, providing an intimate view of Mount Snow rising majestically to the north.

Brill Williams, Rod and Ione's son, was a teenager when the family moved to West Dover. Now, he is the chef and officially one of the owners of the inn. The menu selection and quality of the food has been praised by many national restaurant and food reviewers. The menu changes with the seasons; for example, the fall menu includes grilled marinated duck breasts, backfin crabmeat, fillet of salmon, and a rack of lamb for two. Appetizers include clams Casino, backfin crabmeat cocktail, and cold poached salmon.

With a picture-book Vermont setting like this, accommodations like these, and an almost inexhaustible supply of ideas for sumptuous dining, the idea of being snowbound at the Inn at Sawmill Farm certainly had a great deal of appeal for me.

INN AT SAWMILL FARM, Box 8, West Dover, VT 05356; 802-464-8131. A 26-guestroom country resort-inn on Rte. 100, 22 mi. from Bennington and Brattleboro. Within sight of Mt. Snow ski area. Modified American plan omits lunch. Breakfast and dinner served to travelers daily. Closed Nov. 29 to Dec. 18. Swimming, tennis, and trout fishing on grounds. Golf, bicycles, riding, snowshoeing, alpine and xc skiing nearby. No children under 8. No pets. No credit cards. Rodney, Brill, and Ione Williams, Innkeepers. (See Index for rates.)

Directions: From I-91, take Brattleboro Exit 2 and travel on Vt. Rte. 9 west to Vt. Rte. 100. Proceed north 5 mi. to inn. Or take U.S. 7 north to Bennington, then Rte. 9 east to Vt. Rte. 100 and proceed north 5 mi. to inn.

THE INN AT WEATHERSFIELD
Weathersfield, Vermont (1982)

English hoteliers and innkeepers have a wonderful phrase that describes how they take care of their guests. It is "looking after." Isn't that a wonderful expression! Somehow or other it seems to summarize succinctly what inns are really trying to do, and which some inns accomplish with considerable grace.

The Inn at Weathersfield is a case in point. Ron and Mary Louise Thorburn are very models of innkeepers who "look after" their guests exceptionally well. The inn has a great many of the readily identifiable physical attributes—an ancient building that started as a farmhouse nearly two centuries ago, a history that includes a role as part of the Underground Railroad, an exceptional and bucolic setting in the Vermont mountains, seven fireplaces, and an 18th-century brick beehive bake oven in working order.

Of course, all of these are important, but it is really Ron and Mary Louise who draw people together and provide the generous dollops of congeniality and caring that make a Weathersfield stay so enjoyable.

Please allow me to share with you a translation from Elisabeth Szgeti's article in the French magazine *La Monde,* as a result of her visit a few years ago:

"Gourmet kitchen aromas, four shaggy dogs stretched all over the carpet at the entrance, a big wooden house where Mary Louise and Ron reign. They felt too young to retire and needed the fresh excitement of new faces and the daily accomplishments of a certain sophistication.

"Mary Louise said that spring at the Weathersfield starts around the twenty-first of April, and 'we begin to see a glimmer of bulbs coming through the ground. It's the beginning of the drama, with the trees coming into early leaf and soon after we have lilacs and daffodils and tulips.'

"I have on my mantelpiece in Paris a miniature ceramic picture created by Heather Thorburn, which I received, as do all the guests at Weathersfield, as I was leaving."

Those gourmet aromas mentioned come from Mary Louise's hand, and might be her duck breast in cranberry-orange sauce or pork tenderloin with white wine and mustard, among a long list of great dishes.

The inn is constantly growing and expanding, and includes an aerobic exercise room with two stationary bicycles, a rowing machine, and a Nordic cross-country track exerciser. There is also a slant board, exercise weights, a barre, and a sauna. "This is to satisfy our many guests who enjoy the country but also like to continue on a regular exercise program," Mary Louise said.

There are many places for quiet conversation and reading in the inn, but my favorite is a little front parlor, with a whole corner bookshelf filled with all kinds of novels and books about interests and enthusiasms that I associate with country inn innkeepers and their guests—music, art, sports, theater, history, cuisine. While I was reading Gibbons, Mary Louise came in with a cup of hot cider.

Yes, guests are certainly "looked after" at the Inn at Weathersfield.

THE INN AT WEATHERSFIELD, Route 106 (near Perkinsville), Weathersfield, VT 05151; 802-263-9217. A 17-guestroom Vermont country inn a few mi. west of I-91 and north of Springfield. European plan, with breakfast and a high English tea included in the cost of the room. Dinner also served. Closed for dinner Sun., Mon., and Tues. (although also available on those evenings during the high season). Horseshoes, badminton, croquet, billiards, sauna, exercise room, sleigh riding on grounds. Also a natural amphitheater with music and theater offered during the summer. Many footpaths and back roads. Bicycles available. Berry and apple picking, golf, downhill skiing (Ascutney and Okemo), xc skiing, horseback riding nearby. Children under 8 years old are not conveniently accommodated. No pets. Mary Louise and Ron Thorburn, Innkeepers. (See Index for rates.)

Directions: Traveling north on I-91, use Exit 7 at Springfield and follow Rte. 106. Traveling south, take Exit 8 and follow Rte. 131 to Rte. 106 and turn south. From Boston, leave I-89 and follow Rte. 103 across New Hampshire west into Vermont, where it becomes Rte. 131, and then go south on Rte. 106.

THE INN ON THE COMMON
Craftsbury Common, Vermont (1976)

"We have doubled the size of our cross-country ski trail network. We now have a trail system that will link village-to-village to the Nordic Center. There are all types of terrain—something suitable for any level and a trail system big enough so that it will take the average skier many days to explore it."

Penny and Michael Schmitt of the Inn on the Common were enthusiastically outlining some of the improvements and additions at the inn, which is very close to the Nordic Center, a major cross-country ski center. "As of last fall, we have seventy-five kilometers of groomed and tracked trails, and an additional fifty kilometers of trails marked for back-country touring." This from Michael.

Penny and Michael Schmitt left New York City early in the 1970s and decided to start an entirely new way of life by opening an inn in Craftsbury Common, a beautiful Vermont hill-town, north and west of St. Johnsbury. They had been summering in this section of the state for many years, so the area was most familiar.

According to their brochure (please do not hesitate to write for one), the Inn on the Common is located in a beautiful, peaceful, unspoiled New England town. Each of the three inn buildings dates from the early 19th century and has been handsomely restored. The guest rooms are filled with antiques, folk art, original art, lovely wallpapers, hooked rugs, and custom quilts in wonderful colors. A complete turn-down service is provided, including a change of those big, fluffy towels.

At dinnertime guests are seated at three oval tables and, as the result of a very pleasant pre-dinner social hour, by the time the first course is served almost everybody is acquainted.

Guests get a choice at dinner of first courses and entrées. Penny told me that she has located a great deal of locally raised food. "In addition to vegetables," she said, "we now have quail and lamb raised for us as well as pheasant. A great deal of Provimi veal is raised in Vermont. Our fish supplier brings us superbly fresh fish, ranging from blue-fin tuna to mahi mahi. Among the choices are scallops with herbs and white wine and cream, and chicken served in a spicy wine and nut sauce garnished with shrimp and tomato."

Recognizing that more and more guests are enjoying longer stays, Michael and Penny have, in recent years, provided an expanding program of outdoor recreation that includes a swimming pool, tennis court, and English croquet in summer, extensive walking trails, and cross-country skiing and other outdoor sports in the winter.

For the guests who prefer a contemplative vacation, the bookshelves are most generously stocked with best sellers and mysteries, and the guest lounge with a fireplace is equipped with a library of films on tape. There is also a lovely garden that I have written about many times in the past.

In talking about the inn, Penny said, "People feel good about the inn and good about themselves when surrounded by beauty. Our wonderful, experienced staff backs this up with super food and attentive, caring service. The net result of all this seems to be more and happier guests than ever before, and I think that is what this business is all about. One important plus to that—Michael and I still love our work."

THE INN ON THE COMMON, Craftsbury Common, VT 05827; 802-586-9619. An 18-guestroom resort-inn in a peaceful Vermont town, 35 mi. from Montpelier. Modified American plan omits lunch. Breakfast and dinner served to houseguests only. Open 365 days a year. Swimming, tennis, croquet, xc skiing, snowshoeing on grounds. Golf, tennis, swimming, sailing, horseback riding, canoeing, fishing, xc and downhill skiing, skating, hiking, and nature walks nearby. Attended pets allowed. Michael and Penny Schmitt, Innkeepers. (See Index for rates.)

Directions: From the south take I-91 to St. Johnsbury exit. Take Rte. 2 west, to Rte. 15 west, to Hardwick. Then take Rte. 14 north for 8 mi., turn right and go 3 mi. up long curving hill to inn. From Canada and points north, use Exit 26 on I-91 and follow Rte. 58W to Irasburg. Then Rte. 14 southbound 12 mi. to marked left turn, 3 mi. to inn.

THE MIDDLETOWN SPRINGS INN
Middletown Springs, Vermont (1982)

The Middletown Springs Inn is located on a picturesque green in the middle of this village. The green itself has a brave Civil War laddie on top of a pedestal and an American flag on a slightly bowed flagpole. These are protected by a cannon of some indefinite years. Around the square is the church and a nice Vermont home with a porte cochere, and across the way is a Federal-period brick house. The entire town is on the National Register of Historic Places.

The inn is an 1879 Victorian mansion, built at the time when Middletown Springs was quite a thriving place, mostly because of the springs that still bubble up. At one time the town's reputation for its water rivaled that of Saratoga Springs.

After a three-year search for an inn, Steve and Jane Sax are very happy with their choice. Jane showed me into the parlor with its impressive curved wall on the left of the central hall. This leads into the library, which is a little less formal, and then on into the large center music room with its grand piano.

A handsome carved stairway to the second floor reminds me of the one at the Mainstay Inn in Cape May, New Jersey. Again, there is a center hallway with antique-furnished guest rooms on either side. Terrycloth bathrobes are provided for rooms that have shared baths.

"We brought with us our collection of antique china, glassware, pewter, clocks, and furniture," Jane told me. "Even though the inn retained many of its antiques from previous owners, there was still enough room for our own treasures, including the pictures of my great-great-great-grandparents and their grandfather clock. We added two poster beds and some antique chairs and rockers.

"In November we plan to have a weekend seminar, 'Antiques for Pleasure and Profit.' An antiques dealer friend of ours from Ohio will conduct the activities."

"Our big country kitchen is the heart of the inn," Steve said, "where all our guests find their way in the morning or evening. I am the chef and I make freshly baked bread, blueberry muffins and bubbling homemade soups. We also serve beef Victorian, baked stuffed haddock, and chicken Roquefort. Jane prepares the desserts, with rum torte and English Trifle being the house specialties. A morning favorite is our country breakfast of fruit, cereal, spiced German pancakes and locally produced Vermont maple syrup. We treat all our guests like company.

"For Thanksgiving this year we are inviting our guests to help cook the Thanksgiving meal. All we ask is that they give us a list of ingredients ahead of time so that we can have the supplies on hand.

"We're always delighted to assist in planning the day's activities, arranging bike rentals and sharing our favorite meandering routes. Actually, we're located near some of the best hiking, biking, skiing, and picture-taking in New England, and there's lots of jogging and running, and cross-country or downhill skiing."

I want to make particular note of the fact that the Christmas holidays at the Middletown Springs Inn are most unusual, with sleigh rides, treasure hunts, and gifts. Each evening features the food of a different country, and on the final evening, guests are encouraged to join the innkeepers in wearing Victorian costume.

THE MIDDLETOWN SPRINGS INN, Middletown Springs, VT 05757; 802-235-2198. A 10-guestroom (6 with private bath) Victorian mansion on the green of a lovely 18th- and 19-century village. Modified American plan includes full breakfast and dinner. B&B plan also available. Meals served to public by prior reservation. Open year-round; however, call in advance for reservations. Within easy driving distance of all central Vermont summer and winter recreation. Mt. Killington, state parks, summer theater, trout fishing, hiking, xc and alpine skiing, bicycling, horseback riding, swimming, golf, tennis nearby. Not suitable for young children. No pets. Jane and Steve Sax, Innkeepers. (See Index for rates.)

Directions: From Manchester Center, Vt., follow Rte. 30 to Pawlet and turn north on Rte. 133 to Middletown Springs. From Poultney, Vt., follow Rte. 140 to East Poultney and on to Middletown Springs.

The date in parenthesis in the heading represents the first year the inn appeared in the pages of Country Inns and Back Roads.

MOUNTAIN TOP INN
Chittenden, Vermont (1987)

The first time I visited Mountain Top it was an exceptionally brilliant winter's day; the sky couldn't have been bluer, and the sun on the freshly fallen snow made the road up the mountain positively dazzling. As I pulled into the parking lot in front of the inn, I could hear the sound of sleigh bells, and, sure enough, along the country road came some guests in a horse-drawn sleigh, which was later to carry me to the maple sugar house, where the inn's syrup is boiled down. Particularly in evidence were the skating rink, toboggan hill, and cross-country ski facilities, where there were dozens of skiers of all ages.

On the occasion of my second visit, I went up this very same Vermont road, and the trees, which before had been delicately mantled in snow, now formed a green, arched canopy, and the farms and meadows blended into a midsummer's idyll.

Inside Mountain Top Inn, I gazed in wonderment through the two-story staircase window at the sweeping view of a beautiful lake, where inn guests were canoeing, sailing, and swimming.

"Mount Carmel is the high peak over there," innkeeper Bill Wolfe commented. "There are hiking trails, and that is a five-hole golf course you're looking at."

"We've enlarged things considerably," Bill told me. "Cross-country skiing has really come into its own, and we have 110 kilometers of trails and state-of-the-art grooming equipment, which makes them among the finest anywhere in the world. Our ski shop is in a former barn and has snowshoe furniture and woodburning stoves. We have an excellent staff of instructors also."

Bill and I continued our tour of the inn, and I noticed how nicely the "country inn" atmosphere comes across in the guest rooms, which have reproductions of antiques, very pleasant quilts, quilted wall-hangings, and Shaker-style rockers.

Bill told me that the horseback riding program has been very popular. "We are the only resort that I know of with riding and cross-country skiing included in our rate."

Mountain Top is a deftly orchestrated example of how a country-inn experience can also include a great deal of entertainment and enjoyment for outdoor-minded guests of all ages. With fifty guest rooms it is somewhat larger than the average New England inn included in this book; however, thanks to innkeeper Wolfe, there is a good personal rapport among the staff and the guests.

The modified American plan offers truly gargantuan menus, most of which are very hearty country fare.

Among all the helpful literature is a booklet called "Get Lost in Vermont . . ." with maps and many suggestions for trips to nearby historic and natural attractions. Above and beyond all the possibilities for recreation and diversion, I think the chance to walk to secluded spots where beavers have built lodges in mountain ponds helps make Mountain Top a special place.

MOUNTAIN TOP INN (Romantik Hotels), Mountain Top Rd., Chittenden, VT 05737; 802-483-2311 or 800-445-2100. A 50-guestroom (private baths) four-season resort-inn located in the Green Mountains, between Middlebury and Rutland. Cottages and chalets nearby. Various guestroom categories. Modified American plan. Open year-round. Wheelchair access. Sailing, canoeing, fishing, swimming, horseback riding, tennis, golf, walking, hiking, xc skiing, ice skating, toboggans, horse-drawn sleigh rides, and lawn games all available at no additional cost. Many nearby historical and cultural attractions. Special attention for children. William Wolfe, Innkeeper. (See Index for rates.)

Directions: Chittenden is north of Rte. 4 and east of Rte. 7. After arriving in the village, turn left at the little bridge and stay to the right of the war monument. This is Mountain Top Rd.; follow it up the mountain and to the inn.

"European plan" means that rates for rooms and meals are separate. "American plan" means that meals are included in the cost of the room. "Modified American plan" means that breakfast and dinner are included in the cost of the room. The rates at some inns include a continental breakfast with the lodging.

OLD NEWFANE INN
Newfane, Vermont (1981)

I've got a wonderful job, and I'd be the first to admit it. This time my wonderful job was taking me down a great road that followed a river through the Vermont green-clad mountains. From Route 11 near Stratton Mountain, I continued on Route 30 through Jamaica and Townshend, down to Newfane. This road is one of the crisscross ways of journeying through Vermont.

Townshend is worth special mention for its impressive village green and all the New England white clapboard houses and other very handsome homes.

The Old Newfane Inn is right on the comer of Route 30 and the common, next to the red brick Vermont National Bank. The entrance is on the side, and it is right across the street from the handsome Windham County Courthouse, which was moved from the top of Newfane Hill in 1825, the same year the inn was built.

In mid-July, the vines around the windows of the inn on the first floor and porch were in high profusion, as were the flowers. Befitting Eric and Gundy Weindl's European heritage, the very extensive dinner menus are posted outside, giving visitors a preview of the cuisine.

I was escorted on a tour through every one of the ten meticulously decorated and furnished lodging rooms. It was like visiting a Vermont farmhouse of a hundred years ago. There were elaborate samplers and wall hangings such as I have never seen before. The second-floor rooms, at one time part of a ballroom, are light and airy, and there's a very pleasant little side balcony overlooking the green.

Speaking of the menu, Eric, who was trained as a chef in one of the best hotels in Switzerland, said, "I think we could be characterized basically as Swiss–Continental. Our maitre d' does such dishes as chateaubriand or one of several flaming specialties at the tableside, which is always an extra treat."

"This I can tell you," Gundy said, "Eric is a very good-natured man who loves good fun, but he takes cooking very seriously and is most particular about everything on the menu, including frogs' legs, shrimp scampi, lobster, tournedos of beef, and medallions of veal. He is too modest to say this, but people drive for many, many miles just to enjoy dinner with us. You see, I'm the hostess, so I meet them all."

Dinner was served in the low-ceilinged dining room, with its mellowed beams overhead and windows along one side. The floorboards of varying widths were highly polished and there were pink tablecloths with white undercloths, candles on the table, and pistol-handled knives. The maitre d' was wearing an elegant-looking tuxedo, and the waitresses were in black uniforms trimmed with white.

I was entranced with the salad, which was very simple and served with one of the most extraordinary, but simple, dressings I have ever tasted—just my preference for salads. I've never tasted better calves' liver, served in a Tyrolean sauce, and I had the opportunity to sample the medallions of veal served with creamy mushrooms that were delicious. Everything could be cut with a fork.

On the occasion of the two hundredth anniversary of the Old Newfane Inn, Gundy and Eric held a dinner for the benefit of a distressed family, for whom the town had established a special fund. Needless to say, the community spirit was very high and the dinner was a great success.

Because both Eric and Gundy are highly involved throughout the day with food and dining room preparation, casual visitors cannot be accommodated for tours of the inn. If you have a reservation and find the front door locked, ring the bell and they will be delighted to show you to your room.

OLD NEWFANE INN, Court St., Newfane, VT 05345; 802-365-4427. A 10-guestroom village inn 12 mi. west of Brattleboro, on Rte. 30. European plan. Dinner served to travelers. Closed for rooms on Mondays. Open mid-Dec. to first of April; May to end of Oct. Closed Thanksgiving, Mother's Day. Near many downhill ski areas, Marlboro Music Festival. Backroading, tennis, swimming nearby. No facilities for children under 7. No credit cards. Eric Weindl, Innkeeper. (See Index for rates.)

Directions: From New York, follow 684 to 84 to Hartford; I-91 to Brattleboro, Exit 2. Follow Rte. 30 for 12 mi. to Newfane. From Boston, follow Rte. 2 to Greenfield. I-91 to Brattleboro, Exit 2; follow Rte. 30 to Newfane.

ROWELL'S INN
Simonsville, Vermont (1985)

"How do you make apple pie?" It was a natural question because as soon as I walked through the front door the delicious aroma of baking apples had enticed me through the downstairs hallway and the dining room, with its alternate floorboards of cherry and maple, and into the kitchen where Beth Davis was taking three more pies from the oven.

Without missing a beat, she said, "I make it with a crumb crust, and the filling is my grandmother's recipe. Maybe we can have a piece a little later on."

What an inn kitchen! It's just the kind of a place that guests cannot resist. Fortunately, Beth enjoys their company and is still able to perform all of her varied culinary tasks. There were cookies in a cookie jar, bread cooling, a jar of cinnamon sticks, a long string of pepper pods, bunches of garlic, a little sign that says "Kiss the Cook," an old cabinet with many cookbooks, a big old refrigerator with four doors and jars on the top that said "Apple butter," "Relish," and "Jam." There was everything the accomplished cook needs, within arm's length.

Meanwhile, Lee Davis came down from the second floor where he had been finishing redoing the guest rooms, and we stepped from the kitchen into the Tavern Room, which has all kinds of wonderful things on the walls and tables. There was another old-fashioned refrigerator, not with ice in it, but jampacked with books. There were dried flowers, duck decoys, a moose head, a piano, a mounted fish, all kinds of magazines, a checker game, a big copper pot for holding firewood, and a shoeshine chair. I made a mental note to ask Lee where it came from. There was a present-day cast iron stove, which was radiating heat all over this room and adjacent rooms. The Tavern also has an old-fashioned soda fountain and a collection of syrup dispensers. There's a big tray of peanuts for shelling. Isn't it interesting that one never forgets how to shell peanuts? I went back into the kitchen and asked Beth, "What's for dinner tonight?" She said, "We're going to start out with mushroom strudel, potato and leek soup, orange and grape salad on fresh greens with a homemade dressing, our own bread, beef tenderloin, new potatoes with dill sauce on them, broccoli and cheese—we use a Vermont cheddar. The dessert will be that apple pie with ice cream. We always have a five-course dinner."

Rowell's Inn is an authentic historic inn, built for that purpose in 1820 by Major Simons, who was the founder of the village, located at a bend in Route 11, across from Lyman Brook. This handsome red brick building, with the highly distinctive wooden porches added to the front, is on the National Register of Historic Places. The five guest rooms are furnished in the tradition of the inn's prosperous past, as are the front parlors.

Lee is very proud of the new sun room, just off the dining room and the kitchen. "Our guests are able to enjoy sitting by the fire on a cool morning and yet feel the warmth of the sun while they enjoy coffee or, in the late afternoon, have a cup of hot chocolate or another refreshing drink. They can look out the windows and see all the natural beauty."

As I was leaving, I asked Beth about Christmas at Rowell's Inn. "Well, we start pretty early, along about the 11th or 12th of December, when our inn guests come, and the men go out and cut the trees and the women stay home and pop popcorn and string cranberries. We decorate both trees, one for the sun room and one for the living room. We don't have guests on Christmas Eve, but we do leave the Christmas decorations up through Valentine's Day at the request of our guests."

Everybody was gathered on the porch saying goodbye and I tiptoed back into the kitchen, and as quiet as a mouse I opened the cookie jar and took out one delicious sugar cookie.

ROWELL'S INN, RR 1 Box 269, Simonsville, VT, 05143; 802-875-3658. A 5-guestroom (private baths) inn in the mountains of central Vermont. Mod. American plan with 2-day minimum on weekends. Bed and breakfast also available midweek. Dinner is served by request to houseguests only. Closed 3 wks. in April and 1 wk. in Nov. Convenient to all the cultural, recreational, and historic attractions in the area, including, hiking, biking, trail riding, golf, tennis, fishing, theaters, downhill and xc skiing. Children over 12 welcome. No pets. No credit cards. Beth and Lee Davis, Innkeepers. (See Index for rates.)

Directions: Rowell's Inn is between Chester and Londonderry on Rte. 11.

SHIRE INN
Chelsea, Vermont (1986)

If the word "idyllic" had not already been created, I would certainly have invented it myself just to describe this bucolic scene.

Standing on a sturdy wooden bridge immediately behind the Shire Inn, gazing down on a branch of the White River below, I caught the flash of a trout slipping through the cool, rushing waters. Some early owner of the house so appreciated this scene, he placed a bench long enough to hold eight people here on the bridge.

I had just driven through some exceptionally beautiful Vermont country, following Route 14 north from Lebanon, alongside the White River, to Chelsea. The village is listed on the National Register of Historic Places, and has two commons and several early-18th-century homes and buildings.

Built of Vermont brick in 1832 and surrounded on all sides by gardens and lawns, the Shire Inn, with its fanlight doorway and black shutters, is certainly one of the most attractive of these historic homes.

The entrance hallway is dominated by a handsome circular staircase. On one side of this hallway is a most comfortable living room with deep chairs and sofas, as well as lots and lots of books. "This is the gathering room for our guests," remarked Mary Lee Papa, who with her husband, James, is the innkeeper.

"We're open year around," James told me, "and it's a good base from which guests can explore the variety of recreational and cultural opportunities that abound up here in this area. We've got good cross-country skiing here in Chelsea—actually, right from our own backyard. There's also downhill skiing at the Sonnenberg Ski Area near Woodstock, and there's hiking and bicycling in fair weather, as well as swimming and boating in the summer, and skating in the winter on Lake Fairlee."

The six guest rooms are most attractively furnished and four of them have working fireplaces. Mary Lee referred to the one on the right side of the entranceway as "our toasty room, because the boiler is just underneath." Upstairs, there are two high-ceilinged rooms with fireplaces on the front, one with a delightful canopy bed. Each has a little sign that says, "Good night, rest well. Breakfast at 8:30." Another has a spool bed and ruffled curtains. Very pleasant country bedspreads and comforters are found in each of the guest rooms, and all the beds have triple sheets. The beautiful "pumpkin pine" floorboards have been brought back to their lovely natural finish. All the guest rooms, named after Vermont counties, have a bountiful supply of books and magazines, but each has its own distinctive quality.

Breakfasts are really almost beyond description. There are three courses, and the emphasis is on fruits of all kinds, including baked fruits, as well as all kinds of pancakes and homemade breads. There is also a cream cheese omelet, now and then, served with mint.

Dinner could include scallops in a caraway sauce, veal in vermouth sauce, chicken in a spice or curry sauce, pork chops with caraway stuffing, or fillet of sole in wine. For dessert there might be fresh blueberry pie or an amaretto mousse, chocolate-brandy cake, a grasshopper mousse, or chocolate cheese cake.

You will, as I did, have some fun getting there and after you arrive, I hope you'll agree with me that Chelsea and the Shire Inn have just the kind of "withdrawn New England" atmosphere that you hoped to find.

SHIRE INN, Chelsea, VT 05038; 802-685-3031. A 6-guestroom (4 with private bath) village inn in a beautiful central Vermont setting. Open all year with a vacation break in Nov. and Apr. Breakfast included in room rate. Evening meal available by advance reservation. Bicycles available. The Justin Morgan horse farm, the Joseph Smith memorial, xc and downhill skiing, fishing, swimming, boating, and walking nearby. No children under 8. No pets. No smoking. James and Mary Lee Papa, Innkeepers. (See Index for rates.)

Directions: From I-89 use Exit 2, proceed west on Rte. 14, then northward on Rte. 110 to Chelsea. From 1-91, take Exit 14 and turn left on Rte. 113 proceeding northwest to Chelsea. Both of these roads are extremely picturesque.

THREE MOUNTAIN INN
Jamaica, Vermont (1982)

I have to tell you that I am again smitten with still another daughter of Charlie and Elaine Murray. A few years ago I met Claire, when she was about fourteen and taking care of the inn on a morning when Charlie and Elaine were otherwise engaged. She showed me around the inn and told me all about what it's like to grow up in the inn business. Now, Claire is a young woman with a year in Siena, Italy, behind her and a possible future in international affairs.

Then, incredibly, here I was once again sitting on that very comfortable couch in front of that tremendously impressive huge fireplace at the Three Mountain Inn, talking with another teenage Murray beauty. This one is Sarah, and, like Claire, she was full of news and impressions, and bubbling over with enthusiasm about things that were going on at Three Mountain Inn.

"Well, what I'm doing now is mostly serving here at the inn, but I help out in other areas. I'm a lifeguard, I'm a tour guide in the state park, and I can arrange tennis games, but I don't really play all that well yet myself. You know we're having the Volvo Tournament again this summer, which means that Jimmy Connors, Ivan Lendl, and John McEnroe will be in the vicinity," she chatted. "Would you like to see some of the things that we've been doing?"

Well, I'll confess I would have walked all the way to Manchester, Vermont, just to keep her company. We walked next door to Robinson House, which Elaine and Charlie have purchased and renovated for additional guest rooms. "The lady who owned it was an antique dealer so the house is lovely inside. Don't you agree?" I agreed.

"I get to go on antique trips, which I am very interested in," she said. "I convinced my parents to let me decorate one of these guest rooms.

I like pastel colors because I think that gives the room a gayer touch."

She continued, "Oh, I know something that you will like. On Christmas Eve we're going to have a Christmas party for all our guests, with tree trimming and everything. Normally, we just have our family here, but everybody thinks this will be great fun."

The main house at Three Mountain Inn was built in the 1780s. It's a small, beautifully restored Colonial inn with wide planked pine walls and floors and an original Dutch oven fireplace. It has a wonderful library as well, which is very good for long weekends. Sage Hill House, a small farmhouse across the street, is also part of the inn. With kitchen facilities, it is often used by families.

The inn's location in Jamaica, a very small mountain village, makes it just a short drive from three ski areas—Stratton, Bromley, and Magic mountains—and also within walking distance of hiking, cross-country skiing, and ice skating.

"I hope that you'll mention the fact that we have very good jogging and running here in the mountains. I ran around the University of Virginia campus in Charlottesville when we were there on vacation, and when I graduate from Cushing Academy, I think I would like to go to college there. I like to run and I hope to go into competition next year."

Sarah and I put our heads together over the menu, and she was glowingly complimentary about her mother's cooking, which features freshly baked breads and desserts, as well as Elaine's own salad dressing. Some menu favorites are trout amandine, scallops maison, chicken paprikash, carrot vichy soup, and butter pecan ice cream pie with hot caramel pecan topping.

Sarah was pretty proud of both her parents. "After all," she said, "Kelley, my oldest sister, and Claire and I all turned out pretty well, don't you think?"

You bet I did.

THREE MOUNTAIN INN, Rte. 30, Jamaica, VT 05343; 802-874-4140. An 18-guestroom inn (some rooms in adjacent houses) located in a pleasant village in southern Vermont. Modified American plan (rates include breakfast and dinner). Dinners also served to travelers nightly except Wed. Closed Apr. 15 to May 15; Labor Day to Sept. 10. Swimming pool on grounds. Tennis, golf, fishing, horseback riding, nature walks and hiking trails in Jamaica State Park, downhill and xc skiing, Marlboro Music Festival, Weston Playhouse, all within a short drive. No pets. No credit cards. Charles and Elaine Murray, Innkeepers. (See Index for rates.)

Directions: Jamaica is located on Rte. 30, which runs across Vermont from Manchester (U.S. 7) to Brattleboro (I-91).

THE VILLAGE INN
Landgrove, Vermont (1977)

Don Snyder was telling me about Christmastime at the Village Inn while he whipped up some of his special blueberry pancakes. "Yes," he declared, "there is a berry in every bite." Then he deftly flipped over one of the beauties on the hot grill.

"Well, you know we're really set up to have lots of children here at any time," he told me. "However, at Christmas it's particularly appropriate. The Christmas tree is decorated on Christmas Eve. All the ornaments are put on the table, and everyone has fun decorating the tree. Of course, it's a school holiday then, so we have lots of families here for skiing, and both grown-ups and kids help decorate the tree. There are small trees available for individual guest rooms, and some of our guests have Christmas right in their own rooms. However, we have gifts under the tree, and guests can hang their own stockings. As you might imagine, on Christmas Day we serve a great big Christmas dinner at noon."

The inn is a really family affair, with Don presiding in the kitchen and Else at the front desk. Norma Quinn also helps to serve breakfast, greet guests, and do duties with Else. She tells wonderful stories. Jay and Kathy Snyder and their daughters, Kim and Heidi, who are fast growing up, are also at the inn during the summertime.

In the winter, there are lots of things to amuse guests of all ages and predilections. There is cross-country skiing, right from the inn's back door, as well as downhill skiing at several very prominent ski areas nearby. There is also paddle tennis. In summer, there is tennis on the inn's own court, pitch and putt golf, volleyball, and lots of wonderful trails to hike. The Alpine Slide at the Bromley ski area is very popular with kids of all ages.

Horse-drawn sleigh rides on the snowy roads are offered during the winter and usually start off at sunset, getting back in time for dinner. It's a nice country experience. The inn has some midweek package plans, all of which include various combinations of alpine and Nordic skiing, and skiers particularly find the hot tubs most inviting.

With all of this outdoor activity, as one might imagine, the food is a very important attraction, and among the main dishes are roast duckling with raspberry and orange sauce, prime rib with a popover, lamb chops with fresh herb sauce, broiled swordfish, trout, New York sirloin, and smoked baby coho salmon. Dinner is not served on Wednesdays during the summer. Incidentally, breakfast is included in the rate in the summer, and dinner is an extra charge. In winter, guests are under the modified American plan, and no lunch is served.

I've always been intrigued by the big couch in the living room that holds at least twelve people at one time. It is also known as "the seducery." It's particularly popular with everybody during the winter.

While children find it good fun to be at the Village Inn, adult activities abound, including summer theater in nearby Weston, which is reached by a most agreeable dirt road. They have done such popular plays as *Brighton Beach Memoirs, You Can't Take It with You,* and *A Chorus Line.*

THE VILLAGE INN, Landgrove, VT 05148; 802-824-6673. A 20-guest-room rustic resort-inn in the mountains of central Vermont, approx. 4½ mi. from Weston and Londonderry. Complimentary breakfast in summer. Modified American plan in winter. Dinner served to travelers by reservation during the summer except Wed. Open from Dec. 15 to Apr. 15; June 1 to Oct. 20. Swimming, tennis, volleyball, pitch-and-putt, paddle tennis, xc skiing, fishing on grounds. Downhill skiing, riding, indoor tennis, antiquing, backroading, Alpine Slide, golf, summer theater nearby. Children most welcome. No pets. Jay and Kathy Snyder, Innkeepers. (See Index for rates.)

Directions: Coming north on I-91 take Exit 2 at Brattleboro, follow Rte. 30 to Rte. 11 and turn right. Turn left off Rte. 11 at signs for Village Inn. Bear left in village of Peru. Coming north on Rte. 7, turn east at Manchester on Rte. 11 to Peru. Turn left at signs for Village Inn. Bear left in village of Peru.

A number of inns have nearby airports where private airplanes may land. An airplane symbol at the end of the inn directions indicates that there is an airport nearby. Consult inn for further information.

WEST MOUNTAIN INN
Arlington, Vermont (1984)

Wes Carlson lovingly handed me a potted African violet and said, "This needs bright but never direct sunlight. It prefers temperatures from about 65 to 75 degrees and high humidity. As the air is very dry during the winter months, the violet would benefit from frequent light mistings, but never allow the water to bead up on the leaves or collect around the stems. Water it whenever the soil is dry to the touch with tepid water and a weak mixture of African violet food. Never let the pot sit in water for more than a few minutes; it will rot the roots. You can, however, to provide humidity, place the pot on pebbles with water beneath. Your violet hates drafts and loves classical music and polite conversation."

I think that Wes's advice typifies, if anything could, the real spirit at the West Mountain Inn. In the first place, guests are presented with these precious flowers as they depart. An African violet is put in each bedroom, and the guests may take them home. Is there a more appropriate symbol of hospitality?

Both Wes and Mary Ann personify the very highest spirit of inn-keeping. As Mary Ann explained it to me while we were walking through the snow to see some of the animals: "I think we are all gathered together as one people living on a beautiful planet and we would like to share our part of it with other people.

"Wes likes to feel that he is involved in international peace and love, so our animals are from all over the world. There are dwarf rabbits from the Netherlands, African pigmy goats, and Peruvian llamas. We also have assorted artifacts, including nutcrackers from Germany and Holland, and a collection of Norwegian trolls in our library area. A small collection of African crafts is in the Daniel Webster Room. We like to think of ourselves as including everyone and wanting everyone to be here."

As we walked back across the snow, I noted the wonderful view, looking right down to the Battenkill River, out through the valley, and over to the Green Mountains. Mary Ann told me more than twenty-five species of birds visit here throughout the year, and I enjoyed seeing the birds fluttering around the many bird feeders.

There is a wide variety of outside diversions on the 150 acres of meadows and hills, where wilderness trails abound. The cross-country ski trails have been extended considerably, especially with the novice skier in mind. The area is famous for its fishing, and there is canoeing on the Battenkill.

The guest rooms are in many sizes and shapes: some with outside porches, one with a working fireplace, one with a bedloft for children, two with high, pine-paneled cathedral ceilings, and all attractively and comfortably furnished. There is a room on the first floor equipped for disabled persons.

"We've named our guest rooms for Robert Frost, Norman Rockwell, and Rockwell Kent," Mary Ann told me. "These, and others, are people who lived in the area or had some significance here. We have rooms named after Governor Chittenden, Ethan and Ira Allen, and Dorothy Canfield Fisher, a wonderful authoress. We have a room with about fifty of her books. There is also a room named after Carl Ruggles, a wonderful gentleman who lived here in the fifties. He was an avant-garde composer, and not too many people played his music because it was discordant. There's a wonderful story I'll tell you later about why we named one of the rooms for Booker T. Washington."

There's more to a good inn than food, facilities, and atmosphere. The West Mountain Inn has all of these plus a highly commendable *esprit.*

WEST MOUNTAIN INN, Arlington, VT05250; 802-375-6516. A 13-guestroom (private baths) comfortable hilltop country estate with a view of the Green Mountains. Mod. American plan. Breakfast and dinner served to travelers daily. Open year-round. Wheelchair access. Swimming, canoeing, hiking, fishing, nature walks, xc skiing, and tobogganing on grounds. Special weekend programs from time to time; call for information. Children welcome. No pets. Mary Ann and Wes Carlson, Innkeepers. (See Index for rates.)

Directions: Take Rte. 7 or Historic Rte. 7A to Arlington. Follow signs for West Mountain Inn, ½ mi. west on Rte. 313; bear left after crossing bridge.

BLACK POINT INN
Prouts Neck, Maine (1969)

I drove up the circular driveway to the canopied entrance of the Black Point Inn, and there sat a sedate black London taxicab. I couldn't help but reflect that it was, like the inn itself, a throwback to the days of New England's past.

Normand Dugas, the innkeeper, had seen me through his office window and came out to tell me about "Wally, the cab." "In 1981, an English company sent over a couple of their famous London taxicabs as samples, hoping to corner the market left open by the demise of the Checker Cab Company. However, it all came to naught, and after a number of adventures I acquired one of the cabs. The staff named it 'Wally.' With a four-cylinder diesel engine, Wally has a top speed of fifty miles an hour and gets about fifty miles to the gallon. He seats five people comfortably, and we use him for transporting people back and forth to the airport and for sedate afternoon rides."

We walked upstairs into the lobby, where the grandfather's clock tolled exactly twelve noon, which meant it was thirty minutes before lunch. A few of the guests were on the porch overlooking the bay side of Prouts Neck, and a few others were in the enclosed sunporch, playing cards or knitting. Ordinarily, lunch would be served poolside, but today being a bit too foggy, it was served in the regular inn dining room.

Last summer, twelve-year-old Peter Dugas, who wants to be a writer/historian, put together a one-and-half-hour walking trip on the Cliff Walk, where he gives the history of Prouts Neck, going back to the days of the Indian massacres. He'll repeat his guided tour this year, too.

Another interesting addition to the Black Point is the "Atlantic House Library." The Atlantic House Hotel, also on Prouts Neck, is now closed after 146 years of continuous operation, and the BPI acquired most of their library hooks and some other memorabilia. A lovely outside deck just off the library has been constructed for nice sunny-day reading.

Norm and I walked into the indoor swimming pool room, which he tells me has been extremely well received by all of the inn guests. Those staying slightly off season have particularly appreciated this pool, since the ocean is too cold before mid-June and after mid-September. The walls of the room are lined in beautiful California red cedar, and the pool overlooks the rose garden and the putting green. This also includes a group jacuzzi, sauna, and exercise area.

"Our new 28-foot fishing boat, called *The Blue Lady,* departs with a surprising number of guests at 5 a.m., in order to catch the rascals before they wake up!" Norm said. "Our guests are able to do some fishing and still get back in time for breakfast by 9 a.m. We have mackerel, bluefish, stripers, a few small sharks, and an occasional sea bass."

In many respects, the Black Point is a throwback to the F. Scott Fitzgerald era. Gentlemen wear coats and ladies don colorful dresses for dinner. The small orchestra plays for dancing in the evening and at poolside during lunches.

Rooms are more readily available during the months of June and July. During recent years, the weather in early June has been exceptional, and it is sometimes possible to call and make a reservation a day ahead; however, August is always a full month.

One hundred years ago, the American painter Winslow Homer found in this section of the rocky Maine coastline the inspiration and atmosphere that enabled him to create some of his greatest works. In fact, he walked these sandy shores and climbed these same rocks. His studio is located just a few minutes' walk from the front door of the inn.

Prouts Neck became popular as a summer resort at the end of the 19th century, and time has brought few changes to this lovely neck of land stretching out into the Atlantic. The sea, birds, water, sky, and trees, all of which go to make such desirable tranquility, are still here today.

BLACK POINT INN, Prouts Neck, ME 04070; 207-883-4126. An 80-guestroom luxury resort-inn on Rte. 207, 10 mi. south of Portland. Open May to late Oct. American plan during July and Aug. Optional MAP May, June, Sept., Oct. During high season, 3-night minimum stay. Indoor pool, jacuzzi, and sauna, fresh-water whirlpool, heated salt-water pool, bicycles, sailing, dancing, golf, tennis, and ocean bathing all within a few steps. No children under 8 during July and Aug. No pets. Normand H. Dugas, Innkeeper. (See Index for rates.)

Directions: From Maine Tpke., take Exit 7. Turn right at sign marked Scarborough and Old Orchard Beach. At second set of lights turn left on Rte. 207. Follow 4.3 mi. to Prouts Neck.

THE BRADLEY INN
Pemaquid Point, New Harbor, Maine (1981)

I reached out and put my hands on the firm stone base of the Pemaquid Point Lighthouse. It radiated a wonderful warmth borrowed from the brilliant September sun, so I sat down and rested against it, attempting to draw into myself some of its strength and nobility. It was my lighthouse.

Immediately in front of me, this selfsame sun created momentary jewels where the Atlantic gently lapped against the striated rocks that stretched out toward Spain. Overhead, sea birds wheeled and turned and talked to each other incessantly. I closed my eyes and my thoughts drifted back to my arrival at the Bradley Inn, just a short, pleasant walk from my lighthouse.

This time I had taken Route 32 off Route 1 at Waldoboro, south of Rockland. This is a delightful experience through back-country Maine. Travelers who are trying to get pell-mell from one inn to another may never leave I-95 for Route 1, and that's unfortunate, for here is a good alternate back road that's hard to beat. It comes out just a few moments from the Bradley Inn. If you're traveling north from the Bradley Inn, ask any member of the Ek family and they will put you on Route 32.

Well, I found the Ek family, Ed, Louine, and Grandma, in excellent spirits because many new features had been added to the inn; in fact, the front of it was quite different from the last time I visited. The dining room has also been enlarged to encompass the former old-fashioned screened-in porch, with an addition that forms a lounge with a piano, all done in knotty pine and bentwood chairs. Both the dining room and lounge have a pleasant view across the fields.

A visit to this country inn on the rocky coast of Maine is in many respects a step backward in time. Most of the guest rooms share bathrooms and conveniences "down the hall," and the furniture came from Ed and Louine's former home. Besides decorator sheets and pillowcases in bright colors, these moderately sized rooms have firm mattresses. Smoking, incidentally, is not permitted in the guest rooms.

The menu includes such hearty offerings as prime ribs of beef, several chicken and veal dishes, and much seafood from the local waters, when available, including scallops, sole, swordfish, haddock, and lobster. Sunday brunch is always a happy occasion.

With new areas in the inn and much new decorating, the Bradley Inn has taken on wonderful new dimensions; however, there is a simplicity and purposefulness, in some ways personified by a small plaque in each room, which reads in part: "Let the guest sojourning here know that in this home our life is simple. What we cannot afford we do not offer, but what good cheer we can give, we give gladly. We make no strife for appearance's sake. We will not swerve from our path for you . . .

"For, while you are with us, we would have you enjoy the blessings of a home, health, love and freedom, and we pray that you may find the final blessing of life—peace."

Janice Lindstrom, our artist, has sketched the Pemaquid Point Lighthouse, which I, along with, I'm sure, most of the guests at the Bradley Inn, find delightful.

THE BRADLEY INN, Rte. 130, HC62, Box 361 Pemaquid Point, New Harbor, ME 04554; 207-677-2105. A 13-guestroom (3 shared baths) country inn near Pemaquid Lighthouse on Maine's rocky coast, 15 mi. from Damariscotta. Open mid May to Jan. Continental breakfast included in room rate. Open daily to the public for dinner from mid-June to mid-Oct.; on weekends only Oct. to Jan., March to June. Restaurant is closed Christmas Eve, Christmas Day, Jan., Feb. Tennis, swimming, golf, canoeing, backroading, woodland walks, xc skiing all available nearby. Many cultural, historical, and recreational facilities nearby. No pets. No smoking in rooms. Edwin and Louine Ek and Grandma, Innkeepers. (See Index for rates.)

Directions: From south: Maine I-95 to Brunswick/Bath Coastal Rte. 1 Exit. Follow Rte. 1 through Brunswick, Bath, and Wiscasset. Exit Business Rte. 1 at Damariscotta. Turn right at top of hill (white church), follow Rte. 130, 14 mi. to Pemaquid Pt. From north: Rte. 1; exit at Business Rte. 1, Damariscotta. Turn left at white church onto Rte. 130. Follow 130, 14 mi. to Pemaquid Pt. ◣

THE CAPTAIN LORD MANSION
Kennebunkport, Maine (1975)

I remember it very well: in fact, it was only last summer. It was a Wednesday morning in mid-July and I joined the Captain Lord breakfast group at nine-thirty. (There had been an earlier breakfast group at eight-thirty.) Many of the guests were seated in a large but somewhat formal dining room enjoying coffee and planning the day's activities. A large jigsaw puzzle was on the dining room table and a couple of guests were playing chinese checkers in one corner. The Chippendale chairs, beautiful cabinets, and crystal chandelier were indications that this was indeed an important room during the many years of the mansion's existence.

Meanwhile, the morning breakfast chimes were rung, and almost as one, the waiting guests rose, crossed the hallway, and walked into the ample Captain Lord kitchen, where breakfast is served.

I took advantage of the moment to walk around and admire the handsome woodwork and lovely period wallpapers of this mansion, built during the War of 1812. Captain Nathaniel Lord answered the needs of idle carpenters and sailors by engaging them to build this stately home, using timbers intended for ships.

I walked to the front of the house where a beautiful curving banister led up a rather formal staircase to the third floor. Throughout the mansion, Rick and Bev have collected antiques, oriental rugs, and other tasteful objets d'art. One parlor has been set aside as a gift shop offering attractive mementos of the area, as well as smaller items such as cups, saucers, plates and the like.

Ample use has been made of the generously sized hallways, both on the second and third floors, with handsome cabinets, antique children's sleighs, duck decoys, quilts, prints of sailing ships, a spinning wheel, and even a basket of washed wool. Many of the rooms have been named after ships that probably sailed from Kennebunkport.

I peeked into a few of the spotless guest rooms whose doors were open, and once again fluffy comforters, handmade quilts or 100% wool blankets, and Posturepedic mattresses reigned supreme. There are eight rooms with queen-sized beds and two rooms with king-sized beds.

I returned to the kitchen where the guests were all seated around the lovely harvest table, which provided just the right amount of intimacy. There were lots of laughter and appreciative comments about the break-fast of orange juice, fresh homemade breads, muffins, toast, and coffee, and, if desired, a soft-boiled egg.

It was at this point that Rick came in and started to tell us about the Captain's Hideaway. "It's a beautiful New England Cape Cod cottage with two wonderful guest rooms and working fireplaces," he said. "Although all of our bathrooms are very special and modern, the ones at the

Hideaway are even more so, with whirlpool baths and massage power heads in the showers. One bathroom has a fireplace and a view of the water. The upstairs bedroom has a sitting area and a canopied bed and the downstairs bedroom has a private entrance and patio. They both have working fireplaces.

"Breakfast at the Hideaway is an epicurean delight, with homemade granola, yogurt, fresh fruit, and an egg dish. We make the same fresh muffins you have here but they're mini size." Breakfast is served in the formal dining room at the Hideaway on English china with crystal and silver. "The rates are higher," Bev told me, "but the guests who have stayed there rave about it."

THE CAPTAIN LORD MANSION, Box 800, Kennebunkport, ME 04046; 207-967-3141. An 18-guestroom mansion-inn in a seacoast village. Lodgings include breakfast. No other meals served. Open year-round. Near the Rachel Carson Wildlife Refuge, the Seashore Trolley Museum, the Brick Store Museum, and lobster boat tours. Bicycles, hiking, xc skiing, deep-sea fishing, golf, indoor swimming, and tennis nearby. No children under 12. No pets. No credit cards. Bev Davis and Rick Litchfield, Innkeepers. (See Index for rates.)

Directions: Take Exit 3 (Kennebunk) from the Maine Tpke. Take left on Rte. 35 and follow signs through Kennebunk to Kennebunkport. Take left at traffic light at Sunoco station. Go over drawbridge and take first right onto Ocean Ave., then take fifth left off Ocean Ave. (³/₁₀ mi.). The mansion is in the second block on left. Park behind building and take brick walk to office.

CHARMWOODS
On Long Lake, Naples, Maine (1981)

Charmwoods is a unique type of inn. Set in an area of great natural beauty and maintained by conscientious hosts, the inn provides a perfect setting for an escape to the countryside.

Once a private lakefront estate, Charmwoods radiates all the flavor and ambience of the Maine woods but is a mere 2½-hour drive from downtown Boston.

As hosts, Marilyn and Bill Lewis make for a perfect combination. Marilyn is attractive and vivacious and delights in giving her guests personal attention to ensure the most pleasurable of vacations for them.

Bill, a former editor at the *Boston Globe* and *Boston Herald,* has unusual interests that Charmwoods guests find to be a pleasant diversion. For example, he often entertains with his 1890 Thomas A. Edison phonograph, drawing from a collection of about 500 cylindrical recordings. The newest acquisition is an antique player-piano, complete with rolls of the old favorites. Evenings, it is the center of attraction for guests addicted to sing-alongs with a keen nostalgia for this lusty entertainment of yesteryear.

Marilyn's penchant for decorating is particularly evident in all the spacious bedrooms with their selection of handsome, coordinated sheets, blankets, towels, and other accessories in distinctive colors.

The focus of activity at Charmwoods is frequently the commodious and gracious living room with its massive fieldstone fireplace and panoramic view of lake and mountains. Everything about this room encourages friendly discussions with a free exchange of information and ideas. The striking undersea photographs are provided by the Lewises' son, Jonathan.

Within fifteen minutes of my arrival, Bill and Marilyn had introduced me to their guests and we were immediately on a first-name basis — chatting like old friends. Several guests were regulars at Charmwoods, having returned year after year.

Adjoining the living room and sharing center stage during much of the year is a broad deck with an unobstructed view of Long Lake. It is equally ideal for sunny breakfasts or for chatting under the stars.

A path leads down a few steps to the shoreline of this delightfully clear lake where a rowboat and canoe are docked in the boathouse. Swimming from the white sandy beach or private sundeck is ideal, and a trim cabana provides numerous amenities, including telephone service.

The village of Naples, a short stroll down the road, offers guests some interesting upcountry diversions, not the least of which is a seaplane flight providing an excellent overview of the entire resort area. The *Songo River Queen,* an old-fashioned paddleboat, and the U.S. mailboats run excursion trips across the ten-mile-wide lake. Plenty of backroading and quite a few antique shops can be enjoyed in the immediate area.

During my visit at Charmwoods nearly all the guests clutched tennis rackets, and the all-weather court saw plenty of play. There's a lakeside golf course and riding stables just a few minutes away.

Visiting Charmwoods is like being a guest at a houseparty for friends.

CHARMWOODS, P.O. Box 217, Naples, ME 04055; 207-693-6798. A 4-guestroom (private baths) lakefront bed-and-breakfast inn, plus a guest cottage, on the west shore of Long Lake, approx. ½ hr. from Maine Tpke. Open June into Oct. Breakfast is the only meal served (to houseguests only). Tennis, swimming, boating, canoeing, fishing, shuffleboard, and horseshoes on grounds; horseback riding, golf, para-sailing, and windsurfing nearby. Summer playhouse just down the road. Not suitable for children under 12. No pets. No credit cards. Marilyn and Bill Lewis, Innkeepers. (See Index for rates.)

Directions: From Boston, follow Rte. 1 north to I-95 and take Exit 8 (Portland-Westbrook). Turn right and follow Riverside St. 1 mi. to Rte. 302. Turn left (west) to Naples, which is about 30 mi. ahead. Charmwoods is just beyond the village on the right with an unobtrusive sign. From North Conway, N.H., follow Rte. 302 through Bridgton. Charmwoods sign and driveway off Rte. 302 just before Naples village.

THE CLAREMONT HOTEL AND COTTAGES
Southwest Harbor, Maine (1974)

The year was 1884. Grover Cleveland (Democrat) defeated James G. Blaine (Republican) for president. London opened the first underground railroad. Auguste Rodin created his famous sculpture *Burghers of Calais*. Harry Truman was born. The Ringling Brothers circus was organized in Baraboo, Wisconsin. The Statue of Liberty was completed and presented to the United States. Women first competed in Wimbledon tennis, and the Washington Monument was completed.

It was also the year that the Claremont Hotel was opened. Its creator was Captain Jesse Pease, a native of Rockland and a well-known sea captain. During that first year, 146 names were entered on the register. Many of these came from New York and Boston and enjoyed a simple, modest vacation at the Claremont. There were oil lamps and pitchers and basins in each room. Hot baths were ordered in advance for twenty-five cents.

Considerable contribution to the progress of this now-century-old establishment came during the long tenure of the Phillips family, who owned it for sixty years. During that time, more bedrooms and a new dining room were added, and such improvements as an elevator and a sprinkler protection system were installed.

In 1968, the Claremont was sold to Mr. and Mrs. Allen McCue of Yarmouth, Maine, who have continued in all of the traditions, as well as adding new cottages and making many improvements, including a wing with a spectacular view of Somes Sound.

In fact, the cottages have become so popular they decided just in the past year to add two more, with built-in fireplaces and hardwood floors. Adjacent to the dining room, the rooms overlook Greenings Island and Somes Sound.

The Claremont is situated on the waters of Somes Sound in a most interesting community with an identity of its very own. It always intrigues me that there are two different aspects to Southwest Harbor. On one side of the small peninsula is a working harbor with lots of fishing boats and the hustle and bustle of people who make their living with the cooperation of the sea. On the other side is a more tranquil scene, with sailboats and launches. This view over the water to Northeast Harbor is the one which is enjoyed by Claremont guests as they sit in the boathouse or on the front porch of the inn itself.

On each visit I have been struck by the wide variety of entertainment and recreation available for people vacationing on Mount Desert Island. All of the natural attractions of the area are within a very convenient distance; however, in recent years the Claremont has become well known for an important tournament of 9-wicket croquet—a game which has been played on the lawn of the inn since its earliest days. Players and spectators alike enjoy the Claremont Croquet Classic, a unique event for Claremont visitors. Many guests and staff return year after year to enjoy the serene atmosphere and the beautiful views.

Now the Claremont, on the National Register of Historic Places, is well into its second hundred years!

THE CLAREMONT HOTEL AND COTTAGES, Southwest Harbor. ME 04679; 207-244-5036. A 24-guestroom (mostly private baths) rambling summer hotel with rooms also in two adjacent guest houses; on Somes Sound, Mt. Desert Island, 24 mi. south of Ellsworth. Hotel and dining room open mid-June thru mid-Sept. Breakfast and dinner served to guest and the public. Lunch served in the boathouse during July and Aug. Guest-house rooms and 11 housekeeping cottages available May thru Oct. Hotel and Phillips House rooms available only on mod. American Plan during the season. Off-season, all rooms available either EP or MAP while hotel is open. Tennis, rowboats, croquet, badminton, golf, bicycles, riding, boating, and sailing rental nearby. No credit cards. Personal checks accepted. The McCue Family, Owners; John Madeira, Jr., Manager. (See Index for rates.)

Directions: From Maine Tpke., exit at Augusta and proceed east on Rte. 3 to U.S. 1. At Ellsworth, pick up Rte. 3 again and follow Rte. 102 on Mt. Desert Island to Southwest Harbor. Follow inn signs approaching and in Southwest Harbor.

A number of inns have nearby airports where private airplanes may land. An airplane symbol at the end of the inn directions indicates that there is an airport nearby. Consult inn for further information.

THE COUNTRY CLUB INN
Rangeley, Maine (1981)

Rangeley, Maine, is one of those places in the world that has a special kind of charisma. There are few locations that offer such beauty and grandeur in all seasons. The combination of wide skies, vast stretches of mountain woodland, and the placid aspect of Rangeley Lake have been drawing people to this part of western Maine since long before the roads were as passable and numerous as they are today.

Innkeeper Bob Crory of the Country Club Inn says, "The dramatic lake and mountain scenery surrounding us will tranquilize even the most jangled nerves." At an elevation of nearly 2,000 feet, the Country Club Inn offers a magnificent view. Each of the guest rooms has a picture window, and the dining room and lounge both offer a scenic view of the lake, which reminds me of similar stretches of lake and mountains in certain sections of Scotland—Loch Ness being one. The cathedral-ceilinged living room has heavy beams, wood paneling, and many, many different comfortable sofas, armchairs, and rocking chairs. There are jigsaw puzzles in various states of completion, huge shelves of books, and a great moosehead over one of the fieldstone fireplaces.

We were all gathered at one of the focal points at the Country Club Inn—the deck, with its sweeping panorama of sky, lake, and mountains. There were innkeepers Bob and Sue Crory, their daughter, Margie, and her husband, Steve Jamison, and the Crorys' son, Bob, Jr. Sue mentioned how pleasant it is to have all the family working together. "Our staff is small enough so that everyone becomes part of the family and we find our guests love this kind of atmosphere.

"Of course, we all change hats, so to speak, and move from one job to another, so the guests really receive lots of personal attention."

Bob joined in, saying, "I spent my boyhood summers working in Maine resorts and then went on to major in hotel administration at the University of New Hampshire. Sue and I have had many different jobs, but all the time we knew that what we wanted was to have our own small country inn. We've found that in the Country Club Inn."

Sue elaborated on how they are enjoying being a year-round operation and mentioned the many activities during the summer season—excellent fishing (landlocked salmon and square-tailed trout), hiking the many trails (including the Appalachian Trail, which goes through this area), boating, canoe trips, a swimming pool, and a variety of lawn games. For those who love golf there's a challenging 18-hole public golf course adjacent to the inn. Tennis courts are nearby.

The inn is located in the heart of the northwestern mountains of Maine's ski country, surrounded by Saddleback and Sugarloaf mountains, which offer downhill and cross-country skiing. Margie, Steve, and Bob, Jr., commented on how beautiful Rangeley is during their winter season. "Many of our guests cross-country ski right from our doorstep. Snowmobilers enjoy over 100 miles of well-groomed trails and, at the end of the day, drive right up to their rooms in time to freshen up for a sumptuous dinner."

Sweeping an arm towards the view, Bob said, "September is a golden month. The fall foliage color starts a little earlier in this section of Maine than in other parts of New England. It is a good opportunity to enjoy nature's great show and still experience the wonderful peace and solitude."

THE COUNTRY CLUB INN, P.O. Box 680C, Rangeley, ME 04970; 207-864-3831. A 25-guestroom resort-inn (private baths) on Rangeley Lake in western Maine, 45 mi. from Farmington. Modified American plan. Breakfast and dinner served to travelers by reservation. Open mid-May to mid-Oct. and late Dec. to late March. Near many cultural, historic, scenic, and recreational attractions. Swimming pool and lake swimming, horseshoes, bocci, volleyball, and croquet. A public 18-hole golf course adjacent to the inn. Tennis nearby. Fishing, hiking, and canoeing. Snowmobiling and xc skiing at doorstep. Downhill and xc skiing at Saddleback and Sugarloaf Mts. Bob and Sue Crory, Innkeepers. (See Index for rates.)

Directions: From Maine Tpke., take Auburn Exit 12 and follow Rte. 4 to Rangeley. From Vt. and N.H., take I-91 to St. Johnsbury; east on Rte. 2 to Gorham and Rte. 16 north to Rangeley. From Bar Harbor, Rte. 1A to Rte. 2 to Rte. 4. From Montreal, Rte. 10 to Rte. 112 to Rte. 147 to Rte. 114; then Rte. 26 to Rte 16 to Rte. 4.

THE CROCKER HOUSE COUNTRY INN
Hancock Point, Maine (1987)

Finding a beguiling, secluded place for an overnight stay on a trip to Canada via U.S. 1 would delight many a weary traveler. And it could be the perfect solution for those who enjoy the activity and excitement of Bar Harbor, Acadia National Park, and Blue Hill, but also want a quiet hideaway nearby. On Hancock Point, three minutes from the ocean, the Crocker House Country Inn is all of the above.

The entrance leads into a living room that is eclectic, to say the least, with good comfortable old wicker furniture, a big window seat, some rather striking modern primitive paintings, a very handsome rug of Indian design, a backgammon set, and lots of growing plants. At the very moment I walked in I was greeted with a flute concerto by Jean Pierre Rampal wafting from the stereo. It all seemed quite casual and quite natural.

The guest rooms are bright and cheerful. Almost all of them have been redecorated and some have stenciling on the upper walls. They are large enough to accommodate two people very comfortably.

Innkeeper Richard Malaby told me a little bit about the past history of this part of Maine. "A lot of people think that the most northern part of Maine is Ellsworth and Bar Harbor," he remarked. "Hancock was once a thriving shipbuilding community and also the terminus of the Washington, D.C., to Bar Harbor express train. It was the port from which the famed Sullivan Quarry shipped its cobblestones to pave the streets of Boston, New York, and Philadelphia. I'm afraid that the Crocker House is a lone survivor of those days of the past."

He continued, his eyes alight with enthusiasm, "Up here we're rather out of the way, but we have quite a few of our own activities. For instance, the Monteux Symphony Orchestra performs biweekly in Hancock during June and July and the Somesville Acadia Repertory Theater provides professional theater during the summer. Hancock is the site of one of the two reversing tidal falls in North America.

"We have clay tennis courts available for our guests a short stroll away, and the ocean is just a three-minute walk from our front door. Many guests come to enjoy Acadia National Park and then stay on here an extra day to recover from all of that activity."

One might expect the dinner menu to consist of good hearty upcountry Maine food; therefore, I was quite surprised to find some international dishes such as poached salmon Florentine, coquilles St. Jacques, and veal Monterey, which I ordered. It is very thinly sliced veal, sautéed in madeira with avocado and tomato and topped with Monterey jack cheese. The menu also has baked stuffed lobster, soft-shell crabs, broiled swordfish, broiled halibut Dijon, and other treasures from the sea.

If you happen to be there on Sunday, the brunch is very spiffy indeed, with brandied french toast, eggs Benedict, steak and eggs, and something interesting called "create your own omelet."

In the morning, after a very pleasant continental breakfast, I walked around this little neck of land, enjoying the birch trees and the grass beside the water. It's great for bicycling and running, and I came upon a little harbor with lots of sailboats and mountains in the distance and lobster traps bobbing in the tide. Would you believe that not a single motorcar passed in either direction during my morning walk?

Taken all-in-all, I found the experience at the Crocker House Country Inn most refreshing. I particularly enjoyed my conversation with innkeeper Malaby, who, because of the relatively small size of the inn, can take the time to meet his guests and to share some of his enthusiasm about this quiet, sequestered corner of the Maine coast.

THE CROCKER HOUSE COUNTRY INN, Hancock Point, ME 04640; 207-422-6806. A 10-guestroom (private baths) secluded country inn about 8 mi. north of Ellsworth, Me. Breakfast and dinner served daily. Open from May 1 to Thanksgiving. (Check for possible opening during winter months.) Bicycles and dock moorings available for guests. Tennis, swimming, and walking nearby. Just 30 min. from Mount Desert Island, Acadia National Park, and Bar Harbor. Blue Hill and the east Penobscot peninsula easily accessible. Richard Malaby, Innkeeper. (See Index for rates.)

Directions: Follow Rte. 1 approx. 8 mi. north from Ellsworth. Turn right at sign for Hancock Point and continue approx. 5 mi. ◣

DOCKSIDE GUEST QUARTERS
York, Maine (1975)

"There must be something special that happens here on the Fourth of July; don't I remember that you have a special little celebration?"

Harriette Lusty and I were having a light luncheon on the porch of the dining room at Dockside Guest Quarters. It was a day such as I have experienced here many times in the past, watching the wonderful harbor traffic as all kinds of craft make their way through the harbor to the ocean. Even though it had been a very hot day out on I-95, here on this lovely porch there was a wonderful breeze that made even sitting in the sun a joy.

"Oh, we do some very wonderful things here on the Fourth of July," Harriette exclaimed. "We have a thirty-five-foot-long flag with only thirty-seven stars that is brought out, unfolded, and placed on the lawn, because it is much too large for any flagpole. At noontime we set off our cannon, and the waitresses and all of our chambermaids come over and stand by. It's really quite a ceremony and we leave one of our postcards at each door, inviting all the guests to come up to the shoot. It takes place right over there by the flagpole. We use that little brass one-pounder cannon originally kept in the hallway near the front door. Everybody gets into a wonderful Independence Day mood."

The Dockside Guest Quarters is composed of the original New England homestead of the 1880s, called the Maine House, and four other multi-unit cottage buildings of a contemporary design, with guest rooms that have their own porches and water views. Some have a casual studio feeling and some have kitchenettes.

The innkeepers are David and Harriette Lusty. David is a real "State of Maine" man, complete with a wonderful Down East accent. They have raised four sons at Dockside, and now their second son, Eric, has returned to take a hand in the running of the inn.

Harriette continued, "The days in early June can be spent in many different ways. We have a number of sandy beaches, and swimming is at its best when the sun is highest at midday and in early afternoon. It's also great fun to wander around the stretches of beach and have them almost entirely to one's self. Golf and tennis are available at the golf club, and the marina has rental outboards, great for picnics on the York River. We're doing something very interesting during the month of June; we have arranged a special three-day bargain package that includes a sightseeing cruise with a luncheon stop at Portsmouth Harbor. It also includes a lobster dinner, all at very attractive pre-season rates."

There's always a great deal of history to share in the York area, and this time I learned about the famous statue that is the figure of a Confederate soldier, instead of a "Boy in Blue." David tells me that they have now located the town somewhere in South Carolina where the statue of the

Union soldier has been resting for almost a hundred years. Everybody has decided that they're going to leave the statues the way they are. "After all," said David, "that war has long been over."

So the combination of Dockside life, generous dollops of history, the pleasant vista from Dockside of the harbor craft. and the opportunity to enjoy a good dinner at the Dockside dining room, managed by Steve and Sue Roeder, makes staying at this little seaside inn an enjoyable experience in any season of the year—perhaps just a tad more satisfying in June.

DOCKSIDE GUEST QUARTERS, P.O. Box 205, Harris Island Rd. York, ME 03909; 207-363-2868. An 18-guestroom (some studio suites with kitchenettes) waterside country inn 10 mi. from Portsmouth, N.H. American plan available. Continental-plus breakfast served to houseguests only. Dockside Dining Room serves lunch and dinner to travelers daily except Mon. Open from Memorial Day weekend in May thru Columbus Day (in Oct.). York Village is a National Historic District. Wheelchair access. Lawn games, shuffleboard, badminton, fishing, sailing, and boating from premises. Golf, tennis, and ocean swimming nearby; safe and picturesque paths and roadways for walks, bicycling, and jogging. Credit cards are not welcome for amounts over $75. Personal checks accepted for payment of food and lodgings incurred by registered guests. Eric, David, and Harriette Lusty, Innkeepers. (See Index for rates.)

Directions: From I-95, take the last exit before the northbound toll gate at York to U.S. 1, then to Rte. 1A. Follow 1A thru center of Old York Village, take Rte. 103 (a side street off Rte. 1A leading to the harbor), and watch for signs to the inn immediately after crossing bridge.

GOOSE COVE LODGE
Deer Isle, Maine (1981)

Innkeeper Elli Pavloff's letter, dated August 31, read in part: "Last Friday night we were sitting up in our apartment above the main lodge listening to a group of guests, one of them with a guitar, singing songs. (The Beatles and Simon and Garfunkel seemed to have displaced 'Now Is the Hour' and 'It's a Long Way to Tipperary.') It was after the lobster cookout on the beach.

"I thought: 'There is no other place and no other moment I'd rather be living in!' This is the reward for innkeeping, seeing people happy, relaxed, at peace, at one with the world.

"The Goose Cove environment does it really. We just work along with it—the ocean, the nature trails, the fresh air, the social hour, the family-style meals, the camaraderie and friendships that spring up among the guests—peace flows in and we can actually see people, renewed, recreated in the space of a week. It's wonderful to be a part of the process."

Goose Cove Lodge is a rustic resort-inn on Deer Isle. Elli calls it "the Girl or Boy Scout Camp of the book." It is on the modified American plan, and all guests take breakfast and dinner in the dining room, which has an expansive view of Goose Cove. There is a one-week minimum-stay policy during July and August. Typically, guests arrive about 5:30 on Saturday, which is the beginning of the Goose Cove week. They are shown to their cottage or room and told that hors d'oeuvres have just been set out in the Lodge and that the dinner bell will ring at 6:30. A little later, George and Elli Pavloff greet them and introduce them to other guests. By dinnertime first-timers are beginning to realize that many of the other guests have been coming to Goose Cove for quite a few years.

At breakfast the first morning, everybody is given an orientation to Deer Isle and apprised of the many choices available for various activities. At the Sunday evening buffet they're all eager to share the day's experiences. Perhaps they've gone on a boat ride to the outer islands, taken a drive to Bar Harbor, spent the day walking the nature trails, visited the crafts and antique stores, or had a deep muscle massage or a sailing lesson or expedition.

On Friday night, the lobster cookout on the beach is like the last night of summer camp. Physical and mental tensions are erased, faces are relaxed, and fellowship is high. Guests are exchanging addresses at breakfast the next morning, and George and Elli and their staff are all saying goodbye. The result is obvious and in marked contrast to those guests who are trying to 'do' New England in a week by touching down briefly in a different place each night.

Lest I forget, most of the accommodations are in cottages with native stone fireplaces. Aromatic wood has been used for walls, beams, shelves, bookcases, and the like. Most have a peaked roof and exposed overhead beams, and all of the cottages sit on the great granite rocks adjacent to Goose Cove, and all have wonderful views. Each of the rustic lodges has its own bathroom facilities and in some there is an extra bedroom.

George had a P.S. on Elli's letter: "Another delight of this season is the willingness of our guests to share their talent with one another, these include slide shows, music making, and informal lectures."

GOOSE COVE LODGE, Sunset, Deer Isle, ME 04683; 207-348-2508. A 22-guestroom (60 people) resort-inn on beautiful Penobscot Bay approx. 1 hr. from Rte. 1 at Bucksport. Open mid-June to mid-Oct. Modified American plan mid-June to mid-Sept.; 7-day minimum stay (Sat.-Sat.) in July and Aug.; 2-day minimum stay other times. Meals served to houseguests only. Wheelchair access. Swimming, boating, canoeing, hiking, and bird watching all available at the inn. Other outdoor sports, including backroading, golf, tennis, etc., nearby. Especially adaptable for children of all ages. Elli and George Pavloff, Innkeepers. (See Index for rates.)

Directions: From Bucksport, it is approx. 1 hr. to inn. Drive 4 mi. north on Rte. 1 and turn right on Rte. 15 down the Blue Hill Peninsula to Deer Isle Village. Turn right in village at sign to Sunset, Maine. Proceed 3 mi., turn right at Goose Cove Lodge sign. Follow dirt road 1½ mi. to inn. ⬎

GREY ROCK INN
Northeast Harbor, Maine (1976)

Janet Millet and I were seated in a new, trim sitting room that had been created on the second floor of the Grey Rock Inn since my last visit. Bathed in the afternoon sunshine, it's a perfect place for a quiet cup of tea, and that's exactly what we were having.

"I call it a little upstairs sitting room," she said. "I put on the last of the wallpaper in June, and as you see I've decorated it with other things of which I am very fond. I put some wicker furniture in here, including a Victorian bird cage with some colorful peacocks, and there is some geranium ivy. It's supposed to have pink blossoms, but they haven't come out just yet. That Japanese screen is one of my favorites and it's decorated with jade and mother-of-pearl."

Janet is British and she has an innate admiration for things British. For example, she loves, as do most Britons, "a lovely fireplace." Fortunately, Grey Rock is on the coast of upper Maine and there is plenty of firewood right from her own little forest to supply the two living room/parlor fireplaces with ample wood.

I usually tease her about being British and this time I asked, "What are some British touches that you use here at Grey Rock?"

"Well, we serve a very good strong cup of tea. English breakfast tea," she replied rather firmly. "Another English touch is the unusual reception and drawing room, also used as our breakfast room. We have a very large selection of books and British magazines."

"Is there anything that you particularly remembered from growing up in England that you have introduced in the bedrooms?" I asked.

"Yes, my lovely down-feather pillows. We used to have down-feather mattresses when I was a girl, but I've got the very best down-feather pillows here for Grey Rock. We have all kinds of other English touches too, with lots of flowers and bright and gay fabrics in all of the guest rooms."

I must admit that Grey Rock has a very authentic English country house feeling—the same feeling I enjoy so much when visiting in England. Some of the guest rooms on the second floor have very good views of the corner of the harbor.

One of the focal points is a porch off the reception area that gives one the sensation of sitting in the treetops. There are evergreen trees all around it and big hanging tuberous begonias. It's a very pleasant place for breakfast in the morning.

"Elegant" is an excellent word to describe Grey Rock, and almost immediately new arrivals are struck by Janet's unusual collection of wicker pieces, which are rare art forms. For example, there is a tea table on wheels, a chaise lounge, three or four wicker table lamps, a wicker floor lamp, wicker love seats, a wicker desk, a wicker plant stand for two plants, and wing chairs in wicker. These are all in the main sitting room and another smaller adjacent parlor.

These wicker pieces blend beautifully with the unusual collection of oriental memorabilia that Janet has gathered over the years, making the inn somewhat reminiscent of a New England house of a century ago, when sea captains brought back the wonderful treasure of the Orient on their clipper ships. Particularly impressive are the collection of fans and the exquisite framed oriental paintings on silk. As part of the harmonious whole, fresh flowers complete the picture.

Grey Rock literally sits on a rocky ledge above the town of Northeast Harbor, well within its own forested area, where trails lead into the woods. There is no amusement or recreation on the grounds for smaller children. The entire kaleidoscope of the wonderful natural attractions of Mount Desert Island is literally at the front door.

GREY ROCK INN, Harborside Rd., Northeast Harbor, ME 04662; 207-276 9360. A 12-guestroom village inn adjacent to Acadia National Park and all of the attractions of this unusual region. European plan. Continental breakfast served to houseguests only. No other meals served. Small cottage available for minimum 4-night stay. Season from early spring to Nov. 1. Children 14 yrs. and older preferred. No Pets. No credit cards. No smoking in guest rooms. Janet Millet, Innkeeper. (See Index for rates.)

Directions: Located on the right side of Rte. 198 approaching the town of Northeast Harbor. Note sign for inn. Do not try to make a right turn at this point, but proceed about one block, turn around and approach the inn on the left, up the steep hill.

HARTWELL HOUSE
Ogunquit, Maine (1981)

People in the West who get this book, which is published annually, to learn about inns on the West Coast may also become intrigued with the inns on the East Coast, as well as those in between. Many visitors from the West Coast come to the Northeast each fall to enjoy the storied fall foliage colors and the total New England experience.

On the Massachusetts, Connecticut, and Maine coasts there are several villages whose names alone touch off the desire to come to New England. One such village is Ogunquit, Maine, where the flavor of Old Maine remains zesty and alive, and yet the village has some very contemporary touches.

Seated on the front porch of the Hartwell House with Trisha Hartwell, I was just remarking about how almost everything in Ogunquit is within walking distance, when a very interesting-looking Toonerville Trolley coach came by on its way to Perkins Cove.

"This is an invaluable way for our guests to travel anywhere in Ogunquit during the summertime," she remarked. "One of our problems here is to try to persuade motorists to park and take the trolley down to the Cove and perhaps walk back. It's a very handy type of transportation in the summertime.

"We're delighted to see our guests from the West Coast," she said. "However, I do hope that you will remind them that autumn is a very busy season here in New England and we are booked very tightly during that time. Since we're open year-round I've encouraged many of our guests to come back in late fall, winter, and early spring, because Ogunquit is equally inviting then."

Trisha poured me another glass of iced tea and I settled back in the chair to ogle the many passers-by. "I'm glad you came," she remarked. "because you now have a chance to look at the new guest rooms in the house next door. They're furnished with English country waxed-pine antiques and upholstered with stunning pastel fabrics. We now have three large suites, each with a living room, bedroom, and private bath, plus four delightful guest rooms. They are furnished in the same elegant tones as the main house, and we've taken special care with the landscaping as well. That brings the total of our guest rooms to seventeen."

A complimentary continental breakfast is served either on the patio or in the elegant dining room, or it can be brought to your room, depending on your arrangements.

The little red trolley, which had gone down to Perkins Cove earlier, was now returning, pausing here and there to pick up people who preferred to ride. "Almost all of our guests have heard about and want to walk on the Marginal Way, which is a most pleasant stroll and has many picture-postcard Maine seascapes and rock formations. We have particularly enticing package plans for midweek and weekends, which we have arranged with many of the area restaurants," she continued. "For example, early in December we have a Kennebunkport 'Christmas Prelude,' because all of the many very attractive little shops go out of their way to dress up for Christmas. You can walk the Marginal Way on many of the pleasant days that we have here even during midwinter. There is swimming during the summer on the beach, and it's possible to fish for striped bass or go deep-sea fishing for game fish."

Well, I'm getting carried away with all of the local color, and I did want to say that the guest rooms at Hartwell House are most attractively furnished with many antiques, four-poster beds, and beautiful bedspreads. The tone is set by the front porch area with its beautiful summer furniture, where I was sitting. There are several groups of comfortable chairs and sofas with light-hearted slipcovers, stacks of books and magazines, and many varieties of flowers. It's fun to just sit here and watch the world go by.

HARTWELL HOUSE, 116 Shore Rd., Ogunquit, ME 03907; 207-646-7210. A 17-guestroom (private baths) inn providing a very compatible atmosphere for guests. Complimentary continental breakfast. Open year-round. The ocean, Perkins Cove, the Marginal Way, Ogunquit Playhouse, and churches within walking distance. Fishing, golf, tennis, swimming, bicycles, sailing nearby. Golf privileges available at Cliff Country Club. Not suitable for children under 14. No pets. Trisha and Jim Hartwell, Innkeepers. (See Index for rates.)

Directions: Follow I-95 north through N.H. into Me.; take last exit before Me. toll booth; north on Rte. 1 for 7 mi. to center of Ogunquit. Turn right on Shore Rd., approx. ¾ mi. to Hartwell House on right.

HOMEWOOD INN
Yarmouth, Maine (1973)

"Tell me about the kind of guests who come to Homewood," I said to Fred Webster as we were strolling about the grounds.

"Well, I think that we appeal to a great many people of all ages and preferences," he said. "For instance, we have one guest who comes for three weeks in late June each year and tells us to put through no phone calls and not to bother him and his wife for clambake reservations or anything else. It happens that he's about to leave now and we haven't seen him once! Of course, there are others who like to chat with the staff and the family and who mix well around the pool and the tennis courts with the other guests. One of the things that attracts almost every guest is the L. L. Bean store."

The L. L. Bean store in nearby Freeport is just one of the many reasons to remain several nights at the Homewood Inn. The inn has been operated for a number of years by the Webster family and has a view of some of the 365 Calendar Islands. Many of the single and double cottages that make up most of the inn complex have fireplaces and kitchen facilities and are set among the juniper, cedar, maple, and Norway pine trees. There is a multitude of flowers, including roses, phlox, snapdragons, marigolds, petunias, and dozens of other flowering plants and shrubs.

Guests are frequently delighted to discover that they are sharing their waterside environment with many varieties of land and shore birds. Colleen Webster told me that a few years ago she looked out of her window and saw a moose walking on the property. "It seemed to me to be as big as a house," she declared. "Eventually it strolled down the road, passed some of our cottages, and entered the water and swam off into the distance. We do have seals on our offshore rocks, but this is the first time I've ever seen a moose. As a matter of fact, I hope it's the last time!"

Homewood Inn has been on this particular spot on Casco Bay for many, many years. It was originally started by Fred Webster's mother and father and is being continued by Fred and his wife, Colleen.

In the summer, I've always enjoyed being at Homewood on a Wednesday night so that I can have fun at the regular Wednesday night clambake—a real Down East feast, with lobster, steak, clams, and chicken served outdoors at rustic tables. No other evening meals are offered.

Meanwhile, Fred and I walked over the path he had cut in the field by the woods, through the new pine-tree farm, and we were accompanied by Bonnie, a full-bred collie. She flushed out a pileated woodpecker and a cedar waxwing as we strolled along.

The Homewood is certainly well named; it's very homelike and looks happily settled among the woods, fields, and harbor. Its informal atmosphere invites vacationers, especially those with children, to enjoy a real country resort-inn experience. Sooner or later everyone meets at the lodge, around the pool, or at the tennis courts.

HOMEWOOD INN, Drinkwater Point, P.O Box 196B, Yarmouth, ME 04096; 207-846-3351. A 42-guestroom (including suites and cottages with fully equipped kitchens) waterside inn on Casco Bay, 20 min. north of Portland. Breakfast available for houseguests and travelers. A steak and lobster cookout is held each Wed. night during summer (advance reservation). Open mid-June to mid-Oct. Limited wheelchair access. Bicycles (including tandems), pool, tennis, croquet court, hiking, salt-water swimming on grounds. Golf, riding, fishing, boating, state parks, theater nearby. Fred and Colleen Webster and Ted and Doris Gillette, Innkeepers. (See Index for rates.)

Directions: From the south, take Exit 9 from Maine Tpke. (I-95) to Rte. 1-N, or Yarmouth exit from I-295 to Rte. 1-N and follow signs to inn. From north (Brunswick area) take I-95 to Yarmouth exit. Then take Rte. 88 and follow signs to inn.

"European plan" means that rates for rooms and meals are separate. "American plan" means that meals are included in the cost of the room. "Modified American plan" means that breakfast and dinner are included in the cost of the room. The rates at some inns include a continental breakfast with the lodging.

OLD FORT INN
Kennebunkport, Maine (1976)

"Beaches are fun and I enjoy salt water, but to me there's something very special about having the privacy and quietness of a swimming pool."

A group of us were seated around the pool at the Old Fort Inn when this particular observation was made by a Canadian guest. Someone else had said, "I like to play tennis and I like to know that not only is there a good tennis court here, but there are frequently people who play a good game."

The Old Fort Inn is a very special kind of country inn that provides a complete change of pace from the hustle and bustle of Kennebunkport. A few years ago, the main building of the hotel that originally had been on the property was torn down, and the handsome stone carriage house was converted into twelve large bedrooms with electric heat, fully equipped kitchen facilities, Laura Ashley wallpapers, and daily maid service. The rooms are large enough so that guests can stay for longer periods without feeling cramped.

Guests gather at the main lodge in a converted barn, built around 1880. It has a big fireplace that serves as a focal point on spring and fall evenings, and its open deck next to the swimming pool makes it a very comfortable place where guests may gather in the warmer weather.

The innkeepers are David and Sheila Aldrich, two very attractive people from California, who came here a few years ago and have made the Old Fort Inn and Kennebunkport their new home. They are considerably assisted by their perky daughter, Shana, who must be at least eleven years old by this time.

I think it might be fun if I shared a description of my bedroom at the Old Fort Inn. For one thing, it's large enough to be comfortable for two people, with plenty of room for a third person on the little sofa bed. There is a big double cannonball bed with blue sheets and a harmonizing blue comforter, blue carpeting, and a blue cover on the daybed. There are good reading lights on both sides of the bed. A fully equipped kitchenette, including a stove with an oven and separated from the rest of the room by a divider, gives guests the option of preparing their own meals. A wood table and chairs for two, a Victorian table with an attractive lamp, a wicker armchair, and a beautifully refinished chest of drawers complete the picture. A painting of a duck is part of the great collection of duck decoys and paintings found throughout the inn.

A large over-sized closet contains extra pillows (something I commend at all times). By the way, David and Sheila have provided such thoughtful things as a laundry with a dryer in the same building.

The village of Kennebunkport still retains much of the ambience it had when clipper ships sailed from its shores. The lovely old sea captains' houses remain, and the beautiful streets and winding river make it a very pleasant vacation experience.

During my most recent visit I found that guests spend quite a bit of time in the antique shop that's mainly Sheila's project. "David and I feel that it has added considerably to the attractiveness of the inn," she said. "I'm glad that we put in that lovely English garden. The flowers change with the seasons, and it is the first thing the guest sees upon arrival."

Spring is an excellent time to visit this part of the Maine coast, and between mid-April and mid-June, and November and mid-December, David and Sheila have arranged for a very special midweek "Escape Plan" that I'm sure many of our readers would find most attractive.

OLD FORT INN, Old Fort Ave., P.O. Box M, Kennebunkport, ME 04046; 207-967-5353. A 14-guestroom resort-inn within walking distance of the ocean in a historic Maine town. Includes an ample continental breakfast. Daily maid service. Fireplace lodge. Open from mid-Apr. to mid-Dec. Efficiencies, heated pool, tennis court, shuffleboard and bicycles on grounds. Golf, salt-water swimming, and boating nearby. Not comfortable for children under 12. No pets. Sheila and David Aldrich, Innkeepers. (See Index for rates.)

Directions: Take Exit 3 (Kennebunk) from Maine Tpke. (I-95). Take left on Rte. 35 and follow signs through Kennebunk to Kennebunkport. Take left at traffic light at Sunoco station. Go over drawbridge and take first right on Ocean Ave. Take Ocean Ave. to the Colony Hotel; turn left in front of the Colony, go to the Y in the road, go right ¼ mi. Inn is on left.

THE PENTAGOET INN
Castine, Maine (1988)

For many years I regarded Castine as one of the best-kept secrets in the world. I also discovered that when I ran into other people who knew about Castine, we felt as if we belonged to an exclusive club—something akin to people who have climbed Mount Everest.

I'm sure that many people do stumble on Castine, but it's not on the road to anywhere. Its principal claim to fame is the fact that originally it was settled by British Loyalists, who, after the American Revolution, decided they preferred to remain under King George and so moved, many of them, from Boston up to this lovely out-of-the-way location. There are many markers in the town reminding us that such an exodus did take place.

The Pentagoet Inn has made people sit up and take notice of Castine. I first discovered it quite a few years ago, when it was run by Natalie Saunders. Today, I think it's safe to say the Pentagoet far exceeds her finest dreams under innkeepers Lindsey and Virginia Miller.

One of the first things that Lindsey, Virginia, and I have in common are porches. I've always loved them and I've spent many a happy hour rocking on porches of country inns all over North America. "That's just the way we feel," said Virginia. "As a matter of fact, that's why we have extended the porch all the way to the back of the main building. You'll notice that we've put window boxes and standing flowerpots in as many places as possible, and our new green awning has been a real blessing."

Well, the talk went on from porches to breakfast. "I must step in here," Lindsey declared. "This morning, besides a cup of fresh tropical fruit, we had a creamy, fresh herb omelet. Our french toast is thick homemade slices filled with cream cheese and fresh orange, topped with blueberry sauce. In addition to that there are sausage links or grilled rib eye steak and we continue with the famous Pentagoet muffins that you wrote about when Natalie owned the inn."

In the ensuing conversation we talked about many other interesting changes the Millers had made. "When we first arrived in the fall of 1985 we became aware that the inn needed more dining space and more common areas for the guests. We spent the first winter correcting this by creating a very inviting 'library' with an upright Bosendorfer piano and most of our personal collection of books." I agreed that it provides a good place for guests to relax with a book, play the piano, or listen to some classical music.

"The addition of the back dining room was an inspiration," Virginia said, "and I'm happy to say we are well known for our dinners. Part of this is because we have an excellent chef and we offer a variety of main dishes including Maine lobsters, lobster pie, grilled fresh salmon steak with dilled hollandaise, a peppered rib eye steak, and a roast leg of lamb. It's part of a five-course meal which includes soup and dessert."

Things have happened above the first floor of the Pentagoet which I found very important and exciting. For example, by redesigning the second- and third-floor guest rooms, the Pentagoet now has twelve guest rooms with private baths and two with half-baths. In addition the annex next door, 10 Perkins Street, also has very attractive guest rooms.

"Virginia has a knack for details," Lindsey said, "and guests like such touches as the baskets with a large supply of fresh towels, vases with fresh flowers in each room, and nightly room freshening with beds turned down."

So the Pentagoet is attracting more country inn enthusiasts than ever. I'm very happy to include it again in 1988.

THE PENTAGOET INN, Main St., P.O. Box 4, Castine, ME 04221; 207-326-8616. An 18-guestroom (private and shared baths) inn in a seacoast village on the Penobscot Peninsula, 36 mi. from Bangor. Modified American plan includes breakfast and dinner. Dinner available to outside guests by reservation. Open Apr. 1 to Dec. 1. Tennis, swimming, backroading, village strolling, craft shops, chamber music concerts, Maine Maritime Academy, Acadia Nat'l Park, and Blue Hill nearby. Children over 12 welcome. No pets. Smoking on porches only. Lindsey and Virginia Miller, Innkeepers. (See Index for rates.)

Directions: From the south, follow I-95 to Brunswick and use Rte. 1 exit. Follow Rte. 1 to a point 3 mi. past Bucksport. Turn right on Rte. 175 to Rte. 166 to Castine. Look for Maine Maritime Academy sign; turn left onto Main St.

THE PILGRIM'S INN
Deer Isle, Maine (1980)

Travelers really have to be looking for Deer Isle and the Pilgrim's Inn. It's a good hour's drive from U.S. 1, east of Bucksport, to the Blue Hill Peninsula. Deer Isle sits just off the southern flank of the mainland and no matter how you arrive it's necessary to cross over the suspension bridge at Eggemoggin Reach.

This is really "down home" Maine and even the 1939 bridge has failed to disturb the naturalness of both the islanders and the area.

A four-story, gambrel-roofed red house, this building has overlooked the long harbor on the front and the millpond in the rear since 1793. Jean and Dud Hendrick moved here a few years ago after acquiring the Pilgrim's Inn. Much of the original building has remained almost completely unchanged, with the original Colonial feature of two large rooms and a kitchen on the ground floor still intact. One of these rooms is the Common Room of the present-day inn.

Most of the guest rooms are quite large with richly hued pine floorboards, wood stoves, country furniture, and a selection of books and magazines. They are enhanced by coordinated Laura Ashley fabrics, used for curtains, lampshades, quilts, and cushions.

Although I visited there last summer as part of a hilarious dinner party with some friends from nearby Blue Hill, where everybody vowed that it was "the best time ever," I'd like to share a portion of a yearly letter that Dud and Jean write me.

"We have now purchased and redecorated an enchanting house in the village, which we call 'Number 15.' 'Enchanting' understates it. Number 15 sits over the harbor, affording the occupants unparalleled sunset views from its back deck. It is completely furnished and equipped so that guests may choose to prepare their own meals if they are so foolish as to pass up Jean's fabulous cuisine. It is the quintessential honeymoon cottage or retreat for four friends (it has a hide-a-bed in front of the fireplace in the living room in addition to the upstairs bedroom)."

The letter went on to say that one of the first-floor parlors of the main inn has now been made into a warm reading room and library. "We discovered that guests really don't have a room in which they can quietly read, free of socializing fellow travelers. Now they do."

The Pilgrim's Inn provides far more than can really be done in a single or two-night stay. Guests can bike, hike, sail, canoe, and even learn to kayak in whitewater or the sea with a certified instructor. Guests also play tennis and golf, and do many of the less energetic things. The mail boat run to Isle au Haute is a most romantic day trip, and the sailing here is terrific. There are many, many art galleries and crafts shops a short distance away, and Acadia National Park is just close enough for a day trip.

Pilgrim's Inn, as I said before, is a special place, so tell only your very special friends about it.

THE PILGRIM'S INN, Deer Isle, ME 04627; 207-348-6615. A 13-guestroom (some shared baths) inn in a remote island village on the Blue Hill Peninsula on the Maine coast. Modified American plan, May 15 to Nov. 1, includes a hearty breakfast and a creative dinner. In season, outside dinner reservations are accepted. A 4-day minimum reservation is requested in Aug. Bicycles, badminton, ping-pong, regulation horseshoes, croquet, and a rowboat for the millpond on the grounds. All types of cultural and recreational advantages, including golf, fishing, sailing, hiking, and browsing nearby. No pets. Dud and Jean Hendrick, Innkeepers. (See Index for rates.)

Directions: From Boston, take I-95 to Brunswick exit. Take coastal Rte. 1 north past Bucksport. Turn right on Rte. 15, which travels to Deer Isle down the Blue Hill Peninsula. At the village, turn right on Main St. (Sunset Rd.) and proceed one block to the inn on the left side of the street, opposite the harbor.

A number of inns have nearby airports where private airplanes may land. An airplane symbol at the end of the inn directions indicates that there is an airport nearby. Consult inn for further information.

THE SQUIRE TARBOX INN
Westport Island, Maine (1974)

Karen Mitman and I were walking through the woods behind the Squire Tarbox Inn toward Squam Creek. We were two people being escorted by seven lively, handsome Nubian goats in various shades of brown and beige. It being June, we passed through patches of buttercups and lupine, and our group occasionally paused while one of the goats decided to nibble.

"Come on, Garbo," Karen called. "We call her Garbo because she thinks she's kind of dramatic. Another one is Garbanzo Bean because she has a humorous side to her. Opal is our Southern belle from Luray, Virginia." We arrived at the serene saltwater marsh that has a little dock and a screened-in shed for just sitting and looking through the binoculars provided.

"Most of our guests are from the big city, and it's just nice for them to come here and sit. It is quiet, and the combination of the water and the sky and the clouds and the little marshy island and the trees is so pleasing to them."

The Squire Tarbox is a very quiet inn in a section of Maine that is sufficiently off the beaten track to be unspoiled and natural. The main house has both the wainscoting of the early 1800s and the rustic wide board construction of the 1700s. It is quite small—eleven guest rooms have a cozy "up country" feeling with Colonial prints and colors and some working fireplaces. A large hearth with the original bake oven, pumpkin pine floors, and hand-hewn beams set the tone for this rambling Colonial farmhouse with its hip roof and pale yellow narrow clapboards and apple green shutters.

There are several choices for sitting around in front of fireplaces to enjoy reading or conversation, especially in a captivating barn with large doors that open out on a screened-in sundeck. There is a player piano, an antique music box, Colonial wooden toys, and English wooden puzzles for further amusement.

Karen and her husband, Bill, are very friendly, conversational people, who make innkeeping seem almost deceptively simple. Their background at the Copley Plaza in Boston must have much to do with this.

Karen and I sat in the little shed and continued our conversation while the goats cavorted on the pine needles. "I know you remember when we brought in our first goats," she said. "We were a little hesitant, but they have been a most rewarding experience for our guests. Now we have a new cheese-processing room and have packaged some goat cheese for sale to our guests. The cheese is served every night before dinner as well."

Our conversation turned naturally to food and she mentioned that the Squire Tarbox is on the modified American plan, which includes breakfast and dinner. "Dinner is served at seven o'clock and usually begins with a soup that could be made with fruit or vegetables. The second course is a salad, and the main course is usually fish or chicken and is always served with three vegetables that reflect some creative thinking, such as mint-glazed carrots, cranberries with red cabbage, or broccoli with lemon butter. One of the most popular desserts is a chocolate concoction known as the Squire's 'Sin Pie.'"

Karen had to return to the inn and suggested that I might find it interesting just to sit here and enjoy the sounds of silence. So she took all of the goats and set back up the hill. I mused that this simple little path through the woods down to the saltwater marsh provides guests with the unique opportunity to have the feeling of really being in the country. When one takes all of this "Forest of Arden" atmosphere into consideration, along with the fact that the inn is now on the National Register of Historic Places, it is easy to see why Karen and Bill are proud of what they have accomplished.

THE SQUIRE TARBOX INN, Westport Island, R.D. 2, Box 620, Wiscasset, ME 04578; 207-882-7693. An 11-guestroom (private baths) restored Colonial home midway between Boston and Bar Harbor on Rte. 144 in Westport, 10 mi. from Wiscasset. Modified American plan— includes continental breakfast and full leisurely dinner. Also serving dinner to travelers. Open late May to late Oct. Within a 30-min. drive of beaches, harbors, shops, and museums of midcoast Maine. No amusements for children under 14. Bill and Karen Mitman, Innkeepers. (See Index for rates.)

Directions: From Maine Tpke., take Exit 9 and follow Rte. 95 to Exit 22. Take Rte. 1 to Rte. 144, 7 mi. north of Bath. Follow Rte. 144 to Wiscasset–Westport Bridge. The inn is located 6 mi. south of bridge on Westport Island.

THE WATERFORD INNE
East Waterford, Maine (1980)

Three of us were seated on the screened-in porch, which has a lovely view of the meadows and had actually only been completed the day before, so both Rosalie and Barbara Vanderzanden, innkeepers at the Waterford Inne, were feeling very proud and happy.

"This is something that we've been wanting to do for years," said Barbara. "It seems that we have about one major project every year; one year it was the new kitchen and, of course, this year it's the porch. It also provides us with additional dining space on warm evenings."

My eye happened to travel to what was one of the most sumptuous-looking vegetable gardens I have ever seen, and it prompted a question: "What are some of the things that you grow in your own garden for your kitchen?"

"Well, we grow practically all our own herbs," explained Rosalie, who is Barbara's mother and the cook. "We like fresh herbs in the salad dressing. We also have tomatoes, brussels sprouts, broccoli, peppers, squash, and pumpkins. I'm surprised at how fussy pumpkins are to grow."

Their food has received a four-star rating by the food reviewer of the *Maine Sunday Telegram,* who gave them a rave review.

"We serve baked ham with peach glaze, breast of chicken with heavy cream, various kinds of roasts, and beef Stroganoff. We serve a fixed-price dinner every evening for both houseguests and visitors. We do all our own baking, and our guests seem to enjoy it very much."

At the Waterford Inne, located in the little-known Oxford Hills area of western Maine, "small and tidy" is beautiful. It can be truthfully said that the Waterford Inne is an intimate inn. The inn is small enough to provide a really cozy country inn experience. The original house was built in 1825 and has five upstairs bedrooms that step out of the 19th century. These are augmented by four additional rooms created in a wing leading to a very large barn.

All of the bedrooms have been carefully decorated, usually with some theme in mind. For example, the Chesapeake Room has a fireplace stove and a private porch. The decorations are in the Eastern Shore theme, with duck decoys and waterfowl. Even the sheets and towels have colorful waterfowls on them. All of the rooms have either antiques or attractive country furniture. My bed was a four-poster with a lace canopy.

Guests gather in the main living room, where there are many different books and magazines, including several from England, because Barbara and Rosalie are Anglophiles and in fact followed *Country Inns and Back Roads, Britain and Ireland* in a trip they made to England.

Well, our chat was over, and as Rosalie went to the kitchen, Barbara and I strolled around to take a closer look at the big barn. "The Oxford

Hills section of Maine abounds in much beautiful scenery," she re-marked. "It's hard to drive more than four or five miles without coming to a lake. It's quite a popular area for summer camps, so we are rather well booked in advance for the camp visitation weekends. Many camp parents stay at the inn and then stay on extra days, because it's such a lovely, tranquil experience."

THE WATERFORD INNE, Box 49, East Waterford, ME 04233; 207-583-4037. A 9-guestroom farmhouse-inn in the Oxford Hills section of southwest Maine, 8 mi. from Norway and South Paris. Closed March and April. Breakfast and dinner served to travelers by reservation. European plan. Within a short distance of many recreational, scenic, and cultural attractions in Maine and the White Mountains of New Hampshire. Cross-country skiing and badminton on grounds. Lake swimming, golf, rock hunting, downhill skiing, hiking, canoeing nearby. Alcoholic beverages not served. Well-behaved pets welcome; however, advance notification is required and a fee is charged. No credit cards. Rosalie and Barbara Vanderzanden, Innkeepers. (See Index for rates.)

Directions: From Maine Tpke.: use Exit 11, follow Rte. 26 north approx. 28 mi. into Norway, then on Rte. 118 west for 8 mi. to Rte. 37 south (left turn). Go ½ mi., turn right at Springer's General Store, up the hill ½ mi. From Conway, New Hampshire: Rte. 16 to Rte. 302 east to Fryeburg, Me. Take Rte. 5 out of Fryeburg to Rte. 35 south, thence to Rte. 118, which is a left fork (with Rte. 35 going right). Continue on Rte. 118 east, past Papoose Pond camping area, then watch for right turn onto Rte. 37. Go ½ mi. to Springer's General Store. Take immediate right turn, ½ mi. up hill.

WHITEHALL INN
Camden, Maine (1973)

If ever an inn and a setting were made for each other, the Whitehall Inn and Camden are perfectly matched. The neoclassic buildings of the inn are connected by a large porch filled with plenty of comfortable wicker furniture. The inn sits back from the main street among huge elm and pine trees, and there are many window boxes and arrangements of summer flowers.

Ed and Jean Dewing left Boston with their family and came to Camden in the early 1970s to become innkeepers. Now there are several members of the family who keep this highly reputable village inn thriving. I have seen the Dewings' children, Heidi, Chip, and J.C., grow into professionals and each year take on more and more of the responsibilities of running the inn. Jean's brother, Uncle Don, has maintained a high standard of excellence in the food presentations and Chip's wife, Kathy, and J.C.'s fiancée, Wendy, round out the team.

On the first floor there are several parlors and a large lobby, all of which are furnished with Maine antiques. The lounge has sewing machines ingeniously converted into tables, chess sets that invite competition, and a large collection of unusual shells displayed under glass. Guest rooms are country style.

Ed Dewing says that most of the guests still are interested in the Edna St. Vincent Millay Room, designed as a tribute to her, with many volumes of her poems, along with memorabilia that would be of interest to her numerous admirers. It was here at the Whitehall Inn on a warm August evening in 1912 that young Edna first recited her poem "Renascence."

The inn is just a short, tree-lined walk from the center of the village. An excellent folder provided by the inn has dozens of suggestions about activities in and around this part of Maine, including golf, sightseeing, art exhibitions, boating, swimming, hiking, and fishing.

I believe that a major part of everyone's country inn experience is the food. In reference to the Whitehall Inn, here's a letter I have from a gentleman from Vermont: "Because I have been connected with the food industry most of my life, I instinctively notice the small considerations that lift an establishment head and shoulders above the rest. During the past few years, we have enjoyed quite a few meals at the inn, and this year we were guests for a delightful week. The food is certainly exceptional."

A letter from Ed reads in part: "We find we are serving people who stay longer. Our new parking lot is getting raves from local environmentalists for its natural integrity with the surrounding forest. The plantings and lighting have created an enchanting garden at night. Another innovation that has met with almost 100% enthusiasm is a nonsmoking dining room. Smokers are understanding and are complying. It proves to us that people with different lifestyles can coexist if they reason together."

Many guests comment on the fact that seven members of a family can work together in such harmony. This means there is always a Dewing on the scene at the Whitehall.

As Ed says, "After so many years filled with ups and downs, Jean and I are still glad we chose this way of life and already look forward to our next season. We promise the same beautiful sunrises and sunsets, crisp, clean air, brilliant fall foliage, friendly neighbors, a bountiful table, and lots of people who look out for everybody's comfort and well being."

WHITEHALL INN, Camden, ME 04843; 207-236-3391. A 46-guestroom village inn in a Maine seacoast town, 75 mi. from Portland. Modified American plan omits lunch. Breakfast and dinner served daily to travelers. Open May 25 to Oct. 15. Wheelchair access. Tennis, bicycles, shuffleboard, arrangements for harbor cruises on grounds. Golf, hiking, swimming, fishing, day sailing nearby. No pets. The Dewing Family, Innkeepers. (See Index for rates.)

Directions: From Maine Tpke. take Exit 9 to coastal Rte. 95. Proceed on Rte. 95 to Rte. 1 at Brunswick. Follow Rte. 1 to Rte. 90 at Warren, to Rte. 1 in Camden. Inn is located on Rte. 1, ½ mi. north of Camden.

A number of inns have nearby airports where private airplanes may land. An airplane symbol at the end of the inn directions indicates that there is an airport nearby. Consult inn for further information.

THE BIRCHWOOD INN
Temple, New Hampshire (1986)

"We as a young nation of Americans are really just developing a true nostalgia of our own. Just since the Bicentennial has this craving grown tremendously, and an old country inn allows guests to turn back the clock and immerse themselves almost totally in an atmosphere of the roadside travel of the 18th and 19th centuries in America."

Judy and Bill Wolfe and I were enjoying a quiet moment in the back parlor of the Birchwood Inn, and I could see by the light in his eye that Bill was most enthusiastic about being an innkeeper.

The Birchwood Inn, sitting on one corner of the village green, is listed on the National Register of Historic Places and is believed to have been in operation since 1775. The present Federal-style brick building, along with the adjacent barn, was probably built about 1800, and the records document a history of changing uses that mirror the evolution of the small town tavern in New England.

The small village of Temple has no telegraph wires in the center of the town, and it's pretty much the same as it's been for two hundred years, with the Grange Hall, Congregational Church, village store, Revolutionary cemetery, and old blacksmith shop.

In 1965, probably the most interesting and prized feature of the inn was discovered when some early wall murals were uncovered under layers of old wallpaper. The paintings proved to be the work of the well-known muralist Rufus Porter, painted between 1825 and 1833. Fortunately, they were restored and are now being carefully preserved by Bill and Judy.

Today, the inn is characterized by comfortable furniture, a Steinway square grand piano, wide floorboards, checked tablecloths of yellow, red, brown, and blue, music in the background, and many tiny little areas where guests can enjoy a tête-à-tête. On the other hand, there is much opportunity for sociability. Judy said, "We have developed countless friendships with lovely people from all over the world without ever leaving the comforts of our little inn. The opportunity to reach out to people of all interests is a rare privilege afforded to both innkeepers and their children alike." The Wolfes find that their three children enjoy being involved with inn activities.

There are seven most original guest rooms, five of which have private bathrooms. Each of them has its own theme. For example, the Seashore Room has a lobster trap and shore pictures; the Music Room is decorated with old instruments, including a violin lampstand; the Train Room reflects the fact that Bill is a train buff; and the Editorial Room has a collection of framed original front pages of newspapers with headlines about the moon walk and "Nixon Quits."

The kitchen is handled in an interesting way because Bill does the cooking. Judy bakes breads and desserts, including blueberry-lemon bread, blueberry cobbler, chocolate cake, and various pies and tortes. The evening menu is on a slate blackboard, and on the night of my visit included broiled lamb chops and scallops kabob.

Bill remarked, "Serving meals as innkeepers is like hosting a dinner party each evening, except it's a lot easier since you don't have to sit down with the guests. By the time they're finished, you're nearly finished as well."

Temple is sort of tucked out of the way on a paved back road, and I don't think I would have ever found it on my own, but thanks to one of my readers, I'm glad I did.

THE BIRCHWOOD INN, Rte. 45, Temple, NH 03084; 603-878-3285. A 7-guestroom (private and shared baths) village inn in southern New Hampshire. Open year-round. Breakfast included in room rate. Dinner not served on Sun. or Mon. Wheelchair access. Hiking, xc skiing, hayrides, summer theater, ice skating, superb backroading, and numerous historic houses nearby; also the Cathedral in the Pines. No credit cards. Judy and Bill Wolfe, Innkeepers. (See Index for rates.)

Directions: Take Rte. 3 north to Nashua. At Exit 7W follow Rte. 101 west through Milford to Rte. 45. Turn left 1½ mi. to Temple. From I-91 at Brattleboro take Rte. 9 east to Keene to Rte. 101 through Peterborough, over Temple Mtn. to Rte. 45. Turn right, 1½ mi. to Temple.

COLBY HILL INN
Henniker, New Hampshire (1974)

Following Don Glover's suggestion, I turned off Route 202 just outside Hillsborough, following the sign that says "West Henniker." One of the interesting things about this road is that at one point there are two bridges across the river almost side by side. They are both two-way bridges and I couldn't for the life of me figure out why anyone would want two bridges across the same river at the same point. Later, while standing in front of the long window in the dining room, overlooking the barns shown in Jan Lindstrom's sketch, Don laughed and said that the early inhabitants of New Hampshire certainly had some most interesting ideas.

This dining room was a major change at Colby Hill in recent years, with additional space providing more tables. The atmosphere is enhanced by wide pine floorboards, and the pine furniture causes me to run my hands over the tabletops and backs of chairs. The wood-chunk stove provides comfortable and welcome warmth when needed.

"Oh, I see you're watching our birds," Don said. "Many of our guests are confirmed bird watchers. Yesterday, one of them said that he saw a bobolink—I haven't seen one for many years. The wider window really provides a much more intimate view of the birds."

This classic New Hampshire inn is on the outskirts of the small village of Henniker, the home of New England College. About ten years ago, two Bucknell University friends of mine, Don and Jane Glover, along with their son, Don Glover, Jr., and his wife, Margaret, acquired the inn. A couple of years ago, Don and June decided to retire permanently to Avalon, New Jersey, with occasional visits to Henniker to give Don, Jr., and Margaret a little vacation.

The ceilings of the inn are low, the walls are hung with old paintings and prints, and the furnishings are country antiques. A grandfather clock ticks away in one corner. There are birds during all seasons and a gorgeous flower garden during spring and summer. In earlier times, the living room fireplace was used for baking bread.

Guest rooms at the inn are typical country New England. Many have candlewick bedspreads, hooked rugs, and old bowl-and-pitcher sets, reminiscent of the days when water was brought in from the outside. They all have that wonderful "old home" feeling.

"This is great cross-country skiing terrain," commented Don. "There are forty miles of trails in this vicinity and a great many of our guests, including the children, come up for long weekends, or even, when possible, during the week."

At that moment, I caught the aroma of freshly baked bread coming from the kitchen, so Don and I wandered back there. "We serve chicken Colby House," he said, "and this, along with our fresh seafood, has been received very well. We have specials almost every day and usually a fresh fish of the day." Breakfasts are prepared by Sue, who is now in her tenth year at the inn. Sourdough pancakes with fresh blueberries, eggs, cereal, homemade wheat and graham toast, and corned beef hash, as well as coffee cakes and cinnamon buns are among her specialties.

One of my favorite things at this inn is a delightful swimming pool sheltered by an ell, formed by the two huge barns adjacent to the inn. It is most welcome on the hot days of the southern New Hamsphire summer.

This inn is enjoyable in many seasons because this section of New Hampshire has lakes, state parks, golf courses, summer theaters, and antique shops that add to the attraction for vacationers or weekenders.

COLBY HILL INN, Henniker, NH 03242; 603-428-3281. A 16-guestroom (private baths) inn on the outskirts of a New Hampshire college town. European plan. Breakfast served to houseguests only. Dinner served to travelers Tues. through Sun., except Thanksgiving, Christmas, and New Year's Day. Open year-round. Swimming pool on grounds. Tennis and xc skiing one short block; alpine, 3 mi. Golf, canoeing, hiking, bicycling, and fishing nearby. No children under 6. No pets. The Glover Family, Innkeepers. (See Index for rates.)

Directions: From I-89, take Exit 5 and follow Rte. 202 to Henniker. From I-91, take Exit 3 and follow Rte. 9 through Keene and Hillsborough to Henniker. From the blinking light in town center, go west ½ mi. on West Main St. (Western Ave.) to the Oaks. Inn is on the right.

THE CORNER HOUSE INN
Center Sandwich, New Hampshire (1987)

It had been a long day filled with surprises and a few disappointments. I had been wandering around New Hampshire, visiting inns that I have never seen before, looking for possible new additions to the pages of this book, and I must confess that up to this point there had been more disappointments then surprises.

Then I came to the intersection of many roads in a small village called Center Sandwich, complete with a very nice village green, a library, a shop run by the New Hampshire League of Artists and Crafts since 1925, and many vintage white houses, fences, and several beautiful churches. Best of all, there before my eyes was a village inn called "The Comer House Inn."

Walking in the main entrance, I stepped into a common room where the decorations and furnishings were all in a true New Hampshire country-inn style. There were shining floors, appropriate country furniture, a checker game going on in one corner, and lots of paintings and some quilted wall hangings, along with decorative quilts on the walls.

I soon made the acquaintance of Jane and chef Don Brown, the owners and keepers of this inn. I knew immediately that this was going to be a delight and not a disappointment. And I was right.

Naturally, we took a quick tour of the inn, walking up the front hallway where there is an old spinning wheel, a highchair, and a clothes tree. Around the top of the wall is a stenciled border. All of the guest rooms are immaculate, and furnished in a clean, country-inn style. The front bedroom has a very nice, light feeling with twin beds and posters advertising Renoir and Matisse gallery showings. Another of the four bedrooms has an antique painted headboard and a Monet poster. The back bedroom has a double and a single bed, a wicker rocker, and its own private bath. The fourth bedroom has a brass bed and a post-Impressionist poster. All the wallpapers are different, and the feeling of each guest room is quite different.

I had dinner in the bay window area of one of the four dining rooms. To my delight, I was joined by Fred and Ramona Stafford of Stafford's in the Field Inn. Ramona was extremely enthusiastic about Don's cooking, and we had lots of fun tasting each other's dinners. Later on, both Jane and Don joined us. Incidentally, on that evening I had brandied peach duckling. Other main dishes included such items as lobster and scallop pie and sautéed shellfish. Don pointed out that the seafood is always the freshest available. The breads and desserts are made daily in the Corner House kitchen.

The Corner House Inn has a great lunch menu, served every day, with lots of different kinds of soups and quiches, including a spinach and cheese variety. It's quite unusual to find an inn that also serves lunch, with a bill of fare that looked very, very tempting to me.

"Center Sandwich has one of the largest populations of artists and craftsmen in New Hampshire," Jane remarked. "Our guests can swim in Sandwich Bay on Squam Lake. And, oh yes, that's the very same lake on which *On Golden Pond* was filmed."

Indeed, the Corner House Inn is a great delight!

THE CORNER HOUSE INN, Box 204, Center Sandwich, NH 03227; 603-284-6219. A 4-guestroom (private and shared baths) village inn. Breakfast is included in room rate for houseguests. Lunch and dinner served every day except Mon. and Tues. during winter. Open year-round except Mon. and Tues. during winter. Art galleries, weaving designery, antique and crafts shops, historical museum, tennis, hiking, xc and downhill skiing all available. Not convenient for young children. Jane and Don Brown, Innkeepers. (See Index for rates.)

Directions: From I-93, exit at Ashland and follow Rte. 3 to Holderness; then Rte. 113 to Center Sandwich.

The date in parenthesis in the heading represents the first year the inn appeared in the pages of Country Inns and Back Roads.

THE DARBY FIELD INN
Conway, New Hampshire (1981)

There's a real sense of adventure involved in just making the last stage of the journey to reach Darby Field Inn. I turned off Route 16 and followed the Darby Field sign, plunging into the forest on a wonderful dirt road that seemed to climb ever upward. Following this road through the forest, again I had the great feeling of expectation that something would emerge at the top of the mountain that was going to be grand, and grand it is.

The Darby Field Inn has a most impressive panoramic view from its terrace dining room and many of the bedrooms. On this particular day Marc and Marily Donaldson, the innkeepers, took turns making sure that I saw all of the redecorating that had been accomplished in the inn, and we also had a chance to talk about the great view of the mountains.

"Over there is South Moat Mountain," Marc explained, "and that's Mount Washington just to the right. We can also see Adams and Madison and White Horse Ledge in the center."

The Darby Field Inn sits on the edge of the White Mountain National Forest, where guests can cross-country ski, snowshoe, and hike to nearby rivers, waterfalls, lakes, and open peaks. Fortunately, there's a very pleasant swimming pool on the terrace, providing guests with not only a cooling dip in the hot days of summer, but still another view of the mountains.

Marily and I did a short tour of the rooms. "Each room has its own country personality," she observed. "Some have four-poster beds, patchwork quilts, and braided rugs. Most of them have private baths and, as I'm sure you've noticed, many face our special view of the valley."

There is a cozy little pub, where both guests and Marc and Marily's friends can come together. This is adjacent to the living room, which has as impressive a massive stone fireplace as I have ever seen.

I was curious about the origins of Darby Field Inn. "Samuel and Polly Chase Littlefield first came up here in 1826, when it was hard work farming through all those generations of hard winters and long distances," she recounted. "Later on, the home took in summer guests, and it was then that the innkeeping tradition began. In the 1940s, a man from Boston and his family came here, and the original farmhouse became the living room section of what was to be known as the Bald Hill Lodge. The barn and blacksmith shop came down and in its place the dining room and kitchen section was built. The swimming pool was added and even a small ski lift for guests."

As one might expect, the menu is a bit on the hearty side with lamb chops, filet mignon, veal piccata, and roast duckling satisfying outdoor-oriented appetites.

Marc and Marily met in Venezuela, Marily's homeland, and came to Darby Field in 1979. They saw it as a country home for their children and an opportunity to meet guests from all parts of the world.

Many guests at Darby Field really enjoy going through the three volumes of scrapbooks containing brochures from inns all over New England. They provide a very pleasant few hours of relaxation in the living room in front of the big fireplace, and invariably lead to making new acquaintances among other guests.

As Marc and Marily walked me out to the car, she said, "We can't let you go without pointing out our garden where we get so many of the good things we serve at the inn, including snow peas, peppers, cabbage, corn, lettuce, and brussels sprouts."

THE DARBY FIELD INN, Bald Hill, Conway, NH 03818; 800-426-4147 (NH: 603-447-2181). A 17-guestroom White Mountain country inn, 3 mi. from Conway. Modified American plan. Closed Apr. and early Nov. Bed and breakfast offered at various times and I would suggest checking with the inn in advance. Within convenient driving distance of all of the Mt. Washington Valley cultural, natural, and historic attractions, as well as several internationally known ski areas. Swimming pool and carefully groomed xc skiing trails on grounds. Tennis and other sports nearby. Marc and Marily Donaldson, Innkeepers. (See Index for rates.)

Directions: From Rte. 16: Traveling north turn left at sign for the inn (½ mi. before the town of Conway) onto Bald Hill Rd., and proceed up the hill 1 mi. to the next sign for the inn and turn right. The inn is 1 mi. down the dirt road on the left. ✈

DEXTER'S INN AND TENNIS CLUB
Sunapee, New Hampshire (1978)

What a day! The sky was the bluest of skies, the sun was the sunniest of suns, and New Hampshire during the last week in June was really showing off for the rest of the world. I crested the hill and found Dexter's Inn basking in all of this glory, its bright yellow paint and black shutters blending well with the black-eyed Susans, Queen Anne's lace, and other summertime flowers and the green trees in the background.

After parking my car, I strolled up the granite steps, and stepped into the entrance, over which was the date 1804. Here again was the comfortable library-living room with the handsome antique desk and some appropriate paintings of New Hampshire mountains and countryside. The furniture had been brightly slipcovered, and the room was wonderfully cool after the midday heat. I took a moment and stepped out to a screened-in porch with white wicker furniture and a ceiling painted to look like a canopy. It looked like a wonderful place to spend an evening.

Now I opened the door to the side terrace with its round tables and bright yellow umbrellas, remembering that I first sat here perhaps ten years earlier. There were tennis courts on both sides of the broad lawn and some tennis players were having a lively game. I could hear guests splashing in the swimming pool.

Suddenly, innkeeper Frank Simpson appeared, and true to his promise, recorded in the last edition of the book, he had a pitcher of lemonade. We sat and had a long conversation about innkeeping, including a word or two about Norman Arluck, who at eighty-three was spending his fourteenth consecutive year at Dexter's.

"Shirley and I have turned over the reins to our daughter, Holly, and her husband, Michael, who are now the official innkeepers. I am going to

be known as 'Innkeeper Emeritus,' and I will be doing what I love best—
grounds keeping—and Shirley is very busy decorating our new house."

Now I heard the reassuring sounds of lawnmowers—lawnmowers
always sound wonderful unless you're pushing them yourself, and it's a
sound that perhaps a great many city folk don't hear very often. Frank
continued about Holly. "She's added some very nice main dishes to our
menu, including fresh poached salmon, fillet of sole Capri, and sautéed
scallop linguini with pesto. In addition to some exceptional cheesecakes
and lemon meringue pies, for dessert there's walnut torte and Wellesley
chocolate cake."

Frank was called to the phone and I took a look at the bulletin board.
It's small wonder that this part of New Hampshire is so popular with
country-inn guests because there is always something to do, including a
regular series of band concerts in nearby Sunapee, and drama and music
at the Dartmouth Hopkins Center and the Barn Theater in nearby New
London.

Frank returned, and we went to see some of the guest rooms in the
main house, which are reached by funny little hallways that zigzag around
various wings, and also the guest rooms in the barn across the street.
Everything looked tiptop.

So, there is a changing of the guard at Dexter's. To me it looks as if
nothing is really better, only different. Congratulations to everybody
concerned.

*DEXTER'S INN AND TENNIS CLUB, Box R, Stagecoach Rd., Sunapee,
NH 03782; 603-763-5571. A 17-guestroom resort-inn in the western New
Hampshire mountain and lake district. Mod. American plan; European
plan available in late June and Sept. Breakfast, lunch, and dinner served
to travelers by advance reservation; closed for lunch and dinner on Tues.
during July and Aug. Lunches served only July, Aug. Open from early May
to mid-Nov. Three tennis courts, pool, croquet, and shuffleboard on
grounds. Lakes, hiking, backroading, and championship golf courses
nearby. Pets allowed in Annex only. Michael and Holly Simpson-Durfor,
Innkeepers; Frank Simpson, Innkeeper Emeritus. (See Index for rates.)*

*Directions: From north & east: use Exit 12 or 12A, I-89. Continue west on
Rte. 11, 6 mi.—just ½ mi. past Sunapee to a sign at Winn Hill Rd. Turn left
up hill and after 1 mi., bear right on Stagecoach Rd. From west: use Exit
8, I-91, follow Rte. 103 east into NH—through Newport ½ mi. past
junction with Rte. 11. Look for sign at Young Hill Rd. and go 1½ mi. to
Stagecoach Rd.* ◣

HICKORY STICK FARM
Laconia, New Hampshire (1983)

I'm going to share a letter I received from one of our readers about her trip to Hickory Stick Farm:

"Vacationing by car in Vermont and New Hampshire last month was a great experience, but by the time we reached the resort area of Lake Winnipesaukee, my friends and I were ready for a change of pace from fast motorways, motels, and coffee shops.

"One evening we saw a sign pointing off the main road to 'Hickory Stick Farm' with a carved duck decoy underneath. Turning off into the woods we were immediately in a different world of unbelievable peace and quiet, and we drove 1½ miles of winding roads. 'Round a bend in the road could be seen a picture-perfect red farmhouse on a hill overlooking a splendid panorama. The sun was still shining on the valley and Ragged Mountain in the distance was a misty purple.

"Entering the converted farmhouse was like entering the house of a dream grandmother. We were shown into the living room, which is used as a waiting room, while the hostess checked on the availability of a table for dinner. During the short wait we admired the antiques in the living room, including a spinning wheel, and enjoyed visiting the Gift Shop, where many locally made gifts were for sale.

"Scott Roeder, the innkeeper, introduced himself and recounted the history of the farm, which dates back a number of years when his mother and father first bought it. He invited us to walk around the grounds after dinner and we especially enjoyed the new gazebo, where there is an excellent view of the mountains.

"The atmosphere in the dining room was relaxed and happy, surrounded by antiques and pewter and red accessories. Our waiter, a student from Boston, suggested we order the famous roast duckling, available in quarters, halves, or a whole duck that is carved at the table. I have never enjoyed such a tender and delicious duckling, and Mr. Roeder explained the very special way he has of cooking them so that they have a brown, crisp skin and tender, moist meat. It was served with an orange sherry sauce, stuffing, wild rice, and delicious vegetables.

"After a leisurely dinner Mr. Roeder happened to mention that he had room cancellations for the following night, so we immediately booked the rooms and returned to the farm on the following late afternoon. Our rooms were a welcome sight.

"The Rose Room had a queen-sized cannonball bed and pretty flowered wallpaper. The Gold Room had twin-sized cannonball beds under the eaves, and a comfortable sitting area with antique furniture. Both rooms had large bathrooms with baths, showers, and dressing areas.

"Breakfast was served in the new sun room, which has beautiful white wicker furniture and is very cheerful. Mary Roeder cooked the eggs, bacon, and french toast. She and Scott are very friendly and we all parted most reluctantly."

HICKORY STICK FARM, R.F.D. #2, Laconia, NH 03246; 603-524-3333. A 2-guestroom hilltop country inn and restaurant 4 mi. from Laconia in the lake country of New Hampshire. Guestrooms and breakfast available most of the year. Please telephone ahead. Restaurant open from Memorial Day to Columbus Day; closed Mon. Dinners served from 5 to 9 p.m. Sun. dinner served all day from noon to 8 p.m. Extended hours during fall foliage season—call ahead. Wheelchair access to dining room. The Shaker Village in Canterbury is nearby, as well as the Belknap recreational area (10 mi.) with crafts and antique shows, concerts, Oktoberfests, alpine and xc skiing, and other New Hampshire attractions. Scott and Mary Roeder, Innkeepers.

Directions: Use Exit 20 from I-93. Follow Rte. 3 toward Laconia approx. 5 mi. over bridge over Lake Winnisquam. A short distance past this bridge, turn right on Union Rd. immediately past Double Decker, a drive-in restaurant, and follow Hickory Stick signs 1½ mi. into the woods. If you do not turn onto any dirt roads, you are on the right track. From Laconia, go south on Rtes. 3 & 11 (do not take Rte. 106) and turn left on Union Rd. (about ½ mi. past the Belknap Mall) and follow signs.

"European plan" means that rates for rooms and meals are separate. *"American plan"* means that meals are included in the cost of the room. *"Modified American plan"* means that breakfast and dinner are included in the cost of the room. The rates at some inns include a continental breakfast with the lodging.

THE INN AT CROTCHED MOUNTAIN
Francestown, New Hampshire (1981)

Once again I turned off Route 202 at Bennington, New Hampshire, and followed Route 47 towards Francestown. I noticed that an unusual number of beaver dams had been built by our industrious friends. Admiring the farms on both sides of the road, I wound my way ever upward through the grove of trees, coming once again to the Crotched Mountain Inn, just a few paces from the base of a ski area.

The brilliant sunshine of the day glittered in the waters of the swimming pool and intensified the radiant hues of the uncountable iris. I stopped for a moment to admire the view. One of the intriguing things about this view is that it gets better with each visit.

Rose Perry came around the corner of the inn, and after warm hellos we wandered across the broad back lawn. The subject of how many years the inn had been included in *CIBR* came up. The first entry was in the 1981 edition. Interestingly, some of the things I mentioned then were still true today. I had visited Crotched Mountain early in June, when the late New England spring is most delicious with apple blossoms and lilacs, and I was smitten by the wonderful panorama stretching out for miles.

I made a second visit that year when the fall colors were as magnificent as only they can be in the Monadnock region, where occasionally the full range of color is reached before October 1.

It was during this second visit that I enjoyed a leisurely dinner and the opportunity to see John and Rose Perry and the inn in a different light. There was a glowing fire in the low-ceilinged parlor of the little pub, where after-dinner guests and other couples dropped in during the evening.

The inn was originally built as a farmhouse in 1822. The first owner constructed a secret tunnel from his cellar to the Boston Post Road, incorporating his home as a way station to shelter runaway slaves on the Underground Railroad. During the late 1920s, it was to become one of the most spectacular farms in New England, boasting an internationally recognized breed of sheep, champion horses, and Angora goats.

Unfortunately, the house was destroyed by fire in the mid-30s, rebuilt, and John and Rose came on the scene in 1976.

Rose is an attractive Indonesian woman. She is in complete charge of the kitchen, doing a great deal of the cooking. The menu includes roast duck with plum sauce, sautéed bay scallops, and Indonesian-style scallops with sautéed tomatoes, onions, pepper, and ginger.

Although several years have intervened, both Rose and John looked like the same fresh-faced young innkeepers they were at our very first meeting. I asked John what he thought was the most important thing about innkeeping, and he unhesitatingly replied, "People." He went on to explain that it is really the returning guests who make innkeeping such a joy. "We have had people who have been back every year since we first took over," he said.

As I was leaving, Rose walked out to the car and said, "Do tell your readers that we love children to come here, and we have many things for them to do and see, and they always seem to have a good time."

THE INN AT CROTCHED MOUNTAIN, Mountain Rd., Francestown, NH 03043; 603-588-6840. A 14-guestroom (shared and private baths) mountain inn in southern New Hampshire, 15 mi. from Peterborough. European plan. Open from mid-May to the end of Oct., and from Thanksgiving thru the ski season. During winter, dinner is served on Fri. and Sat., and during holiday periods. Dinner is served from Tues. thru Sat. during the remainder of the year. Within a short distance of the Sharon Arts Center, American Stage Festival, Peterborough Players, Crotched Mt. ski areas. Swimming pool, tennis courts, xc skiing, volleyball on grounds. Golf, skiing, hill walking, and backroading in the gorgeous Monadnock region nearby. No credit cards. Rose and John Perry, Innkeepers. (See Index for rates.)

Directions: From Boston, follow Rte. 3 north to 101A to Milford. Then Rte. 13 to New Boston and Rte. 136 to Francestown. Follow Rte. 47 for 2½ mi. and turn left on Mountain Road. Inn is 1 mi. on right. From New York/Hartford, take I-91 north to Rte. 10 at Northfield to Keene, N.H. Follow 101 east to Peterborough, Rte. 202 north to Bennington, Rte. 47 to Mountain Rd. (approx. 4½ mi.); turn right on Mountain Rd. Inn is 1 mi. on right.

The date in parenthesis in the heading represents the first year the inn appeared in the pages of Country Inns and Back Roads.

THE JOHN HANCOCK INN
Hancock, New Hampshire (1971)

It was raining in Hancock, and the trees arching over the village streets provided a very welcome shelter for many of the umbrella-carrying villagers and visitors. There was a special gleam from many of the white narrow-clapboard Federalist homes. For instance, directly across from the John Hancock Inn there is a pleasant white clapboard with a Victorian porch and next to that is a typical New Hampshire double-galleried peak roofed three-story house in white clapboard with white pillars on the front. The overhang of the third floor creates a sort of cavern effect.

The parking lot for the John Hancock was almost filled. As soon as I walked in the old front door, there was Pat Wells saying, "Oh, it's you!"

It was a busy morning for her, but we managed to have a few moments at the lunch table, and this time, with a choice of four different dining rooms, we decided on the one with the dried flower arrangements hanging from the exposed beams and overlooking the back lawn.

There was a display board showing the day's luncheon specials, and after looking at those and the luncheon menu, which included roast beef hash and poached egg, fried haddock, chicken shortcake, and other assorted unusual sandwiches, I decided on the roast beef hash.

Later, I went outside with Pat and Glynn while they discussed the new landscaping being done on the front of the inn. One of the interesting things about knowing them over these many years is that they always seem to be doing new things—building new dining rooms, redecorating, expanding the grounds, and making additions and improvements to the menu. Because, as Pat says, "You just cannot stand still; you have to move with the times and the circumstances."

When people interested in knowing more about country innkeeping come to visit me, I often suggest that they visit the John Hancock as an example of a certain type of inn located in a village. It is the continuing center for community activity and small enough so that villagers and visitors have the opportunity to get acquainted. It is New Hampshire's oldest continuously operating inn, and all of the guest rooms have been appropriately furnished. Many have double and twin canopied beds.

The inn enjoys the distinction of having murals, not by one, but by two itinerant 19th-century artists, Rufus Porter and Moses Eaton. Pat and Glynn told me Rufus Porter's works were discovered recently while they were doing some redecorating.

Our conversation, taking a circuitous route, arrived at their Sunday brunches. "Instead of having a buffet table, we prefer to offer our guests table service, and in many cases, our Hancock neighbors join with the out-of-town guests—it's becoming a regular stop-off after church or after the 'morning-trip-out-for-the-paper.' "

As I drove away from the John Hancock Inn and my dear friends Pat and Glynn, whom I first met when they visited me in Stockbridge many years ago to talk about the possibility of finding a country inn to buy, I remembered the thought expressed by them a few years ago.

"I think that the whole business of innkeeping has been an act of faith for us. Back in 1972, the realization that we were going to be somewhere else was the controlling factor that led us to Hancock. God has been good these years. We believe that with His strength and guidance we can make the inn what it richly deserves to be—a haven for others, a source of pride for the town, and a deep and rich experience for our family. It is all that, I believe, but never could be without the faith that has supported us in every kind of problem."

THE JOHN HANCOCK INN, Hancock, NH 03449; 603-525-3318. A 10-guestroom village inn 9 mi. north of Peterborough, on Rtes. 123 and 137, in the middle of the Monadnock region of southern N.H. European plan. Breakfast, lunch, and dinner served daily to travelers. Sun. brunch. Closed Christmas Day and 1 wk. in spring and fall. Wheelchair access. Bicycles available on the grounds. Antiquing, swimming, hiking, alpine and xc skiing nearby. Glynn and Pat Wells, Innkeepers. (See Index for rates.)

Directions: From Keene, take either Rte. 101 east to Dublin and Rte. 137 north to Hancock or Rte. 9 north to Rte. 123 and east to Hancock. From Nashua, take 101A and 101 to Peterborough. Proceed north on Rtes. 202 and 123 to Hancock.

LOVETT'S BY LAFAYETTE BROOK
Franconia, New Hampshire (1976)

Charlie Lovett was explaining his philosophy of innkeeping, which he has been practicing here at Lovett's for nearly forty years. "The whole idea is to run a comfortable inn. We think ours accommodates itself to the landscape."

Looking out over the striking White Mountains and then glancing back at the distinctive New England lines of this white clapboard building, I fully agreed with him.

Charlie has become an institution at Lovett's, and even though James Peters, who has been at Lovett's for many years, is now the innkeeper, Charlie is still very much in the picture.

"This is a mountain inn, and you know there are many reasons for coming to the White Mountains and especially to our little village of Franconia. We have antiquing, and flower shows and horse shows, summer theater, auctions, and country fairs. There also is the fall foliage, good winter and spring skiing, and cross-country skiing as well. I think that our guests like to escape from city life by visiting us.

"There are walks all over these mountains and all kinds of places to motor to," Charlie pointed out. "Most of the ski areas run their lifts during the summer and autumn. Shopping seems to intrigue our guests as well. We have several superior places right here in Franconia and a sprinkling of country stores and crafts shops throughout the mountains."

Charlie and I were in the sitting room with its deep couches, overhead beams, and woodburning stove. There is a painting of the inn showing Cannon Mountain in the background.

Lovett's has several country-inn-type guest rooms in the main house and in two nearby houses. There are more contemporarily furnished small chalets on the grounds with living rooms and mountain views, many of them with fireplaces. A few poolside chalets are also available.

With Lovett's impressive reputation for its food, it is difficult to make a choice from the tempting menu.

"We're particularly proud of our cold wild blueberry soup, hot mussel bisque, and curried fresh sorrel soup. The pleasure of three-course breakfasts is heightened by coffee made with Mount Lafayette's purest water," Charlie commented.

The nearby New England Ski Museum is the only ski museum I know of, and it has photographs and films of the early days of North American skiing, which had its beginning at nearby Peckett's Inn on Sugar Hill.

The establishment of the New England Ski Museum was one of Charlie's dreams. "It is for all the New England states and contains much memorabilia and history of some of the great early Austrian ski instructors such as Hans Schneider, who really provided the impetus that eventually resulted in the American ski industry. Lovett's was in on the early part of everything around 1930 and we had our own Swiss ski instructor here. He took the guests up on Cannon Mountain every day, and in those days you herringboned up the side of the mountain because there was no ski lift as there is now."

Winters in this part of New Hampshire are dominated by the presence of ski areas, principally Cannon Mountain, which looms in all of its snow-clad glory just a few minutes from Lovett's. Cannon is one of the principal downhill ski areas in New England, and its well-known tramway carries skiers to the top of the mountain for some really great skiing.

Lovett's is a sophisticated country inn with considerable emphasis on excellent food and service. Many of the guests have been returning for years. Their fathers and mothers came before them. There is a very definite spirit that pulls everybody together. As one guest remarked, "It's almost like a club."

LOVETT'S BY LAFAYETTE BROOK, Profile Rd., Franconia, NH 03580; 603-823-7761. An 8-guestroom country inn with guest cottages in New Hampshire's White Mountains. Modified American plan omits lunch. Box lunches available. Breakfast and dinner served by reservation to travelers. Closed in April. Swimming pool, pond and streams for fishing, xc skiing, lawn sports on grounds. Golf, tennis, alpine skiing, hiking nearby. James Peters, Innkeeper. (See Index for rates.)

Directions: South of Franconia 2½ mi. on N.H. business loop, at junction of N.H. 141 and I-93 South Franconia exit; 2¾ mi. north of junction of U.S. 3 and 18.

THE LYME INN
Lyme, New Hampshire (1971)

On my most recent visit, Judy Siemons showed me the lovely new Lyme Inn notepaper, with a very delicate watercolor of the inn by a local artist, showing all four of the red brick chimneys and the four-plus stories of the inn itself. The second- and third-story open porches in the front of the building are plainly visible. Everything is set off by a trim white fence. It might be that in some future edition of *Country Inns and Back Roads* we would use this for our cover.

I was also pleased to discover the expanding crafts area on the second floor, with many delightful handcrafted gifts by mostly local artisans.

Judy was overflowing with news about the "Garrison stove in our third dining room. What a difference it makes, both in direct heat and warming up the atmosphere. We found a wonderful source of braided rag rugs, and have replaced many of our older rugs and covered previously bare floors with some of the nicest braided rugs I've ever seen. We've also added quite a few Hitchcock chairs and tables to our dining rooms."

The Lyme Inn is an antique-laden gem that sits at the end of a long New England common. The twelve guest rooms with private baths and two rooms with shared baths have poster beds, hooked rugs, hand-stitched quilts, wide pine floorboards, stenciled wallpaper, and winged chairs. I feel certain that children would not be comfortable, because there is no entertainment particularly designed for them.

This inn is a treasure-trove of nostalgic memorabilia; one room displays old farm tools, and reminds us that this is good snowshoeing country. The house boasts a number of antique maps and salt-glazed pottery, and one of its bedrooms is outfitted in a rare suite of 19th-century painted "cottage" furniture, reminiscent of Eastlake.

My attention was drawn to the unusual collection of framed samplers on the wall of the dining room. "Oh, I am definitely into samplers," exclaimed Judy. "I am always anxious to know more about them and sometimes our guests are able to be of assistance.

"Samplers are a form of American folk art," she continued, "and I find that the real old ones are fast disappearing. A friend of mine who lives nearby does most of our framing and we are doing everything we can to preserve them, including using acid-free paper."

Breakfast, included in the room rate, features juice, fresh fruit in season, fried or scrambled eggs, french toast with local maple syrup, and blueberry muffins.

Chef Hans Wickert, trained in Germany and Switzerland, has introduced several Continental specialties, including hasenpfeffer. He offers a different menu for summer and winter, but always a veal dish and a shrimp dish, and always makes his own soups from scratch.

Guests are intrigued with the four sheep, two black and two white ewes. Judy says they are kept as added "lawn mowers." They're sheared every spring and she talked about possibly trading their wool for blankets at one of the crafts shops in the area. These sheep are kept in line by Duffy, the sheep dog, who is well known to almost every guest who stays at the inn. As Judy says of him, "He's just a people's dog and has never led a dog's life."

Although the village feels quite remote, it is nonetheless just ten miles from Hanover, New Hampshire, the home of Dartmouth College, and inn guests have the opportunity to enjoy some of the sporting and theatrical events taking place there. It is just a few minutes from the Dartmouth Skiway, and there's plenty of cross-country skiing nearby. In fact, new snowmaking equipment at the Skiway has caused Fred and Judy to offer a midweek MAP special to take advantage of the uncrowded week days.

THE LYME INN, on the Common, Lyme, NH 03768; 603-795-2222. A 14-guestroom (12 with private bath) village inn 10 mi. north of Hanover on N.H. Rte. 10. Breakfast included in room rate. Dinner served daily to travelers except on Tues. Closed from Sun. following Thanksgiving to Dec. 26, and 3 wks. in late spring. Convenient to all Dartmouth College activities, including Hopkins Center, with music, dance, drama, painting, and sculpture. Alpine and xc skiing, fishing, hiking, canoeing, tennis, and golf nearby. No children under 8. No pets. Fred and Judy Siemons, Innkeepers. (See Index for rates.)

Directions: From I-91, take Exit 14 and follow Rte. 113A east to Vermont Rte. 5. Proceed south 50 yards to a left turn, then travel 2 mi. to inn.

MOOSE MOUNTAIN LODGE
Etna, New Hampshire (1984)

Checking my own directions, I stopped at the Etna General Store and met a very attractive young woman who told me that I should take the second road on the right and follow the road up the mountain and the signs for the lodge. I set off for Moose Mountain Lodge with my heart high, reflecting that on my earlier visits it had been wintertime and sometimes necessary for Peter Shumway, the innkeeper, to come down to the bottom of the last steep incline to pick people up in his four-wheel drive. Up I went to the lodge and its fabulous view.

Moose Mountain Lodge is a rustic building high on the western side of Moose Mountain, built in the late 1930s, mostly of logs and stones gathered from the surrounding forests and fields. The broad porch extends across the entire rear of the lodge, and has foreground views of the rolling New Hampshire countryside and, in the distance, of famed Vermont peaks as far away as Rutland.

I passed through the new entryway and walked into the kitchen, as almost everyone does, joining Peter and Kay Shumway around the big table for a wonderful breakfast visit.

The kitchen is one of the centers of activity at Moose Mountain Lodge. "We run an open kitchen here," Kay said. "I like it when guests wander in and ask 'what's for lunch!' Incidentally, most of the time it's soup and salad." This was Kay's domain and it revealed her many interests besides cuisine, including flowers and plants. In the middle of the big butcher-block table was a copy of *Webster's New Collegiate Dictionary*. How can you go wrong in a kitchen that is also a haven for the intellectually curious!

There are twelve "lodge-type," rustic bedrooms with colorful quilts, lots of books and magazines, bunk beds and conventional single and double beds, and a rustic air that I seldom find these days.

"Many things are different here in the summer, including the menus," Kay remarked. "Summer meals have lots of fish and some meats with light sauces; all of the vegetables from the garden and all the fresh fruits that I can pick; sometimes cold soups. We have salads and home-made breads and generally fruit desserts.

"However, in the wintertime we serve stuffed squash, lots of po-tatoes and big roasts, and always a huge salad and all kinds of desserts. Everything is put out on the buffet table so guests can have whatever they want and they can sit wherever they wish."

In winter there are extensive cross-country ski trails everywhere, and the winter scenery is spectacular. It's great to come in after skiing and grab a cookie from the seemingly bottomless cookie jar.

A recent letter from Kay said, "Peter is enjoying working with a forester to formulate a plan for the best use of our recently acquired over 300 acres of land, including extending our trail system for hiking and cross-country skiing. The Appalachian Trail, about a mile away, inter-sects our new land. In the summer, our spring-fed pond with its sandy beach is a real boon.

"It's a beautiful fall morning here on the mountain, and the fog is covering the floor of the valley below us, looking like a lake, with the hills like islands and the mountains like the far shore. Down in Hanover they don't know what a beautiful day it is going to be yet. The fall colors increase every day, and two days ago we had an early morning blizzard with two inches of snow on the ground for a while. I love this time of year and we feel so fortunate to be able to live here and share our mountain home with people who love it as we do."

MOOSE MOUNTAIN LODGE, Etna, NH 03750; 603-643-3529. A 12-guestroom (5 shared baths) rustic lodge a few miles from Hanover, New Hampshire. Closed April and May, and from Nov. 15 thru Dec. 26. Breakfast, lunch, and dinner served to houseguests only. Xc skiing for all abilities on grounds or nearby. Ski equipment available. Hiking, biking, walking, canoeing, backroading, and many recreational and cultural attractions nearby, including Dartmouth College. No pets. Peter and Kay Shumway, Innkeepers. (See Index for rates.)

Directions: If arriving for the first time, stop in Etna at Landers Restau-rant or the Etna Store and telephone the lodge for directions. The last mile up the mountain is steep, and when the road is icy, guests are met at the bottom parking lot with a 4-wheel-drive vehicle. Etna is on the map, a few miles east of Hanover.

PHILBROOK FARM INN
Shelburne, New Hampshire (1978)

I can't think of another inn in North America that has been under the ownership of the same family for 125 years. In 1986, that is exactly what Philbrook Farm Inn was celebrating—although they were so busy with their innkeeping that nobody remembered it until mid-1986. Then they had a party and invited about sixty guests who had been coming to the inn over many years. In some cases, their guests were members of families who have been coming there over *generations*.

Nancy Philbrook and her sister, Connie Leger, and Connie's son, Larry, have been joined by Larry's sister, Ann, and her friend, Madonna, which has swelled the family members of the staff considerably.

The main house of Philbrook Farm was built in 1834, and the first addition with the blue porch and old-fashioned door was put on in 1861. The east end was built in 1905, and the dining room, along with the "new kitchens" was added when the big barns burned in 1934.

The Philbrook Farm *is* New Hampshire. There are New Hampshire prints, paintings, and photographs, some of them really irreplaceable. There are some tints of old prints, hooked rugs, and many, many books about New Hampshire. A whole library of books is just on the White Mountains, some of them written by former guests of the farm.

In the kitchen there is a *ten-burner woodburning* range built by the McGee Furnace Company of Boston during the 1890s. "Yes," said Nancy, "we do almost all of our cooking and baking on this range. We only use the electric stove in case of emergencies or to keep things warm." Imagine a country inn where almost all of the cooking is done on a woodburning range!

Meals are New England-style home cooking. "It's all homemade with no mixes," said Connie. "There is one main dish each night, and the dinner usually consists of a homemade soup, some type of roast, such as pot, pork, or lamb. The vegetables are as fresh as possible, and we try to stay away from fried foods. Most of the guests enjoy roasts, because these days they are not served as much at home. All of the desserts are homemade. There's pie, ice cream, and pudding.

"For lunches, we serve salads, chowder, hot rolls, hash, macaroni and cheese, and things like that. On Saturday night we have a New England baked bean supper,and we almost always have a roast chicken dinner on Sunday night. We always serve a full breakfast, and on Sunday morning we have New England fish balls and cornbread."

The latest news is that the old barn next door has been put into operation as a stable, and horseback riding, trail rides, instruction, and boarding for horses are now available.

The swimming pool adds one more option to the summertime activities, which include hikes, picnicking, and nature walks on Mount Washington and the Appalachian Trail. In winter, there are cross-country trails on the 900-acre property and downhill skiing nearby.

Guests, friends, and family have been busily making cross-stitch door plaques with the names of many of the long-time returning guests, and another popular pastime is putting together one of the fantastic collection of ninety-eight jigsaw puzzles, all cut by Larry and Ann's great-grandfather and kept in a special cupboard.

Being an official Philbrook Farm "adoptee" (I am the proud possessor of a Philbrook Family Reunion T-shirt, having received it on the eve of one of their huge reunions), I must confess I am a little prejudiced in their favor. Once you've visited this delightful old New Hampshire inn, I think you will be, too.

PHILBROOK FARM INN, North Rd., Shelburne, NH 03581; 603-466-3831. A 20-guestroom country inn in the White Mountains of northeastern N.H., 6 mi. from Gorham and just west of the Maine/N.H. line. American, mod. American, and European plans available. Open May 1 to Oct. 31; Dec. 26 to Apr. 1. Closed Thanksgiving, Christmas. Wheelchair access. Swimming pool, shuffleboard, horseshoes, badminton, ping-pong, croquet, billiards, hiking trails, xc skiing, snowshoeing trails, horseback riding on grounds. Swimming, golf, hiking, backroading, bird watching nearby. Pets allowed only during summer season in cottages. No credit cards. The Philbrook and Leger Families, Innkeepers. (See Index for rates.)

Directions: The inn is just off U.S. Rte. 2 in Shelburne. Look for inn direction sign and turn at Meadow Rd., cross R.R. tracks and river, and turn right at North Rd. The inn is at the end of the road. ◣

ROCKHOUSE MOUNTAIN FARM INN
Eaton Center, New Hampshire (1978)

I'd like to share a letter Libby Edge wrote me that gives a more vivid picture of life at the inn than anything I could do. Here it is:

"The wildflower honey from Johnny's beehives is probably the best ever. We love it; the guests love it; and a certain bear loves it. A month ago the black marauder ambled down from Rockhouse Mountain, demolished two of the hives near the shuffleboard court, and consumed a good portion of the nectar. Johnny was mad, but he was reimbursed for the damage by the state.

"A night ago a marauder, without question the same one, visited two other hives, disregarded the electric fence, scattered the bees, and had another honey feast. Now Johnny has a radio blaring near the rebuilt hive to frighten away nighttime visitors. If ever he returns again, watch out for Johnny's eagle eye.

"While cutting hay in the lower pasture last week, Johnny spotted a small fawn resting in the tall grass. He got as close as ten feet but, of course, didn't have his camera. Since then, he has seen it several times, and knows it must be orphaned. He's hoping to catch it and bring it in to nurture it. Other bucks and does have put on a show for our guests in the Rockhouse fields.

"Mother and Father Peacock have finally hatched out one lone baby, who is being fed in the house. One of the crew members has adopted it, feeds it, and walks around the house with it following.

"Johnny is out cutting hay right now, and it's a beautiful yield. However, his first cutting of the season was rained on four times, and tedded [turned] half a dozen times before it was baled and brought in. Oh, the problems of a farm! Many of our guests help toss the bales, ride in the Jeep, and then help stack the bales on the conveyor belt in the barn.

"John and Libby's two grandsons, Joel, 14, and Orion, 12 (a self-acclaimed half-grandson), are on the 'payroll' this summer, helping with chores, and helping entertain guests. . . .

"All of the young and old guests have pet kittens in the barn, and we often see at least six children sitting in a circle, each mothering or fathering a soft bundle of fur.

"Johnny's tomatoes (grown from seed) are flourishing, while Alana's cucumbers are currently stunted. He never fails to make comparisons. But you should see the rest of her garden, weedless, expanding by leaps and bounds with everything from beans to broccoli to parsnips. Alana's and Libby's flowers are almost in full bloom.

"There's a bucket of pellets near the front door where guests can get cupfuls of feed for the fish in the new pond. It must be loaded with brown trout because no matter where pellets are tossed, the fish rise. Wait 'til next fall for the first big feed. The pond is beautiful now with its surrounding first ground cover of purple vetch.

"The recently planted fruit trees—apples, pears, plums, peaches—should produce a great crop later on. And there's a whole area planted with giant pumpkins which will decorate Rockhouse in the fall.

"John keeps the Rockhouse beach, with its rowboats, canoes, and sailboats, in tiptop shape. In the recent hot weather, the guests have migrated to the cool waters of Crystal Lake, staying down until the dinner bell has rung at the inn.

"The fields are full of wildflowers, Indian paintbrush, daisies, black-eyed Susans, Queen Anne's lace, vetch, red clover, yarrow, buttercups, which Libby uses for house flowers and centerpieces, and which guests photograph.

"Inside—our crew of beautiful girls keeps the house shipshape, and serves the traditionally good and tasty home-cooked food to guests who claim they always overeat and gain weight. . . .

"And there are two pillows for every bed and a reading light."

ROCKHOUSE MOUNTAIN FARM INN, Eaton Center, NH 03832; 603-447-2880. An 18-guestroom (some private baths) country farm inn on 350 acres in the foothills of the White Mountains, 6 mi. south of Conway. Modified American plan. Open from June 15 through Oct. Farm animals, haying, hiking, shuffleboard, private beach on Crystal Lake with swimming, rowboats, sailboats, and canoes—canoe trips planned, stream and lake fishing; tennis and golf nearby. No credit cards. The Edge Family, Innkeepers. (See Index for rates.)

Directions: From I-93, take Exit 23 to Rte. 104 to Meredith. Take Rte. 25 to Rte. 16 and proceed north to Conway and Rte. 153. Continue 6 mi. south on Rte. 153 to Eaton Center.

SPALDING INN & CLUB
Whitefield, New Hampshire (1976)

Many years ago the White Mountains in New Hampshire had numerous summer resorts where "mother and children" might come up early in the season and where "father" joined them for the last four weeks or so. These resorts were wonderful, gay places where everything that was needed for a long, complete vacation was either on the grounds or nearby. The lure of the mountains drew people in great numbers from Boston and New York.

Now, with few exceptions, all of these family-run resorts have disappeared, but not the Spalding Inn & Club, which is thriving under the ownership of William A. Ingram and his partner, Lore Moran. Many of the amenities of earlier times are still preserved; for example, gentlemen wouldn't think of going to dinner without a jacket and tie. The inn is a focal point for the sports of lawn bowling and tennis, with several tournaments scheduled from mid-June to mid-September, including the U. S. National Singles and Doubles Lawn Bowling Championships.

The Spalding Inn & Club is an excellent example of entertainment and hospitality that can be provided for a family with many different preferences. For example, on the inn grounds there are four clay tennis courts, a swimming pool, a nine-hole par-3 golf course, two championship lawn bowling greens, and shuffleboard. Five golf courses are within fifteen minutes of the inn, and plenty of trout fishing and boating and enticing back roads are nearby. The Appalachian Trail system for mountain climbing is a short walk from the inn.

In addition to opportunities for a well-blended balance of vigorous outdoor activity, there are also facilities for quiet times, including an extensive library, a card room, and a challenging collection of jigsaw puzzles. Groves of maples, birches, and oak trees native to northern New Hampshire are on the inn grounds and there are over 400 acres of lawns, gardens, and orchards.

There are real country-inn touches everywhere. The broad porch is ideal for rocking, and the main living room has a fireplace with a low ceiling, lots of books and magazines, baskets of apples, a barometer for tomorrow's weather, a jar of sour balls, and abundant arrangements of flowers.

Those country-inn touches also include the traditional hearty menu items so satisfying after a day of outdoor activities in the White Mountains. Among other offerings in the air-conditioned dining room are delicious clam chowder, oyster stew, broiled scrod, poached salmon, pork chops, roast duckling, roast tenderloin, and sweetbreads. Children love the indian pudding. All of the pies, including hot mince, and the breads and rolls are made in the bakery of the inn.

Bill Ingram and Lore Moran have instilled a really fresh new spirit at this lovely inn. As Bill says, "We are confident that guests of all ages will enjoy our resort. We now have live piano music in the tea room and lounge and a variety of special events is available upon request. With seventy guest rooms we are larger than the average inn in your book, but we are still able to retain a personal touch."

I agree.

SPALDING INN & CLUB, Mountain View Road, Whitefield, NH 03598; 603-837-2572. A 70-guestroom resort-inn in the center of New Hampshire's White Mountains. Full American plan includes lunch. MAP available on request. Open early June to mid-Oct. Breakfast, lunch and dinner are served daily to travelers. Heated pool, tennis courts, 9-hole par-3 golf course, 18-hole putting green, 2 championship lawn bowling greens, and shuffleboard on grounds. Also Sunday night movies. Guest privileges at 5 nearby golf clubs. Trout fishing, boating, summer theater, and backroading nearby. William A. Ingram and Lore Moran, Innkeepers. (See Index for rates.)

Directions: From New York take Merritt Pkwy. to I-91; I-91 to Wells River, Vt./Woodsville, N.H. exit; then Rte. 302 to Littleton, then Rte. 116 thru Whitefield to Mtn. View Rd. intersection—3 mi. north of village. From Boston take I-93 north thru Franconia Notch to Littleton exit; then Rte. 116 thru Whitefield to Mtn. View Rd. intersection—3 mi. north of village. From Montreal take Autoroute 10 to Magog; then Autoroute 55 and I-91 to St. Johnsbury, Vt.; then Rte. 18 to Littleton, N.H. and Rte. 116 as above. The inn is situated 1 mi. west on Mountain View Rd.

STAFFORD'S IN THE FIELD
Chocorua, New Hampshire (1972)

I'd like to share a letter that was written about a visit to this inn. "I have just returned from the most fantastic experience at Stafford's in the Field, Chocorua, New Hampshire. It was almost unbelievable to me that in today's commercial world, it can still be possible to find a haven so well run by such a beautiful family.

"From the moment we left the highway and saw Stafford's, I knew this vacation would be something special. Fred and Ramona Stafford are incredible when it comes to hospitality. And, as you stated in your book, Ramona is a superb gourmet cook. Our stay brought back memories of visiting my grandparents long ago in their big old country home on the farm. This inn is an experience that I will long remember and I will make every effort to go back as soon as possible."

That letter was written in 1972, the first year I included Stafford's Inn in *CIBR*. Since that time, many things have been happening in this inn, which have made it an even more enjoyable experience.

For one thing, cross-country skiing is one of the big winter attractions. There are open fields and practice slopes for novices and marked trails for more accomplished skiers.

Today, as in 1972, still another side of Stafford's in the Field is Ramona's gourmet cooking. I hasten to point out that "gourmet" is a word I never use lightly, but my original conversation with her convinced me that she was not merely a good cook, but a dedicated searcher for true expression in the culinary art. Breads and pastries are home-baked, and there is a very generous selection of Russian, French, Italian, and German dishes with a knowledgeable use of herbs and spices. One of my favorite dishes is the spare ribs cooked in maple syrup.

All of this accumulated knowledge, experimentation, and years of preparing inn meals has culminated in the *Stafford's in the Field Cookbook*. "It has been a family project," declared Ramona. "Fred and our daughter, Momo, worked side by side with me, and even our sons made significant contributions."

Accommodations in the main house are comfortable rooms that have been furnished with country antique furniture. Several rooms have private baths. Other accommodations on the grounds are in cottages that are extremely suitable for families of all ages and sizes.

The guests sit together for the evening meal, and I think this is when the dinner party atmosphere is particularly enjoyable for everyone. Many guests enjoy a stroll through the open fields before dinner, walking down the shady paths in the woods surrounding the inn. Winter transforms these paths into ski trails and guests often spend the whole day out on skis.

In March, it's maple syrup time, and anyone who wants to help, can. I think it adds to the flavor of the blueberry waffles if one has had a first-hand knowledge of the source of the syrup!

During most of the years that I have visited this inn it has been a family affair with twin sons Hans and Fritz participating in the operation and Momo extremely valuable in the kitchen. It is still a family affair except that Momo now has two pet shops, one in North Conway and the other in Berlin, New Hampshire. Fritz married, and he and his wife are taking over more of the innkeeping duties, although Fred and Ramona will be very much on hand, especially in the summertime.

Stafford's in the Field is that inn "at the end of the road."

STAFFORD'S IN THE FIELD, Chocorua, NH 03817; 603-323-7766 (800-332-0355). A 14-guestroom (private and shared baths) resort-inn with 5 cottages, 17 mi. south of North Conway. Modified American plan omits lunch. Dinner is offered to the public with reservations. Open all year. Bicycles, square dancing, tennis, country golf, and xc skiing on grounds. Golf club, swimming, hiking, riding, and fishing nearby. No pets. The Stafford Family, Innkeepers.

Directions: Follow N.H. Rte. 16 north to Chocorua Village, then turn left onto Rte. 113 and travel 1 mi. west to inn. Or, from Rte. 93 take Exit 23 and travel east on Rtes. 104 and 25 to Rte. 16. Proceed north on Rte. 16 to Chocorua Village, turn left onto Rte. 113 and travel 1 mi. west to inn.

The date in parenthesis in the heading represents the first year the inn appeared in the pages of Country Inns and Back Roads.

Southern New England

Eastern Time Zone

Sedgwick Inn, *Berlin, N. Y.*

Mill House Inn, *Stephentown, N. Y.*

ALBANY

PITTSFIELD

Peirson Place, *Richmond*

Village Inn, *Lenox*

The Inn at Stockbridge, *Stockbridge*

Red Lion Inn, *Stockbridge*

Colonel Ebenezer Crafts Inn, *Sturbria*

The Weathervane Inn, *South Egremont*

MASS

NEW YORK

HARTFORD

CONNECTICUT

Bee and Thistle Inn, *Old L*

West Lane Inn, *Ridgefield*

Griswold, *Essex*

NEW HAVEN

Silvermine Tavern, *Norwalk*

Homestead Inn, *Greenwich*

NEW YORK CITY

Windsor House, *Newburyport*

Ralph Waldo Emerson,
Yankee Clipper,
Rockport

• Hawthorne Inn, *Concord*

ongfellow's Wayside Inn,
• *South Sudbury*

y Inn at Princeton
ceton

BOSTON

The Lenox Hotel, *Boston*

ESTER

H U S E T T S

PROVIDENCE

O D E
LAND

CAPE COD

Charles Hinckley House, *Barnstable*

Bramble Inn, *Brewster*

Queen Anne Inn, *Chatham*

The Inntowne, **NEWPORT**

Castle Hill Inn, *Newport*

Larchwood Inn, *Wakefield*

Charlotte Inn,
Edgartown, Martha's Vineyard

Hotel Manisses,
The 1661 Inn, *Block Island*

Jared Coffin House, *Nantucket*

CHARLOTTE INN
Edgartown, Martha's Vineyard, Massachusetts (1979)

It's true. Yes, in last year's edition I said that there was always something new happening at the Charlotte Inn, and my most recent visit confirmed this.

Gery and Paula Conover were taking me on an extensive tour of the fifth dwelling that makes up the ever-growing complex called the Charlotte Inn. This was the Summer House, about which I had written while it was still being redesigned and redecorated.

First, perhaps I will provide a little background about the inn itself. It is located on South Summer Street in Edgartown on Martha's Vineyard Island, off the southern coast of Cape Cod. The main house, like many other Edgartown houses, is a classic three-story white clapboard with a widow's walk on the top. It is the former home of a Martha's Vineyard sea captain. Guest rooms are individually furnished with their own private baths and are very quiet and impeccably clean. Several rooms have working fireplaces and there are many four-poster beds. There are lots of fresh flowers, books, magazines, good reading lamps, and perhaps, most important of all, a very romantic atmosphere.

Besides this main house, there is the Carriage House, with a cathedral ceiling and unusual adornments, about which I wrote several years ago, as well as the Garden House, across the street from the main inn. This has been decorated with a French country look, and, as is the case with the other guest rooms throughout the inn and annex, the furnishings and decorations have been done with great care and taste. This house also provides houseguests with a private lounge of their own, where they may enjoy the fireplace, play games, watch TV, and get acquainted.

Now, back to the Summer House. Entering through a downstairs hallway, I immediately felt as if I were in a British inn. There are English prints, particularly of old London inns and coffeehouses, throughout the hallways and guest rooms, along with some ancient tennis rackets, an old straw hat, and even a hard hat for horseback riding.

The guest rooms in the Summer House are highly individual. There are pineapple bedposts, brass beds, carved antique headboards, beautiful chests, handsome silver, and positively scrumptious bathrooms. One has a tub from 1912 that weighs about a thousand pounds and had to be lifted through the window by a crane.

Mike Brisson and his wife, Joan, are now running "l'etoile," the inn restaurant. I had a chance to talk with Mike about their philosophy. "We try to achieve food that is very simple but is elegant on the plate," he said. "I think our menu is sophisticated but we both feel that it is very palatable. We try to build on the natural ingredients, using flavors and seasonings with subtlety. We like our guests to think of their dinner as a whole rather than picking out one item on a plate."

Among the entrées on this *prix-fixe* dinner are roast supremes of baby pheasant, sauté of lobster and mussels in a puff pastry box, rack of lamb, and grilled swordfish steak with champagne and shrimp sauce. Incidentally, *Travel and Leisure* featured the restaurant and the inn in their spring edition last year.

October is an ideal time to be at Martha's Vineyard. The weather is usually pleasantly chilly in the morning and warms up as the hours go by. The island and the ferries are not crowded, and it's possible to enjoy the Vineyard as a place with its own personality.

CHARLOTTE INN, So. Summer St., Edgartown, Martha's Vineyard Island, MA 02539; 617-627-4751 (after July 1: 508-627-4751). A 25-guestroom combination inn–art gallery and restaurant on a side street, a few steps from the harbor. European plan. Continental breakfast served to inn guests except Sun. Open year-round. L'etoile restaurant open for dinner from mid-March through New Year's Day, also winter weekends. Boating, swimming, beaches, fishing, tennis, riding, golf, sailing, and biking nearby. No pets. Not suitable for children under 15. Gery and Paula Conover, Innkeepers. (See Index for rates.)

Directions: The Woods Hole/Vineyard Haven Ferry runs year-round and automobiles may be left in the parking lot at Woods Hole. Taxis may be obtained from Vineyard Haven to Edgartown (8 mi.). Check with inn for ferry schedules for all seasons of the year. Accessible by air from Boston and New York.

JARED COFFIN HOUSE
Nantucket Island, Massachusetts (1969)

Because I am a great saver of letters and mementos, I ran across this letter from one of my readers, written in 1975, who visited the Jared Coffin House in that year. Let me share some of it with you:

"Having written for our first *Country Inns* . . . while in Frankfurt, Germany (U.S. Army), to ease the homesickness, our enjoyment was limited to paging through to see where we already had visited. Until this Easter week, having five days off together (a rarity on our work schedules), we picked a route to Nantucket by way of Wakefield, Rhode Island, where we enjoyed a delicious meal at the Larchwood Inn. It was certainly a good start.

"But we were totally unprepared for our first visit to Nantucket. Our first surprise was the beauty of the island in early April—crocuses in bloom, sun, and fresh breezes. Mr. Read gave us his front Crewel Embroidery Room in the main house. He was there as we left the next day, and he made us feel so much at home. He is as warm as the inn.

"Being from a family who lived in Oahu, my husband was intrigued by the Hawaiian influences, and as we both love the sea and anything to do with boats we were really incredibly surprised at such a lovely spot in the ocean and yet so close.

"Your book is the best $3.95 we've ever spent. [Well, it certainly was 1975!] We hope you'll be expanding it to some of the European countries." (Our first European edition was published in 1975, and it has been going on ever since.)

Thank you very much, and I'm glad to have the opportunity to share some of your thoughts. If you recognize this letter in this edition do drop me a line; I'd like to know how things are going.

Things are certainly going well at the Jared Coffin House. Phil Read's most recent note points out the fact that he and Peggy have been managing the inn for twenty years and have owned it for ten. "It's been great," he declares. "We still love it and look forward to coming to it each day."

There have been some changes in those years. In addition to the main house of the inn, built in 1845, Phil and Peggy Read have acquired over the years the Harrison Gray House (1841), the Henry Coffin House (1821), the Swain House (1700s), the Eben Allen Wing (1857), and the Daniel Webster House. Three of these are physically connected; the others are only thirty feet away. Each is unique in its own way. All of the rooms have private baths and telephones, and some even have television.

The inn is furnished with period antiques reflecting the worldwide voyages of the Nantucket whalers and a way of life that has now passed forever from the American scene.

To the best of my knowledge, the island of Nantucket, which is thirty miles at sea and can be reached either by ferry or plane, has only one house that has a Victorian design. All other houses pre-date the Victorian era and are either of Colonial or Georgian design.

Shortly after the Great Fire of 1846 burned out most of the center of the town, the English brick walls and Welsh slate roof of the J.C. House resisted the fire and helped stop its spread. During the following year the Nantucket Steamboat Company bought the house for use as a hotel, naming it "The Ocean House."

Nantucket is a very lively place during the height of the summer season, and it is necessary to have reservations at the Jared Coffin well in advance. I suggest a trip in middle-to-late fall or early spring. The cobblestone streets and the shops will not be crowded, and you can enjoy the beauty and intriguing history of both the inn and the island.

JARED COFFIN HOUSE, Nantucket Island, MA 02554; 617-228-2400 (after July 1: 508-228-2400); reservations: 617-228-2405 (M–F, 10–6). A 60-guestroom village inn, 30 mi. at sea. European plan. Breakfast, lunch, and dinner served daily. Wheelchair access. Please verify accommodations before planning a trip to Nantucket in any season. Swimming, fishing, boating, golf, tennis, riding, and bicycles nearby. Philip and Margaret Read, Innkeepers. (See Index for rates.)

Directions: Accessible by air from Boston, New York, and Hyannis or by year-round ferry from Hyannis, MA. Auto reservations usually needed in advance (617-540-2022). However, cars are not recommended for short stays. Inn is a 5-min. walk from ferry dock.

THE QUEEN ANNE INN
Chatham, Cape Cod, Massachusetts (1981)

One of my readers suggested that a good subtitle for this book might be "Conversations with Innkeepers." Actually, I think that's true because in going back over the book now and then, I find that a great deal of what I have written has actually been a result of conversations. That's what I was doing right now, having a conversation with innkeeper Guenther Weinkopf.

This conversation was quite different from the one we had while we were cruising the Chatham Harbor, and he had pointed out the many landmarks and points of natural beauty. On this occasion we were on the deck of my bedroom, overlooking the lovely spacious lawn of the inn and we could just glimpse the players on the tennis courts. Each of the second- and third-floor rooms has its own private deck, and there is a great profusion of flowers of all kinds.

"We've worked very hard to achieve this," Guenther said, "and now after rearranging and planning and re-planning, I think we've finally got it right." My bedroom, typical of most of the bedrooms at the inn, was furnished in beautiful antiques with matching quilts and draperies. The beds have carved headboards and there is a private bath in every room. Some even have a working fireplace and whirlpool bath.

"One of the things that pleases me most," he went on, "is the fact that our guests are enjoying our beautiful and exciting new boats. They can water-ski or enjoy the coastal sightseeing excursions to Monomoy and

Nantucket islands. As you know I have a U. S. Coast Guard Captain's license now and I'm running these trips myself."

Guenther had a surprise for me: "We have restored and renewed another historic inn in Chatham—the Wayside Inn. It already has an excellent reputation, and in the summer people sit on the porch overlooking Main Street."

It's hard for me to realize that Sonja, my first guide at the Queen Anne, whom I met in 1981, has now finished her second year at Tufts. However, Guenther and Nicole's second daughter, Lisa, is now working at the reception desk. Bert, their son, is a ball boy, pro shop operator at the tennis courts, and also doubles as crew on boat excursions. Incidentally, Sandy Dobbrow is a first-rate tennis pro and is available for lessons.

I had dinner in the summer with my old friends, Pete and Jane Johnston, and we were all tremendously impressed by not only the unusual number of offerings but also the delicious food. I particularly enjoyed a special dish called "Atlantic Delicacies," consisting of lobster, scallops, mussels, and shrimp glazed with a white wine sauce. Lobsters are on the menu whenever they are available. The Queen Anne is open every day of the year, and there is a program of fall and winter culinary events, including fowl and game dinners.

As Guenther and I left the deck, heading for the tennis courts, he said, "You know, our new fitness center with the inside lap-pool and sauna is particularly enjoyed by our guests in the winter months. We also have an outdoor fitness trail for running and jogging. It's a wonderful place for an off-season weekend."

THE QUEEN ANNE INN, 70 Queen Anne Rd. Chatham, MA 02633; 617-945-0394 (after July 1: 508-945-0394). A 30-guestroom village inn on Cape Cod on the picturesque south shore. Full American, modified American, or European plans. Open year-round. Breakfast, dinner, Sunday brunch, and Tuesday clambake served to travelers. Restaurant hours limited in fall and winter. Call for reservations. Near all of the Cape's scenic, cultural, and historical attractions. Tennis, swimming, sauna on grounds. Water skiing, deep-sea fishing, sailing, bicycles, backroading, beach walking nearby. No recreational facilities for children on grounds. Nicole and Guenther Weinkopf, Innkeepers. (See Index for rates.)

Directions: From Boston, take Rte. 3 south to Sagamore Bridge, crossing Cape Cod Canal. Continue on Rte. 6 to Exit 11; take Rte. 137 south to Rte. 28 and turn left. This is Chatham's Main St. Turn right into Queen Anne Rd. From New York, take I-95 north to Providence, RI, I-95 to Wareham, and Rte. 6 to Sagamore Bridge (see directions above). 🖎

THE BRAMBLE INN
Brewster, Cape Cod, Massachusetts (1977)

Although Cape Cod is not very large, there is a decided difference between the south shore, traversed by Route 27, and the opposite side, which has Route 6A. The Mid-Cape Highway runs more or less down the middle and is the fastest way to get to most places on either shore.

The Bramble Inn is on Route 6A, which is reached by turning off the Mid-Cape Highway on Route 124. This road leads through some very attractive country scenery, with bike trails off the road that provide another diversion for travelers and natives alike. It's a good example of back roads that are somewhat quiet during many months of the year and are well worth seeking out.

Route 124 joins 6A, which continues on out to exits at Chatham and Orleans with many lovely villages and pleasant views. The Bramble can be seen in the distance on the left side almost as soon as you join 124.

The inn is owned by Ruth and Cliff Manchester, who, in addition to some very practical experience in the hospitality business, also brought with them three very active and attractive daughters. Elise, now nineteen and finishing her sophomore year at Amherst College, is waitressing. Suzanne, seventeen, attends the Culinary Institute in Hyde Park. I'm anxious to talk to her about her experiences there. She's worked in the kitchen with Ruth for six years, including the time they were at an inn owned by Ruth's parents just down the road apiece.

Andrea, sixteen, has taken on the role of pastry chef, making all the bread, rolls, and desserts served at the inn. This frees Ruth's hands quite a bit as she tackles other projects.

I can see that, as in the case of many other inns, the progress of the three Manchester sisters is going to make interesting reading in future editions of *CIBR*. Be sure to ask for them when you visit the inn.

Since taking over the inn a few years ago, the Manchesters have worked hard redoing all of the bedrooms and have put another bathroom in the 1849 House, adjacent to the inn building. It has five rooms, all with private baths. Those, plus three in the main house, make a total of eight.

Guest rooms have flowered wallpapers, antiques, and country furniture, and there's a hint of a tilt to the floors and doors, all of which adds to the fun of staying in a building that is indeed an antique itself.

The continental breakfast, served on the porch every morning and included in the cost of the room, consists of homemade muffins, which are invariably different every day, juice, and coffee or tea.

The evening menu is quite different. It's a four-course fixed-price dinner that usually changes nightly. There's a choice of five items from each course; this gives Ruth, who's a gourmet cook in the true sense of the word, an opportunity to offer some dinners that are quite different. Among the more popular main dishes are tenderloin of beef with Roquefort and a white wine sauce, and rack of lamb with a cracked peppercorn and mustard backing. The most sought-out recipes, also requested by both *Bon Appetit* and *Gourmet,* are the lettuce and scallion bisque and the white chocolate Coeur le Crème.

Dinner is served Monday through Saturday in season and Thursday through Saturday off-season. The restaurant is closed on Sunday.

Cliff has been very busy outside. He painted the main inn last spring and the 1849 House the year before. The shutters are a darker forest green, which adds a crisp note against the white clapboards. The gardens are coming along beautifully—Cliff added window boxes to the front of the inn with geraniums and alpine strawberries. Ruth is quite often seen picking berries to be used for garnish on the desserts.

The Bramble Inn's central location makes it ideal for enjoying all of Cape Cod's recreation and entertainment.

THE BRAMBLE INN, Route 6A, Main St., Brewster, Cape Cod, MA 02631; 617-896-7644 (after July 1: 508-896-7644). An 8-guestroom (private baths) village inn in the heart of one of Cape Cod's north-shore villages. Lodgings include continental breakfast. Dinner served Mon. thru Sat. in season; Thurs. thru Sat. in fall and winter. Open mid-March to mid-Jan. Swimming, sailing, water sports, golf, recreational and natural attractions within a short drive. Adjacent to tennis club. This is a small, intimate inn and does not meet the needs of most children. No pets. Cliff and Ruth Manchester, Innkeepers. (See Index for rates.)

Directions: Take Exit 10 from Rte. 6. Turn left (north) and follow Rte. 124 to the intersection of Rte. 6A (4 mi.). Turn right, $^{1}/_{10}$ mi. to inn.

CHARLES HINCKLEY HOUSE
Barnstable, Cape Cod, Massachusetts (1988)

"What is that wonderful fragrance?" I asked Miya Patrick as we strolled down the little stone path through her wonderful wildflower garden. "Oh, that's thyme," she answered. "I've planted herbs all along the walk, so when anyone comes down the path they'll be surrounded by lovely scents." They will also be surrounded by many, many beautiful flowers—purple cosmos, yellow gladioli, orange nasturtiums, pink alliums, and green bamboo, among many others.

Miya brings her garden into the house, too, with pretty floral arrangements in all the rooms. She even adds the edible varieties to her breakfasts.

Miya and Les Patrick have extended the naturalness and beauty of the gardens throughout this four-square, hip-roofed, Colonial Federal house. As practiced "restorationists," doing most of the work themselves, they stripped, sanded, painted, and polished until the formerly neglected and run-down house looks as bright as the proverbial new penny.

Les, tall, bearded, and amiable, is a skilled carpenter, well versed in traditional building methods. Miya is petite, with a piquant face and a bright smile. Between the two of them, they have created a homey, warm, and hospitable small inn that harks back to an earlier time, with wide pumpkin pine floorboards, original moldings and paneling, and twelve-over-twelve windows with the original uneven glass.

Charles Hinckley, the great-great-grandson of Thomas Hinckley, the last governor of Plymouth Colony, was a shipwright, who built this house in 1809 using some parts from his illustrious ancestor's house, which had been built about 1630. The fine Queen Anne paneling of one wall in the parlor was taken from the earlier house.

The Charles Hinckley House is listed on the National Register of Historic Places, and Miya has kept a feeling of historic integrity in the furnishings and decorations of the inn, with Colonial paint colors, clay pots, hand-dipped candles, and dried-flower wreaths. Along with her antique furniture, there are attractive and unobtrusive upholstered contemporary pieces.

The three guest rooms in the house are refreshingly and simply decorated with pencil-post, curtained beds, shuttered windows, oriental scatter rugs, and lovely fresh flowers. They all have fireplaces and baths. Another guest room in the separate summer kitchen is delightful and cozy with a brass bed and the fascinating original brick cooking fireplace, painted a pristine white. This room has its own private entrance and a skylight.

Miya runs a catering service, in addition to preparing incredibly beautiful breakfast dishes—and I mean beautiful! She had served me a fruit plate with a golden mango ingeniously cut into plump squares, a sliced banana, a small mound of raspberries splashed with Cointreau, and a flame-colored nasturtium, a delicately sweet morsel. There were also cranberry muffins and a wonderful turnover with pears. The sun streaming through the windows had bathed the dining room in a cheery light. The silver and glass sparkled on the polished cherry tables, laid with white placemats and blue napkins. There were fresh flowers on every table, and a beautiful bowl of dried flowers and pewter candlesticks on the painted blue cabinet. "I bake all the breads and pastries and I usually serve eggs or french toast or different kinds of pancakes," Miya said, and Les added, "It's a great time to get together and meet everybody."

They are a winsome and hospitable couple. I wish I could have stayed longer. I am happy to welcome the Charles Hinckley House to the pages of *Country Inns and Back Roads* for the first time.

CHARLES HINCKLEY HOUSE, Rte. 6A, Box 723, Barnstable Village, MA 02630; 617-362-9924. A 4-guestroom (private baths) Federal Colonial circa 1809 inn in the historic district of Barnstable Village, on the unspoiled north side of Cape Cod Bay. Breakfast included in room rate; dinner available on weekends by advance reservation. Open year-round. Cape Cod Bay is a 5-min. walk away. Convenient to many cultural and recreational attractions, including golf, tennis, deep-sea fishing, antiques and crafts shops, restaurants, museums, galleries, and Audubon nature walks. Children over 10 welcome. No pets. No smoking. No credit cards. Les and Miya Patrick, Innkeepers. (See Index for rates.)

Directions: From Rte. 6, take Exit 6, turning left at stop sign, and go ½ mi. to Rte. 6A. Turn right and continue 1½ mi. to inn.

THE LENOX HOTEL
Boston, Massachusetts (1985)

I like Boston. It is really a civilized city. To me the Lenox Hotel and Boston go hand-in-glove.

The time was 7:00 a.m. and the streaks of a mid-October dawn over the city were giving way to a full-fledged day. I was seated in the window of my corner room on the eighth floor of the Lenox, looking east. One by one, the street lamps were flickering out and the tail lights of the early morning traffic were becoming more obscure. There, indeed, was a potpourri of Boston architecture in front of me, with restrained 19th-century business buildings cheek-by-jowl with the single bell tower and spire of a church. The trees on Boylston Street still had a generous tinge of the fall colors. A seagull swooped by my window and perched on the very top of a modern Boston building on the opposite corner. Through the other window I could look down the street towards the Charles River and Cambridge on the other side. The runners and joggers were already out. By the way, the Lenox provides a jogger's guide to Boston.

Now the sun poked its way up over the harbor and I glanced around this most "unhotel" of all hotel rooms. A good substantial Hitchcock-style side chair was augmented by two excellent regular chairs and, of course, a Boston rocker. The furniture, draperies, and wallpaper were all in a most pleasing New England style. There wasn't a single piece of furniture that wouldn't have been in place at one of the *CIBR* country inns found throughout New England.

Perhaps most surprising and gratifying of all was a working fireplace. "This took a lot of doing and designing," Gary Saunders told me. "But we comply with all of the Boston codes and many of our guests can enjoy the fun of actually having a wood fire in their fireplace at a hotel in the city. They should indicate their preference when making reservations; not all of the rooms have working fireplaces."

The Lenox Hotel, a small, turn-of-the-century establishment, conveniently located in the Back Bay area of Boston (next door to Copley Square) is something of a rarity in these days of corporate ownership—a family-run hotel, whose owners are very visible. Gary Saunders and his father, Roger, along with other members of the family, have owned the hotel for the past twenty-five years.

Delmonico's, the main dining room, with a Victorian decor, has an impressive and sophisticated menu. Hearty New England fare is served in the Olde London Pub and Grille, for which the main paneling, posts, and tables were shipped over from England.

Another feature is Diamond Jim's piano bar, which offers young vocalists the opportunity to get a little "on stage" experience. I was pleased to be a judge for the finals of one of the great "Piano Bar Sing-offs."

There is one particular convenience that guests at the Lenox enjoy, which pleases me very much, and that's the airport and limousine service, available at a reasonable charge for guests arriving and departing. This is particularly handy for those of us who have to fly out of Logan Airport in Boston. Incidentally, I must admit that I also enjoyed the valet parking service that eliminates the hassle of finding a garage that isn't full.

I must soon be on my way for a quick trip back to the Berkshires on the Massachusetts Turnpike, but before long I would return again to the Lenox Hotel and my civilized city.

THE LENOX HOTEL, 710 Boylston St., Boston, MA 02116; 1-800-225-7676 (Mass.: 617-536-5300). A 220-guestroom conservative hotel in Boston's Back Bay area. Breakfast, lunch, and dinner served every day. Open all year. All contemporary hotel conveniences provided. Drive-in garage with valet parking service. Convenient to business, theaters, sightseeing, and shopping. The Saunders Family, Innkeepers; Michael Schweiger, General Manager. (See Index for rates.)

Directions: If arriving by automobile, take Exit 22 from the Mass. Tpke., the Copley Square ramp, and turn left on Dartmouth St. for 2 blocks to Newbury St. Take a left on Newbury St. for 1 block to Exeter St., take a left on Exeter for 1 block and the hotel is ahead at the corner of Exeter and Boylston Sts. An airport limo service between Logan Airport and the Lenox is available for a nominal fee.

LONGFELLOW'S WAYSIDE INN
South Sudbury, Massachusetts (1967)

It was my pleasure a few years ago to teach American history to a group of eighth-grade students, and in my endeavor to stay at least one chapter ahead of the class, I found myself once again exploring the fascinating events that preceded the American Revolution. Of course the ideal procedure to follow was to visit the scene of these remarkable events, and this trip took me to Boston, Cambridge, Concord, and other eastern Massachusetts communities that were the sites of so many of the events of 1775 and 1776.

In pursuit of these earlier times, I left the well-traveled roads to search for old buildings, mildewed markers, and ancient trees that might indeed have been witnesses to these events of history. In this way I eventually arrived at Longfellow's Wayside Inn in South Sudbury.

In my wildest hopes I couldn't have expected to find a more ideal setting. Built of red clapboard with white trim, the inn sits off a winding country road, once the stagecoach route between Boston and Albany.

The inn was built around 1702 and originally was called Howe's Tavern. In 1775, the Sudbury farmers, led by innkeeper Ezekiel Howe, were among the men who fought at nearby Concord. Revolutionary War soldiers found sustenance at the inn's tables. Today all musters of the Sudbury Minutemen take place at the inn as preparations are made for their annual reenactment of the march from Sudbury to Concord on April 19th. The 200th anniversary of the Battle of Lexington and Concord was celebrated in 1975.

Henry Wadsworth Longfellow immortalized the inn in 1863 with his

Tales of a Wayside Inn, and thereafter it was known by its new name. Thanks to a grant from the Ford Foundation, the buildings and priceless antiques have been preserved as a historical and literary shrine. The inn is filled with preserved and restored antiques. It combines being a museum with the more practical function of providing lodging and food.

Just up the road, a reproduction of an 18th-century gristmill is in operation grinding flour. Also just a stone's throw away is the famous Martha-Mary Chapel, a reproduction of a classic New England church and the setting for many a marriage these days.

The dining room specializes in good New England fare such as baked Cape Cod scallops, indian pudding served with ice cream, muffins made from meal stone-ground at the gristmill, and Massachusetts duckling in orange sauce.

I must echo the advice of innkeeper Frank Koppeis that anyone who is expecting to visit Longfellow's Wayside Inn either for a meal or lodgings should be sure to make a reservation in advance.

Here is an excerpt from a letter I received recently: "The Wayside Inn was as good as ever. It's got to be the classic in country inns. Probably its only fault is that it is too popular—especially on Sunday afternoon. Our first evening there we tried something new, a swordfish dinner. It was pretty darn good. When we had retired to our room for the evening we heard bagpipes and got up to see what was going on. Unbelievably, a parade of pipers dressed in Colonial uniform was marching through the inn. Quite a treat."

LONGFELLOW'S WAYSIDE INN, Wayside Inn Rd., off Rte. 20, South Sudbury, MA 01776; 617-443-8846 (after July 1: 508-443-8846). A 10-guestroom (private baths) historic landmark inn, midway between Boston and Worcester. European plan. Lunch and dinner served daily except Christmas. Breakfast served to overnight guests. Within a short distance of Concord, Lexington, and other famous Revolutionary War landmarks. Francis Koppeis, Innkeeper. (See Index for rates.)

Directions: From the west, take Exit 11A from Mass. Tpke. and proceed north on Rte. 495 to Rte. 20. Follow Rte. 20 east 7 mi. to inn. From the east, take Exit 49 from Rte. 128. Follow Rte. 20 west 11 mi. to inn.

"European plan" means that rates for rooms and meals are separate. "American plan" means that meals are included in the cost of the room. "Modified American plan" means that breakfast and dinner are included in the cost of the room. The rates at some inns include a continental breakfast with the lodging.

COUNTRY INN AT PRINCETON
Princeton, Massachusetts (1983)

It was an absolutely magnificent day at the height of the fall foliage season. After parking my car, I walked around the north end of the Country Inn at Princeton out onto the lawn, which I shared with some swallows and blue birds, and just stood on the terrace for a moment looking over the rolling northern Massachusetts countryside. The autumn colors of rust, yellow, and orange blended with the high hills in the far distance and were complemented by the perfect blue of the sky. I walked across the terrace, with its handsome white outdoor furniture and glass-topped tables, and onto the veranda, lush with hanging flowers.

Later, enjoying iced tea on the sunny porch, I asked Don Plumridge about the obvious coordination between the furnishings and decorations of the inn and the menu offerings.

"We offer country products of New England, and the game and wild fowl are not only very popular on our menu, but we are using them as artifacts and decorative pieces around the inn. You see, we have bird collections and wood carvings everywhere. This feeling of natural freshness is carried into both of our dining rooms."

"Flowers and floral motifs are essential to us," Maxine declared. "I spend a great deal of time gathering and arranging the flowers, and we have expanded our own garden tremendously."

Interestingly enough, this decorative theme is continued in the Washburn dining room with arrangements of pheasants and with wall mountings of boar heads, deer heads, and others. Mr. Washburn, the original builder, was apparently a good friend of Theodore Roosevelt's and they hunted wild game together.

There are six guest rooms—some are spacious parlor-size suites—each uniquely decorated with authentic antiques and attractive bedroom furniture, and with views of the countryside or forest. Two of them are the largest bedrooms I have ever seen in a real country inn. Since breakfast is served in the privacy of the guest rooms, all have small tables for the continental-breakfast tray.

Maxine and Don are very proud of their French chef, Larbi Dahrouch, who came to them from a successful, twelve-year association as executive sous chef to internationally known chef Jean-Louis Palladin. His American–French nouvelle cuisine will feature such dishes as roasted loin of Vermont lamb with shallot and onion flan and a tajine of mallard duck, cooked by a Moroccan method and served with dates, honey, and cumin.

"Our most exciting innovation is the Private Gourmet Dinner Party evenings," Don declared. "Approximately every six weeks or so we close the inn to all general public dining on a Thursday night. Invitations have been extended to all guests who visit and dine here, and they arrive about seven o'clock for social greetings and introductions. Remember, they all have demonstrated one thing in common: the willingness to explore the uncommon since the entire evening's bill-of-fare has not been disclosed in advance. This dinner is a seven-course meal with wines, and the entire purpose is to provide a social culinary evening for those of our guests whose dining experience and love of adventure make them want to explore an even higher elevation of refined dining, and it gives Larbi a further opportunity to demonstrate his four-star talent."

Put all these factors together in such a romantic setting and one might have what one guest describes in the guest book as "a perfect country inn."

COUNTRY INN AT PRINCETON (Romantik Hotels), 30 Mountain Rd., Princeton, MA 01541; 617-464-2030 (after July 1: 508-464-2030). A 6-guestroom late-Victorian mansion, 50 mi. from Boston and 14 mi. north of Worcester. Open all year except Christmas. Dinner reservations Wed. thru Sun. evenings. Sun. brunch. Closed Mon. and Tues. Near Wachusett Ski Resort, Audubon and Wildlife Society, Mt. Wachusett State Reservation. Tennis, swimming, fishing, hiking, nature trails nearby. Downhill and xc skiing, 3 mi. Lodging for couples only, no accommodations for children. Sorry, no pets. Don and Maxine Plumridge, Innkeepers. (See Index for rates.)

Directions: From Boston, follow Rte. 2 west to Rte. 31 south. From Conn. and Mass. Tpke. (90), follow Rte. 290 north to Rte. 190; then take Exit 5 and continue on Rte. 140. At Rte. 62 turn left 4 mi., and turn right at post office and flashing light. With the town common on your left, the inn is 200 yards up Mountain Rd. on right.

HAWTHORNE INN
Concord, Massachusetts (1980)

First, there was Gregory Burch. No, I'm wrong there. First, there were men like Emerson, Alcott, Nathaniel Hawthorne, and others who sought out the quietude of Concord and established their homes here. Gregory Burch came along about 1976, looking for a place somewhere in New England that needed work and would provide studio space along with some sort of income. In the year of the Bicentennial, he and the Hawthorne Inn were joined.

I think it's only fair to mention that I appeared just briefly on the scene when Gregory was working day and night to whip the inn into the kind of hospitable residence that he would be proud of. In 1980 I included the Hawthorne Inn in *Country Inns and Back Roads*.

However, there are a few more persons to be accounted for in this informal history of the Hawthorne Inn. Next is Marilyn Mudry: "Having met and fallen madly in love, I, too, came to call the Hawthorne Inn my home. We are now a family of five, with Ariel Zoe, Ezra Avery, and Jasper Gardener having arrived on blessed wings from the heavens. Their angelic presence has filled our days with joy and our nights with peace."

The Hawthorne Inn is located in the historic zone of Concord just a short walk from the Alcott House on the road out of Concord toward Lexington. It is the very same road that was neatly named "Battle Road," after the events of April, 1775, when the Minutemen routed the British and sent them in retreat toward Boston.

The inn is situated on land that once belonged to Ralph Waldo Emerson, the Alcotts, and Hawthorne. Bronson Alcott planted his fruit trees and made pathways to the mill brook, and the Alcott family tended their crops of vegetables and herbs here. Two of the original trees, which Hawthorne planted, are still standing and can be seen on the west side of the inn.

The guest rooms, in fact all of the rooms in the inn, have antique furnishings, handmade quilts, and oriental and rag rugs. There are original artworks both ancient and modern, antique Japanese Ukiyoye prints, and sculpture by Gregory. There are floor-to-ceiling bookshelves in the Common Room, which is warmed by a cozy fire in the chilly season.

Breakfast, the only meal served, is taken in the dining room and features homemade baked breads, fruit juice, a selection of teas, or a special blend of freshly ground coffee. In season, there are fruits from the gardens and vines of the inn and honey from the inn's own beehives.

Let me share just a few sentences of Marilyn's most recent letter. "We have an area of land and sky and water where a person can come and think about their life and truly feel who they are and try to learn what they need to do for themselves, their family, and this world of ours. I feel that too often we go from one day to the next, month to month, and year to year and forget to stop. Not only to stop for an early morning walk in the woods or look at a sky emblazoned with stars, but to stop and look at the love and the light and joy which can be if we take responsibility for our lives and our actions."

Henry David Thoreau, another resident of Concord, built a small cabin on the shores of Walden Pond during the 19th century and tried to find out what life was all about. Maybe he would have found a visit with Gregory and Marilyn at the Hawthorne Inn interesting and enlightening, because they would have been happy to share some of the truths that they have discovered.

THE HAWTHORNE INN, 462 Lexington Rd., Concord, MA 01742; 617-369-5610 (after July 1, new area code: 508-369-5610). A 7-guest-room (private baths) bed-and-breakfast village inn approx. 19 mi. from Boston. Breakfast to houseguests is the only meal served. Open all year. Within walking distance of all of the historic and literary points of interest in Concord. Limited facilities for young children but ideal for young people who have an appreciation for history and literature. No pets. No credit cards. Gregory Burch and Marilyn Mudry, Innkeepers. (See Index for rates.)

Directions: The Hawthorne Inn is in the historic zone of Concord, ¾ mi. east of the town center. From Rte. 128-95 take Exit 30B west for 3½ mi. Bear right at the single blinking light. The inn is 1 mi. farther on the left (south side), directly across from Wayside (home of Hawthorne and Alcott).

RALPH WALDO EMERSON
Rockport, Massachusetts (1973)

"When it comes to rocks, ocean, and sky, I think we have more than our share," said Gary Wemyss. Gary pointed out to the breakwater about three miles in front of the "Emerson," as it is known to most of its guests. "In 1946, it was about three times the length it is now, but storms and heavy seas have beaten it down until now in places it is barely visible. The far left end originally formed a harbor of refuge for sailing ships, but the builders ran out of money and gave up the construction.

"There is a reef out there beyond the breakwater known as 'Dry Salvages,' which was an inspiration for the T. S. Eliot poem. The town is trying to get the federal government to rebuild the breakwater because it protects us in winter's heavier storms."

Preoccupation with reefs, the ocean, and the swooping gulls is one of the big attractions at this country inn in Pigeon Cove. It is run by Gary Wemyss, the son of the innkeepers at the Yankee Clipper, about a mile away. The two inns make an interesting contrast, because the Emerson is built along somewhat conventional lines and has many rooms overlooking the water, whereas the Clipper is tucked away among the rocks overlooking the water and is much smaller.

Gary pointed to two lighthouses on Thatcher's Island. "They are the only twin lighthouses on the Eastern Seaboard. However, only one of them has a working light. People like to sit out here in the evening and watch the stars over the ocean and the circling beam from the lighthouse.

"In recent years there's been an increased interest in whale watching, and from May through November there are cruises with naturalists on board. We see some fin-backed whales, but there are humpbacked whales primarily. They come here to feed and they are so tame you can almost reach out and touch them. The naturalists can determine a great many things by looking at the flukes, and they can give you all kinds of information about the whales. The cruises leave primarily from Gloucester, although some leave from Rockport. Plane spotters are often used to determine where the whales are located. You can virtually always see whales. I think it's one of the most thrilling and touching experiences anyone can have to be so close to these wonderful creatures."

Gary explained that the guests include people of all interests and ages. "I think they mix well here," he said. "Everyone seems to enjoy the things that are here—the village, the shore, and of course the proximity to the sea. There is a real feeling of being relaxed and away from urban pressures, and I think that draws a lot of people together. It is such a relief just to have a few days' holiday."

Well, any kind of a holiday usually includes an emphasis on food, and at the Emerson the emphasis is on food from the nearby ocean waters, especially lobster. "People come to this part of New England for lobster, so we try to serve it as frequently as possible," Gary remarked. "Sometimes our guests go up to the Clipper for dinner, or people staying there come down here. It is part of the advantage of having two inns run by the same family."

Ocean, rocks, sky, reefs, lighthouses, bobbing lobster pots, plenty of home-cooked food—all close to Rockport, Massachusetts, one of the most picturesque towns on the New England coast—that's what the Ralph Waldo Emerson is all about. It has provided vacationers with diversion and relaxation for many years.

RALPH WALDO EMERSON, 1 Cathedral Ave., Pigeon Cove, Rockport, MA 01966; 617-546-6321 (after July 1: 508-546-6321). A 36-guestroom oceanside inn, 40 mi. from Boston. Modified American and European plans. Breakfast and dinner served daily from July 1 to Labor Day; bed and breakfast only during remainder of the year. Pool, sauna, and whirlpool bath on grounds. Tennis, golf nearby. Courtesy car. No pets. Gary and June Wemyss, Innkeepers. (See Index for rates.)

Directions: Take I-95 to Rte. 128 to Rte. 127 (Gloucester). Proceed 6 mi. on Rte. 127 to Rockport and continue to Pigeon Cove.

YANKEE CLIPPER INN
Rockport, Massachusetts (1973)

The Yankee Clipper is actually three different buildings. One is The Inn, a gracious ocean-front mansion with antique furnishings, some canopy beds, glass-enclosed porches, and a dining room right on the ocean. All the meals are served in this building. The Quarterdeck, just a few paces away, features unsurpassed views of the ocean through large picture windows and lots of sitting space to enjoy the view. The Bulfinch House was designed by the early-American architect Bulfinch, who also designed the Massachusetts State House. It is a classic early-19th-century New England house of clipper ship days with period furnishings.

The rooms in the Inn and Quarterdeck are offered with breakfast and dinner from mid-May to the end of October under the modified American plan.

The inn is open in winter on a bed-and-breakfast basis in the two ocean-front buildings. Dinner is served on Fridays and Saturdays in winter, and there is a Sunday brunch. Sitting in front of the fireplace in the afternoon, sipping hot mulled cider and munching homemade goodies with the other guests is really a lot of fun. The innkeepers have a better chance to get to know the guests, and many guests come back two or three times during the winter and again during the summer.

Spring in Rockport, one of the most photographable and paintable villages on the New England coast, has become an annual musical treat. Starting in late March through June there are events such as the Rockport Community Chorus, the Cape Ann Symphony, and the annual Rockport Chamber Music Festival. One of the more exciting things for guests to do is to take a whale-watch boat trip out to the feeding grounds off Stellwagen Banks, the main fishing grounds for the local fleet. These boats have naturalists on board who give a commentary on each individual whale sighted, their habits, how often they've been seen, and much other information. These trips last from four to five hours, and at least a two-day stay at the Clipper would be necessary.

There is also much to occupy the time of both the active and more contemplative guests at the Yankee Clipper. A heated salt-water pool is sheltered by lovely garden walls and beautiful shade trees. Many guests spend the greater part of the day in the comfortable deck chairs, looking out over the sunlit waters of the bay.

Whether active or contemplative, guests find their appetites seem to increase, and the menu has always been one of the special features over the past forty years. A New England cuisine is featured, with an extensive menu. Incidentally, lobster dinners are one of the most continually popular reasons that guests return to the Yankee Clipper.

YANKEE CLIPPER INN (Romantik Hotels), P.O. Box 2399, Rockport, MA 01966; 617-546-3407 (after July 1: 508-546-3407). A 27-guestroom intimate inn on the sea, 40 mi. from Boston. Modified American plan from mid-May to end of Oct. The Quarterdeck and main inn open Nov. 1 to mid-May for bed-and-breakfast. Dining room open to the public. Lunch served Sun. only. (Closed Dec. 24 to 26.) Heated outdoor pool in season, ocean view, shoreline walks. Many antique shops and other stores within walking distance. No facilities for infants and children under 3. No pets. Fred and Lydia Wemyss, Owners; Bob and Barbara Ellis, Innkeepers. (See Index for rates.)

Directions: Take I-95 to Rte. 128 to 127 (Gloucester). Proceed 6 mi. on Rte. 127 to Rockport and continue to Pigeon Cove.

"*European plan*" *means that rates for rooms and meals are separate.* "*American plan*" *means that meals are included in the cost of the room.* "*Modified American plan*" *means that breakfast and dinner are included in the cost of the room. The rates at some inns include a continental breakfast with the lodging.*

WINDSOR HOUSE
Newburyport, Massachusetts (1980)

Judith Crumb was telling me how much Newburyport has to offer. "Bird watchers, nature lovers, hikers, and beachcombers love the Parker River Wildlife Refuge with its beautiful beaches, and there are day and evening whale-watch cruises with a marine specialist aboard, as well as harbor tours on a lovely river boat. We can make arrangements for bicycle touring, too, which is more and more popular. Of course," she said as she warmed to her subject, "if you want something really romantic, there's the historic Newburyport tour in a horse-drawn carriage.

"We have a wide variety of comedy, drama, and musicals in our year-round theater in Newburyport, and in the summer we have the Castle Hill Music Festival in Ipswich, the North Shore Music Theatre in Beverly, and the Hampton Playhouse in Hampton, New Hampshire. And there are regular outdoor concerts in our new waterfront park."

I thought she'd told me everything and we'd start our tour of the house, but she put a restraining hand on my arm. "And we mustn't forget that Newburyport is an increasingly important center for fine art, with 18th- and 19th-century painting and antiques, as well as contemporary art, in several excellent galleries. We've definitely moved away from the 'Sunday painter school,' and some very fine work is being exhibited."

Now we headed for the kitchen, as she continued her conversation. "The Windsor House was started in 1785 and completed in 1787 as a private residence. By 1796 it was being used as both a residence and a ship's chandlery. The kitchen here was the original shipping and receiving room, as you can see from those big outside doors.

"The brick wall with the fireplace is part of a firewall that also goes to the top story and separates the warehouse section from the living section. The posts and beams throughout the entire house were built by ships' carpenters, the same men who built the clipper ships."

The kitchen is really the pulse of the Windsor House. Not only do all the guests gather around in the morning to enjoy Judith's prandial skill, but, as she says, "It's the place where we all gather at any time during the day and tell tall tales and get acquainted."

There were interesting contrasts between the rooms on the warehouse side of the firewall and the residential section. The Merchant's Suite on the first floor was the original chandlery. It has its own street entrance and is filled with antiques from 19th-century provisioners, shops, including scales, display boxes, and a bootjack. It's ideal for folks who have difficulty with stairs, or a family with small children.

Rooms on the residential side of the house tend to have wood paneling and other graceful features that would befit a residence.

Judith and her colleague, Jim Lawbaugh, share the breakfast duties, and he has developed his own sausage recipe. Incidentally, his two sons, Richard and Paul, are frequently in residence at the inn. A rather informal supper with the innkeepers may be enjoyed with special advance arrangement.

The door opened and two guests, who had been doing the walking tour of Newburyport with the Clipper Trail folder, returned for a warming cup of coffee and a little conversation. "We decided to stay for two more days, there's just too much to see."

We all readily agreed.

WINDSOR HOUSE, 38 Federal St., Newburyport, MA 01950; 617-462-3778 (after July 1: 508-462-3778). A 5-guestroom inn (private and shared baths) in the restored section of Newburyport. Open year-round. Breakfast served to all guests. Supper with the innkeepers by special arrangement. Located in the Merrimack River Valley, 3 mi. from Plum Island and the Parker River National Wildlife Refuge. A short walk from the restored 19th-century retail area, restaurants, and museums. Also nearby: deep-sea fishing, swimming, art galleries, antique shops, family ski area, horseback riding, and year-round theater. Some trundle beds available for children. Babysitters provided. Small dogs welcome. Judith Crumb and Jim Lawbaugh, Innkeepers. (See Index for rates.)

Directions: From Boston and Maine: From I-95 use exit to Rte. 113, turn right onto High St. (Rte. 1A) and proceed 3 mi. to Federal St., turn left. Inn on left across from Old South Church (Rte. 1A is scenic drive from Boston or New Hampshire).

COLONEL EBENEZER CRAFTS INN
Sturbridge, Massachusetts (1981)

If you're traveling on the Massachusetts Turnpike there are two reasons to stop off in Sturbridge. One is to take advantage of the really exceptional lodgings at the Colonel Ebenezer Crafts Inn and to enjoy dinner or lunch at the Publick House.

The other is to pay a serious visit to Sturbridge Village, a restored 19th-century environment. Such a visit would take at least two and a half hours to skim it and longer to really recognize its significance and appreciate all the work that has gone into it.

The village covers over 200 acres with farms, shops, a tavern, a blacksmith shop, and a working gristmill. All of the nearly forty buildings were moved here from throughout New England and then restored and authentically furnished. Year-round, costumed men and women demonstrate skills that have almost disappeared today.

To get to the Publick House, where one must check in for the Colonel Ebenezer Crafts Inn, if you're coming to Sturbridge from the Massachusetts Turnpike be sure to take the first exit to the right, marked Route 20 West. Follow that to Route 131, turn left, and you're on your way not to old Sturbridge Village, but to today's contemporary Sturbridge Village. On the way you'll pass the Sturbridge Town Hall, the Federated Church, the library, the village green, and the Publick House on your right.

On the June day I arrived at Colonel Ebenezer Crafts Inn, the apple trees on the ridge had shed their blossoms and the small green apples gave promise of good things to come in future months. The lawn was neatly mowed to the edge of the woods and the birds almost seemed to signal my arrival with a pleasant welcome. I walked up the stone steps to the porch with its long deacon's bench and rang the bell. I was greeted by the hostess, Pat Bibeau.

Each of the guest rooms has its own bath and shower, and there's almost always a bowl of apples in each room for guests to enjoy. Pat commented that she frequently turns down the beds in the evening and also leaves cookies. Both of these are nice country inn touches. There is a comfortable terrycloth robe provided for the use of each guest at the poolside or after a shower.

The rooms are very light and airy and are furnished either in antiques or good reproductions. There were a number of chenille bedspreads, including one called "The Pride of Sturbridge."

The living room really invites guests to get acquainted, and I was delighted to find a generously supplied bookcase and also stacks of the *National Geographic,* which makes wonderful bedtime reading.

The exterior landscaping for the inn includes a beautiful brick patio where guests may have morning breakfast or afternoon tea, surrounded by plants and an herb garden. A stone stairway leads from the patio to the pool area, and shrubbery has been planted to form a live sundial around the flagpole.

Because guests at the Colonel Ebenezer Crafts Inn take a great many of their meals at the nearby Publick House, it is of interest to know that luncheons and dinners there include excellent New England clam chowder, as well as New England dishes such as lobster pie, broiled native scallops, double-thick lamb chops, deep dish apple pie—à la mode or with cheddar cheese—and indian pudding served with vanilla ice cream.

COLONEL EBENEZER CRAFTS INN, c/o Publick House, Box 187, Sturbridge, MA 01566; 617-347-3313 (after July 1: 508-347-3313). A 10-guestroom bed-and-breakfast inn in a historic village, 18 mi. from Worcester. Old Sturbridge Village nearby. Lodging rates include continental breakfast and afternoon tea. (Lunch and dinner available at nearby Publick House.) Open year round. Swimming pool on grounds. Tennis nearby. Buddy Adler, Innkeeper. (See Index for rates.)

Directions: From Mass. Tpke. take Exit 9; follow signs to Sturbridge on Rte. 131. From Hartford follow I-84, which becomes 1-86. Take Exit 3.

A number of inns have nearby airports where private airplanes may land. An airplane symbol at the end of the inn directions indicates that there is an airport nearby. Consult inn for further information.

THE VILLAGE INN
Lenox, Massachusetts (1977)

"We're actually beginning our seventh year as innkeepers; it hardly seems possible that that much time has passed." I was having dinner in the Harvest Restaurant at the Village Inn with innkeepers Cliff Rudisill and Ray Wilson. We were reminiscing about their early days here, when they took over the inn in January of 1982, weathered the winter, and worked on learning the ropes and becoming acclimated.

"After Easter that year," Ray said, "we spent two weeks in England and visited seven country house hotels, sampling marvelous cuisine and learning our way around English teas. As a matter of fact, because of meeting Bronwen Nixon at Rothay Manor, we came back and established an English Afternoon Tea, which we've been serving ever since. Rothay Manor is our 'Twin Inn' in England."

These two men, both from Texas, have established their own unique style at the Village Inn, a two-and-a-half-story yellow clapboard building with a basic Federal design. Built in 1771, and ultimately adapted to meet various needs over many years, it became an inn in 1775, and has been one ever since. Two rear wings were once well-constructed barns, forming an L-shaped sheltered terrace with a lawn on which there are a number of beautiful maples. Plantings of iris, daffodils, petunias, roses, and tulips brighten the picture during the warmer weather, and the interior of the inn is enhanced by flowers throughout all months of the year.

On the floors above, authentic New England rooms and suites are available for overnight guests or for those with longer stays in mind. Most of them have their own bathrooms, many have four-poster beds, and some have working fireplaces. All of the rooms have new Colonial wallpaper and new curtains and carpets. They are air conditioned in the summer. There is a separate TV on the first floor as well.

The Tavern in the old cellar is now completely remodeled and features professional entertainment on the weekends.

Cliff and Ray are very happy with their new chef, Steven Anderson, who comes to them with a degree and awards from the Culinary Institute and a practical background, including two years at a former *CIBR* inn, the North Hero House in Vermont. His talents have been recognized by *Gourmet* magazine, which has made seven requests for his recipes, one of which was featured in the fall of 1987. Steven likes to keep the menu homey and "very New Englandish." Some of his specialties include roast chicken breast with thyme and honey glaze, duck with raspberry sauce, and veal medallions with lobster and morels. His bride, Lynn, helps with desserts, and one of her special creations is called Brownie Bottom Bourbon Pie.

But let's return to the style that Cliff and Ray have brought to the inn in the past few years. Two special spring weekends include a "Literary Weekend," featuring the lives and work of Edith Wharton and Herman Melville, with a visit to their homes nearby, and a "Shaker Experience" weekend, which concentrates on the Shaker ethic and crafts, with visits to nearby Shaker centers.

Cliff points out that "Tanglewood is just a mile down the road, and we continue the tradition of good music all year long. We always have good classical music playing in the background, and our grand piano in the large common room is frequently played by guests who share their talent with us." The inn has also been acquiring some very handsome paintings, including those of William and James Hart and other Hudson River School painters.

The Village Inn in Lenox—an inn of graceful style.

THE VILLAGE INN, Church St., Lenox, MA 01240; 413-637-0020. A 28-guestroom inn (mostly private baths) in a historic Berkshire town, 4 mi. from Stockbridge, 8 mi. from Pittsfield, and 1 mi. from Tanglewood. Breakfast and afternoon tea served daily to travelers. Dinner served Wed. thru Sun. Open every day of the year. Lenox is located in the heart of the Berkshires with many historical, cultural, and recreational features. Swimming in pleasant nearby lakes. All seasonal sports, including xc and downhill skiing, available nearby. Children over 6 welcome. No pets. Personal checks accepted. Cliff Rudisill and Ray Wilson, Innkeepers. (See Index for rates.)

Directions: After approaching Lenox on Rte. 7, one of the principal north-south routes in New England, exit onto Rte. 7A to reach the village center and Church St. When approaching from the Mass. Tpke. (Exit 2) use Rte. 20W about 4 mi. and turn left onto Rte. 183 to center of town.

PEIRSON PLACE
Richmond, Massachusetts (1979)

If you are like I am, then I know you enjoy the idea that there are certain places in the world where the past and the present become a continuum. I find it in certain Scandinavian farmhouse inns that have been lived in by the same family literally for centuries, and also in special places in Germany and Austria, where there is this sense of a continuation with the past. At Peirson Place I have the same feeling that the house and the furniture and the grounds and the view and the atmosphere have remained for the most part unchanged.

This point came home to me when I was once again strolling through the grounds of Peirson Place, and Margaret Kingman told me that the Cogswell House was built in 1762 by Joseph Cogswell. A few years later, a tannery was built on the land by Nathan Peirson, starting a connection through a later marriage between the Cogswells and the Peirsons. "Even our groundskeeper, Russell Chapman, who has maintained all of the trails and landscaping for eighteen years, belongs on the place as well. Nathan Peirson was a tanner, Russell's ancestor a harness maker. Each generation has worked on the property since 1790."

Peirson Place is really very unusual, and Margaret and her son, Lou, have created an intimate country inn that is markedly different from other accommodations in the Berkshires, and, in fact, from most other places. She has many guests who have been returning each year because they enjoy the shaded quiet of the Victorian gazebo, the tranquility of the woods, and the quietude of the pond.

Bird watchers have myriad feathered friends to observe, and guests also enjoy riding bicycles and swimming and the use of the sauna.

Peirson Place is open year around, and during the winter it provides very warm and cozy quarters to accommodate cross-country skiers, who actually do not have to leave the grounds to enjoy that favorite outdoor sport. A good point for me to mention is that lunches and dinners are available on weekends at all times; however, special arrangements can be made for midweek repasts with advance notice.

Speaking of those lunches and dinners, I discovered that many people prefer the dinners at Peirson Place, particularly during the summer, and most particularly on the Friday evenings of Tanglewood. For example, the fare might include a chilled fruit soup, chicken, pasta, a fresh vegetable salad, and melon for dessert. Another menu might be minestrone, fetuccini Alfredo, and strawberry shortcake. Still a third might be cream of broccoli soup, a scallop casserole, and dutch apple pie. Each menu has three courses: soup, an entrée, and dessert. By the way, this combination lunch/dinner is served all afternoon; as Margaret says, "People seem to want to eat all day long."

Breakfasts are also rather special, and include whole-grain cereals with honey, maple syrup, milk or cream, raisin bran, various cheeses, toast, muffins, and pastries.

As we continued walking around the grounds, stopping at the grape arbor—a favorite place for weddings—she told me that many guests are fascinated by the fact that her great-grandfather, her mother, and she were all born in the same room in the Peirson house. It has been in the family since the 18th century.

Although Peirson Place is sometimes referred to as an "obscure inn," Margaret insists that she and the guests enjoy the obscurity.

Her latest news is that last spring she visited her "twin inn," the Old Vicarage in Higham, England, and she says, "It was like being home again."

PEIRSON PLACE, Richmond, MA 01254; 413-698-2750. A 10-guest-room (private and shared baths) country house 6 mi. from Pittsfield on Rte. 41. Open year-round. Minimum stay of 2 nights during Tanglewood season and holiday weekends. Complimentary breakfast. Wheelchair access. Near all the scenic attractions of the Berkshire Hills, including Tanglewood, Hancock Shaker Village, and marvelous backroading in 3 states. Pond, sauna, badminton, darts, boating on grounds. Tennis, golf, horseback riding, etc., nearby. No facilities to amuse children under 12. No pets. The Kingman Family, Innkeepers. (See Index for rates.)

Directions: From Boston: Take Mass. Tpke. to Exit 1. Follow Rte. 41 north through Richmond. Peirson Place is on left-hand side. From New York: Leave Taconic State Pkwy. at Rte. 295 and continue east to Rte. 41. Turn left. From Albany: New York Thruway (Berkshire Spur) to State Line Exit; left on Rte. 22 to Rte. 295; right on Rte. 295 to Rte. 41. Turn left.

THE INN AT STOCKBRIDGE
Stockbridge, Massachusetts (1986)

What a wonderful, gorgeous Berkshire afternoon! The last forty-five minutes of an October sun was streaming across the meadows, lighting up the swaying trees and the two-story columns of the Inn at Stockbridge with a wondrous golden light. I pulled around the circular driveway and stood for a moment on the steps drinking in the entire scene, almost reluctant to join Lee Weitz and other guests for the usual afternoon wine and cheese.

Anticipating my mood, Lee opened the front door of the inn and said, "Oh, I know how you feel, it's so wonderful that you almost hate to come inside. But come on in, because we're all having such a good time in here!" Lee introduced me to some of the guests, all of whom had enjoyed a wonderful afternoon walking or driving in the Berkshires.

I trailed off into the library, another very large room furnished in a most comfortable way, quite reminiscent of an English country house with deep chintz-covered sofas and another big fireplace. Then I crossed over to the other side of the house to see the fourteen-place Chippendale dining room table, where I have had breakfast quite a few times myself. You see, I live about a mile away from the Inn at Stockbridge.

I returned and sank down on a sofa, immediately becoming engrossed in conversation with a couple from California who were traveling with CIBR. "We love it here," they said. "It's our third time and it's like coming home again. What we particularly remember is the good time around the breakfast table, when people are so stimulating and fascinating."

Lee came and spirited me upstairs to look at some of the beautiful guest rooms. These are all most attractively furnished and decorated, and all have interesting names. "I like to furnish every room entirely differently," Lee commented, as we moved from room to room. "Fortunately, this was a lovely, spacious private house for many years and so most of the bedrooms are unusually large. All of them have views of the countryside."

Each of them has some little hidden things, such as candy or little flower arrangements or something special to make the room more distinctive.

Some rooms have a view of a spacious patio where, during the warm weather, the tables are set with pink tablecloths and napkins and fresh flowers. It's all very festive. Beyond the patio is a graceful, secluded swimming pool.

As we rejoined the group in the living room I asked Lee about dinners. "We have found that our summer guests are usually headed for a concert at Tanglewood or an evening of theater and have made other plans for dinner. However, we are happy to prepare dinner for a group of eight or more with advance notice. During winter we have a weekend package that includes dinner.

"I have to tell you," she went on, "that people in the summertime love the breakfast out on the patio. Many of them take pictures because the setting is so pretty. Breakfast might include a soufflé or eggs Benedict or a thick slice of french toast with whipped Grand Marnier butter. This makes it taste like crêpes Suzette, but even better. There's also fresh fruit, blueberry pancakes, herbed eggs with cheese and mushrooms, and many other things. We make our own coffee with a French roast blend."

THE INN AT STOCKBRIDGE, Rte. 7, Box 618, Stockbridge, MA 01262; 413-298-3337. A 7-guestroom (5 with private bath) country house about 1 mi. north of the center of Stockbridge. Lodgings include a full breakfast. Dinner for groups by reservation and included in winter weekend package. Open year-round. Convenient to all of the Berkshire cultural and recreational attractions. A summer swimming pool on grounds. No facilities for children under 10. No pets. Lee and Don Weitz, Innkeepers. (See Index for rates.)

Directions: From N.Y.C.: take any of the main highways north to Stockbridge, and continue north on Rte. 7 for 1.2 mi. Look for small sign on the right after passing under the Mass. Tpke. Inn cannot be seen from the road. From Mass. Tpke: exit at Lee, take Rte. 102 to Stockbridge and turn right on Rte. 7 going north for 1.2 mi. as above.

The date in parenthesis in tne heading represents the first year the inn appeared in the pages of Country Inns and Back Roads.

THE RED LION INN
Stockbridge, Massachusetts (1967)

"What is your favorite country inn?"

That's a question I hear literally hundreds of times a year. Quite truthfully I have no favorite. I love them all. If I didn't, I'm sure that I couldn't include them in this book. However, there is one country inn to which I feel very close. That's the Red Lion Inn in Stockbridge.

I feel very close to it for many reasons, not the least of which is that I can see it through my office window, just a half-square away. (A little play on words there.)

I'm close to it for many other reasons as well, because, like all of the residents of my village, I have a proprietary interest in the Red Lion. We who live in Stockbridge were dismayed to learn in 1967 that the old inn, originally erected in 1793, enlarged and improved over many years, then almost completely destroyed by fire in 1896, was possibly going to be torn down and replaced by a gasoline station. We were very much relieved when Jack and Jane Fitzpatrick, owner of Country Curtains, acquired the property, reopened it in 1967, and turned it into a thriving concern.

Like the visitors in Stockbridge, I have spent many a pleasant time rocking on the broad front porch and enjoying lunch at the Widow Bingham's Tavern with my friends. I have attended at least four conferences of *CIBR* innkeepers at the Red Lion over the past twenty-three years. Like many other village inns, it is the center of a great deal of our social activity, including wedding receptions, political gatherings, anniversary parties—in general, a meeting place for villagers.

From the start, the Fitzpatricks have made the Red Lion a family affair, with Jack and Jane being joined by their two daughters, Nancy and Ann. They are all very much involved.

The Fitzpatricks are also the owners of Blantyre, an imposing stone mansion of a former estate, just a few miles from the center of Stockbridge. Blantyre has sumptuously proportioned bedrooms and two proper courts for playing croquet, as well as a swimming pool and tennis courts. In the winter, arrangements may be made through the Red Lion for accommodations there.

One of the most enjoyable times at the Red Lion is Christmas, when the inn is decorated "to the nines" with Christmas greens and trim and 2,000 feet of laurel roping. The ceiling-high tree in the lobby shimmers with hundreds of handmade ornaments.

Ann Fitzpatrick's candy sculptures are restored to their familiar spots throughout the public rooms. During the holiday season, there is afternoon harp music, a visit from Santa, and a concert by bell ringers. Children can hang decorations they have made on the children's tree in the hallway by the gift shop. The Christmas spirit continues with a group of carolers, who gather on the front porch at Epiphany. Incidentally, the Red Lion Christmas trees adorning the top of the porch are kept lighted until long after Christmas.

Betsy Holtzinger, the innkeeper, easily recognizable by her shining blond hair, pointed out to me recently that Stockbridge is a five-season town: winter, spring, summer, autumn, and fall foliage. "It is the first country-inn experience for many people," she commented, "and we want to make it a memorable one. The Berkshire Theatre Festival, the Boston Symphony at Tanglewood, and Jacob's Pillow Dance Festival are open in the summer. In the winter we've got lots of downhill and cross-country skiing. Fortunately, the Norman Rockwell Museum, which contains many of his original paintings, is open every day year-round."

THE RED LION INN, Stockbridge, MA 01262; 413-298-5545. A 95-guestroom historic village inn, dating back to 1773, in the Berkshire hills. European plan. Breakfast, lunch, and dinner. Open year-round. Wheelchair access. Adjacent to Tanglewood, Norman Rockwell's Old Corner House Museum, the Berkshire Playhouse, Jacob's Pillow, Chesterwood Gallery, Mission House, and major ski areas. Outdoor pool. Tennis, golf, boating, fishing, hiking, mountain climbing, and xc skiing nearby. Jack and Jane Fitzpatrick, Owners; Betsy Holtzinger, Innkeeper. (See Index for rates.)

Directions: From the Taconic State Pkwy., take Exit 23 (N.Y. Rte. 23) to Mass. Rte. 7. Proceed north to Stockbridge. From the Mass. Tpke., Exit 2 at Lee, and follow Rte. 102 to Stockbridge.

A number of inns have nearby airports where private airplanes may land. An airplane symbol at the end of the inn directions indicates that there is an airport nearby. Consult inn for further information.

THE WEATHERVANE INN
South Egremont, Massachusetts (1984)

"Good evening, folks, how are you? I'm the innkeeper, Vince Murphy." While I was having a welcome cup of tea in front of the very cozy fireplace at the Weathervane Inn on a midwinter afternoon, Vincent Murphy excused himself at least four times to welcome new guests. Vince is a man who has the knack for making people feel welcome immediately.

Among the things that I look for in an inn are qualities of memorability. Besides innkeeper Murphy, who is, as he says, "a private investigator from the streets of New York," there are many other memorable features.

For example, there's Anne Murphy with the laughing eyes and a most pleasant manner with all of the guests. Then there's Patricia (or Trish), Anne and Vince's daughter, who had just returned from a Florida vacation at the time of my visit and must have knocked them dead on the beaches, because she had a super suntan to go with her Irish good looks.

The Weathervane Inn, listed in the National Register of Historic Places, is a small cluster of buildings set off the highway, with sections dating back to 1785. It is located in the lovely little village of South Egremont in the Berkshires, where there are many pre-1800 houses and a graceful church. Replete with wide-board floors, beautiful moldings, and an original fireplace that served as a heating and cooking unit with a beehive oven, the inn has a comfortable, warm atmosphere.

There are eleven very attractively furnished country inn guest rooms, with private baths, enhanced by Anne's eye for design and her needlework. Antique maple high double beds and some king-sized beds, all with coordinated linens, along with Anne's handmade pierced lampshades, all combine to make each room distinctive. There are many dried flower arrangements, ball fringe curtains, books and magazines, and good reading lamps.

I talked to Anne about the menu at the Weathervane. "Well," she said, "the kitchen is my domain and I'm very proud of the response that our guests have had to our entrées. Our specialties have been Cornish hens with kiwi sauce, veal Dijonnaise, pork tenderloin Normandy, duckling with black cherries, seafood Mornay, and soups like split pea, New England chowders, and a hearty borscht. We've had to print our recipe for celery seed dressing because so many of our diners requested it."

Vince came cruising by and decided to make his contribution: "Let me tell you about our desserts—Trish is the pastry chef par excellence! The best homemade pies with the best crust. All kinds of fresh fruit combinations—blueberry-peach, strawberry-blueberry, peach-nectarine, and pear blueberry. And her cheesecake and chocolate chip walnut pie get nothing but raves!"

There are two dining areas, including a new dining room overlooking the garden and the swimming pool, with a glimpse of the antique shop in a barn that has a feeling somewhat akin to the Sturbridge Village buildings. The shop specializes in early quilts and folk furniture. and inn guests often wander back there to browse.

Eventually, we all sat down in front of the fireplace, next to a sort of little pub corner, and for an hour and a half I was beguiled by the various members of the Murphy family. Vince really is a private investigator, but he takes all of the "Mike Hammer" jokes with exceptionally good grace and even adds a few of his own. "I did that for many years in the city," he said, "and I still go in about one day a week, but all of us have taken up this new life here in the country. As a matter of fact, I'm even a member of the South Egremont Volunteer Fire Department!"

THE WEATHERVANE INN, Rte. 23, South Egremont, MA 01258; 413-528-9580. An 11-guestroom village inn in the Berkshire foothills. Modified American plan in summer; in winter, modified American plan, Thurs. through Sun. Breakfast served to houseguests. Dinner served to travelers Fri. and Sat. Open year-round. Limited wheelchair access. Swimming pool on grounds. Golf, tennis, bicycling, backroading, hiking, horseback riding, fishing. downhill and xc skiing nearby. Tanglewood, Jacob's Pillow, Berkshire Playhouse, Norman Rockwell Museum, and great antique shops all nearby. No pets. Vincent, Anne, and Patricia Murphy, Innkeepers. (See Index for rates.)

Directions; From New York City follow Sawmill River Pkwy. to Taconic Pkwy. to Rte. 23 east. South Egremont and the inn are about 2 mi. past the Catamount ski area. ◢

BEE AND THISTLE INN
Old Lyme, Connecticut (1984)

Although I first visited the Bee and Thistle Inn in 1982, it has taken a succession of visits to bring the inn, the village itself, and, in particular, the lovely ambience created by the Lieutenant River into complete focus for me.

It really happened on my last visit. Bob and Penny Nelson and I strolled out across the broad lawns and fields behind this handsome 1756 building down to the river banks.

"Someday I'm going to have a gazebo here," quoth Penny. "Our neighbor across the river is Roger Tory Peterson, the world-renowned authority on bird life. He has written many guide books, and we have some of his paintings hanging in the inn."

When I remarked on the similarity of this riverside idyll to many French impressionist paintings, Penny was quick to point out that American painters who had gone to France to paint their pastoral settings and then come to Old Lyme, stayed right on this river and decided they didn't have to go to France any more. "The natural beauty of Old Lyme was the ideal subject matter for American artists who painted in the Barbizon and Impressionist styles. Old Lyme was one of the earliest art colonies in this country."

Bob continued, "There are at least fifty houses here, ranging from the late 17th century to the present, which are not only artistically captivating, but also worthy of study for their architectural and historical importance. Lyme Street was designated as a historic district in 1970."

This love of beauty and fine things was reflected throughout the inn. Many of the architectural features enhance an atmosphere of friendly open heartedness. The many fireplaces, antiques, sunlit porches, the lovely carved staircase, the three canopied beds and the four-posters, and the old quilts and afghans plainly show the Nelsons' love for the quality of things in both the past and present.

"I hope you'll return sometime after the first of November," said Penny. "We are serving English tea, November through April, on Monday, Wednesday, and Thursday from 3:30 until 5:00. We have an ever-growing collection of individual china teapots, and the menu includes hot fresh scones with fresh whipped cream and raspberry jam, assorted tea sandwiches, tea breads, and a dessert of the day. Guests have their choice of Darjeeling tea or herbal teas. It's the greatest fun."

As we reluctantly returned to the main inn, passing through the English garden, which is one of Penny's delights, I commented on all the flowers. "There are giant phlox, asters, lupines, iris, peonies, and bleeding heart," she said. "Everyone enjoys the peace and quiet and the lovely colors."

I asked Bob and Penny as we walked through the front door what it was that moved guests to return several times to the Bee and Thistle. "Many of them say that we are what they thought an inn would be like—a gracious home, giving them a chance to sit and talk, have a lovely dining experience with caring people in attendance.

"Bob and I have had a wonderful time," Penny said, "even though there has been so much to do. One of the nicest things is our new head chef, Francis Brooke-Smith. He has the entire staff excited with his superb menus and presentation. Our son, Jeff, is at the Culinary Institute of America, but comes home to help us on the weekend. By the way, Francis received his training at the Ritz in London, which is in your book on England, isn't it? We still want the Bee and Thistle to be the warmest, friendliest, and most traditional New England inn imaginable."

BEE AND THISTLE INN, 100 Lyme St. (Rte. 1), Old Lyme, CT 06371; 203-434-1667. An 11-guestroom (2 rooms with shared bath) inn located in an as-yet-unspoiled Connecticut village, near the border of Rhode Island. Breakfast, lunch, and dinner served daily, except Tues. Sun. brunch. Open year-round. Conveniently located to visit Gillette Castle, Goodspeed Opera House, and Essex steam train and train rides. Mystic Seaport, Essex Village, Ivoryton Summer Theater nearby. No pets. Bob and Penny Nelson, Innkeepers. (See Index for rates.)

Directions: Coming north on I-95, take a left at the bottom of Exit 70. At the first light take a right. At the second light, take a left and then follow Rte. 1 (Lyme Street) to inn.

GRISWOLD INN
Essex, Connecticut (1974)

If you've never been to New England, I could give you a list of towns that are absolute "musts." Right near the top of the list is Essex, Connecticut.

In the first place, each summer, sailors from all over the world make Essex a port of call. A common sight are these yachtsmen, who have moored at the end of the street and come up to do some shopping in their faded jeans and boat shoes, stopping in at the Griswold Inn for lunch.

In fact, that's what I was doing at the very moment. Innkeeper Bill Winterer and I had been strolling for a while on the main street, doing a little window shopping in some of the fine stores of the village, which is another reason for a visit. We had seated ourselves underneath the upstairs gallery on one of the wooden benches that line both sides of the entrance. It was a warm summer afternoon in August, and people-watching was at its best

I like to get Bill started on some of the historical events that took place in Essex. He is a graduate of the Officer Candidate School at the nearby New London Coast Guard Academy and truly a man of the sea himself.

"Only five families have owned the inn since 1776. The Tap Room was built in 1738 and was the first schoolhouse in Essex. It was rolled on logs drawn by a team of oxen down the main street to where we are now.

"The entire fleet of twenty-eight ships was destroyed by fire during a British raid on the town during the War of 1812."

The Gris has a very high historic profile. The Steamboat Dining Room was recently restored to conform to the period of the remainder of the building. Lovely paned windows have been added, and some of the marine collection is now displayed there. It is notable for the mural on the end wall that actually rocks back and forth, creating the impression of being on an old Connecticut River steamship of the 19th century.

Within its many dining rooms and parlors, the inn has a remarkable collection of marine paintings, including some by Antonio Jacobsen. The collection includes prints, ship models, firearms, binnacles, ship's clocks, a potbellied stove, humorous posters and prints, and a genuine popcorn machine. Vicky, Bill's wife, has been working over the past several years organizing everything. "Our plan is to publish a book that can be made available to our guests. This will list each piece in the collection, along with the history of the artist. Oliver Jensen, the founder and publisher of *American Heritage*, has agreed to write the foreword."

Our talk turned quite naturally to the cuisine. "Over the past six months or so we have been doing a considerable amount of research on our New England cuisine and we've added several items to the menu," he remarked. "The deeper we dig into the subject the more we realize how authentically New England our cuisine really is. Menus and recipes have been handed down from year to year, from innkeeper to innkeeper, and from chef to chef. In addition to the New England specialties, we've also added some Creole cooking, following recipes of Sala Griswold's wife, who hailed from New Orleans."

So our chatting eddied back and forth with our shared enthusiasm for history, good books, and good inns. It was a wonderfully pleasant summer's day for two old friends.

GRISWOLD INN, Main St., Essex, CT 06426; 203-767-1812. A 22-guestroom inn in a waterside town, steps away from the Connecticut River. European plan. Complimentary continental breakfast served daily to inn guests. Lunch and dinner served daily to travelers. Hunt breakfast served Sun. Closed Christmas Eve and Christmas Day. Near the Eugene O'Neill Theatre, Goodspeed Opera House, Ivoryton Playhouse, Gillette Castle, Mystic Village, Valley Railroad, and Hammonasset State Beach. Day sailing on inn's 44-foot ketch by appointment. Bicycles, tennis, and boating nearby. Victoria and William G. Winterer, Innkeepers. (See Index for rates.)

Directions: From I-95 take Exit 69 and travel north on Rte. 9 to Exit 3, Essex. Turn right at stoplight and follow West Ave. to center of town. Turn right onto Main St. and proceed down to water and inn.

THE HOMESTEAD INN
Greenwich, Connecticut (1969)

As frequently as I have visited the Homestead over the years, I'm always delightfully re-surprised at the truly residential nature of its location. There's been an inn here for a very long time with a long procession of different innkeepers and many different types of accommodations; now, however, I believe the Homestead has reached the pinnacle of its success.

Today, the inn reflects the sensitivities and tastes of Lessie Davison and Nancy Smith, two attractive and talented women who saw the possibilities in restoring this 185-year-old farmhouse that is just a few moments from I-95.

The inn began its life as a farmhouse, built in 1799. In 1859 it was sold to innkeepers who completely remodeled it in the distinctive "Carpenter Gothic" architecture of the Victorian era.

The inn is set back from the road in a lovely old orchard and gardens, and the sloping lawn is highlighted by handsome hydrangea bushes. There are now twenty-three guest rooms, all with different decorative themes. They are handsomely furnished, including many antiques and such comforts as clock radios, electric blankets, two pillows for every head, lots of books and magazines, and very modern bathrooms. In many ways, the guest rooms resemble those at Rothay Manor in the Lake Country of England.

Although many of the guest rooms are in the main house, some very careful attention has been given recently to the remodeling of other buildings on the property, and guests may now enjoy a variety of rooms, some with queen sized beds and balconies or porches, as well as a queen-bedded suite, with a lovely, large, cathedral-ceilinged bedroom and a front porch overlooking the neighbor's apple orchard.

The Homestead is the perfect alternative to the busy, noisy New York hotels, and provides a very pleasant country-type atmosphere for city dwellers who want to leave the canyons of steel for the peaceful lanes of Greenwich.

One of the main reasons for the continuing success of the Homestead is La Grange Restaurant. The chef is Jacques Thiebeult from Paris, who trained in France, Switzerland, England, and at Le Cirque and Le Cygne restaurants in New York. He has recently joined Lessie and Nancy as a partner and has the title of vice-president.

The *New York Times* restaurant reviewer awarded three stars to La Grange, pointing out that the restaurant "pays attention to every detail: salads, warm, crusty rolls, even a choice of loose tea, all are part of the seamlessly smooth dining performance."

The menu offerings include french country paté, many marvelous soups, especially the mussel bisque, called Billi-Bi, tender sweetbreads of veal, lobster done several ways and duck with cassis sauce. Desserts made by the inn's pastry chef often include fresh fruit tarts, triple chocolate layer cake, or Linzer torte.

Incidentally, I learned recently that William Inge wrote *Picnic* here during the 1950s. This, of course, was long before Lessie and Nancy arrived on the scene, bringing with them impeccable taste and a gratifying attention for detail. I'm sure, were he to revisit now, Mr. Inge would find the atmosphere and cuisine even more inspiring.

THE HOMESTEAD INN, 420 Field Point Rd., Greenwich, CT 06830; 203-869-7500. A 23-guestroom inn located in the residential area of a suburb, 45 min. north of New York City. Lunch served Mon. thru Fri.; dinner served daily except Labor Day, Christmas, New Year's. Wheelchair facilities for restaurant. Located a short distance from Conn. countryside and shore scenes. Accessible by train from New York City. No amusements for children under 12. No pets. Lessie Davison, Nancy Smith, Innkeepers. (See Index for rates.)

Directions: The inn is 3 min. from Rte. I-95. Take Exit 3 in Greenwich; from NYC, turn left; from New Haven, turn right off ramp. Turn left onto Horseneck Ln. at light, just before railroad overpass. Go to next traffic light; turn left onto Field Point Rd., and continue approx. ¼ mi. to inn on the right. ⌐

The date in parenthesis in the heading represents the first year the inn appeared in the pages of Country Inns and Back Roads.

SILVERMINE TAVERN
Norwalk, Connecticut (1975)

I wish that everyone could visit the Silvermine Tavern on a day like that of my last visit. It was mid-August, but a high-pressure system from Canada cooled our hot, humid air to a more bearable temperature. The sunshine was brilliant, and the sky was a clear blue as I drove down a tree-lined street through the residential section of Norwalk to the crossroads where the Silvermine Tavern and Country Store are located. The Silvermine can be difficult to find, and the first-time traveler has to follow the directions very carefully.

It was late afternoon, still a bit early for dinner. I walked through the lobby and found my way to the outer deck, which overlooks the millpond and waterfall. I watched the ducks circle and play in the vicinity of a single white swan that floated serenely, apparently unaware of the majestic effect he was creating. The sun shone through the trees as they towered over the deck, creating a dappled pattern on the tables and gleaming silverware.

The deck was built around the trees, with holes cut in the floor to allow the trees to continue to grow comfortably. There were even rubber cushions lining the holes to prevent injury to the trees as they swayed in the wind. What a pleasant place to relax in the warm afternoon sun.

During the chilly months guests can enjoy the cozy atmosphere of the several different dining areas, all of which are decorated with antique oil paintings, prints, wooden farm implements, and other artifacts of our agrarian heritage. There are fireplaces and many old tables and booths available for quiet conversation.

The guest rooms at this inn are typical of many country inn rooms I have seen. They are from medium to small in size, furnished with antique country furniture, and have neither televisions nor telephones. Lodgings are scattered through the various buildings of the Tavern complex.

The menu, which is quite large, can best be characterized as American cuisine with New England specialties. It's one of the few places I know north of Virginia that actually serves genuine Smithfield ham. Other menu offerings include indian pudding, bread pudding, native scrod, lobster, and scallops. On various nights during the week there are special buffets, and a brunch buffet is offered on Sunday.

Whenever I visit the Silvermine, I never miss taking home a dozen of the absolutely scrumptious honey buns. I freeze them and enjoy them very sparingly, one at a time, to stretch out the memory of my visit.

A word about desserts: save room for cream pies, homemade fruit pies, and superior cakes!

This trip was particularly enjoyable because I ate outside on the deck, but this inn is also a great place when the wind is whistling around corners and the snow is sifting down through the bare branches of the trees.

SILVERMINE TAVERN, Perry Ave., Norwalk, CT 06850; 203-847-4558. A 10-guestroom country inn in the residential section of Norwalk. European plan includes continental breakfast. Lunch and dinner served to travelers daily. Open year-round. Closed Christmas Day and Tuesdays during winter. Long Island Sound and beaches 6 mi. away. Golf, tennis, and fishing nearby. Francis C. Whitman, Innkeeper. (See Index for rates.)

Directions: From New York or New Haven via I-95, take Exit 15. Pick up the new Rte. 7 going north. At the end of Rte. 7 (approx. 1 mi.) turn right, go to first stoplight, turn right. At next stoplight by firehouse turn right onto Silvermine Ave. Proceed down Silvermine Ave. about 2 mi. to Tavern. From I-84 and Danbury take old Rte. 7 south to Norwalk. Watch for Kelly Greens, ½ mi. south of Merritt Pkwy. on the left, and turn right on Perry Ave., opposite Kelly Greens. Follow Perry Ave. 2 mi. to Tavern. From Merritt Pkwy. take Exit 39 south on old Rte. 7 and follow directions above.

"European plan" means that rates for rooms and meals are separate. "American plan" means that meals are included in the cost of the room. "Modified American plan" means that breakfast and dinner are included in the cost of the room. The rates at some inns include a continental breakfast with the lodging.

WEST LANE INN
Ridgefield, Connecticut (1980)

"Basically, I think that we have three different types of guests that find their way to our little inn." Maureen Mayer and I were seated on the broad front porch of the West Lane Inn enjoying a generous continental breakfast. "By the way," she added, "if you'd like a bigger breakfast, we have an à la carte breakfast menu that offers, among other things, grapefruit, sliced bananas, berries, yogurt, corn flakes, and poached eggs."

I might add that this breakfast was served at a table with real linen tablecloths and napkins.

One of the things that sets West Lane Inn apart is the many additional amenities this attractive innkeeper provides for her guests. For example, there is a clock in every guest room, as well as a computerized phone system, a radio-TV, individual heating and air conditioning controls, and one-day laundry and dry-cleaning service, and a basket of fruit, cheese, and crackers is presented to newly arrived guests.

"Among our guests are families being relocated to the Ridgefield-Fairfield-Danbury area who need a comfortable, roomy place in which to stay while they look for a new home. Many come and stay for a week or two. I decided that they would be much more comfortable if we had accommodations that reflected the feeling of the area, so we have rooms with decks overlooking our lawn and the forest in the rear. Some of these have fireplaces and kitchen facilities. You see, guests can literally establish a little home for a short time. One of our bathrooms is designed for the handicapped, similar to the one at the West Mountain Inn in Vermont."

I observed that Ridgefield itself would be an ideal suburban place in which to live. Within commuting distance of New York and driving distance of the many corporations which are relocating in Fairfield County, Ridgefield is a most pleasant town with large graceful trees and excellent small shops. "There's also a very active community here," Maureen remarked. "We have a historical society, a library, the Ridgefield Symphony, the League of Women Voters, and various men's service clubs, sports groups, and business groups."

West Lane Inn is set back from the village street with a broad lawn enhanced by azaleas, tulips, roses, and maple and oak trees. It was originally built as a mansion in the early 1800s and the guest rooms are unusually commodious.

The other types of guests are commercial travelers, both men and women, and vacationers who enjoy country-inn hospitality. "I think we understand commercial travelers very well and we've done everything possible to have them feel that this is really a 'home away from home.'

"As far as the country-inn travelers are concerned, we're at sort of a crossroads for north-south, east-west travel, and many couples on their way to or from New England come back and stay every year."

The West Lane could well be a model for other bed-and-breakfast inns everywhere. Every lodging room is spotless and the furnishings and decorating are all part of a harmonious color scheme. Overnight guests are coddled even further with heated towel racks and wonderful, new, large, fluffy bath sheets.

One of the things that also appeals to me is the 100%-cotton sheets on every bed in the inn. When was the last time you slept in a bed that had 100%-cotton sheets? Outstanding!

WEST LANE INN, 22 West Lane, Ridgefield, CT 06877; 203-438-7323. A 20-guestroom (several suites with kitchens) inn approx. 1 hr. from N.Y.C., in a quiet residential village in southwest Connecticut. Open every day in the year. Breakfast and light snacks available until 10:30 p.m. Wheelchair access. Convenient to many museums and antique shops. Golf, tennis, swimming, and xc skiing and other outdoor recreation available nearby. No pets. Maureen Mayer, Innkeeper. (See Index for rates.)

Directions: From New York City: Westside Hwy. to Sawmill River Pkwy. Take Exit 6, going right on Rte. 35, 12 mi. to Ridgefield. Inn is on left. From Hartford: Exit I-84 on Rte. 7 south and follow Rte. 35 to Ridgefield.

HOTEL MANISSES
Block Island, Rhode Island (1982)

Joan Abrams was waxing poetic about the Hotel Manisses. This in itself was nothing unusual, because she has been waxing poetic about the Manisses ever since the day, several years ago, when I first walked through the old building with her and she told me what the Abrams family had in mind in terms of restoring this old Block Island hotel. Built in 1870, the Manisses was then known as one of the best summer vacation hotels in the East. In those days families and groups of friends arrived at Block Island by private yacht and stayed for weeks.

I've been visiting the Abrams family at the other *CIBR* inn on Block Island, the 1661 Inn, for quite some time. Each year there would be more to say about the Manisses, until finally Joan and I agreed that it should have its own special place in *CIBR*.

"We all loved the task of restoring the Manisses, and almost every week there was some decorative or furnishing highlight that was very exciting," Joan said. "For example, the twenty-three-foot-long bar, dating back to 1870, was in a Boston saloon. The century-old stained-glass inserts come from the same historic era, and the lighting fixtures are holophane glass invented by Thomas A. Edison.

"From the renowned 19th-century Plimpton House estate in Norwood, Massachusetts, we acquired many impressive Victorian items, such as the hand-grooved arches, including the one in the library lounge. We were able to purchase some handsome hooped doors from a judge's chamber in Boston.

"In keeping with the natural beauty of Block Island, natural products have been integrated with the decor. Most of it is the brick, wood, and stone of the original building. That includes the antique wood washtub divider in the dining room, now decoratively filled with green plants and fresh flowers.

"Many of our guests ask about the weathervane, mounted on the tower, which stands six feet high and is hand-forged wrought iron, about 250 years old, from a castle in Cardiff, Wales. The figure is a griffin, a mythical creature feared and admired in past centuries."

Each bedroom and bathroom at the hotel is decorated in a different wallpaper. Almost all of the furniture is of the late 19th century, and the beds are copies of that era but in king and queen sizes. Some of the smaller rooms have the original beds; all have private baths. Flowers, hanging plants, and large plants adorn every room.

The dining room is on the ground floor and includes a delightful deck area with colorful umbrellas. The luncheon menu is lively, imaginative, and satisfying. The dinner menu offers a wide choice of appetizers and entrées appealing to both the trencherman and gourmet alike. Courses include many different beef items, as well as swordfish, flounder, scallops, lobster, and bouillabaisse. The vegetables come from a 1½-acre garden, just a few paces away.

The hotel is on the National Register of Historic Places. It is an eloquent testimony to American hospitality and a tribute to what dedication, hard work, good taste, and much investment capital can accomplish.

HOTEL MANISSES, Spring St., Block Island, RI 02807; 401-466-2421. An 18-guestroom (private baths) strikingly restored and preserved hotel on Block Island Sound, off the coast of R.I. and Conn. Some rooms have jacuzzis, ocean views, and private decks. Breakfast available at 1661 Inn. Open from 1st week of Apr. thru mid-Nov.; weekends only thru Memorial Day. Tennis, bicycling, ocean swimming, sailing, snorkling, scuba diving, salt- and fresh-water fishing nearby. Located on the Atlantic flyway. No facilities for children under 10. No pets. The Abrams Family, Innkeepers. (See Index for rates.)

Directions: By ferry from Providence, Pt. Judith, and Newport, R.I. and New London, Ct. Car reservations must be made in advance for ferry. By air from Newport, Westerly, and Providence, R.I., New London and Waterford, Ct., or by chartered plane. Contact inn for schedules.

The date in parenthesis in the heading represents the first year the inn appeared in the pages of Country Inns and Back Roads.

INN AT CASTLE HILL
Newport, Rhode Island (1976)

I was enjoying a few moments of quiet on the porch of one of the Harbor Houses at the Inn at Castle Hill watching the water traffic on Narragansett Bay. In the foreground, a young fisherman wearing very high orange boots was taking in his nets, and in the middle distance I counted at least seventeen sailboats, including one of the famous twelve-meter yachts that are used in the America's Cup Races. In the far distance there was the presence of the famous Newport Bridge, which soars over the bay to Jamestown.

Each one of the Harbor Houses is beautifully furnished with its own bathroom and is roomy enough to accommodate three people comfortably. All of them are newly decorated and the bright white walls and gay curtains and bedspreads are just perfect for the waterside atmosphere.

In addition to these lodgings, there are several rooms in the main mansion of the Inn at Castle Hill. This was once the property of the eminent naturalist Alexander Agassiz, who built Castle Hill in 1865 as a summer residence. It has remained unchanged in character and many of the original furnishings, including oriental rugs and the handcrafted oak and mahogany paneling, are still intact. "This was done before Newport really became a chic society hideout," said Paul McEnroe, the innkeeper at Castle Hill. "Agassiz built this mansion for himself and was really one of the forerunners of Newport's later resplendence."

Paul and I strolled along the grassy bank to the deck of the main house where luncheon was served in full view of the everchanging panorama of sea, sky, and ships. The menu featured several enticing offerings, including a variety of omelets, crêpes, quiches, and salads.

Our conversation naturally led to the dinners at the inn, and Paul explained that the inn takes a limited number of diners each night. "They must be spaced just right. Dinner takes two to two-and-a-half hours, so we naturally cater to people who are not in a hurry. Our dinners are now 98 per cent by reservation, and we only hold a table ten minutes. We always request that they not be late in order to avoid any misunderstandings.

"The evening meal is oriented to French cuisine and includes hot and cold hors d'oeuvres, soups, salads, fish, fowl, lamb, veal, and beef, all cooked and served in the continental manner. We also have a nonsmoking dining room. Guests arriving on Sunday should be prepared for a very crowded brunch. Sunday arrivals will not find the Castle Hill a quiet country inn until after 8 p.m. This applies to Sunday only."

The European flavor of the Inn at Castle Hill is considerably reinforced by the road that leads from Ocean Drive through a small section of woods. It reminds me of the Barbizon Forest, about two hours south of Paris, which inspired a school of French painters, including Millet. When I remarked to Paul on this resemblance to inns that I have visited in Europe, he responded enthusiastically, "That's exactly what we've tried to achieve. After all, this inn was built as a mansion and we're trying to recreate the elegance of Newport's past by having a menu, service, and furnishings that best suit our ideals. Jackets are required at dinner and no jeans, not even designer style, are allowed in the dining rooms. I'm sure that's the way it was eighty years ago."

INN AT CASTLE HILL, Ocean Dr., Newport, RI 02840; 401-849-3800. A 20-guestroom mansion-inn on the edge of Narragansett Bay. European plan. Continental breakfast served to houseguests only. Lunch and dinner served daily to travelers. Dining room closed from Dec. 1 to week before Easter. Guestrooms open all year. Lounge open winter weekends. Near the Newport mansions, Touro Synagogue, the Newport Casino, and National Lawn Tennis Hall of Fame, the Old Stone Mill, the Newport Historical Society House. Swimming, sailing, scuba diving, walking on grounds. Bicycles and guided tours of Newport nearby. No pets. Jens Thillemann, Manager; Paul McEnroe, Innkeeper.

Directions: After leaving Newport Bridge, follow Bellevue Ave., which becomes Ocean Dr. Look for inn sign on left, about 2 mi. out of town.

"European plan" means that rates for rooms and meals are separate. "American plan" means that meals are included in the cost of the room. "Modified American plan" means that breakfast and dinner are included in the cost of the room. The rates at some inns include a continental breakfast with the lodging.

THE INNTOWNE
Newport, Rhode Island (1982)

No matter how many times I've done it, it still gives me a tremendous lift to cross over the bridge from Jamestown to Newport, Rhode Island. Not only is this approach one of the most convenient ways to reach Newport, it affords a wonderful view of Newport Harbor.

It was a lovely day in mid-May, and as soon as I parked the car I spied Paul McEnroe, well tanned and as young-looking as the day I met him in 1966. He immediately took me into the Mary Street House, a new addition to the main inn since my last visit. Each of the rooms has been decorated with care and subtlety by Ione Williams, who with her husband, Rod, is also the owner of the Inn at Sawmill Farm in West Dover, Vermont.

The Mary Street House proved to be a fitting complement to the Inntowne, and all of the decorations and furnishings were a continuation of the earlier themes that had been established a few years ago when Paul and his wife, Betty, relocated in Newport after living for many years in New York State. Paul is also the innkeeper of the Inn at Castle Hill. After spying the architectural integrity of the original, old, dilapidated brick building on the corner of Mary and Thames, he decided to convert it into an elegant bed-and-breakfast inn and call it the Inntowne Inn.

The lobby-living room area has some handsome antiques, including an old grandfather's clock in a beautiful inlaid antique case, and one wall is a bookcase decorated with ivy plantings and a beautiful model ship. It's like being in a living room of a very elegant house of two hundred years ago, because the atmosphere is decidedly Colonial, rather than Victorian.

Betty joined us, and while we were having a cup of afternoon tea, a regular event at the Inntowne, I heard the receptionist responding to a phone call, explaining that there were no TV's and no elevators. Upon checking in, guests are advised that arrangements can be made for parking in a special lot just up the street.

Breakfast at the Inntowne includes very tasty croissants and muffins, and something I am always delighted to find: freshly squeezed orange juice.

I asked Paul about the best time to come to Newport. "If someone is looking for a nice quiet time and a nice quiet country inn within the city, I think the fall or even the winter is lovely. The crowds are gone and you can get into all of the restaurants and there is still much to see and do.

"We're taking more and more reservations for people in the wintertime," he continued. "There are three mansions open on weekends in the winter. The indoor tennis facilities are open, the shopping and wharf areas, and the fine restaurants are all at their best. The drive along the ocean is magnificent."

Betty added, "Christmas in Newport is a wonderful time to come. The city is very active with many events scheduled, including parades, Christmas tree decorations, and there are candles in all the windows. The town is most tastefully decorated. There is a special calendar published for December, and there is something happening every day. Although we are closed Christmas Eve and Christmas Day, we are open throughout the rest of the Christmas season."

As I departed after a really pleasant visit with Paul and Betty, it occurred to me that there was a distinct resemblance between the Inntowne and the Residence du Bois in Paris. Each has a soothing air of quietude, somewhat away from the hustle and bustle of the city.

THE INNTOWNE, 6 Mary St., Newport, RI 02840; 401-846-9200. An elegant 20-guestroom bed-and-breakfast inn in the center of the city of Newport overlooking the harbor, serving continental breakfast and afternoon tea. Telephones in all the rooms. Open every day. Reservations by telephone only between 9 a.m. and 11 p.m. Convenient for all of the Newport historical and cultural attractions, which are extremely numerous. No recreational facilities available; however, tennis and ocean swimming are nearby. Not adaptable for children of any age. No pets. Betty and Paul McEnroe, Innkeepers. (See Index for rates.)

Directions: After crossing Newport bridge, turn right at first exit sign, and right again at bottom of ramp. Drive straight to Thames Street; Inntowne is on corner of Thames St. and Mary St., across from Brick Marketplace.

LARCHWOOD INN
Wakefield, Rhode Island (1969)

Frank Browning and I were talking about lobsters, a subject that is near and dear to the hearts of those of us who are fortunate enough to live near New England's coastal waters. The Larchwood Inn certainly qualifies in this respect, since it's just a few minutes from the great beaches of southern Rhode Island.

"We buy from one source, and we know we're getting the best," he told me. "On Monday, we have special dinners of either twin lobsters or prime rib, and it is one of our most popular nights in the week. We always have a full-sized lobster every night and twin lobsters on Monday. I hope your readers will reserve ahead for lobsters because there's always a great demand. By the way, on Mondays in the summertime we have Al Conte, who is a cabaret performer and a piano player. It really livens things up."

I wandered into one of the dining rooms, where there is a mural depicting the southern Rhode Island beaches. The tables were very attractively set for the next meal with green tablecloths. I noticed the living room had been redecorated since my last visit. It was very pleasant, with comfortable chairs and a fireplace with a very impressive ship's model on the mantel. There was also an exotic bird in a cage.

At this point, Frank returned, and I asked him about the ship's model. "That is a three-masted schooner, called *L'Astrolabe,* and everything was built to scale by a friend of mine. See the little boys on the deck — he thought of everything."

The Larchwood is a large mansion, dating back to 1831, in the village of Wakefield, set in the middle of a large parklike atmosphere with copper, beech, ginkgo, pin oak, spruce, mountain ash, maple, Japanese cherry trees, evergreens, dogwoods, and a very old mulberry tree. In all, there are three acres of trees and lawn.

The interior has many Scottish touches, including quotations from Robert Burns and Sir Walter Scott, and photographs and prints of Scottish historical and literary figures.

The conversation naturally turned once again to menu items, since Frank was the chef here for many years and is now carefully supervising the kitchen and dining room.

"We're in the process right now of working with the South County Hospital. They are coming out with low-cholesterol items, and they came to us to ask if we could cooperate with them. We're working on seven or eight items in our restaurant for their program. There will be lighter things, including different ways to serve chicken and fish."

I asked him about breakfasts, and I'm very glad I did. "We make the french toast with our own bread and offer it with either sour cream or whipped cream and warm strawberries. The strawberries make it absolutely fantastic. It's something that our guests really appreciate, along with our selection of different omelets."

Besides guest rooms in the main inn, there are additional attractively furnished guest rooms in the Holly House, a 150-year-old building across the street from the inn. Guests at the Holly House can enjoy breakfast, lunch, and dinner at the Larchwood Inn dining room.

My eye caught a card on the table that had a Catholic, Jewish, and Protestant grace, and also one from Robert Burns, which I am going to share with everyone.

> *Some ha'e meat and canna eat*
> *And some ha'e nane that want it,*
> *But we ha'e meat and we can eat,*
> *So let the Lord be thankit.*

LARCHWOOD INN, 176 Main St., Wakefield, RI 02879; 401-783-5454. A 19-guestroom (some shared baths) village inn just 3 mi. from the famous southern R.I. beaches. European plan. Breakfast, lunch, dinner served every day of the year. Swimming, boating, surfing, fishing, xc skiing, and bicycles nearby. Francis Browning, Innkeeper. (See Index for rates.)

Directions: From Rte. 1, take Pond St. exit and proceed ½ mi. directly to inn.

THE 1661 INN
Block Island, Rhode Island (1976)

A few years before my first visit to Block Island, Joan, Justin, Rita, Mark, and Rick Abrams had discovered the 1661 Inn during one of their many sailing adventures from Providence. At that time it was a small hotel named the Florida House. Later, it was renamed the 1661 Inn by the Abramses, in honor of the year that Block Island was settled by colonists from New England.

"At that time, we gave each of the bedrooms the name of one of the original brave settlers," Joan explained. "Our family spent many hours consulting books for authentic New England decor and redoing all the rooms. We decorated with many of our own antiques and Early American paintings."

A few years later, after Rita Abrams and Steve Draper were married, the house next door to the 1661 Inn was acquired. Steve, who is a natural-born planner and builder, set about completely remodeling what was to become the 1661 Guest House. All of the bedrooms were done over and private decks were added. The guest house is completely heated and is open all year.

Perhaps Steve did not know the Abrams family's penchant for re-modeling and rebuilding, but he soon found out about it! Joan and Justin decided to restore one of the island's historic summer hotels, the Manisses Hotel, also owned by the Abrams family.

The two accommodations offer interesting contrasts: the 1661 House has a distinctly Colonial and early-19th-century atmosphere, while the Manisses has a mid-19th-century-resort opulence.

In recent years, three of the bedrooms overlooking the dining deck at the 1661 Inn were enlarged and now enjoy glorious views of the ocean from their own decks. Directly above them, three second-floor bedrooms also have their own decks, so that there are seven rooms with sea views and decks. Joan tells me thay have added canopies over the decks so that guests can now sit outside and enjoy the pure Block Island air in almost any season. Each room has been decorated in Colonial-period furniture, wallpaper, and draperies. There are Winslow Homer prints and quite a few original watercolors and drawings of Block Island houses.

Breakfast is an extravaganza with fresh fruit, corned beef hash, scrambled eggs, quiche, choices of breakfast meat, small, red potatoes, roasted first, then baked in the oven with spices, and at least one or two special dishes, such as chicken tetrazzini and vegetable casseroles. All the muffins, jams, and breads are homemade.

The evening menu features such regional dishes as Block Island clam chowder, flounder, lobster, swordfish, johnnycake, indian pudding, and blackberry flummery. I must say that the baked stuffed flounder with mussels and clams is a joy. There is also a lobster boil every Saturday night. Guests may take lunch at the Manisses.

May I take a moment to point out that Block Island is a very singular experience during what is usually known as the "off season." This is any time after the middle of October. There are wonderful beaches to walk, bikes to ride, and the island, with a population of only 600 during the winter, becomes a very private experience. Rita and Steve and their two boys are always on hand in the Guest House to help island winter visitors make it a really beautiful experience.

THE 1661 INN, Box 367, Block Island, RI 02807; 401-466-2421 or 2063. A 25-guestroom island inn off the coast of R.I. and Conn. in Block Island Sound; 11 private baths. Open from Memorial Day thru Columbus Day weekend. Breakfast served to travelers daily. (Guest House open year-round; continental breakfast included in off-season rates; dinner upon request.) Lawn games on grounds. Tennis, bicycling, ocean swimming, sailing, snorkeling, diving, salt and fresh water fishing nearby. Block Island is known as one of the best bird observation areas on the Atlantic flyway. The Abrams Family, Innkeepers. (See Index for rates.)

Directions: By ferry from Providence, Pt. Judith, and Newport, R.I., and New London, Ct. Car reservations must be made in advance for ferry. Cars are a convenience, but not needed on the island. By air from Newport, Westerly, and Providence, R.I., New London and Waterford, Ct., or by chartered plane. Contact inn for schedules.

Mid-Atlantic

LAKE HURON

O N T A R I O

TORONTO ● The Briars, *Jackson's Pt.*

LAKE ONTARIO

Oban Inn,
Niagara-On-The-Lake

● Asa Ransom House,
Clarence

Holloway Hou
East Bloomfie

STRATFORD

LAKE ERIE

N E W

P E N N S Y L V

Gateway Lodge, *Cooksburg* ●

Tara, *Clark* ●

INTERSTATE 80

WILLIAMSP

Tavern, *New Wilmington* ●

■ PITTSBURGH

Smithton Inn, *Ephrata* ●

PENNSYLVANIA

HARRISBURG

TPK.

Century Inn, *Scenery Hill* ●

Hickory Bridge Farm, *Orrtanna*

Eastern Time Zone

BARLEY SHEAF FARM
Holicong, Pennsylvania (1982)

I sat on the terrace of Barley Sheaf Farm looking down across the lawns over the old stone fence, bordered by gorgeous spring flowers and covered with vines, into what could best be described as the next lower level of lawn, where the pond and the swimming pool are.

Ann Mills told me that I should not miss the pair of Canada geese who herd their four goslings in and out of the pond every morning. "The mother and father arrive every spring and stay long enough to produce the eggs and guide the family, and then a few weeks later they all fly away. The parents come back again every year."

Earlier that morning, lying abed in my room, which had been fashioned out of one of the original outbuildings of the farm, I became aware of the fact that Barley Sheaf was a series of foregrounds and backgrounds. For example, on the walls and window sills beside my brass bed there were several country artifacts. Then out of one of the windows, I could look over the red brick walks and farm fence in the foreground across the fields to the line of trees in the background. The other window provided a wonderful view of the old barn on the property. This handsome building, which saw service on this property for most of the 19th century, if not longer, has the recognizable earmarks of an early Pennsylvania antiquity. The stone pillars and walls support the second and third floors, constructed of long plank siding. Meanwhile, the sounds of the mourning doves and busy birds filled the Bucks County morning air with their anticipation of another busy day.

Located in the heart of Bucks County, north of Philadelphia, Barley Sheaf Farm has been designated a National Historic Site; the original part of the farm dates back to 1740. There are chickens and horned Dorsets on the property, and the eggs that are eaten for breakfast are often straight from the nest. There are also beehives, and the wildflower honey they yield is often taken home by the guests. Almost everything comes from the farm and the bread is baked fresh every day.

The emphasis of Barley Sheaf Farm is more on knowledgeable hospitality than on farming. The living rooms and reception areas are adorned with impressive Early American oils and prints, and there's a decided interest by all the Mills family in Early American antiques.

Guest rooms indicate a continuous labor of love, as country antiques abound and personal touches, such as the international doll collection in one of the bedrooms, provide a homey feeling. Each room has its own distinct character and flavor; one has a mahogany sleigh bed with a Hitchcock dresser and still another has an antique iron bed with a very handsome quilt. There's an antique brass bed and a fireplace in the master bedroom suite, with a lovely view of the terrace.

Plans are afoot to put aside a corner of the old barn for antiques and local artwork to be enjoyed and purchased by guests.

Now, what about my Canada geese? I hadn't seen them yet. Could they have indeed flown off on the very morning of my arrival? Ah, I could now see a long graceful neck among the grasses along the edge of the pond and, sure enough, a four-gosling flotilla was heading out across the placid waters. Whatever else might happen today, the geese would be at Barley Sheaf Farm.

BARLEY SHEAF FARM, Box 10, Holicong, PA 18928; 215-794-5104. A 9-guestroom (private baths) bed-and-breakfast inn, 8 mi. from Doylestown and New Hope, Pa. A full breakfast is the only meal served. Open Valentine's Day thru weekend prior to Christmas; weekends only mid-Jan. to mid-Feb. Minimum 2-night stay on weekends; 3-night minimum on holiday weekends. Near Delaware River, Bucks County Playhouse, George Washington's Crossing. Croquet, badminton, swimming pool, farm animals on grounds. Tennis, boating, canoeing, and horseback riding nearby. Near all of the natural and historical attractions of Bucks County, Pa. Recommended for children over 8. No credit cards. Don and Ann Mills, and Don Mills, Jr., Innkeepers. (See Index for rates.)

Directions: Barley Sheaf Farm is on Rte. 202 between Doylestown and Lahaska. ✈

A number of inns have nearby airports where private airplanes may land. An airplane symbol at the end of the inn directions indicates that there is an airport nearby. Consult inn for further information.

CAMERON ESTATE INN
Mount Joy, Pennsylvania (1982)

Betty Groff was telling me about the history of the Donegal Presbyterian Church, which adjoins the Cameron Estate Inn property. We had been wandering around the parklike grounds of the inn and quite naturally gravitated toward this historic spot.

"Founded by Irish settlers prior to 1721, this is the church with the famous Witness Tree. On a Sunday morning in September, 1777, an express rider came to the church with the news that the British Army under Lord Howe had left New York to invade Pennsylvania. Challenged to show proof of their patriotism, they joined hands around the historic tree and declared their loyalty to the new cause of liberty and to the founding of a new nation."

As we walked beside a woodland stream, she pointed out the many trout darting about in it. "We stock this stream with trout, for which our guests may fish." Standing for a moment on an old stone bridge, she continued the narrative. "As you know, Abe and I live right here in Mount Joy and we've been operating the Groff Farm Restaurant for quite a few years. But we've always wanted to own an inn and we had our envious eye on this estate for a long time."

Agreeing to meet for dinner later on, Betty and I separated at the front door of the inn, a most impressive red brick mansion, built in 1805, with attractive dormer windows on the third floor. I speculated mentally that the broad veranda running around three sides of the inn probably had been added later in the 19th century.

Stepping inside, I found the interior to be exactly what one would have expected in a mansion: large living rooms, a library, generous-sized bedrooms, some with canopy beds and a great many with fireplaces. There are many oriental rugs and period furnishings chosen by Abe and Betty to define the historical significance of the inn. These are fitting complements to the fine paneling and marble embellishments.

Dinner that evening in the main dining room was another baronial experience, with excellent service, delicate china, and fine silverware against pristine napery. The menu included roast Long Island duckling with a mandarin orange sauce; chicken sauté "Simon Cameron" served with ham and complemented by a wine-and-cheese sauce, and white asparagus; and a succulent Steak Diane. These are an interesting contrast to the family style dinners offered at nearby Groff's Farm Restaurant, which specializes in Pennsylvania Dutch food. Inn guests also eat there.

Betty Groff is the author of three best-selling cookbooks: *Good Earth Country Cooking, Betty Groff's Country Goodness Cookbook,* and *Betty Groff's Up-Home-Down-Home Cookbook.* She's also been seen on many TV programs and featured in magazine articles.

CAMERON ESTATE INN, R.D. #1, Box 305, Donegal Springs Rd., Mount Joy, PA 17552; 717-653-1773. An 18-guestroom (16 with private baths) elegant inn in a former mansion, 4½ mi. from Mt. Joy and Elizabethtown. Complimentary continental breakfast. Lunch and dinner served every day except Sun. and Christmas. Open year-round. Convenient to all of the attractions in the Pennsylvania Dutch Amish country, as well as the Hershey and Lancaster museums, art galleries, crafts shops, and theaters; halfway between Gettysburg and Valley Forge. No children under 12. No pets. Abram and Betty Groff Innkeepers. (See Index for rates.)

Directions: The inn is situated in the heart of the triangle formed by Harrisburg, York, and Lancaster. Traveling west on Pennsylvania Tpke. take Exit 21. Follow Rte. 222 S to Rte. 30 W to Rte. 283 W. Follow Rte. 283 W to Rte. 230 (the first Mt. Joy exit). Follow Rte. 230 through Mt. Joy to the 4th traffic light. Turn left onto Angle St. At first crossroads, turn right onto Donegal Springs Rd. Go to the stop sign. Turn left onto Colebrook Rd. Go just a short distance over a small bridge. Turn right, back onto Donegal Springs Rd. Follow signs to inn—about ½ mi. on the right. Traveling east on the Pa. Tpke. take Rte. 72 at Lebanon Exit to the Square in Manheim. Turn right on W. High St. This becomes the Manheim-Mt. Joy Rd. Follow directly into Mt. Joy. At the first traffic light, turn right onto Main St. Follow Main St. to the next traffic light. At light turn left onto Angle St. Follow above directions from Angle St. ✈

CENTURY INN
Scenery Hill, Pennsylvania (1972)

"So this is a joggling board," I observed. "Yes," responded Megin Harrington, "we've had it here for a number of years and the guests really like it."

Megin and I were sitting on this great long, suspended board that "joggles," and that's all I'm prepared to say about it. "It's been tempering for at least seventy-five years," she said. "You just sit on it and it goes up and down."

Pointing to a magnificent black locust tree, she said, "Lafayette and Andrew Jackson probably passed under the branches of that tree. The Century Inn was built before 1794, and is the oldest continuously operating tavern on the National Pike, most of which is today's U.S. 40. Consequently, the inn has played an important role in the history of southwestern Pennsylvania. Lafayette stopped here on May 23, 1825, and Jackson was a guest twice, once on the way to his inauguration as President of the United States."

The inn remains what it has been for so many years: the pride of the community and a place sought out by true lovers of country inns. They've been coming for many years to enjoy stuffed pork chops, roast turkey, seafood, whipped potatoes, sweet potatoes, absolutely scrumptious cole slaw, and homemade pies.

As many times as I have visited the inn I always delight in visiting Room 5, which will probably never be occupied because it is jampacked with dolls of all sizes and descriptions.

Guests stopping at the inn today are attracted as much by the vast array of antiques as they are by the bill of fare. All of this restoration was started by Gordon and Mary Harrington, the parents of Megin's late husband, Skip Harrington. Gordon and Mary purchased the inn in 1945, and restored and furnished it with rare and valuable antiques collected during their lifetime.

I had arrived at high noon on a beautiful warm September day. There were generous flowers in the front of the inn and large potted geraniums interspersed with rocking chairs and benches on the porch.

The room on the right, off the main hall, has the Whiskey Rebellion flag, just as it was during the time of my first visit many years ago, when I met Gordon and Mary Harrington. We talked all through dinner and far into the night of the things that inn-seekers enjoy so much: history, music, art, and the lovely countryside.

"Let's go down the street and look at our new shop," Megin said. "There are twenty-three little shops in Scenery Hill, and we are gaining a wonderful reputation among people who like to have a personal shopping experience." Well, walk we did, and when I stepped into It's Always Christmas, Megin's shop, I realized I was in a place where Christmas never ends. It has all kinds of Christmas everythings, including a Christmas tree hung with miniature dolls, a corner cupboard with more of the same, still another tree decorated differently, toys, paintings of ducks, and dozens of things one can mix with Christmas. Each of the little rooms of the shop, which is a former house, has been decorated differently.

After a chance to see a few of the other shops, we walked back up the street, returning to the inn to enjoy lunch in the Keeping Room, with its huge fireplace and truly astonishing collection of old tools and artifacts decorating the mantel. It's a cozy dining room, and many a lovely meal have I enjoyed in this pleasant atmosphere.

All of this and a joggling board!

CENTURY INN, Scenery Hill, PA 15360; 412-945-6600 or 5180. A 10-guestroom village inn on Rte. 40, 12 mi. east of Washington, Pa., 35 mi. south of Pittsburgh. European plan. Breakfast served to houseguests only. Lunch and dinner served to travelers daily. Open Mar. 16 to Dec 23. No pets. No credit cards. Personal checks welcome. Megin Harrington, Innkeeper. (See Index for rates.)

Directions: From the east, exit the Pa. Tpke. at New Stanton. Take I 70W to Rte. 917S (Bentleyville exit) to Rte. 40E and go 1 mi. east to inn. From the north, take Rte. 19S to Rte. 519S to Rte. 40E and go 5 mi. east to inn or take I-79S to Rte. 40E and go 9 mi. east to inn. From the west, take I-70E to I-79S to Rte. 40E and go 9 mi. east to inn.

EVERMAY-ON-THE-DELAWARE
Erwinna, Pennsylvania (1982)

One of the subheads for an article in *Philadelphia Magazine* just happened to catch my eye. It read: "Evermay-on-the-Delaware: The crown jewel of Bucks County country inns." The author went on to praise the horses, sheep, geese, and the long-haired red Scottish West Highland cattle, and the beautiful lawns and impressive trees. Furthermore, it had a very apt description of the inn itself, its antique furnishings and its delicious breakfast, and dinners. I was quite in agreement with it.

Long before Ron Strouse and Fred Cresson discovered and explored the full potential of this lovely property, Evermay had existed as an accommodation as far back as 1871. The original part of the house was built in 1700 by a prominent family in the valley. A 1905 photograph in the parlor of the inn shows that it has hardly been changed since then.

A recent letter from Ron and Fred pointed out that the animal population has increased, but with a slightly different bent: "We now have two horses, Canton and Flow Blue, the two Scottish West Highland cows, Eunice and Flyn, and a host of sheep, as well as the peacocks and geese." Animals are an important part of Ron's life, and plants and flowers are important to Fred.

"Our 7:30 dinner, served on Friday, Saturday, and Sunday, has become a very special experience. It is now six courses. We begin with champagne and hors d'oeuvres, and then serve an appetizer, soup course, salad, entrée, cheese and fruit, and dessert. Some of the entrées include sautéed Muscovy duck on onion marmalade with lingonberries, and roast loin of veal with mushroom sauce. All of the desserts are homemade. There are a couple of dishes we would like to test on you when you visit next time. We also serve on Thanksgiving, Christmas Day, and New Year's Eve."

One of my favorite times at Evermay is very early morning, when I can watch the sun coming up over the river and hear the geese and other birds heralding the first streaks of daylight. This scene is especially available to rooms on the top floor facing the river. At that early hour there are few cars on the river road, and I feel as if I am very much in my own private world.

Beside the snug rooms on the top floor, Evermay has larger, second-floor master-sized guest rooms, many with fireplaces. The views from the front of the inn include the Delaware River, but I find that the views from the rear are equally inviting. These include the meadows and gardens that Ron and Fred have developed, as well as the hills beyond. Additional guest rooms are now available in the recently remodeled carriage barn.

I think the readers might be interested in Ron's comment on his travels with Fred in Europe: "During the September lull, we traveled from

Vienna to Venice and back, staying at some fine inns and hotels. I guess there are not really many new major ideas to be discovered as innkeepers travel to other inns, but there are a whole host of details and refinements to be discovered, many of which we hope to incorporate into Evermay. I guess, after five years here and ten years as innkeepers, there is an Evermay 'style' which will not change, but hopefully can always be enhanced and improved."

I actually visited Evermay before the first guest had been escorted to a guest room, and it's been a pleasure for me to see how Ron and Fred have made this such a wonderful country inn experience. It is a "crown jewel."

EVERMAY-ON-THE-DELAWARE, Erwinna, PA 18920; 215-294-9100. A 16-guestroom riverside inn in upper Bucks County. Breakfast and afternoon tea included in the room tariff. Box lunches available for houseguests. Dinner served Fri., Sat., Sun., and holidays at 7:30 p.m. by reservation. Open every day for lodging except Dec. 24. Wheelchair access. Convenient to all of the Bucks County natural and historical attractions, including handsome mansions, museums, and amusements for small children. No pets. Ron Strouse and Fred Cresson, Innkeepers. (See Index for rates.)

Directions: From New York City, take I-78 west to Exit 15 (Pittstown). Follow Rte. 513 thru Pittstown to Frenchtown. Cross river and turn south on Rte. 32 for 2 mi. From Philadelphia, follow I-95 north to Yardley exit and Rte. 32 north to Erwinna. There are several other routes also.

GATEWAY LODGE
Cooksburg, Pennsylvania (1983)

In the past two editions I have begun the account of my visit to the Gateway Lodge by sharing a conversation I had with innkeepers Linda and Joe Burney about the black bears in Cook Forest. This time, as we were enjoying a candlelit dinner, we talked about the other animals in the woods. "Besides the bears," Joe said, "we also have bobcats, raccoons, porcupines, skunks, deer, turkeys, rabbits, chipmunks, gray squirrels, and an uncountable number of birds."

It had been a typical day for me on the road, starting with waking up at the Benn Conger Inn in Groton, New York, continuing on for an elaborate breakfast at the Rose Inn in Ithaca, and then arriving at the Gateway Lodge about four o'clock. After saying hello, I donned my bathing trunks for a dip in the new indoor swimming pool.

I must point out that since 1981 it has been the lodge's custom to allow the first caller who makes a dinner reservation to set the menu for that evening. The choices might include chicken Cordon Bleu, thick pork chops with bread stuffing, country-style barbecued spareribs, chicken and biscuits, or baked trout, among others. On that particular night the main choice, which had been chosen by an earlier telephone caller, was braised sirloin steak.

Gateway Lodge is a rustic country inn in Cook Forest, where the pine and hemlock may be seen in all their majesty, towering 200 and more feet above the pine-needle-carpeted forest. Hundreds of years of growth, untouched by human progress, has preserved for us some of the most magnificent forest scenery east of the Rocky Mountains. The pine and hemlock logs of the lodge suggest the ruggedness of our pioneer forebears.

The big living room of the main lodge has log walls and a beautiful big fireplace, with lots of deep, comfortable chairs gathered around it. The guest rooms have beds with chestnut headboards, and all have comforters and dust ruffles. Most rooms with baths "down the hall" also provide fluffy robes for the trip.

In addition to the rustic guest rooms in the main lodge, there are six cabins across the road in the forest, which require a minimum two-night stay. These cabins have kitchen conveniences, porches, and fireplaces, and are very snug with lots of firewood. Some guests decide to return to these for longer stays.

The Cook Forest really serves as the recreational motivation to visit this rustic hideaway. It has twenty-seven miles of hiking and over seventeen well-marked trails for good cross-country skiing. It's possible to fish for trout and warm-water fish in the Clarion River, and there are over ninety species of birds that have been identified in the park. Canoeing and inner-tubing can also he enjoyed, as well as golf, horseback riding, swimming, superb backroading, and there's even a summer theater nearby.

After dinner I strolled down to the Mountain Greenery Gift Shop, a little rustic building just a few steps away, where there are all sorts of gifts, made mostly by local craftspeople. "It makes a very nice place for our guests to browse in both before and after dinner."

"Our winters are very active here," Joe commented, as we wandered back up to the front porch of the lodge. "We have all kinds of carefully maintained cross-country ski trails, ice skating, miles of snowmobile trails, and one of our new things is sleigh rides, starting right here from our front porch." "Yes," Linda chimed in, "as a matter of fact, winter is one of our busiest times."

Linda made a sign to me and put her finger to her lips. She pointed down the forest road to where three deer were crossing. "It happens all the time," she whispered, "but it always gives me a big thrill."

GATEWAY LODGE, Rte. 36, Cooksburg, PA 16217; 814-744-8017 (Pa.: 800-843-6862). An 8-guestroom (some private baths) rustic lodge in the heart of Cook Forest in western Pa. Cabins require 2-night minimum stay. Open year-round, except Wed., Thurs., and Fri. of Thanksgiving week and from Dec. 22 to 25. Indoor swimming pool. Beautiful backroading and many trails in forest. All types of seasonal outdoor recreation available. The Burney Family, Innkeepers. (See Index for rates.)

Directions: Because Cooksburg is accessible from all four directions, locate Cook Forest State Park on your map of Pa., and find Rte. 36. The lodge is on Rte. 36, 15 min. north of I-80.

HICKORY BRIDGE FARM
Orrtanna, Pennsylvania (1978)

Once again I was taking the road from Fairfield to Orrtanna and Hickory Bridge Farm. It is one of my most favorite back roads.

There are great cornfields on one side and apple orchards on the other and, in the midst of all, a large farmstand with a wonderful collection of pumpkins out in front, and every imaginable type of the fresh farm produce that is abundant in this highly agricultural area.

I turned at the inn sign, passed over the railroad track, and was in sight of Nancy Jean and Doctor Jim Hammett's Hickory Bridge Farm. There were the big red barn, the many flower gardens, the old farmhouse, and the ever growing collection of old farm machinery and carts. The newest addition was a natural swimming pond with a diving platform. All of this was set against the background of beautiful, swaying trees, which in late September were beginning to take on their autumnal colors.

Walking through the gate, I was greeted with open arms by Nancy Jean. We stepped into the house, where there was a beautiful, welcome fire in the huge stone fireplace, over which a musket was hung. Nancy Jean proudly pointed out the decorations in the dining room, done by her son, David, who now has full-time charge at a church just east of Gettysburg. Breakfast was well in progress, and on the sideboard was a selection of dry cereals, some hot oatmeal, granola, and orange juice.

As usual, Nancy Jean was overflowing with energy and exuberance. "The apple butter is made right here on the farm," she said. "The vegetables are from our garden, and the peaches, from our neighbor's orchard. We have honeydew melons and cantaloupes from our own farm, too."

The bedrooms in the main house are Pennsylvania farm bedrooms. Many have washstands and one even has an old-fashioned radio on the shelf. There are many additional touches, such as good country-type fixtures on the walls, that make the bedrooms very pleasant, including a rocking chair for two in one room.

The guests take breakfast out on the deck, overlooking the island and the covered bridge over the creek. "Sometimes they stay out here so long I have to shoo them out so that we can get the breakfast dishes done," Nancy Jean said. "This is a wonderful place for birders, and guests come out with their spyglasses."

We took a little tour around the grounds, ably assisted by one of the eight grandchildren. One of the points of interest is a country store museum, where there is penny candy, molasses, sarsaparilla, and apple butter for sale. However, it is basically a museum store, with an old post office money window, and it provides a great deal of amusement for guests.

Additional accommodations are in two cottages beside the brook in the woods. Plans are also in the works to build a guest lodge and garden breakfast room as an addition to the restaurant.

HICKORY BRIDGE FARM, 96 Hickory Bridge Rd., Orrtanna, PA 17353; 717-642-5261. A 7-guestroom (private baths) country inn on a farm (with cottages) 3 mi. from Fairfield and 8 mi. west of Gettysburg. Open year-round except Dec. 20 thru Jan. 1. Deposit required. Full breakfast included in rates. Dinner served to guests and travelers some weekdays and every weekend by reservation. Less than 2 hrs. from Wash., D.C., Baltimore, Lancaster, Amish country, and Hershey, Pa. Near Gettysburg Battlefield Natl. Park, Caledonia State Park, and Totem Pole Playhouse. Hiking, biking, fishing, and country store museum on grounds. Swimming privileges at local country club. Golfing, horseback riding and antiquing nearby. The Hammett Family, Innkeepers. (See Index for rates.)

Directions: From Gettysburg take Rte. 116 west to Fairfield and follow signs 3 mi. north to Orrtanna. From south, take U.S. 81 north to Green-castle, Pa. Then east on Rte. 16 to 116 east to Fairfield. From south, take U.S. 270 to Rte. 15 to Emmittsburg, Md., then west on 16 to Rte. 116 east through Fairfield. From west of Pa. Tpke., get off at Blue Mt. exit and go south on Rte. 977 to Rte. 30 east for 9 mi. Turn south at Cashtown, Pa., and follow the signs.

A number of inns have nearby airports where private airplanes may land. An airplane symbol at the end of the inn directions indicates that there is an airport nearby. Consult inn for further information.

THE INN AT STARLIGHT LAKE
Starlight, Pennsylvania (1976)

The orchestra was playing "Moonglow." The peepers were peeping and the sunset afterglow was lighting the western sky. I had wandered out on the front porch of the Inn at Starlight, speaking, as everyone else did, to the mother cat and her two brand-new kittens. I wandered down the steps through the little grove of trees next to the lake and out onto the long dock, off of which were moored boats and sailboats.

I turned around to look at the lights of the inn and could hear the voices of some of my innkeeping friends from Pennsylvania and New York, who had gathered here to enjoy the opportunity to exchange experiences, tell good stories, and perhaps lend encouragement and counsel to each other. The trees along the shore created lacy silhouettes against the darkening blue sky. Then I noticed that several other innkeepers had decided to take a walk along the shore of the lake to help digest the wonderful evening meal. The small orchestra changed to a bit more up-tempo with "String of Pearls."

My evening meanderings also brought me within sight and earshot of four ducks who had taken up residence in the lake near the inn. Three of them were feathered in beautiful hues and the fourth was an ordinary white barnyard duck. They all had names and, as Judy McMahon explained, they had "just sort of all arrived and never left. They are busy morning and night rooting in the lush green grass at the edge of the lake for some succulent tidbits, and then cruising energetically to this end of the lake, occasionally diving down into the depths after some elusive fish."

This inn is on a back road, overlooking beautiful Starlight Lake. It is a rambling, old-fashioned, comfortable place with an accumulation of furniture from over the years. The combination lobby/living room has a fireplace in one corner, and there are reminders that the McMahons are originally from "show business." Besides the piano and the guitar, books of plays or sheet music may be found on the tables or on the bookshelves.

Guest rooms are in the main building and also in adjacent cottages that have been redecorated and winterized. The inn is on the modified American plan, meaning that dinner and breakfast are included in the room rate. Lunch is offered every day at an additional charge.

There's a TV room, a game room in the main house, and lots of outdoor activity, from canoeing, sailing, swimming, and bicycling to ice skating on the forty-five-acre lake and cross-country skiing on eighteen miles of marked trails. There is a very pleasant lakeside play area, and many lovely walks and dirt roads for backroading in the picturesque woods. By the way, the McMahons have a fabulous collection of old films.

Some of my favorite reading is country inn menus and this one is particularly extensive. There are several different beef dishes, including filet medallions Bordelaise and sirloin steak au poivre. One of several veal dishes is a really tasty Wiener schnitzel. Roast duckling always makes a hit with me, and there is fresh local trout from a trout farm just six miles away.

The newest feature is Starlight's occasional murder mystery weekend. I've been offered a small role in a future production—probably the victim!

Now I could hear Jack McMahon's high tenor voice wafting out from the living room and I knew it was time to go back for a very pleasant evening at the Inn at Starlight Lake. It's always a pleasure to visit.

THE INN AT STARLIGHT LAKE, Starlight, PA 18461; 717-798-2519. A 28-guestroom resort-inn, 5 mi. from Hancock, NY. Modified American plan. Breakfast, lunch, and dinner served daily between May 15 and Apr. 1. Closed Apr. 1 through Apr. 15. Wheelchair access. Swimming, boating, canoeing, sailing, fishing, hunting, tennis, hiking, bicycling, xc skiing, and lawn sports on grounds. Golf nearby. No pets. Judy and Jack McMahon, Innkeepers. (See Index for rates.)

Directions: From N.Y. Rte. 17, exit at Hancock, N.Y. Take Rte. 191S over Delaware River to Rte. 370. Turn right, proceed 3½ mi.; turn right, 1 mi. to inn. From I-81, take Exit 62 at Tompkinsville. Follow Rte. 107 east 4 mi. to Rte. 247N and Forest City. Turn left on Rte. 171 (the main street), and continue 10 mi. north to Rte. 370. Turn right and go 13 mi. east to Starlight. Turn left, 1 mi. to inn.

THE OVERLOOK INN
Canadensis, Pennsylvania (1975)

Boy, oh, boy — a letter from Lolly Tupper at the Overlook Inn! Here's part of what it says:

"Teatime is and always will be an important part of an Overlook visit! Saturday, with 'ol' Lol' pouring is indeed a 'proper tea' (Bronwyn would be pleased with it!), complete with cucumber sandwiches, hot scones, lemon curd, cakes, and cookies (of course, homemade).

"With the fire crackling, the camaraderie is, well, just too splendid to describe. And, don't you know I love every minute of it. In the fall hot mulled cider fills the inn with an aroma that can't be topped.

"Our holidays have become an *Overlook Must* to so many. Thanksgiving, our only buffet, is sumptuous, sparkling, splendidly supplied with turkeys and trimmings, along with some surprises, tasty and traditional.

"Christmas has trees decorated with handmade ornaments from guests through the years and outside trees with lights and pine boughs aglow. We hope each year for snow to add its glory to it all.

"New Year's Eve is festive, complete with midnight fare, and our one and only brunch in the year is on New Year's Day. The nucleus of returners grows each year. As they check out, it is this group (and always a few new ones) that about fills the inn for the next New Year.

"Our daily eighteen-entrée menu, along with three specials each night, gives our guests lots of choices.

"Our breakfasts of special omelets, pancakes, and homemade muffins are still a great drawing point for a stay at the Overlook. But what really get the all-time raves are Pierre's popovers . . . hot, huge, spectacular, and yummy!

"Generally speaking, I think people are discovering how much there is to do in the Poconos—two hours from major metroplitan areas—yet so unspoiled in so much of it. We have our own very homemade maps that take our guests to whatever they wish to do—lots of 'druthers.'

"There are neat gift shops (unusual ones), antiques, factory outlets, hiking, biking, short walks, falls, views, lakes, mountain streams, trout fishing, canoeing, boating, water skiing, museums, jazz gatherings, steam railroad trips, golf, tennis, riding, rifle ranges, and biplane rides right next door. To top this, the people of the Poconos do not resent the casual visitor. They are super friendly and warm. Do I sound like the Chamber of Commerce? Sure I do. But, it is all a fact."

Well, that's Lolly Tupper for you. She's been innkeeping for twelve years and, if anything, her enthusiasm has increased rather than waned!

The bedrooms and suites at Overlook are the kind that you hope you will find when you go to a country inn. They have books, original paintings, plants, colorful afghans, two pillows for every head, comfortable furniture, and some have walls of aromatic cedar shakes.

Ultimately, what sets the Overlook apart are Bob and Lolly Tupper themselves. They have a keen understanding of and a wonderful rapport with their guests, and this is what is mentioned most frequently in letters I have been receiving since the first year the Overlook Inn was included in *Country Inns and Back Roads*.

THE OVERLOOK INN (Romantik Hotels), Dutch Hill Rd., Canadensis, PA 18325; 717-595-7519. A 20-guestroom (private baths) resort-inn in the heart of the Poconos, 15 mi. from Stroudsburg, Pa. Modified American plan. Breakfast and dinner served to travelers; jackets requested. Open year-round. Pool, shuffleboard, bocci, horseshoes, hiking on grounds; golf, tennis, antiquing, biking, backroading, summer theater, downhill and xc skiing nearby. No children under 12. No pets. Bob and Lolly Tupper, Innkeepers. (See Index for rates.)

Directions: From the north, exit from I-84 to Rte. 390 south thru the town of Promised Land about 12 mi. to traffic light in Canadensis. Make right-hand turn on Rte. 447 north, go ¼ mi. to Dutch Hill Rd. and turn right. Inn is 1½ mi. up hill, look for sign on right. From New York City, take Geo. Washington Bridge to I-80 west. Turn off at Pa. Exit 52. Follow Rte. 447 north straight past Canadensis traffic light about ¼ mi. to Dutch Hill Rd. Follow above directions from Dutch Hill Rd. From Philadelphia, take Pa. Tpke. to Northeast extension to Exit 35. Follow I-80 east to 380 west to Mt. Pocono Exit 8. Turn right on Rte. 940 to dead end. Make right and quick left; you're still on 940. Continue to 390. Make left and follow 390 to traffic light in Canadensis. Make left and go ¼ mi. to Dutch Hill Rd. Turn right 1½ mi. up hill.

THE PINE BARN INN
Danville, Pennsylvania (1976)

From the very first edition of *Country Inns and Back Roads,* which I wrote in 1966, I've maintained that innkeepers and their growing families were every bit as important to me as the changes and developments in the inns themselves

The Pine Barn Inn is a case in point. I've been visiting and writing about it now for many years and I've seen some interesting developments—originally in the concepts and new ideas shared by innkeepers Shube and Marty Walzer. Later on, as Shube more or less retired to Florida, Barbara Walzer entered the picture, saving Marty from complete dissolution by marrying him a few years ago.

The inn began life in the 1870s as a wonderful Pennsylvania barn and later served for a long time as a riding stable, and then as a private home. It was transformed in 1950 into the Pine Barn Inn, and in 1967 it was purchased by the Walzers, father and son. Today, it is an inn and restaurant of considerable reputation.

The residents of that area of Pennsylvania think most kindly of the Pine Barn as a restaurant, with its menu that includes roast beef and roast leg of lamb, as well as homemade pies, breads, and rolls. Travelers speak highly of the accommodations. Even though they are somewhat "motel" in style, the rooms are furnished with attractive cherry reproductions and have many thoughtful touches that I always enjoy finding in a country inn, such as plants and magazines and books for guests to read in each guest room.

For the past few years I have shared Marty's yearly letter with readers, in which he brings us up to date on their six-year-old son Christopher. They had visited the Robert Morris Inn in Oxford, Maryland, where Ben and Kent, the innkeeper's sons, have for a long time made

extra pocket money by selling packets of corn to guests who feed the ducks on the bay. "Christopher is trying to find the same paying situation and has been awarded all the receipts from people who pay a penny to weigh themselves on our old weighing machine. The only trouble is that at a penny a shot Christopher is not getting rich.

"Barb finished redecorating one of our private dining and conference rooms with a library theme. Oak paneling and oak floor-to-ceiling book-shelves, with reproductions of old photographs of Danville, have given the room an all-new look and it's excellent for private parties.

"The inn looks wonderful even if we can't brag of any great additions. We're taking a breather right now and looking at our priorities. Flowers adorned the grounds despite my entire ignorance of horticulture. Craig, who heads our maintenance department and who Christopher says can fix anything, managed to keep everything seeded, watered, and growing.

"Chef Ralph Richardson with the able assistance of Larry Horne and Scott Smith has kept the menu varied and fresh. I am also ready to put forward to the scientific world a new law of physics, which is: 'No one can possibly lose weight as long as they are a patron of Rose's soups or Polly's pies.'

"Our proximity to Geisinger Hospital is a great convenience for our guests who are friends and families of patients. We are within walking distance."

And now, dear reader, thus endeth the yearly report on the Pine Barn Inn. I will mention one more thing: when you visit ask Marty to tell you about the time he swam against Johnny Weissmuller.

THE PINE BARN INN, Danville, PA 17821; 717-275-2071. A picturesque country restaurant with 75 attractive motel rooms in central Pennsylvania. European plan. Breakfast, lunch, and dinner served daily except Christmas, New Year's, July 4, Labor Day, and Memorial Day. Near Geisinger Hospital and several colleges and historic sites. Golf, tennis, waterskiing, sailing, and canoeing nearby. Pets allowed in some rooms. Martin and Barbara Walzer, Innkeepers. (See Index for rates.)

Directions: From Exit 33 of I-80, go south 3 mi. to Danville. Take a left at the first traffic light. Proceed 10 blocks and follow signs to Geisinger Medical Center. Pine Barn adjoins the Center.

The date in parenthesis in the heading represents the first year the inn appeared in the pages of Country Inns and Back Roads.

1740 HOUSE
Lumberville, Pennsylvania (1973)

As often as I have driven up the so-called River Road, in reality Route 32, on the Pennsylvania side of the Delaware, it never ceases to wonder me (as our Pennsylvania Dutch friends would say) just how beautiful it is. Especially visible before the trees are in leaf, are the hills sloping up from the road on one side, and on the other, the canal and long stretches of the Delaware River. The road has a roller coaster quality, lifting up to the top of the hills, and dropping down beside the river. The laurel is green and welcome at all seasons, and here and there in April I could see errant tufts of grass that enjoyed a little more sunshine than others beginning to push up along the river bank.

It is a small wonder that many years ago, my friend Harry Nessler, the innkeeper at the 1740 House, came to this section of Pennsylvania and saw the possibilities of opening what at that time was a rather remarkable phenomenon, a country inn in the cluster of barns and other farm outbuildings. Each of the bedrooms at the 1740 House has either a balcony or a terrace with a full view of the canal and the Delaware River beyond. All are furnished with exceptional care and taste.

The inn abounds with bushes, shrubs, flowers, trees, and birds. A portion of the building is covered with beautiful green ivy. There is a sort of natural division between the buildings, separated by a small swimming pool.

A typical menu at the 1740 House includes a choice of three appetizers—things like mushroom soup, herring in cream sauce, and fettucini Alfredo. Typical entrées are filet mignon, chicken Marsala, crab Imperial, broiled scallops, and a baked fish. Desserts usually include crème caramel and always ice cream. Although there are several restaurants in the area, many of the returning guests have found it most convenient and quite enjoyable to have a quiet dinner at the 1740 House. It is most necessary to make reservations for that dinner in advance.

There is a bridge over the river in Lumberville—a single-passenger bridge—and it's possible to go across to New Jersey on the other side. There is also a preserved canal lock, which shows exactly how boats were assisted through the canals in the old days.

Of course, backroading is one of the favorite pastimes of visitors to Bucks County. The back roads here not only have a great deal of history connected with them, but they have the historic old buildings, homes, barns, and sheds that make it even more enjoyable. There is something about the quarried stone in this part of Pennsylvania that mellows and weathers in a most handsome way.

Harry pointed out that one of the additional sports guests may enjoy is canoeing and tubing on the river, and there are places where canoes and inner tubes are available for this purpose. "The Delaware during the time when the water would be warmest is a relatively placid experience," he said, "with none of the hair-raising elements that we hear about on other rivers."

1740 HOUSE, River Rd., Lumberville, PA 18933; 215-297-5661. A 24-guestroom riverside inn, 6½ mi. north of New Hope, in the heart of historic Bucks County. Lodgings include breakfast, served to houseguests daily; dinner served daily except Sun. and Mon. by reservation only. Open year-round. Weekend reservations must include 2 nights. Pool and boating on grounds. Golf and tennis nearby. Superb backroading in an area rich in American history. Harry Nessler, Innkeeper. (See Index for rates.)

Directions: From N.Y.C., travel south on N.J. Tpke., and take Exit 10. Follow Rte. 287 north to another Exit 10. Proceed west on Rte. 22 to Flemington, then Rte. 202 south over Delaware Toll Bridge. After an immediate right U-turn onto Rte. 32N, drive 5 mi. to inn. From Pa. Tpke., exit at Willow Grove and proceed north on Rte. 611 to Rte. 202. Follow Rte. 202 north to Rte. 32 and turn north to inn. From Phila., take I-95 to Yardley-New Hope Exit, follow 32N through New Hope and 7 mi. to inn.

"European plan" means that rates for rooms and meals are separate. "American plan" means that meals are included in the cost of the room. "Modified American plan" means that breakfast and dinner are included in the cost of the room. The rates at some inns include a continental breakfast with the lodging.

SMITHTON INN
Ephrata, Pennsylvania (1987)

"We want our guests to have a great Lancaster County experience. The people who live in this part of Pennsylvania are our forebears and it is an opportunity to see who our forebears were, because here their customs have remained unchanged. It's like being in touch with your own past."

I was to ponder that thought, expressed by Dorothy Graybill, many, many times during my visit to the Smithton Inn and the surrounding countryside at Ephrata, a predominantly Pennsylvania Dutch community.

"Unfortunately, the image of the Pennsylvania Dutch has been considerably distorted over the years, largely because of the efforts to commercialize some of the customs, language, and artifacts. We have developed a booklet with suggestions for touring and shopping that completely eliminates any of these places," Dorothy continued. "Both Allan and I make extensive and continuing trips throughout the countryside to make certain that our guests see the 'real' Pennsylvania Dutch life."

Dorothy was speaking of her associate at the Smithton Inn, Allan Smith, who is, among many other things, an excellent architect and woodcraftsman. We were having a chat in the truly handsome Great Room of the inn, and I couldn't help but feel that this room, with its fireplace, hooked rugs, comfortable furniture, and brightly polished hardwood floors, was an excellent place to start any adventure of this nature.

The inn is a pre-Revolutionary inn and stagecoach stop, built in 1763, and has been an inn for most of its many years. Each of the guest rooms has its own working fireplace and can be candlelighted during the evening hours. Beds have canopies, soft goosedown pillows, and bright handmade Pennsylvania Dutch quilts. Red flannel nightshirts are an amusing touch for guests to wear if they wish. All of the guest rooms have fireplaces or cast iron stoves. Allan is pleased to escort inn guests through the inn, pointing out many of the marvelously designed and constructed features, not only in the original building, but in the additions that are being made. He has a wonderful sense of history and an obvious affection for good craftsmanship.

In a recent note from Dorothy, she mentioned that they have finished redecorating a four-room suite and also the Gold Room, which sounds very elegant, with gold velvet draperies, a gold velvet and black leather chair and couch, and a queen-sized, canopied bed. This room is on the first floor and faces the garden and is most convenient for guests who cannot use steps.

"We serve a full country breakfast and a rather simple but nourishing evening meal at our guests' request," Dorothy told me. "It consists of an appetizer, soup, salad, and a meat pie. Dessert is a homemade ice cream with our exceptional chocolate sauce, which is a story in itself."

The well-known Ephrata Cloister, an 18th-century German Protestant monastic settlement, is situated just a few steps away. It is the scene of *Vorspiel,* a musical drama presented throughout the summer.

The entire area abounds in museums, crafts shops, antique shops, summer and winter theater, concerts, winery tours, art exhibits, and Renaissance fairs. Many are located in old mills, inns, historic hotels, and on Mennonite farms. There are several Pennsylvania Dutch restaurants.

I strongly suggest that our readers plan on staying at the Smithton Inn for a minimum of two nights and, if possible, three or more. The expert and caring guidance from the innkeepers provides every one with a "real Lancaster County experience."

SMITHTON INN, 900 W. Main St., Ephrata, PA 17522; 717-733-6094. A 7-guestroom (private baths) pre-Revolutionary inn in Pennsylvania Dutch country near Lancaster. Breakfast included in room rate. Dinner served to houseguests by advance reservation. Open all year. Wheelchair access. Convenient to all of Lancaster County's cultural, historic, and recreational attractions. Ephrata Cloister nearby. Dorothy Graybill, Innkeeper. (See Index for rates.)

Directions: From north or south, take Rte. 222 to Ephrata exit. Turn west on Rte. 322 for 2.5 mi. to inn.

A number of inns have nearby airports where private airplanes may land. An airplane symbol at the end of the inn directions indicates that there is an airport nearby. Consult inn for further information.

STERLING INN
South Sterling, Pennsylvania (1974)

I could not resist it any longer—I had been listening to the gurgling waters of the Wallenpaupack Creek for about twenty minutes on a warm, lazy afternoon. I was sitting on a lawn chair about fifty paces from the back of the Sterling Inn, just two feet from the bank of the creek. The smell of the freshly-cut lawn mingled with the scent of the forest on the other side of the water.

I kicked off my shoes, rolled up my pants, and waded out to stand on the flat, smooth shelf of rock in the middle of the creek. The water was clean and cool. There was a little pool about twenty-five feet away, deep enough for someone to sit in and have the water come up to his chest. A flash of red and another of blue signaled a cardinal and a bluejay darting into the woods, deep in the Pocono Mountains of Pennsylvania.

I climbed back on the bank and was drying my feet, when one of the other guests came and plunked down on a nearby chair. "I think this is one of the best-kept, neatest places that I have ever visited," she said. "It's as American as apple pie and fresh vegetables. The rooms are so comfortable, and I'm very glad I came. Don't you just love it here?"

Even if her enthusiasm hadn't been catching, I would have had to agree.

This was the friendly and unpretentious atmosphere that Alice Julian had in mind over a half-century ago when she acquired the Sterling Inn. That is the way her daughter and son-in-law, Carmen and Henry Arneberg, kept it, and the same way that the present owners, Ron and Mary Kay Logan, are keeping it today.

The Sterling Inn is on a back road in the Poconos. There are enticing hiking and walking trails on the inn property and nearby. One of them, Ron told me, leads to a waterfall on the ridge behind the inn. There is a very pleasant nine-hole putting green, a swimming area with a sandy beach, and a little pond with willow trees and a few ducks.

Guest rooms are in several very attractive buildings, all beautifully situated in the parklike surroundings. Some handsome new suites have been furnished with beautiful antiques, Franklin woodburning fireplaces, and decks overlooking the creek that I was wading in.

The menu includes such entrées as roast lamb, pot roast, and standing rib roast because, Mary Kay Logan says, "This is the kind of food that people serve only when they are having guests for dinner." All the baking is done in the warm, friendly kitchen.

In many ways this Pocono Mountain inn personifies the things that I find most delightful in country inns. For example, fresh flowers are on the dining room tables at all times, and there are books and magazines in all parlors and sitting rooms. When guests advise the inn of their arrival time, the inn automobile will meet buses and airplanes. Special diets can also be accommodated.

The inn is open year-round, and the setting is like a picture postcard. Winter activities include cross-country skiing and lessons, ice skating, sledding, winter hikes, and roasting chestnuts or marshmallows by the open fire. The horse-drawn sleigh rides are very popular.

In the blaze of autumn colors there are incredibly beautiful nature walks along Wallenpaupack Creek and hikes on woodland trails. Spring and summer at the Sterling Inn, of course, offer all sorts of outdoor enjoyment.

STERLING INN, Rte. 191, South Sterling, PA 18460; 717-676-3311. From Ct., N.Y., N.J., Md., Del., Wash., D.C.: 800-523-8200. A 60-guestroom secluded country inn-resort in the Pocono Mountains, 8 mi. from I-84 and 12 mi. from I-380. Mod. Amer. plan. Bed-and-breakfast rates available. Reservation and check-in offices close at 10 p.m. Breakfast, lunch, and dinner served to travelers daily. Jackets required for dinner. Open year-round. Swimming, putting green, shuffleboard, all-weather tennis court, scenic hiking trails, xc skiing and lessons, ice skating, and sledding on grounds. Golf courses, horseback riding, major ski areas nearby. Gift shop and print gallery. No pets. Ron and Mary Kay Logan, Innkeepers. (See Index for rates.)

Directions: From I-80, follow I-380 to Rte. 940 to Mount Pocono. At light, cross Rte. 611 and proceed on Rte. 196 north to Rte. 423. Drive north on Rte. 423 to Rte. 191 and travel ½ mi. north to inn. From I-84, follow Rte. 507 south through Greentown and Newfoundland. In Newfoundland, pick up Rte. 191 and travel 4 mi. south to inn.

TARA
Clark, Pennsylvania (1986)

Inspired by the world's most renowned movie, *Gone With the Wind*, Jim and Donna Winner restored a beautiful antebellum mansion located midway between Cleveland, Ohio, and Pittsburgh, Pennsylvania. They named it "Tara."

When I first saw Tara from the rolling highways of western Pennsylvania I wondered if magically I'd been transported in time to the Old South of the early 1800s—the era before the Civil War, when grace and grandeur, honor, fine clothes, plantations, and Southern hospitality were the lifestyle.

The house was built in 1854 and is one of western Pennsylvania's most famous historic landmarks. The mansion, with its two-story Grecian columns, overlooks 4,000-acre Lake Shenango surrounded by rolling hills of maple and pine.

Incurable romantics, Jim and Donna knew from the first time they saw what was to become Tara that it should definitely be a country inn. They have made it their home and have lavishly displayed their entire collection of antiques, art, rare china, and crystal throughout, including crystal chandeliers from Austria and a hand-painted Dresden chandelier from Germany. An antique brass chandelier featuring Steuben shades graces the circular stairwell.

There are fourteen guest rooms, all with working fireplaces. Each room has been carefully decorated to reflect the personality of a character from the book. For example, "Miss Melanie's" room is all feminine and fluffy in yellow and pink, with bows and wicker furniture. Overlooking the lake, it boasts one of the best views in the house. "Rhett's" room is masculine and strong. Its focal point is a center-island bed with a canopy that rises to the nine-foot ceiling. The "Katie O'Hara" room has an 18th-century hand-carved bed and a hand-painted ivy floor. The "old maid's" stairwell descends to the lovely antique private bath below.

There are two main dining rooms, a tavern, and a patio café for outdoor dining in clement weather. "Ashley's" is for formal dining, with such offerings as medallions of beef, Norwegian salmon, and rack of lamb, an array of tantalizing desserts, and special gourmet coffees, all served on antique tables set with crystal and silver. The "Old South Room" is a true-to-life Southern-style dining room, serving fried chicken, smoked ham, grits, cornbread, and other Dixie favorites, all served family style. "Stonewall's Tavern" has walls of hand-hewn stone with beamed ceilings and offers a lighter, more informal menu.

Tara is just fun to browse through. There is an authentic, primitive slave kitchen, a primitive bedroom with a genuine rope bed, and a collection of antiques that date back to 1760. One of the pieces on display is a table that belonged to President James Buchanan and was used in the White House during his administration, just before the Civil War. The library itself is most impressive, with both old and new books, and one can read on the veranda or in "Miss Pittypat's Parlor."

The day after Thanksgiving, 100,000 tiny white lights will be draped in the trees and bushes. The trees in the parlor are decorated in a Victorian mode, and those in the Old South Room will be done in an old-fashioned style. Bows and holly adorn the crystal chandeliers.

A letter I received from one of my Canadian readers said in part: "On our return from a trip to Washington, D.C., we were truly transported to the period when hospitality was a very special thing in the South and we experienced this at Tara. Every trip should include at least one outstanding and memorable experience and indeed our visit to Tara will be remembered for many years."

TARA, 3665 Valley View Rd., Box 475, Rte. 18, Clark, PA 16113; 412-962-3535. A 14-guestroom mansion, 8 hrs. west of New York and 8 hrs. east of Chicago. Breakfast, lunch, and dinner served. Open year-round. Croquet, bocci, boating, fishing, swimming, carriage rides, bicycling, backroading, xc skiing, and golf, Not suitable for children. No pets. Jim and Donna Winner, Innkeepers. (See Index for rates.)

Directions: Just inside the Pa. border on I-80 take Exit 1N and follow Rte. 18 north for 8 mi. Tara is located on the east side overlooking Lake Shenango. ✔

THE TAVERN
New Wilmington, Pennsylvania (1974)

The sheltered cot, the cultivated farm,
The never-failing brook, the busy meadow,
The decent church that topped the neighboring hill,
The hawthorn bush, with seats beneath the shade,
For talking age and whispering lovers made.

These words from Oliver Goldsmith in many ways express the beautiful countryside and ambience of New Wilmington, which is in the rolling country of northwestern Pennsylvania. I was here to visit Mary Ellen Durrast and the Tavern, which has offered hospitality for well over fifty years. Most of that time the innkeeper was Mary Ellen's mother, Cora Durrast.

I enjoyed my trip down from the Berkshires, especially the drive through the beautiful farm country of Pennsylvania. The early corn was up, and farmers were harvesting the wheat and oats. The first cutting of hay was baled and waiting to be collected and put in the barns. As I drove, I kept my eye peeled for Amish buggies, and before long I spotted two or three.

At one farm an entire Amish family, dressed in their traditional clothing, was outside. Next to the road were tables piled high with the fresh eggs and produce they were selling to passersby. The corn on the cob looked particularly tempting, but I reminded myself that in just a few minutes I would be at the Tavern enjoying some wonderful country food.

And country food aplenty there was. The luncheon menu included chicken salad, chicken pie, ham loaf, pork chops, liver, flounder, ham, shrimp, and scallops. The appetizers were chicken noodle or potato soup, fruit cup, a variety of juices, and white grape, cranberry, or pineapple fruit shrub. A tossed green salad and a pear salad with a strawberry-pineapple whipped topping were also on the menu.

While I was making up my mind, two warm honey buns with whipped butter were placed in front of me. It took all of my resolve not to eat them both immediately.

The people at the adjoining table were being served chicken pie. It looked delicious. Two waitresses passed bowls of vegetables; there must have been four or five different kinds. I decided on the smoked pork chops, which came with a side order of very crisp pork dressing and a fresh spinach salad with Cora's egg-and-cheese dressing. The desserts included cherry crisp, butterscotch pie, and many different kinds of ice cream and sherbert.

Meanwhile, some expected guests had arrived and Mary Ellen was hurrying about, making certain that everything was just right. After they finished lunch and their bus departed, Mary Ellen and I had a chance for a little chat. She said that she just loved "Berkshire Travellers," they were her kind of people.

There are several dining rooms, all bright and cheery, with crisp linens and fresh flowers on the tables. In one room, there is the largest collection of recipe books I've seen in a long time; in another is a big stone fireplace.

The Tavern maintains some very simple bedrooms across the street in a building called the Tavern Lodge. They're reasonably priced and provide sleeping quarters for overnight guests.

There is no breakfast provided at the Tavern; however Mary Ellen sends all of her overnight guests to a town restaurant about two blocks away. This is a town meeting place, and on the morning of my visit there were several Amish patrons.

THE TAVERN, Box 193, New Wilmington, PA 16142; 412-946-2020. A bustling country restaurant on the town square with 5 sleeping rooms in a lodge directly across the street. European plan. Lunch and dinner served daily except Tues. Reservations required. Closed Thanksgiving, Christmas, and July 4. Sports and cultural events at Westminister College nearby. No diversions for small children. No credit cards. Mary Ellen Durrast, Innkeeper. (See Index for rates.)

Directions: From I-80, take 1-S and follow Rte. 18 south to Rte. 208. Proceed east on 208 to town square. From I-79, follow Rte. 208 west for 14 mi. to New Wilmington.

The date in parenthesis in the heading represents the first year the inn appeared in the pages of Country Inns and Back Roads.

ASA RANSOM HOUSE
Clarence, New York (1976)

The letter was typical of several I have received from readers who have stayed at the Asa Ransom House: "A delightful surprise; we didn't realize that such a wonderful old place existed near Buffalo. Here we were treated as personal guests. Our bedroom was really beautiful, furnished with old pieces and decorated with exquisite taste. The bathroom was one of the prettiest and cleanest I have ever seen. The dining room was crowded, but our table was kept for us until we arrived and then we sat down to one of the finest meals I have had for years. The next morning a complimentary breakfast was served because we were remaining overnight. Everything seems to be homemade and from organically grown produce. We intend to return."

As long as I am at it, let me quote till another reader's letter: "Driving down the main street of Clarence at dusk on a December day my spirit was brightened when I saw the warm glow of the lights of the inn reflected on the snow. I could see through the windows that everyone was thoroughly enjoying themselves. Upon entering I was greeted by Judy Lenz who showed me to my bedroom and gave me a bowl of fruit.

"I had a real treat on the first night of dinner. It was fillet of sole in parchment, which is a sole with mushroom stuffing and wine sauce, baked in parchment. It was most unusual.

"An evening by the fire near the Franklin stove and a good book was a change of pace (without television) and most enjoyable. While I was reading, one of the waitresses asked if she could bring me some tea or coffee."

The unique printed menu also includes the Asa Ransom News, which provides interesting historical and gastronomic observations. Besides an impressive assortment of main dishes, such as salmon steak baked in puff pastry, baked sole Florentine, and country inn veal, the dinner includes steaming soup from the kettle, tossed garden greens, fresh vegetables, and freshly baked bread and muffins.

The inn has two distinctly different dining rooms and four totally different guest rooms. The Lavender/Green Room had a king-sized bed and a deep antique bathtub. The larger Gold Room is outfitted with twin iron-and-brass beds with coordinated patchwork coverlets, and originally designed stenciling on the upper walls, whose theme is old-fashioned American hospitality. The Blue Room has a canopy bed, and the Green Room has two double beds, a sitting area with a love seat, a bookcase, and a view of the herb garden.

Each of the two dining rooms has its own decorative theme, and one room is set aside for nonsmokers.

The Asa Ransom House menu reflects the Lenzes' innovative flair, as well as some deep convictions about their life. For example. their religious persuasion prohibits serving pork and shellfish. As a pork substitute, "one of our favorite dishes," Bob comments, "is chicken breasts with raspberry sauce. This was discovered last winter on one of the gourmet nights held frequently during the winter season."

Breakfast for houseguests consists of fresh fruit, muffins, and a beverage, as well as Judy's special breakfast egg pie.

The Asa Ransom House is closed on Fridays and Saturdays because of the religious beliefs of Bob and Judy, who are members of the Church of God. Friday provides them with the opportunity to spend time with their families or to set off with their daughters for some point in western New York or southern Ontario to enjoy many scenic attractions. As Bob says, "We frequently end the day with a fine dinner at an old favorite or sometimes discover some new country inn."

ASA RANSOM HOUSE (Romantik Hotels), Rte. 5, Clarence, NY 14031; 716-759-2315. A 4-guestroom village inn approx. 15 mi. from Buffalo near the Albright Knox Art Gallery, the Studio Arena Theatre, the Art Park, and Niagara Falls. European plan. Dinner served on Mon. through Thurs., 4:00 to 8:30 p. m.; Sun., 12:00 to 8:00 p.m. Jackets required. Lunch is available on Wed. only. Closed Fri. and Sat. Wheelchair access to dining room. Tennis, golf, fishing, swimming nearby. Limited amusement for children under 12. No pets. No credit cards. Bob and Judy Lenz, Innkeepers. (See Index for rates.)

Directions: From the New York Thruway traveling west, use Exit 48A-Pembroke. Turn right to Rte. 5 and proceed 11 mi. to Clarence. Traveling east on the N.Y. Thruway, use Exit 49; turn left on Rte. 78, go 1 mi. to Rte. 5 and continue 5¼ mi. Coming from the east via Rte. 20, just east of Lancaster, N.Y., turn on Ransom Rd., go to end and turn left. ✒

BARK EATER LODGE
Keene, New York (1985)

The most welcome comment I can receive about this book is "The inn was exactly the way you wrote about it." I try to do that in every inn-stance (little play on words, there). In this case, I'm going to let Joe-Pete Wilson and Harley McDevitt describe Bark Eater themselves.

"The lodge is a modest, 150-year-old farmhouse, preserved to give the guest a true feeling of 'life back when.' We offer good home cooking, sometimes done on our wood stove, informal family-style meals, and relaxed evenings with good conversation around the fireplace. Occasionally, we schedule talks and advice on ski waxing, mountain safety, or skiing technique.

"We maintain several miles of cross-country ski trails; some to entice the beginner, others to challenge the expert. We have certified instruction, tours, and rentals or sales from our own ski shop. We also have moonlight tours, citizen races, and guided picnic trips into the wilderness.

"In summer, we switch to exploring the great outdoors on foot or horseback, mountain or rock climbing, or just strolling around nearby country roads or trails. There is great trout fishing nearby and plenty of opportunity for swimming, canoeing, sailing, tennis, golf, and other sports.

"We have forty-five horses and we offer picnic trips, trail rides, and lessons. Our horses range from well-trained Western horses to well-trained English riding horses.

"A visit during the Adirondack autumn, with its spectacular colors, is unbelievable."

Bark Eater Lodge is a year-round country inn specializing in cross-country skiing in the winter, and enjoyment of the outdoors in all seasons of the year. It is situated on 250 acres of beautiful rolling meadow with a delightful pond, in the High Peaks region of the Adirondacks.

It is homey and informal, and at the same time, eclectic. The magazines and newspapers include the *New York Times, Architectural Digest, Natural History, Backpacker,* and *Gourmet,* to name a few. There are stacks of books on a wide diversity of subjects. I've always been able to tell a great many things about an inn by the nature of the books that are available to the guests.

The kitchen is wide open for everyone to enjoy. There are a couple of old-fashioned stoves and modern ones, as well. Guests are welcome to sit down at the table and talk with Harley while dinner is being prepared. By the way, these dinners are a feature of the inn and, because of the great outdoor activities, are often very hearty. Everybody sits down about seven o'clock in the evening around the big table.

Guest rooms have rocking chairs, many old-fashioned wash stands, double and single beds, over and under bunks, wooden chests, and a wonderful old fashioned feeling.

New guest rooms with private baths have been added in the Carriage House next to the inn. They have been most tastefully designed by Harley with a more modern flavor.

Bark Eater is on a special "inn-to-inn" program, described in a special folder, that begins with the Garnet Hill Lodge, which is also in *CIBR,* and full details are available at either inn.

To illustrate just how "up country" Bark Eater is, if you don't succeed in making a telephone connection on the first try, keep trying. It's a real country telephone system.

When you visit Bark Eater Lodge, bring a great sense of expectancy.

BARK EATER LODGE, Alstead Mill Rd., Keene, NY 12942; 518-576-2221. A 12-guestroom (some with shared baths) rustic mountain inn in the Adirondacks. Rates include a full country breakfast. Open all year, but check in advance during April. Dinners served. A wide variety of mountain recreation available at the inn or nearby, including High Peaks climbing, Hudson River Gorge whitewater rafting, and self-guided hiking tours. Horseback riding, swimming, tennis, golf, canoeing, sailing available nearby. Children welcome. No credit cards. Joe-Pete Wilson and Harley McDevitt, Innkeepers. (See Index for rates.)

Directions: From the Northway take exit 30, follow Rte. 73 for 1 mi. past the village of Keene and turn right on Alstead Mill Rd. Inn is ½ mi. beyond.

BEEKMAN ARMS
Rhinebeck, New York (1967)

"I've heard lots of explanations for the name 'Rhinebeck' or 'Rynbeck,'" said Chuck LaForge, as we sat down for dinner in the low-ceilinged Tap Room of the Beekman Arms, "but recently I learned that on the same ship with Peter Stuyvesant was a German, William Beckman, who originally came here from the Rhine Valley. His son received a land grant here in 1703 from Queen Anne of England, and he named the property Rhinebeck. 'Beckman' could have been changed to 'Beck' through a clerical error in later years."

By 1769, the Beekman Arms, which started from rather humble beginnings, had increased in size to two full stories with a roomy attic that later became a ballroom. When trouble arose with the Indians in the area, the entire community would take refuge within the inn's walls.

During the Revolution, George Washington and his staff enjoyed the fare of the inn, and the window from which he watched for his couriers is still in place. Those were anxious days also for Lafayette, Schuyler, Arnold, and Hamilton, who spent many hours at the inn. In fact, over the years hundreds of men who have helped fashion the destiny of our nation partook of the inn's hospitality.

Tonight, the light from the flickering candles was reflected in the varnished tabletops and overhead beams. The walls were hung with ancient documents and prints and sabres and muskets, many of them dating back to the days of the American Revolution. This was the same place where pioneer families and early tradesmen enjoyed a roaring fire and perhaps took a pipe similar to the white clay pipes that also adorned the walls.

While earlier Colonial Beekman Arms menus probably included such items as roast beef, venison, bear steak, pheasant, quail, and turkey, tonight chef Dan Smith's menu had varieties of boned roast duckling (raspberry sauce or hunter's style), fresh seafood, scrumptious veal preparations, as well as a few select recipes from other inns featured in *CIBR*. Casual but elegant country dining is the fare.

During most of the more than twenty years I have visited the Beekman Arms, Chuck has been kind enough to share news of the ongoing new developments with me. These have included the creation of a greenhouse dining area in the front of the building, the Antique Barn with thirty shops, and the growth of still another adjunct to the Beekman Arms—the Delameter House, built in 1844.

Chuck suggested that we take a stroll to the Delameter House to see all of the recent developments. "This is the Delameter courtyard," he commented, as we walked into an open-ended square area. There were buildings on three sides, including one that had been there earlier and a Federal house of batten-and-board design similar to the original Delameter House, which had been moved from another point in the village.

The guest rooms in this section are furnished with a very pleasant restraint; each has a four-poster bed and a fireplace, and there is split wood for the fire. Each of them has its own little refrigerator. There are thirty-one rooms in this complex.

"I think that these rooms add a completely new dimension to what we offer at the Beekman Arms," Chuck declared, as we walked back through the courtyard past the Carriage House, which also has some additional attractive guest rooms. "We have attempted to emulate the early designer, Alexander Jackson Davis, as much as possible."

The Beekman Arms today is more than a historic inn where thousands of guests enjoy its fascinating and authentic Colonial decor and menu; like many other country and village inns, it is still the community meeting place.

BEEKMAN ARMS, Rhinebeck, NY 12572; 914-876-7077. A 12-guest-room village inn with an additional 31 rooms and 2 suites in nearby guest houses. European plan. Breakfast, lunch, and dinner served to travelers daily. Open year-round. Wheelchair access at Delameter House. One mile from Amtrak station at Rhinecliff (2-hr. train ride from Grand Central Station). Short drive to Hyde Park with F.D.R. home and library, Rhinebeck World War I Aerodrome, and Culinary Institute of America. Golf, tennis, swimming nearby. No amusements for young children. Chuck LaForge, Innkeeper. (See Index for rates.)

Directions: From N.Y. Thruway, take Exit 19, cross Rhinecliff Bridge and pick up Rte. 199 south to Rte. 9. Proceed south on Rte. 9 to middle of village. From Taconic Pkwy., exit at Rhinebeck and follow Rte. 199 west 11 mi. to Rte. 308 into village. ⬏

BENN CONGER INN
Groton, New York (1983)

"That is the world's greatest rocker." I'll admit that I was somewhat skeptical about Mark Bloom's adamant statement. It looked like a lot of other rockers I had seen. Well, maybe it was a bit more sturdy and perhaps wider, but beyond that it looked like your everyday rocking chair. Mark and his wife, Pat, and I were seated in the library of the Benn Conger Inn. They were telling me of their adventures in finding the Benn Conger, and also how they happened to have made such a good reputation in a relatively short time. "In 1981 Mark took a job as the head chef at a very fine restaurant in Chicago's Lincoln Park. We were already married and had begun to dream of owning our own country inn. We scouted many places, and then in 1984 we saw the real estate listing for the Benn Conger Inn, came East to take a look at it, and immediately fell in love with it." This from Pat.

"We worked long and hard just to get things open and going," Mark said, "and the inn is furnished with a combination of our furniture and treasures we've found at antique shops. It's our home and we're happy to share it with our guests."

Pat continued, "Mark does all the cooking, baking, and kitchen management, and he's terrific. His food is made with the finest ingredients and prepared with real style. We think of ourselves as a European *auberge*—we specialize in the country cooking of France and Italy. Mark makes stews and roasts that taste like heaven in a bowl. Our guests tell us that our food is different, and we've developed a sizable following."

While we were chatting, a black Labrador retriever named Riff, who was about the size of a small pony, came in the library. "He's not allowed in during the dinner hour, but he is around among the guests at other times and he's very lovable. We also have a big calico cat who has become a pet of the guests, too. She's unpredictable and saucy."

The Benn Conger is a stately Greek Revival mansion, built in 1921, overlooking the village of Groton. There are eighteen acres of rolling land, great for cross-country skiing and nature walks. Extensive plantings complement the front entrance. I noticed marigolds, snapdragons, asters, primroses, roses, Canterbury bells, red salvia, purple and green basil, pansies, and Johnny-jump-ups.

The first thing a guest sees upon gaining entrance to the impressive front hallway is a sweeping, curved staircase that leads up to the second floor, where, among other things, there's a spacious window seat, perfect for reading a good book. This nook has a group of video cassettes, including some of those movies you thought you'd never be able to see again, like *Casablanca* and *The Maltese Falcon*.

The guest rooms are furnished with antique wood and brass beds, flannel sheets, warm comforters, and period furniture. "We wanted it to be comfortable, more elegant than a home but not museum quality," Pat told me.

Whether by chance or design, I think that Mark and Pat have caught the spirit of the 1920s in portions of the interior decorations of the inn. The use of period posters from various art museums, as well as some other selective original works of art, placed with care and taste, have recreated a certain ambience of the 1920s and 1930s.

"Well, so far, all you've done is to look at the 'world's greatest rocker.' Why don't you try it?" I did and they were absolutely right. It is the world's greatest rocker.

BENN CONGER INN, 206 West Cortland St., Groton, NY 13073; 607-898-5817. A 4-guestroom (private and shared baths) village mansion in a quiet community in the Finger Lakes District. Complimentary full breakfast. Dinner served nightly except Sun. and Mon.; reservations are necessary. Open Apr. thru Feb. Cornell University and Ithaca College nearby, as well as golf, tennis, swimming, downhill and xc skiing, and backroading. No entertainment for children under 10. Mark and Pat Bloom, Innkeepers. (See Index for rates.)

Directions: From I-81, take Exit 12 (Homer), turning south on Rte. 281 for 3 mi., and west (right) on Rte. 222. Continue 10 mi. to Groton, crossing Rte. 38 and making no turns. The Benn Conger is up the hill on the right.

A number of inns have nearby airports where private airplanes may land. An airplane symbol at the end of the inn directions indicates that there is an airport nearby. Consult inn for further information.

BIRD AND BOTTLE INN
Garrison, New York (1972)

I had awakened to the joyous sound of the birds and had lingered under the covers at the Bird and Bottle for just a few more minutes, noting with appreciation the handsome overhead beams made of mellowed, weathered barnboard and the rest of the furnishings in my room in one of the outbuildings of the inn. Out the window I could see the high spreading branches of one of the huge old trees against the blue spring sky, with just a wisp of a white cloud.

There was much to do that day, so a few minutes later I ambled over the red brick walk to the main building of the inn for breakfast. Some birds flew overhead and one of them landed on the chimney of this yellow clapboard house that has played host to so many travelers and guests over the years. I opened the Dutch door with its heavy cast-iron hardware and stepped into the main reception area where the polished, wide pine floorboards seemed almost to reflect an oil portrait of a young lady dressed in Colonial costume.

To my right was the low-ceilinged dining room, where the previous night there had been gleaming white napery with candles and many diners seated side by side—a very romantic idea, indeed. The menu on the blackboard had announced that there was ratatouille au froid, also smoked trout, french onion soup, and then a supreme of chicken, roast duckling Bigarade, and rognon de veau moutarde.

For breakfast, innkeeper Ira Boyar suggested the small dining room with a crackling fire against the chill of the early spring morning. There were fresh flowers on the table.

I had selected my breakfast order the night before from a menu that included all kinds of eggs, sausage, and fruit juice. I chose scrambled eggs and sausage and noticed some other houseguests were having beautiful french toast served with syrup or honey. We soon began to talk with one another because it's that kind of atmosphere.

Breakfast completed, I leaned for a moment on the window overlooking a little terrace and stream, where a light spring rain was making punctuation points in the small puddles. The trees were in early bud and I could well imagine what magic the entire scene would reveal in another two or three weeks.

Ira suggested that I might like to see more of the bedrooms in the main building, and as I walked up the stairs I realized that I was looking at the same Colonial wallpaper that I have in my own dining room. However, it seemed much more appropriate in this setting, here on the second floor where the floorboards creaked a little and were slightly aslant.

All of the bedrooms are furnished in Early American antiques and have either a canopy or a four-poster bed. All have private baths and woodburning fireplaces. There are two double rooms and a suite which includes a cozy sitting room.

The Bird and Bottle goes back to the mid-1700s, when it was a stagecoach stop on the New York to Albany route. Its nearness to West Point undoubtedly made it a meeting place for Benedict Arnold's emissaries to the British, prior to his defection.

Today, the Colonial atmosphere is preserved with narrow clapboards (quite unusual), low ceilings, and rich paneling. The inn is beautifully decorated with many duck decoys, period wallpaper, pewter, old paintings, and many wooden accessories. It is indeed like stepping back into an earlier time.

BIRD AND BOTTLE INN, Garrison, NY 10524; 914-424-3000. A 4-guestroom country inn, rich in antiquity, located on Rte. 9, a few miles north of Peekskill, N.Y. MAP rates include both a full breakfast and dinner. From April 1 to Nov. 1 lunch and dinner served daily. From Nov. 1 to April 1 dinner served Wed. thru Sun. Sunday brunch served year-round. A short distance from Boscobel Restoration. U.S. Military Academy at West Point, and Sleepy Hollow Restorations. Ira Boyar, Innkeeper. (See Index for rates.)

Directions: From NYC: cross Geo. Washington Bridge and follow Palisades Pkwy. north to Bear Mtn. Bridge. Cross bridge and travel on Rte. 9D north 4½ mi. to Rte. 403. Proceed on Rte. 403 to Rte. 9, then north 4 mi. to inn. From 1-84, take Exit 13 and follow Rte. 9 south for 8 mi. ✈

The date in parenthesis in the heading represents the first year the inn appeared in the pages of Country Inns and Back Roads.

GARNET HILL LODGE
North River, New York (1980)

September in the Adirondacks! It's hard to imagine a more gorgeous place. I was having a morning cup of coffee on the balcony of my bedroom, one of the six recently remodeled guest rooms at Garnet Hill. All of them have an excellent view of Thirteenth Lake, below the ridge on which the lodge sits.

I thought of my last visit in late March, when I had joined George and Mary Heim and a group of CIBR innkeepers for a meeting and some of the last cross-country skiing of the season. Now it was early September and one of the best times to travel, when the weather is marvelous with just a slight chill in the air.

I reluctantly left my vantage point, collected my tape recorder and camera, remembering that George had told me that all of these rooms in the Log House have private baths and are finished in a nice combination of original pine paneling and wallpaper. There were also fresh flowers adding a pleasing touch.

Garnet Hill Lodge is an all-season resort-inn. The Log House was built in 1936, and it is a true rustic lodge, with a big combination living/ dining room of varnished Adirondack white pine in a post-and-beam construction—the bark has been left on in many cases. Guests gather around the big fireplace for some good conversation and fun.

Even on rainy days there are things to do in this lodge, including watching movies, television, or the VCR, or playing games. And there are books and books and books. The room is big enough to accommodate several different groups comfortably.

While we were taking a short tour of the property, George and Mary expressed great pride in the new nature trail. "All the trees have been carefully marked," Mary told me, "and one of the trails is used for skiing in the winter."

Besides walking and hiking, there is canoeing and fishing. Among the many other outdoor activities are white-water rafting trips on the upper Hudson River through a fifteen-mile gorge, which has some of the most spectacular rapids and scenery in the Adirondacks. "Fishing is another big thing here," George commented. "We have land-locked salmon and brook trout right here on the lake, and the nearby lakes and streams have lake trout, rainbows, brownies, bass, walleyes, and pickerel.

"I'd say we have two faces up here on the mountain," George said. "Our wintertime face is cross-country skiing. The Adirondacks offers some of the best snow in the East. We get over 125 inches here, and there is downhill skiing at Gore, Whiteface, and Lake Placid. Our own cross-country skiing includes forty kilometers of scenic, groomed trails, and we have a well-equipped ski shop with an experienced staff for lessons and tours."

Winter or summer, the evening meal is a big event at Garnet Hill Lodge. The menu includes a sizeable group of appetizers—paté, shrimp cocktail, and soups. Entrées might be fish, shrimps, scallop Provençale, baked stuffed shrimp, fillet of tenderloin, chicken in many different forms, or center-cut pork chops broiled and then sautéed in a savory brandied apple sauce.

I asked George about the animals one might see on a walk in the woods. "Well, we have black bear, although they are very seldom seen; however, you can see white-tailed deer, red foxes, minks, an occasional beaver, and the other day a coyote came right up on the ski trail. You don't see them very often, but they're out there."

GARNET HILL LODGE, 13th Lake Rd., North River, NY 12856; 518-251-2821. A 20-guestroom rustic resort-inn high in the Adirondacks, 32 mi. from Warrensburg. Mod. American and European plans available. Breakfast, lunch, and dinner served to travelers. Open year-round except 2 wks. in June and Nov. Wheelchair access to dining room. Swimming, boating, hiking, fishing, and xc skiing on grounds. Downhill skiing, long-distance hikes, Hudson River white-water rafting trips, and beautiful Adirondack drives nearby. The area has many museums, arts and crafts centers, and historical points. No pets. No credit cards. Taxi service provided to bus stop 30 mi. away. George and Mary Heim, Innkeepers. (See Index for rates.)

Directions: From the Northway (I-87) take Exit 23 and follow Rte. 8 north 4 mi. Take left fork (Rte. 28) 22 mi. to North River. Take second left (13th Lake Rd.) 5 mi. to lodge. For more explicit directions, write for brochure.

GREENVILLE ARMS
Greenville, New York (1975)

To me one of the most exciting things about my visits to country inns for the past twenty-three years is the spirit of innovation expressed at many inns. This is particularly true at the Greenville Arms in the northern Catskills. Besides having a family tradition of innkeeping extending at least forty years into the past, for the past few summers the inn has been hosting special painting workshops, which I'll discuss in just a moment.

A Victorian country mansion with several interestingly fashioned porches, cupolas, gables, and corners, the inn is well shaded with tall trees and beautifully landscaped with bushes and shrubs. Throughout, the atmosphere could best be described as "homey and inviting."

Another dimension to be found at the Greenville Arms is its role as a very comfortable resort-inn. Behind the main house, with its several bedrooms with private and shared baths, is the Carriage House, where there are more contemporary rooms, all with private baths. There is a large, beautiful lawn with shuffleboard, ping-pong, horseshoes, badminton, lawn bowling, and a swimming pool.

The innkeepers at Greenville Arms are two sisters, Barbara and Laura Stevens. They are carrying on the family tradition, since Greenville Arms was originally owned by their mother; their aunt and grandmother still own inns in the Catskill Mountains.

The main house at the Greenville Arms was built in 1889 and has the feeling of being almost frozen in time, with the same type of furniture, decorations, and lifestyle. There are even button switches for some of the lights. One of the most delightful things for me was the many different types of bedspreads. Off the second floor is a porch that you always wanted and never had.

Dinner is single entrée and is really typical Catskill Mountain home cooking with lots of turkey, baked ham, roasts, and fresh vegetables from the garden.

Greenville Arms is located in a region rich in history and resplendent with natural beauty. The northern Catskill Mountains, the Hudson River, and the rural farmland in the valleys between have attracted travelers and inspired artists for generations. This is the land of Thomas Cole, Frederick Church, and the renowned Hudson River school of art.

I had the opportunity to attend for a brief time one of the art classes being conducted by Sygmund Jankowski. While I didn't have the opportunity to take any lessons, I talked to some of the students, all of whom were most enthusiastic about not only the instructor but the opportunity to take advantage of the limitless subject matter in the area and to work one-on-one with such a splendid communicator. As one student told me, "He said, 'I'll walk with you along every step of the way.' And he did. I found it fascinating."

For a special brochure with all the details about the Hudson River Valley painting workshops call either Laura or Barbara. I have seen the schedule for 1988, and also the list of the artist-instructors and, believe me, nothing would give me more pleasure than to be able to take an entire week and participate myself.

GREENVILLE ARMS, Greenville, NY 12083; 518-966-5219. A 20-guest-room Victorian country inn in the foothills of the northern Catskill Mountains, 25 mi. south of Albany, 120 mi. north of New York City. Modified American plan rates include a hearty breakfast and a specially prepared single-entrée country dinner. Bed-and-breakfast rates also available. Open May 1 to Oct. 31. Pool and lawn sports on grounds. Antiquing, country auctions, historic sites, horseback riding, golf, tennis nearby. Pets accommodated in nearby kennels. No credit cards. Laura and Barbara Stevens, Innkeepers. (See Index for rates.)

Directions: Exit N.Y. State Thruway at 21B (Coxsackie–New Baltimore). Turn left on 9-W south 2 mi. to traffic light. Turn right on 81 west, 13 mi. to Greenville. Turn left at traffic light on 32S. You will see Greenville Arms on the right. Via Taconic Pkwy.: Exit at Ancram on Rte. 82W, over Rip Van Winkle Bridge and follow Rte. 23W to Cairo. Turn right on 32N, 9 mi. to Greenville. ◢

THE HOLLOWAY HOUSE
East Bloomfield, New York (1976)

It was a beautiful sunny day in western New York. The corn was up, covering the rolling hills off Route 20. The sky was blue without a cloud, and the silos and barns of this beautiful farming country were constant reminders of its rich yield.

This time, I was coming east after paying an overnight visit to the Asa Ransom House in Clarence, and entered East Bloomfield just about noontime. East Bloomfield is a village of elms, maples, oak trees, and lovely old homes. It is a relatively short distance from Rochester.

At the Holloway House, Doreen Wayne told me some of its history. Jonathan Child, who was elected Rochester's first mayor in 1834, had opened a store in 1812 in part of Peter Holloway's tavern. In 1818 he married Sophia Eliza, the daughter of Colonel Nathanial Rochester, who lived a mile west of the tavern when he established his city at the falls of the Genesee.

"In those days, of course, the road was just thin ruts created by stagecoaches and farm carts," said Doreen. "Now Route 20 moves along the northern edge of what we call in these parts the 'Bristol Valley.' A great many people find their way to our door, just as they did when Peter Holloway, the village blacksmith, built this as a tavern in 1808."

The inn was doing a brisk business for lunch, but Fred and Doreen promised to visit with me as soon as things got quieter, and showed me to a corner in the Peter Holloway Room, which has a view of the village through the beautiful trees. The waitress recited the lunch menu for me and brought a wonderful variety of hot fresh breads, for which the inn is quite famous. Doreen was able to visit for just a few moments and to tell me about the buffet dinner, served on Friday nights during July and August.

"We have seafood, shrimp, scallops, oysters, creamed mushrooms, and various types of Newburg dishes. Everybody always oohs and aahs over the way the big table is decorated. It is very popular with the people who live in the area. On Saturday night we have a prime roast beef dinner.

"Incidentally, we have two kinds of dinners, either a complete dinner or a plate dinner. The plate dinner includes the entrée, two vegetables, a salad, potato, our well-known Sally Lunn bread, and homemade rolls. The complete dinner includes a choice of appetizers, entrée, choice of potato, two vegetables, a choice of salad and salad dressing, the Sally Lunn bread, homemade rolls, beverage, and a choice of dessert."

There are several very interesting nearby attractions, according to Doreen Wayne. First is the Wizard of Clay pottery and workshop, which is housed in a complex of geodesic domes where all the pottery pieces are handmade on the potter's wheel by the "Wizard" and his staff of skilled craftsmen. It is located on Route 20A, three miles east of Honeoye Lake, and is open year-round. The second, within walking distance of the Holloway House, is the restored 1833 Bloomfield Academy, bordering on the historic Civil War Park. Inside the academy is the unique Communications Museum, which is particularly enjoyed by ham operators. It has one of the first collections of early radio apparatus—actual equipment associated with Marconi, DeForest, Armstrong, Edison, and other pioneers. A feature of this museum is a replica of a 1925 radio store completely stocked with hundreds of parts and tubes for building one's own radio set.

"Our guests particularly enjoy visiting these places after lunch," remarked Doreen.

THE HOLLOWAY HOUSE, Rtes. 5 and 20, East Bloomfield, NY 14443; 716-657-7120. A country restaurant 8 miles west of Canandaigua, N.Y. No lodgings. Lunch served daily 11:30 to 2 p.m.; dinner 5:30 to 8:30 p.m. Sunday—12 to 7:30 p.m. Closed Mon. Open April 1 thru Thanksgiving. Sonnenberg Gardens, golf courses, and Finger Lake Racetrack nearby. The Wayne Family, Innkeepers. (See Index for rates.)

Directions: From N.Y. State Thruway, take Exit 45 and Rte. 96S. Continue 3 mi. to Victor, N.Y. At the third traffic light go south on Maple Ave., 5 mi. to Holcomb. Turn right at light and then take second left to Rtes. 5 and 20.

LINCKLAEN HOUSE
Cazenovia, New York (1968)

If an old-time stagecoach driver were to pull up his team in front of the Lincklaen House today, he would find the hotel looking almost the same as it did in 1835, at least outwardly. The locally made brick, the fine chimneys, the broad front steps, and the columns flanking the doorway were built to last—and they have. Twenty or more stagecoaches passed through Cazenovia each day traveling over the Third Great Western Turnpike, and the snap of the drivers' whips was a familiar sound. The stages carried the mail and as many as fourteen passengers, and the Lincklaen House must have been a welcome respite from hours spent in those lumbering horse-drawn conveyances.

Guests staying at the Lincklaen House and meeting innkeeper Helen Tobin for the first time, frequently say, "Oh, I feel as if I have known you for a long time." This is because Helen has genuine warmth and consideration, and the Lincklaen House reflects this feeling.

"I try to visit with everyone while they're here," she said. "Many become good friends and stop off many times. We always get lots of Christmas cards from them.

"We have been working for the past year repainting and stenciling as many guest rooms as possible. We've also refurbished the front of the building with fresh paint. As a matter of fact, I think we look quite 'spiffy.'"

The Lincklaen House has been called one of the best examples of early-19th-century architecture in central New York State. Its Greek Revival lines are in harmony with other buildings in this college town. The inn was named after the founder of the village, and over the years, many famous guests have enjoyed its hospitality.

Cazenovia is one of the attractive towns along Route 20 in central New York State. This road, by the way, is a very interesting alternative to traveling across the state entirely on the Thruway, just a few miles to the north.

"We are getting to be a very special-event-minded community," Helen remarked. "We have the winter festival every February; the Lorenzo needlework exhibit the whole month of June; arts and crafts on our village green; plus a parade and fireworks over the 4th of July; the Lorenzo driving competition, which takes place in July; the Franklin car reunion each year in August; and our own events here at the Lincklaen House at Christmastime."

Cazenovia provides a wide variety of sports and diversions. Swimming, fishing, sailing, waterskiing, and in winter ice skating and ice fishing are available on the lake, and there is also tennis, horseback riding, and skiing nearby. A small folder outlines five lovely motor tours in the vicinity of the town, and eventually all roads lead back to the Lincklaen House for afternoon tea.

"We serve afternoon tea every day," Helen told me, "and it's the one time of the day that I make every effort to be back here to meet my guests and introduce them to each other. It's one of the nicest times of the day at the Lincklaen House, when we are all sitting around the fire or in the courtyard."

LINCKLAEN HOUSE, Cazenovia, NY 13035; 315-655-3461. A 27-guest-room village inn, 20 mi. east of Syracuse. European plan. Modified American plan upon request. Breakfast, lunch, and dinner served to travelers daily. Open year-round. Near several state parks, the Erie Canal Museum, and the Canal Trail. Tennis, golf, bicycles, alpine and xc skiing nearby. Helen Tobin, Innkeeper. (See Index for rates.)

Directions: From west on NY Thruway, take Exit 34A, follow Rte. 481 south, take Exit 3E and follow Rte. 92 east to Cazenovia. From east on NY Thruway, take Exit 34 and follow Rte. 13 south to Cazenovia. From Rte. 81, take Exit 15 (Lafayette) and follow Rte. 20 east, 18 mi. to inn.

"European plan" means that rates for rooms and meals are separate. "American plan" means that meals are included in the cost of the room. "Modified American plan" means that breakfast and dinner are included in the cost of the room. The rates at some inns include a continental breakfast with the lodging.

MILL HOUSE INN
Stephentown, New York (1979)

I love apple strudel. I'm particularly fond of Ronnie Tallet's apple strudel because she puts extra goodies in its crisp blanket and each bite is a real delight. Oddly enough, Ronnie and I took a course in baking a few years ago and one of the things we worked with was phyllo dough. She makes her own phyllo dough for her strudel, and each layer is so thin you could read this book through it.

The apple strudel is occasionally served during afternoon tea at the Mill House Inn, so inn guests have the fun and pleasure of many of Ronnie's different concoctions.

The Mill House (formerly the Millhof) now has not only a new name, but a new look. Frank explained it like this: "The major project we've had in the last two years is our new roof. We had a flat roof before, but now we have a regular full-pitched roof designed in a European style with the hip in front, and it gives the building a lot more mass and somehow a great deal more credibility. The reason I say this is because we've had quite a few people pass and say, 'Oh, I never knew you were here.' Now we have people look at the building when they come and it just gives it a much more substantial appearance because it actually adds another floor. We're not using that floor but it's a very convenient storage space."

Ronnie explained the change from Millhof to Mill House. "This place always was a mill house and we've expanded it several times and added new dimensions. The European word for house is 'hof' so we've simply Americanized it."

I've written many times that a country inn is actually an extension of the personalities of the innkeepers. Frank and Ronnie make an interesting combination. She is from Yugoslavia and occasionally returns there. Ronnie is a most accomplished artist and has done a number of the paintings that are in many of the inn guest rooms. Frank is from a French background and has done all of the designing and a great deal of the actual work on the many additions to the inn over the years.

Their three children had extensive training in all phases of innkeeping. Debbie now works in the hospitality world. Lisa will complete college in June 1988, and Gregory is a vital part of the innkeeping team.

The inn has a European Alpine theme, and the guest rooms are individually decorated and furnished with plants, books, fresh flowers, and magazines. They have a definite mid-European feeling.

Smoking is restricted to the downstairs common room, which also has some games and a TV set.

Since it is the only real meal served, breakfast is most notable at the Mill House. It starts off with juice, toast from homemade breads, a cheese wedge, beverage, and some very enticing homemade jam. Every guest may enjoy this continental breakfast as part of the room rate; however, the regular à la carte breakfast, served at a reasonable price, consists of eggs, juice, toast, jam, bacon or sausage, and stone-ground wholewheat cakes and may even include blueberries or cheese omelets. One of Ronnie's specialties is shirred eggs with cheese and sausage.

We visited in the cozy living room, whose walls are adorned with reminders of mid-Europe again—some very handsome, intricately carved pipes from Yugoslavia and Switzerland, a collection of bells, and some antlers. I saw quite a few antlers in Swiss and Austrian country inns.

"We're attracting people who want a quiet place, a place to relax," explained Ronnie. "The swimming pool, the rock garden, and the extensive plantings and flowers all have a soothing effect, and even though we are a very convenient distance from Tanglewood, where the Boston Symphony plays every summer, many of our guests find the atmosphere of rest and relaxation very pleasing."

MILL HOUSE INN, Route 43, Stephentown, NY 12168; 518-733-5606. A 10-guestroom middle-European-style country inn, 14 mi. from Pittsfield and 12 mi. from Williamstown. A pleasant drive from both Tanglewood in the summer and Jiminy Peak and Brodie Mountain in the winter. European plan. Full breakfast menu served daily. Afternoon tea served to guests. Many fine restaurants nearby. Open every day from May 26 thru March 31. Swimming pool on grounds. Hiking, skiing, backroading, and all of the famous Berkshire recreational and cultural attractions nearby. No pets. Frank and Ronnie Tallet, Innkeepers. (See Index for rates.)

Directions: From New York: exit the Taconic Pkwy. on Rte. 295. Travel east to Rte. 22, making a left turn and continuing north to Rte. 43. Turn east (right) on Rte. 43 toward Williamstown. The inn is 1 mi. on the left. From Boston: exit Mass. Tpke. at New Lebanon. North on Rte. 22 to Rte. 43, as above.

THE REDCOAT'S RETURN
Tannersville, New York (1977)

I think it's fair to say that every inn I have written about in my books is unique. Each has its own personality and its own particular brand of hospitality. However, I have noticed certain similarities among various inns. In the case of Redcoat's Return, I am reminded of some British inns. One is the Royal Oak in Yattendon, another is the Collin House in Broadway in the Cotswolds, and still another is the Pheasant in the English Lake District.

I suggest that one of the reasons I see similarities is that Tom Wright, who with his wife, Peggy, is the innkeeper at Redcoat's Return, is a true Britisher. He was brought up in England, apprenticed at the Dorchester Hotel in London, and was at one time with the Cunard Line as a chef on the Queen Mary.

The furniture and decorations at Redcoat's, as it is familiarly known, could well be at home in many English pubs. For example, the paintings in the pub room include a bravura treatment of the Battle of Waterloo and an oil painting of a young boy coming home with a mess of fish and a fishing pole over his shoulder. Another oil painting could well be of a thatched cottage in the Cotswolds. Adding to this wonderful "hands across the sea" feeling is a family room with a solarium and a group of Hogarth prints.

For regular readers and followers of Redcoat's progress there is good news and bad news. First of all, the new dining room and deck has been very successful, and, as Peggy Wright points out, the air conditioning is certainly a blessing during the summer. The room faces west towards some beautiful sunsets, and the deck is very popular as a gathering place in the summer, and for an occasional wedding as well.

The bad news is that Rex, the Irish setter who loved to take Redcoat's guests on hikes, is no longer at the inn. However, his place has been taken by Humphrey, a Swiss mountain dog, who is learning the routes already.

There are twelve guest rooms in the inn, most with wash basins and several with private baths. "We've tried to preserve the best of what is really appropriate for the building," Tom says, "and have made a few major changes that will provide more bathrooms." These guest rooms are rather small and cozy and definitely of the country inn variety.

The Wrights' preoccupation with things artistic also includes their sign in front of the inn, on one side of which is a red-coated soldier, looking surprisingly like Tom, and on the other side, a pretty woman in a period costume, who looks surprisingly like Peggy.

The British thing includes the menu, where steak-and-kidney pie is one of the most popular items, along with prime ribs of beef, usually served on the weekends. Beef Stroganoff is another hearty favorite, as is the duckling.

The inn is built at an elevation of 2,000 feet, and there's plenty of both downhill and cross-country skiing nearby, particularly at Hunter Mountain. This is the kind of countryside that creates hearty appetites.

Whenever I visit Redcoat's, I like to sit down in front of the fireplace and soak up some of the atmosphere. I also positively have to go look at my favorite painting of the Indian maiden with a headband and a coy look, wearing an Indian costume that includes knee-length stockings. "That's one of our prize possessions," Peggy says. "She's a kind of Hiawathan Betty Boop."

THE REDCOAT'S RETURN, Dale Lane, Elka Park, NY 12427; 518-589-6379. A 12-guestroom English inn approx. 4 mi. from Tannersville, N. Y., in the heart of the Catskill Mts. Lodgings include breakfast. Dinner served daily except Thurs.; no lunches served. Open from Memorial Day to Easter. Closed 1 wk. in early Nov. Please call for details. Wheelchair access to restaurant. Within a short drive of several ski areas and state hiking trails. Nature walks, trout fishing, croquet, skiing, swimming, ice skating, riding, tennis nearby. No pets. Tom and Peggy Wright, Innkeepers. (See Index for rates.)

Directions: From the New York Thruway, going north, use Exit 20; going south, use Exit 21. Find Rte. 23A on your map and follow it to Tannersville; turn left at traffic light onto County Rd. 16. Follow signs to Police Center, 4½ mi. Turn right on Dale Lane.

The date in parenthesis in the heading represents the first year the inn appeared in the pages of Country Inns and Back Roads.

THE ROSE INN
Ithaca, New York (1986)

Perhaps it is because I am so attuned to the characteristics of Central New York State that the flat-topped cupola of the Rose Inn attracted my eye. Many 19th-century homes have such cupolas. I was driving north from Ithaca along the shore of Cayuga Lake, and there on top of a small hill was a gorgeous mansion with the easily recognizable, graceful lines of a mid-19th-century Italianate home. Innkeeper Charles Rosemann met me as I was parking the car, and together we started on a lovely tour of the inn.

About the first thing I learned is that the Rose Inn is known locally as "the house with the circular staircase."

As Charles explained, "The house is a gem of woodcraft, built of heavy timbers with large, heavy handcut doors of chestnut. The floors are laid with quarter-sawed oak, inlaid in parquet fashion. It was built and completed in 1851, with the exception of a center staircase that would have led to the cupola. No one capable of completing it could be found. Hundreds of feet of priceless Honduras mahogany were stored for over half a century. In 1922 a master craftsman appeared, and he worked for two years building a circular staircase of that solid mahogany, which extended from the main hall through two stories to the cupola."

The inn displays the ambience of its period. High ceilings, the warm glow of woods from indigenous American trees long gone, marble fireplaces, and period antiques provide an elegant but surprisingly comfortable setting. Sherry Rosemann said, "Telephone callers sometimes ask us what the atmosphere of the inn is like, and we tell them that we have an elegant country mansion that is at the same time intimate and relaxed. To illustrate the point, guests feel as comfortable coming for dinner casually dressed as they do in formal attire."

Because I have a space limitation, please take my word for it that all of the guest rooms are done in the same beautiful but comfortable fashion. Several new guest rooms have been added, and all have the same high ceilings and fine millwork found throughout the inn.

Dinner is something special. Sterling silver settings and candlelight set the mood for such four-course, single-entrée dinners as rack of lamb with an herbed sauce or scampi Mediterranean, cooked in a light curry and cream sauce. For larger parties there is chateaubriand grilled over charcoals. Eclectic and ethnic meals are also available, and since dinners are served only with advance reservations, the innkeepers have a chance to create something quite different.

My visit was true to form and I was delighted. At breakfast (Sherry cooks the evening meal and Charles cooks breakfast), Charles explained, "We like to give our guests a good start, and so we have full breakfasts, including hand-squeezed orange juice, our own blend of coffee, home-made jams and jellies, along with fresh fruits, German apple pancakes, french toast, or eggs Benedict."

There are many, many more things to share about the Rose Inn, but I think the best way for such sharing is a visit to the inn itself. It may be known as the inn with the circular staircase, but I think the second most wonderful thing is that Sherry and Charles Rosemann appeared on the scene — just the right people to maintain this beautiful building and permit those of us who love inns to enjoy its hospitality.

THE ROSE INN, 813 Auburn Rd., Rte. 34 — P.O. Box 6576, Ithaca, NY 14851; 607-533-4202. A 10-guestroom (9 baths) elegant New York State mansion just a few minutes from Cornell University. Breakfast included in room rate; dinner offered by advance reservation. Open all year. Conveniently situated to enjoy the beautiful Finger Lakes scenery and attractions, including Cayuga Lake, wineries, and college campuses. No facilities for children under 10. Arrangements can be made for pets. No smoking anywhere in the inn. Charles and Sherry Rosemann, Innkeepers. (See Index for rates.)

Directions: From N.Y. State Thruway take Exit 40 and Rte. 34 south about 36 mi. The inn will be on your left before arriving in Ithaca. From I-81 use Exit 11 (Cortland) to Rte. 13 to Ithaca. Take No. Triphammer Rd. right, 7.4 mi. to inn.

THE SEDGWICK INN
Berlin, New York (1985)

There is a small but cleverly contrived booklet on each dining room table at the Sedgwick Inn. It not only contains an extensive list of the appetizers, soups, entrées, and desserts that are frequently offered, but its pages also have some extremely unique Victorian-style cartoons and some quotes from various food writers and travel authors who have found Bob and Edie Evans' establishment noteworthy.

As I have written (and they quoted me): "Mr. Currier and Mr. Ives would have loved the Sedgwick Inn. It has beckoning windows framed by wooden shutters and the traditional white clapboard walls reminiscent of homey farmhouses and buildings seen so often in Currier and Ives colored prints. Although the central part of the building was constructed in 1791 during the Colonial period, the principal architecture is Victorian."

On this particular evening in late October, Virginia Rowe, the editor of this book, and I had driven the short hour over from the Berkshires. The colors were still holding because as yet there had not been a killing frost. Berlin nestles in a valley, which has a wonderful patchwork quality, between two ranges of respectably high hills. The trim little houses looked very neat and comfortable. Many of the farmhouses had flowers in their yards as well as pumpkins and cornstalks on the porches. This was just a few days before Halloween.

Again approaching the Sedgwick Inn, I was struck by the feeling of brightness and vitality. The windows of the Coach Room Tavern revealed a scene resembling a Dickens party. The low-ceilinged room, with its antique chairs and tables, was filled with diners. The candles, flickering in their solid brass holders, created a warm, intimate glow.

The Sedgwick Inn is located on one of the main roads between New York and Montreal. The building once served as a stagecoach stop, a summer house for a prominent New York City family, and for many years had a good reputation in the area as a restaurant. Bob and Edie have added a considerable dimension to the establishment. They've created some excellent Victorian country inn guest rooms in the main house, and there is an antique shop housed in a beautiful one-room building with a historic designation. This was once used as a Civil War recruiting station and had later lives as a dentist's office and a feed store. An art gallery in an old converted carriage house displays old prints and modern paintings, as well as some of Edie's sculptures. There is also a gift shop featuring carefully selected gifts and jewelry.

On this evening the menu on the blackboard offered three different kinds of soups, including apple pumpkin, which I tried, and it was super delicious. Appetizers included Scotch eggs, Baltimore crabcakes, and stuffed mushrooms. The choices for entrées were fillet of sole Picasso and veal Vulpera, orange shrimp tempura, chicken in plum sauce, and filet mignon. The desserts were key lime pie, apricot almond crêpes, frozen chocolate mousse pie (sinful), and a selection of coffees and teas. These are all listed in the booklet that I mentioned earlier, and the list is most impressive. The menu changes weekly, beginning on Thursday. Tables are reserved for the entire evening.

After dinner, we had a chance to see the newest bedroom in the inn, furnished in a Victorian style and featuring a lovely stenciled bedboard. It has its own private stairway leading down to the dining room.

One final note: On the last page of the little booklet, Bob and Edie display their puckish sense of humor by quoting the last words of Union Army General John Sedgwick during a battle in the Civil War. When his officers urged him to duck behind a parapet, the general ignored the warnings. "Nonsense," he declared. "They couldn't hit an elephant at this dist—"

THE SEDGWICK INN, Rte. 22, Berlin, NY 12022; 518-658-2334. A 6-guestroom (private baths) country inn almost midway between Tanglewood, Shaker Village, and Williamstown. European plan. Breakfast, lunch, and dinner served daily, except Mon. and Tues. Open all year except Nov. Conveniently located to enjoy all of the recreational and cultural activities of the Berkshires. Motel accommodations also available. Bob and Edie Evans, Innkeepers. (See Index for rates.)

Directions: The inn is located on Rte. 22 between Petersburg and Stephentown, New York.

1770 HOUSE
East Hampton, Long Island, New York (1980)

"Aquiring the 1770 House was part of a longtime dream for us," recounted Sid Perle. "We spent many months searching outer Long Island for just the right place for the ideal country inn." Sid and I were seated in the main living room of the inn, where some of the most recently acquired pieces are from the old Easthampton Post Office. They have been used very cleverly. There was one window labeled, "General Delivery." Another one for money orders now has a tiny television set that disappears completely, if necessary.

We were joined momentarily by Miriam Perle, who is the chef at the inn. She formerly ran a cooking school in Great Neck for twelve years and studied earlier at the Cordon Bleu in Paris.

The menu changes weekly and, with the exception of desserts and beverages, it is a complete meal. There are such appetizers as spaghettini with a robust fresh tomato sauce, fresh poached salmon served with three sauces, stuffed artichoke Siciliano, crabcake Edna Lewis—lump crabmeat cake sautéed in a butter and mustard dressing. The salads are different every week, as are the salad dressings.

I asked Miriam about the main dishes. "Well, as you know, we're here on the end of Long Island, where there is lots of fresh fish available. So, our entrées very frequently include stuffed fresh swordfish, lobster creole, and other fish dishes. Tonight, we also have stuffed filet mignon, rack of lamb, roast loin of pork with a lemon-garlic marinade, and your favorite, roast duck with a lingonberry glaze." She knows my great love of roast duckling and knew that she had, indeed, made a conquest.

Downstairs in the Tap Room there is a beautiful beehive fireplace, and many old trivets and other artifacts on the wall. The atmosphere is quite similar to an English pub, and the room is now used as an antiques shop for their guests.

The bedrooms are delightful. Several of them have canopied beds and combinations of French and American Victorian antiques, including several bedside tables with marble tops. They are all very romantic, and one in particular on the ground floor overlooking the garden struck my fancy as being an ideal honeymoon suite.

Incidentally, guests at the 1770 House can also be booked at the Philip Taylor House, a few doors away. It's an English manor house with canopied beds and fireplaces in three luxurious guest rooms.

Sid said there have been several references to my quotation from Owen Meredith, which is occasionally used on their menus:

We may live without friends, we may live without books, but civilized man cannot live without cooks.

Sid put an arm around Miriam. "I always tell them that I'm the luckiest guy in the world because my wife and daughter, Wendy Van Deusen, are two of the world's great cooks."

1770 HOUSE, 143 Main St., East Hampton, Long Island, NY 11937; 516-324-1770. A 7-guestroom elegant village inn near the eastern end of Long Island. Open all year. Dinner served Thursday thru Sunday during the summer months. During the off-summer months, dinner served Friday and Saturday only. During July and August weekends, 4-day minimum reservations are required; mid-week, 3-day reservations are required. Convenient to many cultural and recreational diversions, including antiquing and backroading. Not comfortable for children under 14. No pets. The Perle Family, Innkeepers. (See Index for rates.)

Directions: From New York City, take the Long Island Expressway to Exit 70, and then turn south to Rte. 27 East, the main street of East Hampton. The inn is located diagonally across the street from Guild Hall.

THE SHERWOOD INN
Skaneateles, New York (1979)

Skaneateles is the eastern gateway to New York State's scenic Finger Lakes area, and the inn makes an ideal touring center for a stay of several days while visiting the many lakes, nearby vineyards, and other western New York places of interest, such as Ithaca, the home of Cornell University. It is also possible to visit other *CIBR* inns in the area for lunch or dinner.

From time to time I enjoy sharing with my readers letters from the innkeepers of the various *CIBR* inns. Here is one from Ellen Seymour at the Sherwood Inn:

"I'll start with our pumpkin carving contest. A lot of the kiddies in town participated, and the jack-o-lanterns were displayed all over the inn during the Halloween week. Another touch we added for our guests was a big basket of apples in the lobby. We also hosted the Skaneateles Hunt Club Breakfast, doing a full English spread, including such items as trifle, 'bangers' with grilled tomatoes and 'mash,' mock wild boar, lemon curd tartlets, sweet and savory scones, and much, much more.

"Christmas was the best ever! The staff got together and strung popcorn and cranberries, as well as making pomanders, which were used all over the inn. Our big Christmas tree in the lobby was trimmed with papier-mâché Santas and was graced underneath with an antique toy display (some were mine as a kid).

"The old year went out in style with a very elegant menu for our guests that included such items as poached salmon with a tangerine hollandaise and beef Wellington.

"Winter being our slowest season, we all buckle down and plan for the upcoming spring and summer. We did, of course, throw our annual Superbowl party in January, and we hosted the Merchants' Fashion Show with what I dubbed an American tea, featuring coconut bars, white chocolate chunk shortbread, and tea sandwiches.

"Spring started with an Easter Egg Hunt in the park across the street. We supplied hot chocolate because it was a little chilly. And, our best wedding season ever started this April.

"I hosted a venison dinner for a local wine-tasting group, featuring organically raised venison from Robinia Hill Fallow Deer Farm, located at the south end of the lake.

"As I'm writing this, the lake's shore is lit by flares, as it is the Fourth of July weekend in Skaneateles. Today was also the kickoff for Friday night band concerts in the park. Skaneateles will be getting a facelift this fall with all its wiring being placed underground and the addition of new brick sidewalks and old-fashioned benches and lamp posts. The town is sporting a number of new shops, including an all-New-York-State gourmet and crafts shop, a homeware store of gifts from around the world, and a shop dealing exclusively in kites!

"A new fountain was installed in the park across the street. Also across the street is the recently built *Judge Ben Wiles,* a replica of an old lake steamer that used to grace our shores years ago. It now takes guests for dinner cruises every night, weather permitting. Our own boat, *Stephanie,* is going out evenings with cocktail cruises accommodating up to eight people. The last noteworthy item about town is that we have several hot air balloonists hanging around, taking people for rides over the countryside. It's almost become old hat to see the balloons floating over the lake. *National Geographic* included a shot of a hot air balloonist in their edition of *America's Great Hideaways.*

"Many of our guest rooms have a view of the lake, and almost all of them were completely redecorated within the past year. A community open house was held to show off these rooms and over 350 people attended! Skaneateles is certainly proud of its inn."

In reading over Ellen's letter, it looks to me as if the Sherwood Inn has learned how to make a holiday for every month of the year.

THE SHERWOOD INN, 26 West Genessee St., Skaneateles, NY 13152; 315-685-3405. A 17-guestroom (private baths) village inn on the shore of Lake Skaneateles in the Finger Lakes district of New York State. Continental breakfast included in room tariff. Lunch and dinner served daily to travelers. Open every day except Christmas. Tennis, swimming, boating, golf, and indoor winter ice skating available nearby. Near Everson Museum, Barrow Art Gallery, and William Seward House. William Eberhardt, Owner; Ellen Seymour, Innkeeper. (See Index for rates.)

Directions: From N.Y. State Thruway use Weedsport exit and follow Rte. 34 south to Auburn (6 mi.). Turn east on Rte. 20, 7 mi. to Skaneateles. From the south use Rte. 81 to Cortland, then Rte. 41 to Skaneateles, turning left on Rte. 20 for about 1 mi.

SPRINGSIDE INN
Auburn, New York (1971)

Once again the familiar red clapboards of the Springside Inn, with beautiful hanging flowers on the front porch and more hanging flowers on the little lamps flanking the graceful drive that circles the broad lawns, came into view. It occurred to me that with all of these flowers, plus those in the window boxes, in the gardens, and in the various dining rooms, this could be known as "the inn of the flowers."

I had driven across New York State on Route 20, after a short visit with Helen Tobin at the Lincklaen House in Cazenovia and Bill Eberhardt at the Sherwood Inn in Skaneateles. Nearing the center of town, I kept my eye out and turned left on Route 38, proceeding to the traffic circle and then down the west shore of Owasco Lake.

Many years ago when I was about eight years old, my father and mother drove from where we lived in Elmira, New York, to this very spot on the shore of the lake, where there was a wonderful amusement park. What a great day that was to ride the then world-famous roller coaster. The park is no longer in existence, and I must say I really haven't enjoyed roller coasters since.

Bill Dove, who said he had been keeping a weather eye cocked for me, was waiting on the porch and suggested that it would be time to have some "breakfast in a basket" fruit and homemade muffins, offered to every Springside Inn guest as a part of the room rate. "The first person down plugs in the coffee pot," he said with a smile. "Norman, you'd be surprised at how many guests send us thank-you notes for this breakfast."

Springside Inn is in the heart of New York State's Finger Lakes District. I've been visiting it for many years, and each time Bill has some more news for me about activities at the inn.

"My family and I have done a few things to improve the atmosphere and lovely grounds we have here," he told me. "We have installed carpeting throughout all our guest rooms, giving them a sense of warmth and color. We also have followed your suggestion of leaving a couple of rooms open for viewing by our guests.

"One project still tucked away in our minds is a gazebo. This would be ideal not only for wedding ceremonies, but also for entertainment. Our dinner theater, begun at least fifteen years ago, has been increasingly popular every year. The current production is *George M.*

"I'll tell you who's been doing a wonderful job here, and that's Abe Eberhardt, my daughter Missy's husband. He is a real 'jack-of-all-trades' and is a great asset to the inn. He can fix everything from leaky faucets to refrigeration units. During the busy summer months, he works in the kitchen behind the broiler."

Our breakfast completed, we walked inside and up the red-carpeted stairway to the second floor to look at several of the guest rooms. Each of them is decorated to give a different feeling; one is in shades of pink, with a pink bedspread and matching curtains. There are friendly rocking chairs in front of the window overlooking the small pond and the lake beyond. Still another guest room has twin beds, Victorian furniture, and lamps with red bows. By way of contrast, the room on the top floor is done in shades of beige and yellow with formal valances on the windows, a Tiffany-type lamp, hooked rugs, and twin beds.

I noticed that there were small baskets of cheese and Finger Lakes wine in each of the guest rooms.

We wandered into the main dining room, the Surrey Room, and from my first visit I remember the authentic turn-of-the-century lamps that lend a pleasant feminine elegance to what otherwise might be considered a masculine room. By the way, the Sunday brunch and the family dinner, served for many years at the inn, still continue to be real culinary treats.

"You know, Norman, I'm always surprised and happy to see so many of our guests from Canada. Many of them come from Toronto and Montreal, and some have been coming back for years."

SPRINGSIDE INN, 41 West Lake Rd., Auburn, NY 13021; 315-252-7247. An 8-guestroom (some shared baths) country inn, 1 mi. south of Auburn with a view of Owasco Lake, in the heart of the historical Finger Lakes. Lodgings include continental breakfast. Open every day; however, may be closed during the month of Jan. Boating, swimming, bicycling, golf, riding, alpine and xc skiing nearby. The Dove Family, Innkeepers. (See Index for rates.)

Directions: From N.Y Thruway, take Exit 40 and follow Rte. 34 south through downtown Auburn to Rte. 38. Follow Rte. 38 south to traffic circle at lake and take 2nd exit right at west shore of Owasco Lake. Drive ¼ mi. to inn.

THREE VILLAGE INN
Stony Brook, Long Island, New York (1972)

On a fresh August morning, I was sitting in one of the beach chairs under a tree on the terrace in front of my cottage at the Three Village Inn. Seagulls circled over the scene, which included the broad lawn leading down to the marina, with its many sailboats and cruisers, to the marshes beyond and the low cliffs on the northern shore of Long Island in the distance. A friendly robin lighted on the rustic fence and began poking his way through the entangled rambler roses.

The previous afternoon, I had taken the ferry from Bridgeport, Connecticut, to Port Jefferson, Long Island, a trip that took an hour and thirty minutes, and then followed Route 25A through one or two villages, arriving at Stony Brook just about six-thirty in the evening. Once again it was Whitney Roberts, who has literally grown up in this inn, who greeted me with the news that his mother and father, Monda and Nelson, along with his brother, Larry, would be joining me for dinner a little later on.

The Three Village Inn is, at all odds, a Long Island institution and tradition in one of the most interesting and well-preserved towns on Long Island. The Roberts family has a background of innkeeping which began with Whitney's grandfather, who came from Rockland, Maine, and opened a restaurant called "The Maine Maid" in nearby Jericho, Long Island.

Originally, accommodations were found only in the main house of the inn, but since 1971, the year of my first visit, several cottages have been refurbished or built to accommodate guests, some of which face the yacht club and marina. These are furnished with Colonial reproductions, and some have fireplaces. Monda Roberts says that they are quite a favorite with honeymooners.

From my very first visit I realized that Nelson (he's the head chef) and

Monda Roberts have placed great emphasis on the food. They are very particular about some things, including not using foil for baked potatoes, and baking them in rotation through the evening. Vegetables are fresh whenever they are available. The menu is quite extensive and includes a great deal of beef, pork, veal, and lamb, as well as the fresh seafood. The extra touch of serving sherbet with the main meal is something I have always enjoyed. Desserts include such things as apple crisp, homemade cakes, indian pudding, and delicious fruit pies and tarts. They are all made in the inn's kitchen.

In addition to walking along the sandy beach behind the inn and watching the boats from the marina, there are many things to do on the north shore of Long Island, which is rich in Colonial history. There's quite a gathering at twelve o'clock noon each day at the Stony Brook post office where an enormous carved wooden eagle with a twenty-foot wingspread slowly flaps its wings.

"In the off-season we have a lot of people from Manhattan come out for a restful weekend, because everyone is working at such a pace these days," Monda told me. "During the week visitors to SUNY at Stony Brook are frequent guests. By the way, it is possible to come from Kennedy Airport to the Three Village Inn by limousine for a relatively reasonable rate. We can make arrangements." The inn is about sixty miles from New York City.

Nelson and Monda Roberts and their sons have been at the Three Village Inn since 1946, and since 1978 they have been the innkeeper/ owners. It's given me a great deal of pleasure to be visiting it since 1971.

THREE VILLAGE INN, 150 Main St., Stony Brook, L.I., NY 11790; 516-751-0555. A 9-room village inn with 23 adjacent cottage motel accommodations, 5 mi. from Port Jefferson, on Long Island's historic north shore. European plan. Lunch and dinner served to travelers daily. Closed Christmas. Wheelchair access. Near the museums of Stony Brook. Golf, swimming, and boating nearby. Special attention given to handicapped persons. No pets. Nelson and Monda Roberts, Innkeepers. (See Index for rates.)

Directions: From L.I. Expressway, take Exit 62 and travel north on Nichols Rd. to Rte. 25A. Turn left on Rte. 25A and proceed to next light. Turn right onto Main St. and travel straight ahead to inn. Accessible from New England via L.I. ferries from Bridgeport during the summer. Ferry reservations advisable. (N.Y.: 516-473-0286; Conn.: 203-367-8571.)

COLLIGAN'S STOCKTON INN
Stockton, New Jersey (1983)

"Yes, I know that we are very well known as the inn said to have inspired the song 'There's a Small Hotel,' but I think that a great many of our guests are returning because of all of the additional features and attractions that we continually offer throughout the year."

I was talking with Todd Drucquer as we strolled through the many dining rooms and accommodations at Colligan's Stockton Inn. He was—as is his wont—waxing very enthusiastic. "We have a cabaret every Friday in the Garden Room and we have jazz every Saturday in Colligan's Silver Dollar Bar," he said. "On every Sunday we have a brunch that would knock your eyes out. And new this year, Norm, is our jazzy Fox Restaurant."

Coming across the bridge from Pennsylvania to New Jersey, you can see the double gallery of Colligan's Stockton Inn. There are old stones, white pillars, and a mansard roof on the third floor. Evidently, there's been an accommodation here since about 1790, although the present building, or most of it, dates back about 150 years. The stone walls have the wonderful weathered look that comes with Pennsylvania–New Jersey stone.

We passed through the dining room that has the unusual murals that have been there for years. "These were painted on the plaster walls and depict the countryside as it was during the early part of the 19th century," Todd said. "As you see, we have carefully restored some of them. These murals are the very first things that attracted me when I visited for the first time."

I asked him about some of those events that made the inn desirable for revisits. "Well, for one thing we have two-night midweek getaways," he told me. "These have been augmented by the introduction of a 'romantic overnight' as well. We also make special events out of Veteran's Day weekend, Election Day, and the Fourth of July. You know my family, and you know how enthusiastic we are about things that bring families together.

"There's also the antique show and sale at Prall's Mill during August, as well as the New Hope Auto Show. We also have ethnic dining on Fridays throughout the winter months."

By this time we had visited all of the guest rooms, including those in the main inn, the Carriage House, the Wagon House, and the Federal House. Most of the guest rooms are suites with fireplaces, but they are all handsomely furnished and most comfortable.

We ended our stroll in the tavern. "This has been here for the entire life of the inn," Todd said. "It's where the local townspeople come at the end of the day, and we don't want to change it very much because we think it's lovely just the way it is. It belongs to the town, and like an Englishman's pub, it's 'their' place."

There's a good-sized menu at the inn, with at least a dozen entrées. Besides the deviled crabcakes, for which it is famous, there's also rack of lamb and something that I like very much—boneless lacquered duck.

With Bucks County, Pennsylvania, just over the Delaware River, it's no wonder that a great many of the inn guests return to the small hotel with the wishing well.

COLLIGAN'S STOCKTON INN, Route 29, Stockton, NJ 08559; 609-397-1250. An 11-guestroom (mostly suites) traditional inn in a Delaware River village. Lunch and dinner served every day. Open all year except Christmas Day. Weekend minimum 2-night stay; holidays, 3 nights. All of the scenic, historic, and cultural attractions of nearby Bucks County, Pa., and New Jersey are within a very short distance. No pets. Todd and Karen Drucquer, Innkeepers. (See Index for rates.)

Directions: From New York City: Take New Jersey Tpke. south to Exit 10, then follow I-287 north of Somerville, exiting to Rte. 22 west. Go 2½ mi. and then take Rte. 202 south, past Flemington to the Delaware River. Use the last exit in New Jersey, marked "Rte. 29, Lambertville and Stockton." Go 3 mi. north on 29 to Stockton. From Philadelphia: Follow I-95 north to the Delaware River. Cross the Delaware to the first exit in New Jersey, marked "29 Trenton/Lambertville." Follow 29 north through Lambertville, approx. 17 mi. to Stockton.

THE MAINSTAY INN & COTTAGE
Cape May, New Jersey (1976)

"What is Renaissance Revival?" I inquired of Tom and Sue Carroll as we were sitting on the side porch of the Mainstay Inn having a cup of tea in the afternoon.

"It's interesting that you should mention that," remarked Sue, "because our furniture here is almost all Renaissance Revival. It's flowing to the eye with graceful curves. Walnut was used extensively during the 1870s, and there are very tall mirrors, tall headboards and wardrobes. They're a shock compared to things today. I think the fun of staying here is that you are seeing furniture that would probably never go in your house, and it can be very exciting."

While we were chatting, I noticed an occasional horse and carriage clip-clopping by the inn. "Oh, yes," Sue said, "Cape May has regular horse-and-carriage and antique auto tours of the town."

In a community that has gained a great reputation for Victorian restoration and revival, the Mainstay Inn is an outstanding example. It was built in 1856 by wealthy Southern planters as an elegant gambling club. The first operator of the club, a Mississippi showboat minstrel, employed a lady to rock on the front porch, watching for the police. If she rocked violently, the gamblers inside would quickly stash their evidence, and when the police arrived, they would be having a harmless musicale.

Today, the Mainstay is a lovely guest house in one of the most unusual remaining Victorian environments: the town of Cape May, New Jersey. Tom Carroll had pointed out to me that there are over 600 Victorian buildings in Cape May in various stages of restoration and preservation.

The drawing room has Victorian wallpaper, which can be seen in the Bradbury & Bradbury wallpaper catalog and also in some of their advertising. This is a carefully researched, authentic Victorian reproduction.

Tom and Sue have created one of the most dramatic Victorian hallways in the country, with ceiling decorations, stenciling, oriental carpeting with brass rods on the staircase, and gold cording as a rail. They've refinished floors, repaired wood, and found old brass hinges, among other things.

Upstairs, the guest rooms have such dramatic furnishings as ten-foot mirrors, ornately carved headboards, and marble-top dressers. Under some of the beds are chamber pots that roll out on wooden trays, and other beds have the original mosquito nets attached to small pulleys in the ceilings.

The only meal served at the Mainstay is breakfast, offered in warm weather on the broad veranda, and on cool mornings in the Grand Dining Room. The house tour is conducted every day at 3:30 p.m. for both houseguests and interested visitors. Everyone is invited for tea after the tour.

Tom and Sue have renovated the beautiful old house next to the Mainstay, and now provide a total of twelve guest rooms in the two houses. They are all decorated in the Victorian manner and named for famous Americans who visited Cape May.

The lighthouse that Tom worked so hard to preserve has come into full flower now. Guests can tour it for a nominal sum, and it is one of the real landmarks of Cape May.

THE MAINSTAY INN & COTTAGE, 635 Columbia Ave., Cape May, NJ 08204; 609-884-8690. A 12-guestroom inn in a well-preserved Victorian village just one block from the ocean. Breakfast served to houseguests. Open every day from Apr. to Dec. 10. Open in Dec. for Christmas house tours. Boating, swimming, fishing, bicycles, riding, golf, tennis, and hiking nearby. Not suitable for small children. No pets. No credit cards; personal checks accepted. Tom and Sue Carroll, Innkeepers. (See Index for rates.)

Directions: From Philadelphia take the Walt Whitman Bridge to the Atlantic City Expy. Follow the Atlantic City Expy. to exit for Garden State Pkwy., south. Go south on the Pkwy., which ends in Cape May. The Pkwy. becomes Lafayette St.; turn left at first light onto Madison. Proceed 3 blocks and turn right onto Columbia. Proceed 3 blocks to inn on right side.

A number of inns have nearby airports where private airplanes may land. An airplane symbol at the end of the inn directions indicates that there is an airport nearby. Consult inn for further information.

ite Gull Inn,
ish Creek

Stafford's Bay View Inn,
Petoskey

LAKE HURON

● White Lace Inn, *Sturgeon Bay*

LAKE MICHIGAN

MICHIGAN

The National House Inn,
Marshall

DETROIT

Botsford Inn, *Farmington*

LAKE ERIE

Patchwork Quilt,
Middlebury

Wooster Inn, *Wooster*● **CLEVELAND**

OHIO

Welshfield Inn,
Burton

The Inn at Honey Run,
Millersburg

INDIANA

COLUMBUS ■ ●

Buxton Inn, *Granville*

INDIANAPOLIS
■

Golden Lamb, *Lebanon*

■ **CINCINNATI**

THE BUXTON INN
Granville, Ohio (1976)

Ever since I learned about the connection between Granville, Massachusetts, and Granville, Ohio, on my first visit to the Buxton Inn in 1975, I've been fascinated by it. The fact is that Granville in western Massachusetts, just above the Connecticut border, is a very attractive town that happens to be well known in the area for having exceptionally fine cheese.

Granville, Ohio, the home of the Buxton Inn, has been called "Ohio's best kept secret." "It was founded in 1805 by a mass migration from Granby, Connecticut, and Granville, Massachusetts," Orville Orr told me. "The community is laid out like a typical New England village, as you can see, with broad tree-lined streets, a town square where pioneers built four churches, and the Denison University campus."

He continued, "We have over one hundred buildings on the National Register of Historic Places. Most of the businesses are located in the restored downtown area, where three blocks are dominated by the Avery Downer House, which houses the Robbins Hunter Museum, furnished with 18th- and 19th-century American and English furniture, paintings, and decorative accessories."

If I had only one word that might describe the Buxton Inn, it would be "flair." On each of my visits since that now memorable first one, when a very young Amy Orr conducted me on my first tour of the inn and the town, there has been something exciting either accomplished or in the developmental stage. It seems that all of the Orr family, including Audrey, Orville, Amy, and Melanie, have unusual talents that are expressed in the inn.

The Buxton was originally built in 1812, and the Orr family has recreated the atmosphere of an inn of that period, even to the point of having waitresses and hosts and hostesses dressed in carefully researched costumes of the time.

Actually, the inn is a reflection of 175 years of changing styles, with the tastes and fashions of owners and innkeepers of different eras represented in the fabrics and designs. "We tend to collect things from different periods anyway," Audrey told me, "and we've furnished our bedrooms and dining rooms with different themes. Originally, we used period chairs in one of the dining rooms and discovered that they were too small; people were sliding off. So we reluctantly took them out and put in new, larger chairs."

I've always been intrigued by the printed menu at the Buxton Inn, not only because it contains the very interesting history of the inn, but also because it has far more offerings than the average menu, including many varieties of seafood, and such hearty offerings as veal sweetbreads, baby beef liver à l'orange, and Louisiana chicken with artichoke hearts. Be sure to ask about the spareribs with a most marvelous barbecue sauce.

Perhaps it's the atmosphere of a college town that encourages the Orrs to reach out beyond the visible horizon. Many things have been done here over the years I've been visiting. There was the creation of the Wine Cellar and the Tavern downstairs, where the original drivers and settlers would be fed when this was a stagecoach inn after 1812. The gazebo and the fountain, the columns and colonnades in back of the inn, all create a feeling of Roman baths.

The most recent addition is a beautiful dining room, glassed in on three sides and with a glass roof, giving the room a greenhouse feeling. Still more of the nearby homes have been converted into further guest rooms, including the Warner House on the corner.

It is obvious to me that the Orrs are people with dreams and a capacity for inventiveness that has allowed them to continue to turn their dreams into realities—realities that fortunately become wonderful benefits for inn guests at the Buxton.

It's a bit of a distance from Granville, Massachusetts, to Granville, Ohio, but a trip to the Buxton is always a great pleasure for me.

THE BUXTON INN, 313 E. Broadway, Granville, OH 43023; 614-587-0001. A 16-guestroom inn in a college town in central Ohio near Denison University, the Indian Mounds Museum, and the Heisey Glass Museum. European plan. Lunch and dinner served daily. Closed Christmas Day. Golf, tennis, horseback riding, cultural activities nearby. No pets. Orville and Audrey Orr, Innkeepers. (See Index for rates.)

Directions: Take Granville exit from I-70. Travel north 8 mi. on Rte. 37 into Granville.

THE GOLDEN LAMB
Lebanon, Ohio (1970)

Sandra Reynolds and I were seated in the lobby of the Golden Lamb, waiting for Jack Reynolds to finish a telephone call, and then we were all going to walk up the street to the Warren County Museum.

Just to be in this lobby is to partake of a generous helping of the American past. Among other things, there was a lamp, the base of which was made out of a candle mold, and a curly maple table. An old coal stove that was used 100 years or more ago is still in use today. Always on hand is a big punch bowl, where guests and friends may enjoy a modicum of refreshment. There are quite a few examples of Shaker crafts in the lobby and elsewhere in the inn, including Shaker boxes, dowels, chests, and Shaker-style furniture in the dining room.

"The Shakers came to this section of Ohio during the 19th century and attracted buyers from all over the country with their fine farm stock, medicinal herbs, furniture, and other household essentials," explained Sandra. "Their community, Union Village, was sold by them over a half century ago, but we have a lot of local interest in their culture, and the Warren County Museum has a considerable area devoted to Shaker memorabilia."

If Ohio could be called the "mother of presidents," the Golden Lamb might be called the "mother of country inns," because it is a significant force in providing inspiration for many innkeepers to preserve the best of the old, and at the same time to back it up with good innkeeping. Throughout the inn are found artifacts, furniture, and furnishings that have been collected from America's past that in a sense give us a real feeling of appreciation for what our forebears thought was beautiful, useful, and promising.

The building dates back to 1815 and was built on the site of an original log cabin erected by Jonas Seaman, who was granted a license in 1803 to operate "a house of public entertainment." Even before roads were built many guests came on foot or horseback to the inn. Here, in the warmth of the tavern's public rooms, they exchanged news of the world and related their own experiences. Many famous people have stopped here, including ten United States presidents as well as Henry Clay, Mark Twain, and Charles Dickens. Overnight guests may stay in rooms that are named for some of the great and near-great, both national and international, who have enjoyed accommodations here in the past.

Since this lovely old inn is a part of the heartland of America, it stands to reason that the main dishes would be representative of American cooking. There is beef in many forms, rainbow trout, and fried Kentucky ham steak. Roast duckling with wild rice dressing, flounder, Warren County turkey, and pork tenderloin are some of the principal entrées. When possible, vegetables from the nearby verdant Ohio countryside are used.

Each guest room is named for a famous guest and is filled with antiques. When the rooms are not occupied, visitors may stroll through the halls and peek at the collection of chests, wardrobes, tables, and beds.

One of the most rewarding times to visit this inn is during the Christmas holiday season, when it is decorated literally "to the nines." Planning starts in July, with decisions on the theme and the menu. It is also the scene for the Cincinnati Art Club annual show.

THE GOLDEN LAMB INN, 27 S. Broadway, Lebanon, OH 45036; 513-932-5065. A historic 20-guestroom (19 private baths) village inn in the heart of Ohio farming country on U.S. Hwys. 63, 42, and 48. European plan. Complimentary continental breakfast. Lunch and dinner served daily except Christmas. Golf and tennis nearby. No pets. Jackson Reynolds, Innkeeper. (See Index for rates.)

Directions: From I-71, exit Rte. 48N, 3 mi. north to Lebanon. From I 75, exit Rte. 63E, 7 mi. east to Lebanon.

A number of inns have nearby airports where private airplanes may land. An airplane symbol at the end of the inn directions indicates that there is an airport nearby. Consult inn for further information.

THE INN AT HONEY RUN
Millersburg, Ohio (1984)

It was about 6:45 a.m. I was taking a short walk before joining Marjorie Stock for breakfast at the Inn at Honey Run. It was one of those magic times of the day when the moon is still out and the sun is on the rise. In fact, the moon was directly overhead, and the fleecy morning clouds had the wonderful pink, grey, and white tones caught by some of the 18th century French court painters.

In a sense, I guess that Marjorie is like an artist who had an ideal and set out to accomplish it. The Inn at Honey Run was her ideal, and now on this, my third visit, I told her it has come to full fruition.

"Oh, don't say that," she had said the night before. "I have ideas in my head that haven't even been discovered yet, and here at the inn we are always finding more things to do."

Designed to harmonize completely with the rolling countryside and set amidst a stand of maple, ash, oak, poplar, black walnut, butternut, and hickory trees, the inn is a bird watcher's delight. It is multilevel, with many rooms that give the impression of actually dwelling in the forest.

The guest rooms are a potpourri of styles, including Shaker and Early American. The woods used in the guest rooms reflect the trees of the forest. Everything has been made in Ohio, much of it in Holmes County. Many of the woven and quilted wall-hangings are also done by Ohio craftspeople.

My morning walk had taken me to some of the places where I had joined Marjorie the evening before, with even further views of this rolling countryside, which would have delighted Grant Wood or Thomas Hart Benton. My moon, at the quarter, was still brilliant but I could see it was losing out to the sun. Around me the many trees that have been carefully preserved by Marjorie, as well as the shrubs and bushes, which so beautifully augment the architecture of the inn, would be in their full autumn glory in a few short days. I couldn't help but reflect on how patient she has been, waiting for all of these things to come together.

This particular area is also to be the locale for "Honeycombs," which will undoubtedly be featured in our next edition.

My morning walk had stirred my breakfast yearnings, so I headed back to the dining room, where meals are made from scratch and include freshly squeezed orange juice in the morning. In the evening there are such things as pan-fried trout from Holmes County waters, vegetables carefully steamed to perfection, and a menu that is impressive for both its offerings and its reasonable prices.

Marjorie's idea of having "Tuesday Tastings," a buffet of about twenty seven items, has continued to make an impression on the guests, who also provide a continued source of testing to update food.

The newest thing this year is the "Raid the Kitchen" Sunday supper. All the tables are pushed together in the kitchen and guests help themselves from trays of cold meats, local cheeses, salads, fresh fruit, soup, and any leftover desserts. Everybody has a lot of fun.

I walked through the main lobby with its massive chimney fireplace and stepped for a second out on one of the many decks, which seem literally to thrust themselves into the forest. Here, looking toward the eastern sky, I saw that the sun had made its full appearance, and the hues and tones of early fall could now be more easily distinguished.

The Inn at Honey Run is not a quaint, old-fashioned country inn. It is a bold, modern concept that might well be setting the pace for future inns. Instead of reproducing an old inn, Marjorie Stock has built a contemporary inn that makes its own statement, and this statement will be telling something to the inn-goers of 100 years from now about what was contemporary in the 1980s and 1990s.

THE INN AT HONEY RUN, 6920 County Road 203, Millersburg, OH 44654; 216-674-0011. A 25-guestroom country inn located in north-central Ohio's beautiful, wooded countryside. Breakfast included in room rate. Lunch and dinner served Mon. thru Sat. Advance reservations only. Sun. breakfast and eve. buffet served to houseguests only. Closed Jan. 1 to 15. Wheelchair access. Ample opportunities for recreation and backroading in Ohio's Amish country. No facilities for small children. No pets. Marjorie Stock, Innkeeper. (See Index for rates.)

Directions: From Millersburg, proceed on E. Jackson St. (Rtes. 39 and 62) past courthouse and gas station on right. At next corner turn left onto Rte. 241. At 1 mi. the road goes downhill. At 1³/₄ mi. it crosses the bridge over Honey Run; turn right immediately around the small hill onto Rte. 203 (not well marked). After about 1¹/₂ mi. turn right at inn sign. (Watch out for the Amish horse-drawn buggies.)

WELSHFIELD INN
Burton, Ohio (1973)

I was standing in the kitchen at the Welshfield Inn talking with owner-chef Brian Holmes about two things very near to his heart. One was the preparation of baked and mashed potatoes, and the other was his philosophy of keeping a restaurant.

"Norman, when I bake potatoes I believe in having the skin clean enough to eat; I like to eat the skin myself, especially because it contains so many minerals. First we scrub the potatoes thoroughly and put shortening or oil on them. We put them in the oven at about 400° to 425° and after they've been in the oven for an hour and a quarter they should be ready—I test the doneness by inserting a fine-tine fork.

"We're known far and wide for our whipped Idaho potatoes. We whip them in an electric mixer which puts more air into them and makes them much whiter. These are also made in small batches so they're fresh. One of the secrets of good food is preparing in small quantities. I learned that from an old-time restaurant man."

I've been visiting the Welshfield since the late 1960s. Skillet-fried chicken, baked ham, fresh fillet of sole, salmon, and apple pie are some of the specialties. Brian says, "We never use mixes. Our rolls and bread are made from scratch." This is a real country restaurant with real country cooking.

A raisin sauce for the baked ham was bubbling on the stove and the wonderful aroma of apple pies already in the oven filled the kitchen. There were pans with baked acorn squash, stuffed zucchini, and the makings of fresh strawberry shortcake. "Our recipe for indian pudding came from Cape Cod," Brian said. "We took it as a compliment when one of our customers said it tasted exactly like the pudding at the Red Inn at Provincetown."

One of the waitresses, dressed in an attractive early American costume complete with a white duster cap, carried a tray of fresh rolls into the dining room.

We took a few minutes to walk through the many dining rooms and I even stopped to drop a coin in the famous nickelodeon. "I hope you've had a chance to visit our Country Store," he said. "It's expanding all the time and Polly is very much involved with that."

The Welshfield Inn is about thirty miles from Cleveland and is extremely well known in the area as *the* place to go for Easter, Mother's Day, Thanksgiving, and Christmas. On the day of my visit a great number of families were dining at tables of eight and ten.

Brian paused long enough at the front door to bid me goodbye and he had a final thought for me:

"I'm known for being fussy and particular," he said. "I believe if you're in the restaurant business, the main thing in that business is *food*. Food preparation and serving of food are most important, and Polly and I feel that nothing is too good for our customers. I'm happy to say that we seem to be able to please more people every year, and a great many of them arrive with your book tucked underneath their arms. You've extended your territory since your first visit in 1972 and we're even more pleased than ever to be included."

Brian, it is we who are proud to have you.

WELSHFIELD INN, Rte. 422, Burton, OH 44021; 216-834-4164. A country restaurant on Rte. 422, 28 mi. east of Cleveland. No lodgings. Lunch and dinner served weekdays. Dinner only served on Sundays and holidays. Closed the week of July 4th and three weeks after Jan. 1. Closed Mondays except Labor Day. Near Sea World and Holden Arboretum. Brian and Polly Holmes, Innkeepers. (See Index for rates.)

Directions: On U.S. 422 at intersection of Ohio 700, midway between Cleveland and Youngstown, Ohio.

"European plan" means that rates for rooms and meals are separate. "American plan" means that meals are included in the cost of the room. "Modified American plan" means that breakfast and dinner are included in the cost of the room. The rates at some inns include a continental breakfast with the lodging.

WOOSTER INN
Wooster, Ohio (1988)

The soccer ball came toward me in an arc, and for just a moment I thought perhaps I was back at college again myself. There was a fair-sized crowd for this soccer game at Wooster College, where some co-eds stood on the edge of the field. In the near distance the Gothic buildings were somewhat reminiscent of my college in central Pennsylvania.

Meanwhile, the ball hit the ground right in front of me. I considered all the possibilities and then gave the ball a sort of half-hearted kick that returned it to the referee.

It was early fall and the rolling countryside between Akron and Millersburg had beautiful tints and hues of autumn. The cornfields were fallow in their own shades of beige, and the roads across the Ohio countryside followed the contours of the land, where cattle peacefully grazed and occasional small villages gave me the unmistakable feeling of being in America's heartland. The town of Wooster is actually the hub for many highways leading off in all directions.

I had arrived a bit earlier than anticipated, and Willy Bergmann, the manager of the Wooster Inn, suggested that since there was going to be a soccer game I might get a kick out of it, little knowing the accuracy of his prediction.

The Wooster Inn, which offers full services, reflects a great deal of the town-and-gown spirit with its furnishings and location right on the edge of the campus. During the college year the cultural events on the campus, such as lectures, concerts, plays, and art exhibits, are open to the public, and of course that includes the inn guests. During the summer the Ohio Light Opera performs several productions in the college theater. There are also various types of athletic events, providing an interesting diversion for the pleasure of business travelers who might find themselves in Wooster.

The architecture of the inn has generous amounts of what I guess is American Georgian, and it fits very well with the campus buildings. One of its attractive aspects is its view of the college golf course, which is open to guests throughout the year. All-weather tennis courts are also nearby.

The newly decorated lobby is most attractive, with comfortable chairs and tables arranged in conversational groupings, where guests who are waiting to be called to dinner or perhaps waiting for someone to join them can take in this collegiate atmosphere.

The dining room is straight off the lobby, and the big bay windows have a splendid view of the rolling golf course. The tables are set with crisp white tablecloths, fresh flowers, and candles. I asked Willy Bergman to tell me about some of the main dishes on the menu. "We are well known for serving fresh rainbow trout," he said. "Our guests also enjoy veal scallopini Dijon. I guess our tastes out here represent the Midwest because our pork chops basted with honey are very popular. The students also like the fettucini with scallops and shrimp." Those are just a few of the over sixteen items on the dinner menu. That night I had a most enjoyable dinner with Willy and found the pork chops basted with honey much to my taste. I decided to try them at home at the next opportunity. Breakfast features such specialties as pecan waffles, and there is a wide selection on the luncheon menu.

Guest rooms at the inn have been very tastefully furnished. All or most of them have views of the golf course, the soccer field, or the nearby residences. There certainly was no disturbing noise during the evening.

As we were finishing off the dessert, Willy said, with a twinkle in his eye, "I happened to be looking out the window of my office when that soccer ball landed in front of you, and I wondered why you didn't give it a good healthy kick."

"Well, to tell you the truth, soccer never was my game."

THE WOOSTER INN, Wayne Ave. and Gasche St., Wooster, OH 44691; 216-264-2341. A 14-guestroom (private baths) pleasant inn on the campus of the College of Wooster, about 60 mi. southwest of Cleveland. Air conditioning, telephone, and TV in room. Breakfast included in room rate. Breakfast, lunch, and dinner served every day. Open year-round. Convenient to all of the college cultural and athletic events. Golf and tennis nearby. Willy J. Bergmann, Innkeeper. (See Index for rates.)

Directions: Wooster is the hub of U.S. Rtes. 30 and 250 and Ohio Rtes. 3, 585, and 83. Locate the college and then ask for directions to the inn.

The date in parenthesis in the heading represents the first year the inn appeared in the pages of Country Inns and Back Roads.

PATCHWORK QUILT COUNTRY INN
Middlebury, Indiana (1971)

The news here is that a new owner-innkeeper has taken over. Arletta and Milton Lovejoy have retired and turned over the inn to their daughter, Michele Goebel.

Almost every year since 1970 there has been special news from the Patchwork Quilt. I say 1970, because that was the year I first visited the Patchwork Quilt and met Arletta and Milton Lovejoy and Treva and Herb Swarm. First, a word of explanation:

The Patchwork Quilt is a real working farm in the rich agricultural area of northern Indiana, and has been in the Lovejoy family for over a hundred years. Five-course farm-style dinners are served in the large farmhouse in the center of the 260 acres.

In recent years the inn has offered bed-and-breakfast accommodations for overnight guests in three double guest rooms with shared bathrooms. However, thanks to some very cooperative local people, there are many more guest rooms available nearby for Patchwork Quilt guests.

For many years the excellent reputation of the Patchwork Quilt came from the truly munificent evening meals, which include a zesty home-made soup or chilled fruit appetizer and a trip to the buffet that is loaded with many more salads than I could possibly mention here. The main course might include such offerings as herbed roast beef, open-hearth baked ham, burgundy steak, or Arletta's great prizewinning buttermilk-pecan chicken. The main course is accompanied by a vegetable, potatoes, hot homemade rolls and jams, and coffee or tea.

I always recommend that, if possible, dinner guests save room for one of the fantastic desserts—coffee-toffee pie, three-layer German chocolate cake, lemon meringue pie, old-fashioned custard pie . . . ad infinitum.

Among the many services that have been offered by this farmhouse–country inn is the Back Road Adventure package, which includes a four-hour back road tour through the Amish country, lunch, a five-course dinner, and overnight bed-and-breakfast.

Over the years the Patchwork Quilt has received much recognition in national magazines. Articles and stories have appeared in many different media. I guess the first real recognition came just about the time of my very first visit, when Arletta's famous pecan chicken recipe (still on the menu) won a national award.

I have known Michele Goebel since she was a little girl and I know that her mother's accomplishments have been a great inspiration to her. "I am proud to follow in her footsteps," she says. Although Michele is full of plans and has already been busily refurbishing and redecorating the guest rooms and dining rooms, she says "we haven't changed Mom's great recipes." That is good news, indeed.

We send our warmest regards to Arletta and Milton, and very best wishes to Michele in her new endeavor.

PATCHWORK QUILT COUNTRY INN, 11748 C.R. 2, Middlebury, IN 46540; 219-825-2417. A 3-guestroom working farm restaurant and bed-and-breakfast inn about 20 mi. east of Elkhart. Dinner served by reservation only. Guest rooms available Tues. thru Sat. Rates include continental breakfast. Closed Sun., Mon., Thanksgiving, Christmas, and New Year's. Wheelchair access. No smoking. Michele Goebel, Innkeeper. (See Index for rates.)

Directions: From east or west, exit Indiana Toll Rd. at Middlebury (Exit 107) and go north ¼ mi. to Country Rd. 2 and proceed west 1 mi. to inn. From Middlebury, follow Indiana Rte. 13 for 8 mi. north to Country Rd. 2 and west 1 mi.

"European plan" means that rates for rooms and meals are separate. "American plan" means that meals are included in the cost of the room. "Modified American plan" means that breakfast and dinner are included in the cost of the room. The rates at some inns include a continental breakfast with the lodging.

SEVEN GABLES INN
Clayton, Missouri (1988)

Looking every bit as if it had been spirited away from a 17th-century European town and set down in the middle of high-rise buildings in downtown Clayton, on the outskirts of St. Louis, the Seven Gables Inn is truly, as its innkeeper-chef, Bernard Douteau, says, "a country hotel in a small city."

The original builders were influenced by England's Tudor architecture and also by Hawthorne's famed novel, *The House of Seven Gables,* so I guess it was inevitable that they built a half-timbered Tudor-style building with seven gables. In 1926 the rambling three-story building was intended as apartments with ground floor offices and shops. Today it has been turned into a small European-style hotel.

In addition to being listed on the Register of Historic Places, Seven Gables has also been awarded membership in the prestigious Relais et Chateaux, which has brought a number of European visitors to the inn.

The day I visited, Bernard was dressed in his chef's whites and although he had lots to do in the kitchen he took time out for a chat. We were standing in the lobby, which is actually a very wide hallway with whitewashed plaster walls and a tile floor. "This was originally an open walkway between the two wings of the building," Bernard said, with a slight French accent. "As you probably noticed, there are all sorts of interesting architectural features—gables, nooks, crannies, and jogs in the walls, and we did not want to lose any of that special character."

I think they've done a great job. The entrance hall has some nice paintings and a few pieces of antique furniture along its length, including a spinet piano, and at the end there is a very pleasant sitting area with chairs grouped around a table. Tall bay windows look out on a garden courtyard, which is enclosed by a high white latticework fence. "They thought that the old mulberry tree in the courtyard would not survive, but it is doing very well and it adds a beautiful presence," he said.

The garden courtyard, with its brick flooring, European street lamps, white garden tables and chairs, and all the plantings, is certainly a most attractive place. "This is really one of the focal points of Seven Gables," he said. "Of course, outside dining is very European and being a Frenchman, I feel this is a very typical touch."

He explained that there were guest rooms overlooking the courtyard, and these are called Garden Court rooms; others are called Gables rooms and, being under the gables, they come in a variety of sizes and shapes. All of the guest rooms are decorated differently with furnishings imported from France, and they are all equipped with color cable television and the very latest in telephones, along with a number of other amenities.

Bernard's abiding interest lies, naturally enough for a chef, with his two restaurants. "I would say Bernard's is a café or bistro like you would have in Paris, a kind of intellectual gathering place," he told me. "All the art work on the walls and the comfort and simplicity make everyone feel at ease." Bernard's serves a varied menu. "We do everything ourselves," Bernard declared, "our own doughs, our breads, all our pastries."

Chez Louis is more formal, with crystal and silver table settings and a decidedly French cuisine. For my dinner I decided on an appetizer of broiled goat cheese with rice vinegar and lime-orange jicama, a main course of goose, lightly spiced and smoke grilled to crisp the skin, served in a shallot and elephant garlic confit and Pernod. They were both incredibly delicious. Dessert was called La Gavroche de Chocolat à la Crème Anglaise, and describing it requires some kind of divine language that I don't have. As Margaret, our lovely hostess, said, "You come to Chez Louis to enjoy a wonderful meal and for the very special service we give you." I agree.

I could see that other guests were enjoying their stay, and I think you will, too.

I am happy to welcome Seven Gables Inn to the pages of *Country Inns and Back Roads* for the first time.

SEVEN GABLES INN, 26 No. Meramec Ave., Clayton, MO 63105; 314-863-8400. A 32-guestroom European-style hotel with two restaurants in a small city, the administrative center of St. Louis County. Breakfast, lunch, and dinner served to the public. Open year-round. Within 15 min. of downtown St. Louis, with all the cultural and recreational attractions, including Missouri's famous botanical gardens, and shopping or business matters. Children over 10 welcome. No pets. Bernard Douteau, Innkeeper. (See Index for rates.)

Directions: From I-70, turn south on I-170 and continue to Clayton.

THE ST. JAMES HOTEL
Red Wing, Minnesota (1981)

The original St. James Hotel was built in the mid-1870s and according to the history of the hotel, was a very impressively designed and decorated building with various reception rooms, parlors, and a large ballroom, and was well known for its excellent food and service.

However, even at the top of its form it could not begin to approach today's *restored* St. James Hotel.

The entire project is a tribute to the fact that American ingenuity, capital, and know-how are able to reproduce successfully almost every type of furniture, ornamentation, decoration, and design of a hundred years ago, and still maintain the very best quality.

Almost all the furnishings in the St. James are copies of lamps, bureaus, tables, chairs, beds, and carpets originally manufactured during the Victoran era. All of this furniture is solid, well made, and sturdy, and doesn't have the rickety feeling that sometimes occurs. Even the small details have been considered, including brass soap holders, towel racks, doorknobs, hinges, and the like.

The hotel is a modern accommodation of today, but serves as a reminder of opulent days gone by. In addition to excellent reproductions, the photographs and prints taken in a bygone era are further reminders of the past. Many of the walls are hung with pictures of Red Wing, taken over a hundred years ago, both of the town and of the river steamers that made the town a regular stop.

What excites me most is that this small hotel in the heart of America could have been torn down and gone the way of so many others, but instead, it is making a contribution that bids fair to endure for at least another hundred years.

Turn-down bed service and the morning newspaper at the door are a couple of the niceties that add to the pleasure of a visit to the St. James. Bed linens and towels are of first-rate quality and the quilts for each bed were especially designed and made to harmonize with the furnishings and colors of the room. Many of the rooms look out upon the Mississippi River, where the unending flow of barges provides constant entertainment. An excursion boat is available for guests who would like a closer look at the river.

The Amtrak station is just across the street from the St. James and many of the guests arrive in this most convenient fashion.

The lobby of the old original hotel has been restored, but it is not used as the lobby of today's St. James. Instead, it has been set aside for parties, banquets, and special occasions. Photographs of the original 1870s investors, who put up all of $60,000, look down upon today's travelers with a certain undisguised smugness.

A most unusual and fascinating history of the old St. James Hotel, recounted in the words of staff members who worked there in the earlier years of this century, has been compiled with great attention and loving care. Entitled *If Walls Could Talk,* the booklet has some wonderful photographs ranging from 1875 to 1980, and provides an interesting glimpse not only into the workings of a hotel, but also of life in days gone by.

The new-old St. James, always a familiar landmark in Red Wing, has made even greater strides in the 1980s.

ST. JAMES HOTEL, 406 Main St., Red Wing, MN 55066; 612-388-2846. A 60-guestroom restored country town hotel on the Mississippi River, 50 mi. from Minneapolis. Open all year. Breakfast, lunch, and dinner served to travelers. Wheelchair access. This is an in-town hotel with no sports or recreation on the grounds, but swimming, tennis, hiking, golf, bicycling, backroading, and river sightseeing trips are all very convenient. No pets. Gene Foster, General Manager. (See Index for rates.)

Directions: From Minneapolis/St. Paul Airport take Hwy. 5 east, exit on Hwy. 55 to cross Mendota Bridge. Follow Hwy. 55 to Hastings where it joins Hwy. 61. Follow Hwy. 61, 22 mi. south into Red Wing. Accessible by Amtrak. ▄▄◣

A number of inns have nearby airports where private airplanes may land. An airplane symbol at the end of the inn directions indicates that there is an airport nearby. Consult inn for further information.

SCHUMACHER'S NEW PRAGUE HOTEL
New Prague, Minnesota (1979)

John Schumacher, who is one of the most energetic and cheerful people I've ever met, was telling me about some of the main courses at his inn. "Our game menu includes pheasant, quail, venison, and rabbit served in various ways. In addition, there is a full poultry menu, lots of fish and seafood, some Czech dishes, including sausages, and several veal dishes. As a matter of fact, I think there are about fifty-six main offerings on the menu.

"There's a special 'healthy heart cuisine' menu for people who are so inclined and also a menu for lighter appetites, including sauerbrauten sandwiches. Of course, desserts like apple strudel, torte, and cheesecake will cancel out all of your good intentions."

John is a very innovative chef, having graduated at the top of his class from the Culinary Institute of America. He and Kathleen are young innkeepers who gain great satisfaction and personal fulfillment in running a country inn. As he says, "It's been a wonderful experience since I first came to New Prague, and right from the start there were many things that had to be done, but it's been a highly satisfactory arrangement. Fortunately, I'm a chef and I feel that a great deal of our reputation centers around the fact that the food is something that I can control."

The building for Schumacher's New Prague Hotel was built in 1898 and originally was called the Broz Hotel. It was designed by Cass Gilbert, the same man who designed the George Washington Bridge, the Supreme Court building in Washington, and the State Capitol in Saint Paul.

If the menu and the food are impressive, then the inn's guest rooms are equally so. Each is named for a different month and has an atmosphere and personality all its own. For example, "January" has "three-bear beds"—two beds put together to make a king-sized bed. Many of the guest rooms have a folk art theme; however, "April" departs and features an antique Victorian three-piece settee and a king-sized custom round bed with a mirrored headboard.

There's a high canopied bed in "May," and the mustard-colored walls are decorated with white Bavarian daisies. "October" is in a deep mulberry, accentuated by painted pink chrysanthemums. (Now that I've got all those names straight, John tells me they are thinking of changing them.)

"We've been to Europe several times," John pointed out, "and I believe the decorations and cuisine here reflect my identification with Germany and Czechoslovakia. We have imported cotton-covered goose-down comforters and pillows, and there are many central-European decorative touches, such as wood carvings and stenciled paintings.

"Some rooms have television, and they all have telephones, plants, and magazines, and we even put candy under the pillows."

New Prague is just thirty-five miles south of the Minneapolis/Saint Paul metropolitan area, and besides the fun of staying at Schumacher's, there is a surprising number of things to do nearby, including golf and tennis. Cross-country skiing is twenty minutes away, and there are a number of lakes within a thirty-minute drive. The Minnesota River is just nine miles away and is ideal for canoeing. The area is excellent for biking as well as running.

SCHUMACHER'S NEW PRAGUE HOTEL, 212 West Main St., New Prague, MN 56071; 612-758-2133. (Metro line: 612-445-7285.) A 12-guestroom (private baths) Czechoslovakian-German inn located in a small country town, approx. 35 mi. south of Minneapolis and St. Paul. European plan. Breakfast, lunch, and dinner served to travelers all year except 2 days at Christmas. Wheelchair access to restaurant. Good bicycling and backroading nearby; also xc skiing, tennis, and golf, No entertainment available to amuse children. No pets. Kathleen and John Schumacher, Innkeepers. (See Index for rates.)

Directions: From Minneapolis, take Rte. 494 west to Rte. 169 south to Jordan exit. Turn south on Rte. 21 for 9 mi. to New Prague. Turn left to Main St. at the stop sign, and the hotel is in the second block on the right.

"European plan" means that rates for rooms and meals are separate. "American plan" means that meals are included in the cost of the room. "Modified American plan" means that breakfast and dinner are included in the cost of the room. The rates at some inns include a continental breakfast with the lodging.

OLD RITTENHOUSE INN
Bayfield, Wisconsin (1980)

"Jerry was still working on his music degree at the University of Wisconsin, and I had just gotten a teaching job. We came to Bayfield on our honeymoon in 1969, and as soon as we saw this lovely old house we fell in love with it."

At first I thought Mary Phillips was speaking of the present building that houses the Old Rittenhouse Inn, but I soon realized she was really speaking of what was known for many years in Bayfield as "The Mansion."

"In 1973, we came back on a visit and noticed *this* house and wondered how we could have missed it on previous visits. We bought it for a song, and it's been our expanding home ever since." The Old Rittenhouse Inn is a Queen Anne-style mansion with an unusually wide veranda, decorated with hanging flowers and wicker furniture.

The sequel to this interesting episode is that the Phillipses did eventually buy the Mansion and have done it over with the aid of their partner, Greg Carrier. It has been renamed Le Chateau Boutin, and it is now a part of the Old Rittenhouse Inn.

There have been exciting things happening here ever since my first visit in 1979. These two musician-innkeepers have refused from the very start to accept the idea that Bayfield was simply a summertime resort area. They began by staging Christmas and Valentine's Day dinner concerts at the inn, and these developed into many more activities. The success of their programs made it necessary to expand, and so today the original five guest rooms have been augmented with another ten, and Mary finally has a full and proper kitchen.

Antiques being one of Jerry's sidelines, each of the guest rooms has been handsomely outfitted with antique furniture, and a few of them have their own fireplaces.

It may be that Jerry and Mary are best known for their dinners. Jerry, resplendent in a Victorian tailcoat, describes the menu to his dinner guests, and it is also given in detail by the waitress later on. The fixed-price dinners start with several soups and a variety of entrées, including Lake Superior trout cooked in champagne, lamb, seafood crêpes, scallops, or chicken Cordon Bleu. The breads and preserves are all home-made. Their gourmet foods are also on sale at the inn and through a mail-order business that includes jams, jellies, marmalades, candies, fruit cakes, and many other delicious gifts.

The Phillipses have prepared a splendid new brochure entitled "The Old Rittenhouse Inn: An Innside Outlook." My copy lists every special event, seminar, festival, workshop, concert, and island adventure that can be enjoyed in Bayfield or on nearby Madeline Island throughout the entire year. Just to give you a quick idea, there's a quilters' retreat in June, the Christmas Dinner Concerts in December, ski touring under the auspices of the Audubon Society, and summer-day sails galore. The brochure continues with two cooking workshops, Valentine Sweetheart specials, two Murder-at-the-Mansion Mystery Weekends, a Bed and Breakfast Workshop in February, and, of course, the famous Apple Festival in October. The Phillipses will be glad to send you your copy.

It has certainly been a pleasure for me to visit and revisit the Old Rittenhouse Inn and enjoy good fun, good eating, and wonderful hospitality.

OLD RITTENHOUSE INN, Box 584, 301 Rittenhouse Ave., Bayfield, WI 54818; 715-779-5765. An 18-guestroom Victorian inn in an area of historic and natural beauty, 70 mi. east of Duluth, Minn., on the shore of Lake Superior. European plan. Breakfast, lunch, and dinner served to travelers. Open May 1 to Nov. 1; weekends through the winter. Advance reservations most desirable. Extensive recreational activity of all kinds available throughout the year, including tours, hiking, and cycling on the nearby Apostle and Madeline Islands. Not comfortable for small children. No pets. Jerry and Mary Phillips, Innkeepers. (See Index for rates.)

Directions: From the Duluth Airport, follow Rte. 53-S through the city of Duluth over the bridge to Superior, Wis. Turn east on Rte. 2 near Ashland (1½ hrs.), turn north on 13-N to Bayfield.

SEVEN PINES LODGE
Lewis, Wisconsin (1981)

I parked my car among the tall pine trees and immediately became aware of the sounds of the woods—a combination of water, birds, and wind. The front door of the lodge opened and out scampered a beautiful little golden Labrador retriever, and to the forest sounds were added the delighted and welcoming squeals of what Joan Simpson refers to as "our official greeter."

Joan, Moses the Labrador, and Rascal (the inn's rent-a-cat) are the innkeepers, with help from her children, Tina and John, during school breaks. This rustic hideaway in a natural setting on fifty-two acres was built in 1903 by Charles Lewis, a grain broker and financier from Minneapolis. Constructed of handhewn logs, the lodge has retained its original appeal and surprising elegance, including an array of interesting antiques that are an integral part of the decor. Ninety percent of the furniture and decorations have been here since Mr. Lewis's time. It is now listed on the National Register of Historic Places.

Immediately upon my arrival I took a pleasant stroll with Joan, scuffing through the dried leaves to the trout stream, and we passed through a grove of original pine trees, some of which are 115 feet high. Passing over a rustic bridge beside a melodious waterfall, we entered an almost pagodalike, two-story building with a full screened porch around four sides of the second floor. This is a summer sleeping porch, and I can just imagine the good times enjoyed here by families.

We followed the stream a short distance and came to a sylvan pool with a stone statue of a young Indian boy. As we were drinking in the quiet loveliness of the scene, Joan pointed to a finny denizen and said, "There goes a dinner." She explained that the brownies, rainbows, and brook trout, all of which are raised on the property, often appear on the menu. Joan does all the cooking.

Guests frequently sit at the kitchen table while she prepares the Scandinavian bread, desserts, trout dinners, and the hearty meals that are welcomed by guests, who usually have spent most of the day outdoors, whether it be summer or winter. "When guests make reservations they are given a choice of one of three main dishes, although most returning guests like the trout."

Accommodations at Seven Pines Lodge are in the main building, where there are five year-round bedrooms, and also in log outbuildings, used only during temperate weather. These have a real "woodsy" feeling.

That evening I joined the other guests around the dinner table, and then we all adjourned to the friendly confines of the living room, where there is a big oval table with an overhead lamp that provides convenient lighting by which to enjoy albums of fascinating photographs of the lodge as it was in earlier times. Some *Portland Oregonian* newspapers for 1922 provided us all with a good deal of entertainment and laughs.

Joan and a friend had done a wildflower study that catalogued 181 different wildflowers. The fly fishermen oohed and aahed over the brand new fly display case with beautiful specimens tied by David Crooks. And so the evening passed quite pleasantly in the big rustic living room, where there is no television. There is only one telephone in the lodge. There's nothing to disturb the peace and serenity at Seven Pines Lodge.

SEVEN PINES LODGE, Lewis, WI 54851; 715-653-2323. A 10-guest-room rustic resort-inn (some rooms have shared baths) in the Wisconsin woods about 1½ hrs. from Minneapolis. Open year-round. Closed Thanksgiving and Christmas Day. Trout fishing on grounds. St. Croix Falls, Taylors Falls, National Wild River Scenic Waterway nearby. Tennis, swimming, golf, woodswalking, xc, downhill skiing, backroading nearby. Very attractive for children of all ages since the innkeeper also has children. No pets. No credit cards. Joan Simpson, Innkeeper. (See Index for rates.)

Directions: From Minneapolis/St. Paul: follow 135W or 135E north to U.S. 8 at Forest Lake, Minn. East on U.S. 8 through Taylors Falls, Minn./ St. Croix Falls, Wisc., to Wisc. 35 north to Lewis. Turn right at gas station to T, right 1 mi. to fork in road and turn left ½ mi. to Seven Pines Lodge entrance.

THE WHITE GULL INN
Fish Creek, Wisconsin (1979)

This is actually going to be a tale of not one inn, but two inns. One is the White Gull Inn, where I have been visiting Jan and Andy Coulson and their two daughters, Meredith and Emilie Lindsley, for quite a few years. The other inn is the Whistling Swan, which the Coulsons purchased and have remodeled and redecorated. Both inns are located in the heart of Fish Creek's historic section.

The White Gull is a full-service inn, built as part of a large resort area more than seventy-five years ago, when hundreds of tourists would arrive in Fish Creek from Chicago and Milwaukee aboard steamships. Nowadays, guests drive or fly to Fish Creek because the beautiful waterfront, the main street, and the sparkling atmosphere have remained unchanged.

The main inn is a white clapboard, three-story building with an air of informality. The rooms, which have been increasing in numbers over recent years, are tidy and neat, and have been undergoing a steady redecorating program.

In the Midwest, the White Gull is justifiably famous for its traditional Fish Boils, featuring freshly caught lake fish, boiled potatoes, homemade cole slaw, fresh-baked bread, and cherry pie. Russ Ostrand has been the master boiler for over twenty years. He prepares a roaring fire, and the fish are boiled in two huge iron cauldrons. He also plays the accordion and leads everybody in lots of singing and clapping of hands.

Besides the Fish Boils, the White Gull also has a more familiar evening menu.

The Whistling Swan, a bed and breakfast inn, has four bedrooms and three suites with antique beds and dressers, comfortable reading chairs and reading lights, carpeting and wallpaper that matches the fabrics. Most of the bathrooms have the original meticulously reglazed tubs, pedestal sinks, and brass fixtures.

A continental breakfast featuring fresh-squeezed orange juice and freshly baked pastry is served in the summer on the huge veranda, and guests take their ease in wicker chairs and rockers. Wintertime guests have a full breakfast at the White Gull, and dinners are taken at the White Gull by Whistling Swan guests, if desired.

Jan and Andy have also opened two shops in the Whistling Swan, one of which sells unusual gift items plus a distinctive line of women's and children's clothing, elegantly displayed in antique armoires and dressers, and the other features more masculine items and gifts for men.

And so Jan and Andy and Joan Holliday and Nancy Vaughn and the remainder of the staff at the White Gull and the Whistling Swan continue to make progress in some respect with each passing year. I'm sure it won't be long before Meredith, ten years old, and Emilie Lindsley, four and a half, will be taking over some of the innkeeping duties themselves.

Door County is a wonderful place to visit in any season of the year and, thanks to the presence of two fine inns, it's a great place for a holiday.

THE WHITE GULL INN, Fish Creek, WI 54212; 414-868-3517. A 14-guestroom inn with 4 cottages (private and shared baths) and additional guestrooms in the Whistling Swan in a most scenic area in Door County, 23 mi. north of Sturgeon Bay. (Bookings for the Whistling Swan: P.O. Box 193; 414-868-3442.) Open year-round. European plan. Breakfast, lunch, and dinner except Thanksgiving and Christmas. Fish Boils: Wed., Fri., Sat., Sun. nights May thru Oct.; Wed. and Sat. nights Nov. thru April. All meals open to travelers; reservations requested. Wheelchair access to restaurant. Considerable outdoor and cultural attractions; golf, tennis, swimming, fishing, biking, sailing, xc skiing, and other summer and winter sports nearby. Excellent for children of all ages. No pets. Andy and Jan Coulson, Joan Holliday, and Nancy Vaughn, Innkeepers. (See Index for rates.)

Directions: From Chicago: take I-94 to Milwaukee. Follow Rte. I-43 from Milwaukee to Manitowoc; Rte. 42 from Manitowoc to Fish Creek. Turn left at stop sign at the bottom of the hill, go 2½ blocks to inn. From Green Bay; take Rte. 57 to Sturgeon Bay; Rte. 42 to Fish Creek. ◣

The date in parenthesis in the heading represents the first year the inn appeared in the pages of Country Inns and Back Roads.

WHITE LACE INN
Sturgeon Bay, Wisconsin (1988)

The first time I visited Dennis and Bonnie Statz at the White Lace Inn a number of years ago, I was doing some research for one of my other books, *Bed and Breakfast, American Style.*

At that time Dennis was working on the Garden House in the rear of the Main House, and we had a long talk about his plans for the garden area.

Since then not only is the Garden House a *fait accompli,* with fireplaces in the six guest rooms, but all the wonderful things associated with its name have actually come true, with myriad flowers everywhere.

So now, with the Garden House and another more recent addition, the luxurious Washburn House, the White Lace Inn offers fifteen guest rooms in three historic Victorian houses. Each room has period wallcoverings, floral print fabrics in roses, peaches, and earth tones, polished hardwood floors, and many antiques. There are thick towels, good linens, warm comforters, extra pillows, good lighting, and many other things I like to find in country inns. The Washburn House boasts double whirlpool bathtubs, too.

I was curious about the name "White Lace." I suggested that perhaps it was just a nice, pleasant, evocative term, but Bonnie assured me that indeed there was "something of white lace in every one of the guest rooms." It's kind of fun to find the white lace in each room. In one room it's the hand-knotted lace canopy on a bed; in another it's the Battenberg lace border on the cloth covering a table; in another, it's filmy lace curtains.

Bonnie and Dennis are both originally from Wisconsin. He had graduated from the Engineering School at the University of Wisconsin at Madison and she had studied interior design before they were married. They had moved to Connecticut, and when the "inn idea" got too strong to be ignored, they looked all over New England without success, until a friend suggested that they visit Door County in Wisconsin.

They found what they'd been looking for on a quiet street in the residential area of Sturgeon Bay, within five blocks of the bay and two blocks of the downtown National Historic District. Bonnie and Dennis put many hours of hard work into bringing three nearly ruined houses back to life, and they have succeeded in creating a very special inn with a warm and intimate atmosphere.

A word or two about Door County, which is sometimes called one of the the best-kept secrets in the country. Lots of Wisconsin natives have never been there. I know of people who always look heavenward when extolling Door County's virtues. It's a good four-season resort area. Winter days can be spent cross-country skiing on the trails in the state parks or snowshoeing in the woods. After returning to the inn, it's fun to stand in front of the crackling fire and exchange information and enthusiasms with other guests. Of course, being on the lake, Door County in the summertime offers ever-expanding vacation delights, including sailing, windsurfing, fishing, and swimming.

I thought that it might be a bit quiet during the winter, but Bonnie assured me they have many full weekends between January and March, when people bring their cross-country skis and make a wonderful time of it.

Guests at the Garden House and the Washburn House enjoy continental breakfast at the Main House. Different kinds of home-baked muffins and Scandinavian fruit soup are featured each day, as well as juice and plenty of aromatic hot coffee. The coffee pot is always on the stove at other times as well. "No one has ever left the table hungry at breakfast time here," Dennis said.

We're delighted to welcome the White Lace Inn to the pages of *Country Inns and Back Roads* for the first time in 1988.

WHITE LACE INN, 16 N. Fifth Ave., Sturgeon Bay, WI 54235; 414-743-1105. A 15-guestroom (private baths) bed-and-breakfast inn in one of Wisconsin's attractive resort areas. Open year-round. Conveniently located near all of the cultural and recreational attractions in Door County. Special 3-, 4-, and 5-night packages available from Nov. to May. No pets. Dennis and Bonnie Statz, Innkeepers. (See Index for rates.)

Directions: From the south take the Rte. 42-57 bypass across the new bridge, turn left on Michigan, and go right on Fifth Ave.

BOTSFORD INN
Farmington Hills, Michigan (1969)

I go back a long time with the Botsford Inn, but not way back to 1836 when it was first built by Orrin Weston as a home, or to when the famous Botsford family took it over and converted it into an inn. But I have been visiting it for quite a few of the more recent years.

I can remember when I first heard of the Botsford Inn, my reaction was, "Who would expect to find a New England country inn in Detroit?" I soon learned that it wasn't really in Detroit, but Farmington Hills, and the people in Farmington Hills will tell you that there's quite a difference. It's a very pleasant residential town. The inn was a stagecoach stop on the road from Grand Rapids on Lake Michigan, and, in fact, at one time the Grand River plank road followed an Indian trail that went on to Lansing and Detroit.

I strolled around the surprisingly spacious grounds and the rose garden, which was originally created by Mrs. Henry Ford, admiring the towering pine, maple, and elm trees. I realized that some of the more elegant features of the 19th century have been preserved at the Botsford, many by Henry Ford, who restored it in the 1920s. I think it is remarkable that such a valuable piece of property has not gone the way of the wrecking ball and bulldozer long before now.

One of the principal reasons for this must be attributed to the devotion of the present innkeeper and owner, John Anhut, who has a weakness for country inns. Following Mr. Ford's example, John has succeeded in holding back time. For example, in two sitting rooms there are many furnishings from Henry Ford's house, including a beautiful little inlaid spinet, a horsehair sofa, music boxes, inlaid mahogany tables, and spinning wheels.

The older sections of the inn have very low ceilings, huge beams, and handsome fireplaces with big andirons. One of the more celebrated features of the inn is the second-floor ballroom, where, at a country dance, long ago, Henry Ford first met the young lady who was to become his wife.

I'm certain that innkeeper Botsford and preserver Ford would approve of the contemporary changes that innkeeper Anhut has made, including guest rooms with reproductions of Colonial furniture, air conditioning against the Detroit summer heat, and tennis courts.

It's also certain that the farmers, drovers, and traveling men of the past century would nod their heads in approval at the hearty offerings from the Botsford kitchen today. These include braised short ribs of beef with jardinière sauce, frogs' legs sautéed in chablis, Botsford old-fashioned chicken pot pie topped with flaky buttered crust, and roast prime rib of Western beef, au jus. Their cherry cobbler has become so famous it was featured in a cartoon in the *Detroit News*.

Many birds can be glimpsed through the floor-to-ceiling windows of the restaurant, which overlook a garden courtyard, and cards on the tables help guests to identify the feathered visitors.

What appeals greatly to me about this inn is John Anhut himself. As busy as he is, he makes a concerted effort to meet every one of his guests. "Some of them have really become old friends to me," he said. "I think it's the best part of having a country inn."

The Botsford tradition of hospitality, begun during the Indian trail days, is continuing now with the Anhut family. In 1836, it was a day's journey from the banks of the river, where Detroit was a burgeoning city; today, it is just a short drive from the hustle and bustle of the Motor City. Worthwhile reminders of the past have been preserved and, best of all, the spirit of country innkeeping and community service is very much alive.

BOTSFORD INN, 28000 Grand River Ave., Farmington Hills, MI 48024; 313-474-4800. A 62-guestroom (private baths) village inn on the city line of Detroit. European plan. Dinner served daily except Monday. Breakfast and lunch Tues. thru Sat. Sun. brunch. Closed Christmas and New Year's Day. TV, telephone, and air conditioning in rooms. Wheelchair access. Tennis on grounds. Greenfield Village, skiing, and state parks nearby. John Anhut, Innkeeper. (See Index for rates.)

Directions: Located in Farmington Hills on I-96, easily accessible from major highways in Michigan.

THE NATIONAL HOUSE INN
Marshall, Michigan (1978)

Barbara Bradley, the innkeeper at the National House Inn, was helping me to assimilate the experience of the unusual town of Marshall. "Mr. Brooks was the most important factor," she said. "He was the man who had the vision for Marshall. But everybody in the town has joined in. We are proud of the homes and the museums, and we all work together. I'm sure the National House could not have been restored if it hadn't been a community effort. People helped out in so many ways.

"This is probably the oldest remaining hotel building in Michigan," she remarked. "We learned that it was open in 1835 and undoubtedly was the first brick building of any kind in our county. It is now listed on the National Register of Historic Places.

"At one time it was a windmill and wagon factory and more recently an apartment building," she continued. "Restoring it was hard work, but underneath the dirt and grime of dozens of years there was the solid, beautiful structure of the original brick as well as irreplaceable wood-work. The apartments from the old building were converted into sixteen guest rooms and baths.

"As you can see, Marshall is very much a Victorian restoration, and we have had a great deal of fun discovering new Victorian pieces for the inn, among which is an antique wooden cash register that was discovered in the cellar. There is also country stenciling in the Andrew Mann bedroom and some other rooms. Our gardens continue to attract more and more attention."

To me, one of the most striking features of the National House is the passionate attention to detail. For example, each guest room has its own ambience and there are colorful comforters, old trunks, marble top tables, bureaus, dried-flower arrangements, electric lamps that are reproductions of gas lamps, candle sconces with reflectors, little corner sofas, and special care with doorknobs. Special attention is also given to the linens. The bedroom windows overlook either the residential part of town or a beautiful fountain in the center of the town park.

Breakfast is the only meal served and is offered every morning in the dining room, where there is an interesting collection of chairs and tables from great-grandfather's day. The color tones are warm brown and beige. The breakfast, included in the room tariff, offers home-baked goods, selected teas, and the best coffee in Calhoun County.

The inn has a very interesting and well-designed newsletter containing much information about the town of Marshall and the inn itself. It also has a generous sprinkling of the recipes that enhance the breakfast menu. I'm sure they would be happy to send you one on request.

In the years since I began visiting Marshall, a great many of the buildings and homes of the town have been added to the State of Michigan Historic Sites and to the National Register. The town contains the finest examples of 19th-century architecture in the Midwest.

Marshall is situated on Interstate 94, Michigan's historic highway, which started as an Indian trail. There are six historic sites that can be visited along this road on which the development of the territory can be traced.

The National House has five weekend specials, which include visits to private homes by candlelight. The inn will be happy to supply any reader with further details, including the dates.

I am happy to welcome the National House back to the pages of *Country Inns and Back Roads* in 1988.

THE NATIONAL HOUSE INN, 102 South Parkview, Marshall, MI 49068; 616-781-7374. A 16-guestroom (private baths) elegantly restored Victorian-period village inn. European plan includes continental breakfast. No other meals served. Open year-round. Closed Christmas Eve and Christmas Day. Marshall is the finest example of 19th-century architecture in the Midwest, with 15 State Historic Sites and 6 National Register Sites. Tennis, golf, swimming, boating, xc skiing nearby. Barbara Bradley, Innkeeper. (See Index for rates.)

Directions: From I-69, exit at Michigan Ave. in Marshall and go straight 1½ mi. to inn. From I-94 use Exit 110 and follow old Rte. 127 south 1½ mi. to inn.

STAFFORD'S BAY VIEW INN
Petoskey, Michigan (1972)

First, a little background: Stafford's (as it is known in the area) is on the edge of the Bay View section of Petoskey, which is a summer resort community that grew up around a program of drama, music, art, and religious lectures and services. The community began in the late 1800s, when people rode on the Grand Rapids/Indiana Railroad or on lake steamers to reach this part of Michigan. The early residents built Victorian homes that are scattered throughout Bay View today.

Stafford met his future wife, Janice, at the inn, where both of them were on the staff. Since that time, their family has grown to include Reg, who attended the Cornell University Hotel School and is now with a fine restaurant in Cincinnati, Mary Kathryn, who is also involved in the hospitality field, and the youngest, Dean, who was always a big hit as a small boy wearing a tuxedo helping his father at the famous Sunday brunches.

Now, to continue. A recent letter from Janice reads as follows: "Bay View is about to be declared a significant historic district by the Department of the Interior. Bay View has been on the National Register for some time, but this new distinction has only been given to two other locations in Michigan."

Janice continues with news of the reopening of the third floor: "Norman, we were finally able to restore and rebuild ten new rooms on the third floor and thanks to Judy Honor, because it was her project, they are lovely. New windows, new walls, and a new floor plan. The only 'old' that remains are the outside walls, and some nooks and crannies.

"No two rooms are alike. Each is wallpapered in exciting Clarence House prints with a Victorian flare and bright, bright flowers. All the antique furniture and rocking chairs that we've been saving all this time have been refinished and are in the rooms. We have even created a mini-lobby for our guests to gather in up there. All is very cozy and comfortable.

"My favorite room, which Judy calls Grandmother's room, because it is blue with pink rosebuds, is located in the tower and incorporates my old room when I was a hostess and I first met Stafford. That part is a lovely sitting room that overlooks the bay; even the old dresser that I used has been refinished and fits right into the decor."

I would like to return to a portion of an earlier letter from Janice. "Constant hard work and dedication to people, service, and to quality have been our watchwords. The inn is no longer a quaint, homespun, charming hotel. We have become a first-class sophisticated delight—a pleasure to own and to share with the discriminating guest. That nice young couple that took over this business in 1961 have matured, and so has their business."

This is a good time for me to point out that Janice and Stafford have grown in several ways, including in the establishment of two other restaurants, one in Boyne City, Michigan, and the other in Harbor Springs.

Incidentally, as if he didn't already have a full work-load, Stafford is also president of the CIBR Innkeepers' Association, and his dedication to and enthusiasm for the high standards of the association have contributed considerably to its success.

STAFFORD'S BAY VIEW INN, Box 3, Petoskey, MI 49770; 616-347-2771. A 30-guestroom (private baths) resort-inn on Little Traverse Bay in the Bay View section of Petoskey. Bed-and-breakfast plan includes full breakfast. Breakfast, lunch, and dinner served daily to travelers. Open daily May 6 to Nov. 1; Thanksgiving weekend; Dec. 26 to Mar. 24. Wheelchair access. Lake swimming and xc skiing on grounds. Historical Festival events, 3rd weekend in June. Bay View cultural programs in July and Aug. Golfing, boating, tennis, fishing, hiking, alpine ski trails, scenic and historic drives, and excellent shopping nearby. Stafford and Janice Smith and Judy Honor, Innkeepers. (See Index for rates.)

Directions: From Detroit, take Gaylord exit from I-75 and follow Mich. Rte. 32 to Rte. 131 north to Petoskey. From Chicago, use Rte. 131 north to Petoskey.

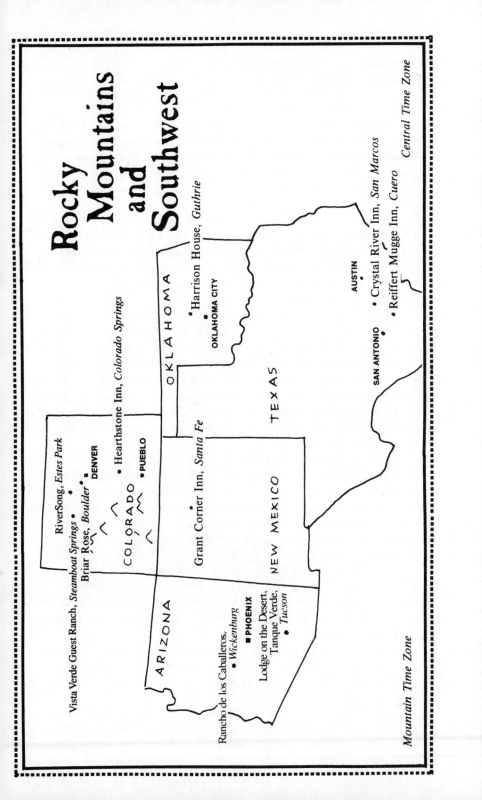

Rocky Mountains and Southwest

Vista Verde Guest Ranch, *Steamboat Springs* •
RiverSong, *Estes Park* •
Briar Rose, *Boulder* •
DENVER ■
• Hearthstone Inn, *Colorado Springs*
• PUEBLO

COLORADO

ARIZONA
Rancho de los Caballeros. •
Wickenburg
PHOENIX ■
Lodge on the Desert, *Tanque Verde,* •
Tucson

NEW MEXICO
Grant Corner Inn, *Santa Fe* •

OKLAHOMA
• Harrison House, *Guthrie*
OKLAHOMA CITY ■

TEXAS

AUSTIN •
SAN ANTONIO •
• Crystal River Inn, *San Marcos*
• Reiffert Mugge Inn, *Cuero*

Central Time Zone

Mountain Time Zone

BRIAR ROSE BED & BREAKFAST
Boulder, Colorado (1983)

I'm going to share a part of a sparkling letter I received from Emily Hunter, the innkeeper at the Briar Rose:

"Briar Rose is filled with people who have come to see the CU–Ohio football game. There is a bouquet of autumn leaves in the Briar Rose window seat, screening the bird feeder from the activity at the dining room table. A flock of grosbeaks has taken up residence in the lilac bushes and lost all hesitations, sitting for hours, sharing pounds of sunflower seeds with Rusty the squirrel.

"We built the first fire of the season yesterday. The big poplar out front is turning that great marigold yellow that I look forward to every year. The fire alarms are all checked, the firewood ordered and to be split next week, and the down puffs go back on the beds tonight. It feels like all the appropriate gestures have been made to stave off the cold and dark and snow for a few more months."

The ground floor exterior of the inn is a beautiful rose-colored brick, with Queen Anne shingles on the second story. I noticed several other small houses in Boulder that featured some of the same basic design.

The Briar Rose has also undergone some extensive redecorating in the public rooms, dining rooms, and some of the bedrooms in a small building immediately adjacent. Almost all of the furnishings are Regency Victorian, and there are splendid additional touches, such as roses in the guest rooms, baskets of fruit on the nightstands, and the aforementioned down puffs on the beds.

More as an accommodation to the guest than anything else, the Briar Rose offers a modest dinner consisting of a single entrée of different types of casseroles with puff-pastry tops. There's usually a choice of beef with onion, wine, and mushrooms or turkey with cream, onions, and carrots. This is augmented by a simple dessert that goes along with dinner.

As Emily says, "Boulder is a great restaurant town, and there are good restaurants within walking distance, but we want to be able to offer dinner to those guests who are arriving really tired from a long trip and who don't want to take the trouble to go out for dinner. This is particularly true of businessmen, and if they want to have dinner in front of the fire or at the table — or even on the back porch in the summertime — they can take their tray and enjoy it wherever they like."

During the past few years Emily has gained a considerable reputation for conducting conferences and seminars whose basic subject is "how to open a bed-and-breakfast inn." These are held several times a year and I'd suggest contacting her to find out all of the details.

Emily's letter went on: "We have an ideal climate here in Boulder with four distinct and wonderful seasons. There are over 300 sunny days a year and many things for visitors to enjoy, both recreational and artistic. Of course, the mountains offer everything, including climbing, hiking, cross country skiing. Some people say that the powder snow offers the best downhill skiing in the world. Biking is also very popular here in this part of Colorado and there are bicyclists everywhere, as well as joggers and runners."

Emily's letter continues: "At this moment my dining room here at home is filled with six-foot-long cardboard boxes, in turn filled with dried whole roses that I dried in my attic. A friend, who is a floral designer, has begun just this week to market 'Briar Rose Potpourri.' A friend gave me a plastic pink flamingo that now resides hidden in the water lilies of the fish pond. Only the most observant guest is treated to the sight of our own 'Loch Ness Flamingo.' "

BRIAR ROSE BED & BREAKFAST, 2151 Arapahoe Ave., Boulder, CO 80302; 303-442-3007. A 12-guestroom (some shared baths) inn located in a quiet section of a pleasant, conservative Colorado city, approx. 1 hr. from Denver. Open all year. Breakfast included in lodging rate. Evening meal available upon request. Afternoon tea served. Convenient for all of the many recreational, cultural, and historic attractions nearby. Limousine service available to and from Denver airport. Emily Hunter, Innkeeper. (See Index for rates.)

Directions: From Denver, follow I-25 north and Rte. 36 to Boulder. Turn left on Arapahoe Ave. Briar Rose is on the right on the corner of 22nd St.

THE HEARTHSTONE INN
Colorado Springs, Colorado (1979)

It was a most agreeable early August morning at the Hearthstone Inn. This time I was paying a visit in midsummer, when I could see the inn's beautiful lawn and flowers at their very best, and also sit on the front porch in one of the new handsome Tennessee country rockers.

I watched with amusement while a father, mother, and their four-year-old boy romped on the lawn, and then one of the staff came out and set up the croquet set. I had arrived just a few moments earlier, driving down from Denver and Boulder, and was immediately offered my choice of coffee or iced tea. "The coffee is on from early in the morning," explained Dot Williams, who with Ruth Williams (no relation), is the innkeeper at the Hearthstone.

Now I watched the few cars go by on Cascade Avenue, one of the most impressive streets in Colorado Springs, and reflected on the many changes I have seen in the considerable number of years since the first night I landed in Denver. I had been picked up by Dot and Ruth and driven out to the "Springs." These two women had opened up the first inn in Colorado Springs, overcoming many difficulties. At that time there was only one house; now there are two houses, cheek-by-jowl.

The most recent development is the completion of Sheltering Pines, a totally different type of accommodation in nearby Green Mountain Falls. I had visited it when it was just a bit more than a gleam in the innkeepers' eyes.

"It is slowly developing its own following," Dot said. "The cool of the mountain evenings and the clear air of our mountain days make this part of Colorado a real boon for those who suffer from heat or allergies. Family reunions or groups are enjoying the patio, barbecue grill, and the many trees. It's quite a bit higher than Colorado Springs."

Sheltering Pines is actually a duplex with two completely separate living areas. Each has a completely equipped kitchen with everything provided, including all of the bedding and towels. In the summer it is rented only by the week, but the rest of the year it's available for shorter stays with a two-night minimum.

The Hearthstone itself is well known from coast to coast as being one of the truly impressive Victorian restorations. Every room has been furnished entirely with Victorian furniture and decorations, and the outside of this wonderful combination of two rambling houses has been finished in carefully researched Victorian colors. Visitors will be surprised, as was I, to see how gracefully they reflect the Mauve Decades.

I always look forward to breakfast at the Hearthstone, and there is a wide variety of hearty breakfast offerings, not just the usual. "We never serve the same guest the same breakfast twice," Ruth declared.

Dot and Ruth joined me on the front porch, and we watched the squirrels, Minnie the Moocher and Pearl the Squirrel, and their friend, Jaws, eat themselves silly on sunflower seeds.

"I've always hoped that you would come out during Christmas some year," Ruth said. "Our guests all gather around for eggnog and the tradition of decorating the tree. Many guests bring a homemade ornament, and we tag each one with their name and the year, and it becomes a permanent part of each tree's decorations. Why don't you plan to come next year?"

I certainly would enjoy that experience very much!

THE HEARTHSTONE INN, 506 N. Cascade Ave., Colorado Springs, CO 80903; 303-473-4413. A 25-guestroom bed-and-breakfast inn within sight of Pike's Peak, in the residential section of Colorado Springs. Complimentary full breakfast is the only meal served. Open every day all year. (Housekeeping units also available in Green Mountain Falls.) Convenient to spectacular Colorado mountain scenery as well as Air Force Academy, Garden of the Gods, Cave of the Winds, the McAllister House Museum, Fine Arts Center, and Broadmoor Resort. Golf, tennis, swimming, hiking, backroading, and Pikes Peak ski area nearby. Check innkeepers for pet policy. Dorothy Williams and Ruth Williams, Innkeepers. (See Index for rates.)

Directions: From I-25 (the major north/south hwy.) use Exit 143 (Uintah St.); travel east (opposite direction from mountains) to third stop light (Cascade Ave.). Turn right for 7 blocks. The inn will be on the right at the corner of St. Vrain and Cascade—a big Victorian house, tan with lilac trim.

RIVERSONG
Estes Park, Colorado (1987)

As I meandered through the grounds in front of RiverSong, I noticed that the grass had been allowed to seek its own level, along with the wildflowers and various flowering bushes. I noted, too, a couple of ponds and pools and a gazebo with a fireplace for cooking out. Through the trees I could see to the top of the great Continental Divide, which in August was still snowcapped. This view is even better from several of the guest rooms in RiverSong. It is reminiscent of an Albert Bierstadt painting.

Now I crossed a narrow little stone bridge into a lovely tiny glade of evergreens, with two benches, and wandered to the edge of still another pool. There is a series of connecting pools where all the wonderful music of splashing water can always be heard. It reminded me of the same wonderful tinkling sounds I've heard in the fountains of Spanish *paradores*.

The first time I walked through the front door, I knew that this was a small, intimate inn whose owners understood what it means to provide a place for guests to come together and exchange ideas and conversation. In the middle of the living room was a large, crescent-shaped couch, which faced the fireplace at one end and a spectacular view of the great peaks of the Rockies at the other end. It was a room with many, many books of all kinds—books indicating an active literary and intellectual curiosity on the part of Sue and Gary Mansfield. As Gary says, "Although we are an inn that basically appeals to outdoor-minded people — they want to hike on the trails or ski or just go outside and smell the fresh air after a rain — we know that when the day is through there are times when a good book is exactly what is needed."

Every one of the guest rooms has been furnished most uniquely. I'll just describe the honeymoon suite, which has a queen-sized bed, a working fireplace with a raised hearth, a semi-cathedral ceiling with a skylight, and a little unicorn. In fact, there are unicorns in all of the guest rooms. This suite has its own patio, looking up through the ponderosa pines. The bathroom has a sunken tub and a double redwood shower with a skylight. A few steps away is a carriage house with some very attractive additional rooms.

Sue told me that almost all of the antiques in the inn have been handed down through her family; the carved bed and dresser in one room belonged to her father's parents, and the quilts were made by her maternal grandmother. The antique silver and dishes have come from both sides of the family. As she says, "It's nice to be able to share these things with other people who really appreciate them."

The talk turned to breakfast. Apple pan dowdy, blueberry and rhubarb cobblers, baked cinnamon apples, along with such favorites as cinnamon rolls, bran muffins, and homemade raspberry jam or Emily Hunter's lemon curd are some of the offerings.

Very special candlelit dinners are served on advance request. Guests have the choice of a beef or chicken entrée, and the rest of the meal is set by the chef. This is a pleasant solution for those guests who do not want to drive "downtown" to Estes Park for the evening meal.

"Oh, I wish you could come here at Christmas!" Sue exclaimed. "It is truly a magical time, with the deer and the elk returning and the serenity and beauty of our little inn on the banks of the Big Thompson River. I do wish you could join us." I've never had a better invitation.

RIVERSONG, P.O. Box 1910, Estes Park, CO 80517; 303-586-4666. An 8-guestroom (private and shared baths) mountain inn at the foot of the great Continental Divide, 70 mi. from Denver. Breakfast included in room rate; simple dinners offered on advance request. Open all year. Downhill and xc skiing, hiking, walking, golf, tennis, antiquing, and exploring, all most convenient. Boarding kennel nearby for pets. No smoking. Gary and Sue Mansfield, Innkeepers. (See Index for rates.)

Directions: From Denver: Estes Park is only 70 mi. from central Denver with no mountain passes to cross. Any choice of roads is wonderfully scenic. Ask the inn for directions from the center of Estes Park.

VISTA VERDE GUEST RANCH
Steamboat Springs, Colorado (1987)

There seemed to be a ruckus in the side yard next to the main lodge at the Vista Verde Guest Ranch, where some children were practicing with the lariat. There was a great deal of shouting and laughing because they had lassoed one of the wranglers, and he was now on the ground. They were all standing around him like the Lilliputians stood around Gulliver. The other adult guests in the dining room and I crowded to the window to see what was going on. One of the mothers seated at my table noted somewhat wryly that this was the first night her young daughter hadn't worn bluejeans, and it was obvious that her little flowered frock was going to be grass-stained.

Afterward we all drifted back to the tables and most of the talk was about the day's rafting trip down the Colorado, and the guests who had been here previously said that it was always a different adventure.

Vista Verde is an activity-oriented guest ranch, with the major focus centered on horseback riding. However, as Frank Brophy pointed out, "We have lots of things like gold panning and guided hiking expeditions for people who may not care for riding."

It was my first real Colorado guest ranch experience, and I must say that I was tremendously impressed. It is situated at an elevation of 7,800 feet, surrounded by a national forest and a wilderness area. Guests share the environment with elk, deer, bears, foxes, coyotes, beavers, porcupines, and golden and bald eagles.

Lodgings are in individual hand-hewn cabins with hooked rugs, calico curtains, and Early American furnishings. All of them are carpeted, with spacious living rooms, cozy fireplaces, kitchens and baths, and from one to three cheerful bedrooms.

Guests are on the American plan rates, which include three meals a day, and what meals they are! Everybody is summoned by a ranch dinner bell, and, as you might imagine, home cooking is the rule. There are homemade breads, pies, and pastries, and fresh eggs from the henhouse. Meals are served family-style in the main lodge or on picnic tables near the outdoor fireplace. Breakfast cookouts, steak barbecues, and fish fries all add to the fun. There's evening entertainment almost every night, with such diversions as a rodeo, square dancing, sing-alongs, story-telling, and even some guest talent as well.

There is an extensive children's program with a children's counselor. As Frank says, "In short order, we can have a five-year-old riding better than an eighteen-year-old."

For both the summer and winter guests, there is a spa and exercise center with a whirlpool, sauna, and exercise facilities to help them relax after a day out of doors, either in the saddle, on hiking trails or on skis.

In winter, there is cross-country skiing, horse-drawn sleigh rides, snowshoeing, and ice fishing right on the ranch, or just relaxing in front of the fire.

This account of Vista Verde's virtues must of necessity be somewhat limited, and I hope that it will pique your interest enough to write for a brochure, which contains far more extensive suggestions. I can assure you that it is right on the mark.

VISTA VERDE GUEST RANCH, Box 465, Steamboat Springs, CO 80477; 303-879-3858. A 40-guest-capacity working ranch, high in the Colorado Rockies. Full American plan includes breakfast, lunch, and dinner. Open year-round. Inquire about minimum stays. Horseback riding and instruction; xc skiing on grounds and nearby in winter. Colorado River float trips, hunting, fishing, hot-air ballooning, tennis, swimming, golfing, and other summer sports nearby. No pets. Special cancellation policy. Mr. and Mrs. Frank Brophy, Innkeepers. (See Index for rates.)

Directions: American Airlines and PSA will have nonstop jet service to Steamboat Springs during the winter with access from fifty major U.S. cities. In summer, the best plan is to fly to Denver and transfer to Continental Express Airways or drive to Steamboat Springs. Once there, telephone the ranch for further instructions.

HARRISON HOUSE
Guthrie, Oklahoma (1988)

In the rousing finale of that grand musical *Oklahoma!* is the line "You're doing fine, Oklahoma—Oklahoma, okay!" And after a visit to the lively town of Guthrie, smack in the middle of state, I'll have to echo those sentiments.

I was greatly inspired by the pioneering spirit of community in Guthrie, originally the capital of both the Oklahoma Territory and later the state.

The Harrison House is a perfect example of that spirit. Phyllis Murray was a volunteer in the restoration of one of the buildings in the downtown historic district. Her husband, Ron, was one of the local investors in the project to develop an inn in what had been a handsome bank and office building. They needed someone to furnish and decorate the rooms, and Phyllis took on the job.

Little did she realize how involved she would become. Today she is the innkeeper, and she loves it. "I wanted this inn to be special," she told me, "and I have always been partial to the Victorian period, so the idea of decorating it really appealed to me." And this is where the feeling of community comes in. Phyllis found everything she has used in the inn within the immediate area. This includes every piece of antique furniture, all of the fabrics and wallpapers, even the mattresses, made by a local company to fit the various-sized old beds.

"I felt that it was really important to have furnishings and the feeling of what Guthrie was like at the turn of the century, and also I wanted this restoration to benefit the local economy," Phyllis declared. "It has been wonderful to see the interest that people in town have taken in this project."

By the time she had finished her splendid job of decorating, she decided to stay on as its innkeeper. Phyllis is a very warm and hospitable lady, who seems to make her guests feel very much at home.

The Harrison House is a handsome red brick and sandstone building with an impressive arched entrance at the corner. The lobby is elegantly decorated with marble-topped tables, velvet upholstered chairs, deep green carpeting, and plum-colored draperies.

Upstairs is a parlor and dining area where a continental breakfast is served at tables set with old china and silver plate. "None of our china or silver matches," Phyllis laughed, "which makes it more fun — like being at Aunt Susie's or Grandma Murray's."

The guest rooms are all decorated differently with original antique beds and other interesting pieces, and they all have their own bathrooms.

I had a brief chat with Ron Murray, a slow-talking, soft-spoken gentleman, and he told me how the town had accomplished the restoration of the Pollard Theatre, right next door to the inn. In fact, some of the guest rooms extend over the theater.

"It's the only full-time professional repertory theater in Oklahoma," he said. "It opened in October with *Guys and Dolls,* and there will be ten musicals and plays presented throughout the year.

"We have a lot of history right here in Guthrie," he added. "You know, this town was established during the famous 'Run of '89,' when the Oklahoma Territory was opened to settlers, and next year will be our 100th year."

Phyllis took up the thread, "Nearly everything of interest is within walking distance. Oh, there are all sorts of things to do and see here."

Looking over all the brochures and folders listing various events and sightseeing possibilities, I had to agree with her.

I'm happy to welcome the Harrison House to the pages of *Country Inns and Back Roads* for the first time.

HARRISON HOUSE, 124 W. Harrison St., P.O. Box 1555, Guthrie, OK 73044; 405-282-1000. A 23-guestroom (private baths) in-town bed-and-breakfast inn in the historic district of a bustling southwestern town, about 20 mi. north of Oklahoma City. Continental breakfast included in room rate. Open year-round. Museums, theater, concerts, rodeos, territorial home tours, special events nearby. Well-behaved children welcome. No pets. Phyllis Murray, Innkeeper; Patricia Holland, Assistant Innkeeper. (See Index for rates.)

Directions: Guthrie is located on I-35, about 20 mi. north of Oklahoma City. The inn is at the corner of West Harrison and First Sts.

CRYSTAL RIVER INN
San Marcos, Texas (1988)

Cathy Dillon has the right idea. I was very taken with her vivacity and enthusiasm when I paid her a surprise call on an October afternoon, and when I saw what a nice job she and her husband, Mike, are doing with the inn, I was convinced. "It was very important to me to make it as comfortable and beautiful as we could," she told me.

But it's not just the pleasingly decorated rooms or the warm and inviting atmosphere that impresses me, it's their imaginative approach to offering diversion, entertainment, and just plain pampering to their guests. In addition to the ever-popular Murder Mystery weekends, which in this case include a sunset champagne cruise on a lake, you can enjoy a Country Gourmet weekend, complete with cookery demonstrations, samplings, and a full-fledged, fourteen-course feast on Saturday night. There is also a Romantic Interlude weekend with such options as a llama trek into the Texas hill country with a picnic basket full of gourmet goodies, or a dawn or sunset balloon flight, or a massage and facial in the privacy of your room. You can spend a whole week having massages and visiting a spa for aerobics and water workouts on their Spa week, which also includes manicures, pedicures, makeup and color analysis, as well as "lots of time for reading and resting."

They will arrange white-water rafting, canoeing, tubing, and river trips at any time, and this is something that Cathy and Mike know a lot about since they are avid canoeists themselves.

Five Ionic columns supporting the second-story veranda give the house an impressive facade, which perhaps the original owners felt was important, being close to the courthouse square. It was built in 1883 in a kind of Greek Revival style by one of the founders of Southwest Texas State University. Cathy and Mike bought the house 100 years later in 1984 and have spent a lot of time renovating and decorating.

Their five guest rooms, two downstairs and three upstairs, are named for the clearest and most beautiful Texas rivers and have canopied, four-poster, and white iron beds. The colors are soft and restful, the wallpapers and fabrics are attractive, and there are piles of pillows, fluffy towels, interesting old magazines, and fresh flowers. Three rooms have fireplaces. There are three similarly decorated guest rooms in the 1885 Young House across the street, each with a clawfooted tub in the bathroom, and a telephone and TV.

Cathy, who was formerly a nurse, is a very busy person, involved with a number of civic and personal activities, one of which is catering. Mike manages an office complex in Austin and is involved with real estate projects. They're a handsome couple, and with their little four-year-old, Sarah, they provide a pleasant, easy atmosphere for their guests.

"I think how welcome a guest feels is very important," Cathy told me. "I encourage our guests to socialize, to gather and talk over coffee in the family room, or to read or listen to music in the library, and they're always welcome in the kitchen. Of course, there's always our upstairs veranda where you can have breakfast or take a picnic or have a glass of wine." I rather enjoyed just sitting and rocking there.

Cathy told me she bakes all the breakfast pastries, and her weekend brunches sound positively scrumptious, with such delicacies as stuffed french toast with apricot sauce and bananas Foster crêpes with crème fraiche. If you make advance arrangements, she will serve dinner. "Our house dinner specialty is beef Wellington with a ripsnorting béarnaise!"

I am happy to welcome Crystal River Inn to the pages of *Country Inns and Back Roads* for the first time.

CRYSTAL RIVER INN, 326 W. Hopkins, San Marcos, TX 78666; 512-396-3739. An 8-guestroom (private and shared baths) country inn in a small resort city 40 min. from both San Antonio and Austin. Breakfast included in room rate; dinner available with prior arrangements. Open year-round. Cultural and sports events at Southwest Texas campus, Aquarena Springs, canyon recreational area, Spring Lake, glass-bottom boat, swimming, fishing, canoeing, golf, hiking, riding, caveing, and ballooning nearby. Children over 12 welcome. No pets. Smoking with restrictions. Cathy and Mike Dillon, Innkeepers. (See Index for rates.)

Directions: From I-35, take Exit 205 west, which becomes Hopkins St. The inn is 3 blocks past the courthouse.

REIFFERT MÜGGE INN
Cuero, Texas (1988)

There's a picture of a guardian angel in the Nursery in the Reiffert Mügge Inn, and perhaps it is the same angel who must have been watching over the house during the hurricanes of 1875 and 1886. At that time the house stood in Indianola on Matagorda Bay, and it was one of the few buildings that remained standing amidst the wreckage of the prospering seaport town. Emil Reiffert, a German immigrant who had made his fortune and built his home there, decided to move his house and family out of harm's way. Along with other survivors with salvageable buildings, he had the house dismantled and shipped sixty miles inland to the peaceful town of Cuero.

As I pulled off the very wide, tree-lined, residential avenue and into the Reiffert Mügge (pronounced "Rye-fert Miggy") grounds, I was most taken with the expanse of green lawns and the many huge, beautiful old trees. Gil Becker later told me there were twenty-seven live oaks and many pecan trees on the grounds, as well as bougainvillea, lantanna, rose bushes, and other exotic plants.

The Beckers are a personable young couple who fell in love with this house and actually spent several years researching and studying how to restore it before they finally bought it in 1985.

They have really immersed themselves in the history of the Reiffert and Mügge families, who owned the house until 1980. As Gil said, "What makes the house significant is the family, and it's so important to keep that history alive."

"There were so many family things still here," Lecia said. "For instance, we found Christmas lists in the attic of what each child was to receive, and some of the toys are still here. In fact, many of them decorate the Nursery."

"Yes," Gil added, "we even know the Christmas customs they brought from Germany, where children were not allowed to see all the presents and decorations until Christmas morning."

I could well imagine the cries of excitement and peals of laughter that must have echoed in the grand parlor with its fourteen-foot-high ceiling, magnificent parquet floor, crystal chandelier, and original wallpaper. Gil explained that the family had kept furnishings in this room to a minimum as it was mainly used for parties and dancing.

The sitting room is cozier, with a comfortable white upholstered sofa and chair around a coal fireplace, which has a carved oak mantelpiece with a mirror and columns on either side. This is where the Beckers serve their guests hors d'oeuvres in the afternoon.

A full Texas breakfast of fresh fruit, juice, fresh homemade biscuits, bacon or sausage, and eggs or pancakes is served in the sunny white and blue dining room, where a large ficus plant stands in the tall bay window, and there are fresh flowers on the lace-covered tables.

The guest rooms are charmingly decorated, each with its own bathroom down the hall.

Lecia and Gil are very involved with the community. Friends and neighbors have brought them many turn-of-the-century items, and they open the house for special community events sponsored by different organizations several times a year. "We've had quilt shows, flower shows, and art shows," Lecia said. "Some of the people in town get a kick out of being involved in our Mystery Weekends, too."

There is certainly a lot of history in this section of Texas, called the Golden Crescent. There are many reminders here of the early Spanish and Mexican settlers. La Salle established a brief beachhead at Fort St. Louis, and battles for Texan independence, Civil War skirmishes, and some bloody local feuds have all added to a turbulent history.

That was all long ago and far away, I thought, as I sat under a great old tree, enjoying the flowers and the birds and the smell of new-mown grass. "Everything is so peaceful here now."

I'm happy to welcome the Reiffert Mügge Inn to the pages of *Country Inns and Back Roads* for the first time.

REIFFERT MÜGGE INN, 304 W. Prairie St., Cuero, TX 77954; 512-275-2626 (after 6 p.m.). A 6-guestroom (private baths) bed-and-breakfast inn in a quiet and historic residential section of Cuero, the county seat for DeWitt County, about 60 mi. from the Gulf of Mexico. Breakfast included in room rate. Other meals by arrangement. Open year-round. Telephone and TV available. Air conditioning and heating. Arrangements for special interest tours—wildlife, wildflowers, history, antiques, and back-country; horseshoes, croquet, tandem bicycle on premises. Mission Espiritu Santo, golf, tennis, swimming, fishing, hiking, racetrack, zoo, and museums nearby. Children over 12 welcome. Smoking outside only. Gil and Lecia Becker, Innkeepers. (See Index for rates.)

Directions: From I-10, take U.S. 183 south to Cuero. Turn west on Indianola and continue 2 blocks to Prairie St. and the inn.

GRANT CORNER INN
Santa Fe, New Mexico (1988)

While the overhead fan in the dining room whirled lazily and morning conversations rose and fell, I took in my surroundings with pleasure. Sun streamed in the large windows, the rose-colored woven mats with blue napkins in white rabbit napkin rings and the little vases of fresh daisies made a pretty pattern on the polished oak tables. The aroma of fresh-brewed coffee scented the air, and my fruit-filled pancakes were delicious. "What a way to start the day," I thought.

I leafed through Louise Stewart's cookbook, with over 300 of the recipes that she and her husband, Pat Walter, have used for their breakfasts, which have become so famous that local people make reservations just for breakfast. The Southwestern and Mexican influence makes for some exciting combinations — poached pears with raspberry sauce, spicy *huevos rancheros,* scrambled eggs with jack cheese and coriander, peach or pumpkin-raisin pancakes, wholewheat burritos brushed with butter and served with jalapeño jelly and sour cream, stuffed french toast, blue corn waffles, asparagus frittatas, strawberry frappe, and always the delicate sopapillas. Sopapillas, in case you've never tried them, are delicious fried pastries dusted with powdered sugar and served with butter and honey. I understand Pat is the creator of many of the breakfast specialties. There are also all kinds of homemade breads, fresh fruit, juices, various cereals, and still other choices.

Later, talking to Pat and Louise, I realized that they made a perfect combination and had both come to this challenge with especially tailored backgrounds. Pat was a builder and had taught space planning and design, and Louise had a degree in hotel management and was an interior designer. Between the two of them, they have whipped what was a dilapidated 1905 "ugly duckling" of a house into an elegant and delightful bed-and-breakfast inn.

Throughout the inn they have placed many of their personal belongings—family antiques and heirlooms, Indian and Mexican folk art, and other treasures they have collected over the years. "Our guests enjoy the special things and always take good care of them," Louise told me. "I think it's the extra touches that people remember—I know I do."

Every guest room has a personality all of its own, and each one is quite different from the others. One sunny room has a very southwestern feeling with Indian rugs, a natural pine bed with a handmade antique country quilt, and natural muslin bed curtains. Another room, with french doors opening onto a private porch, is more formal, with a white iron and brass bed, a handsome antique quilt and matching ruffled pillow shams and curtains, a European-style white telephone, and a beautiful bentwood upholstered settee. I noticed baskets of fruit on bedside tables. Thick robes in rooms where the bathroom is "down the hall," and telephones, TV, and ceiling fans in all the guest rooms.

Conversation is easy in the cozy parlor, where afternoon refreshments are served. Although no other meals are served, Louise assures me that arrangements can be made for an elegant picnic lunch, and both she and Pat are always happy to help map out day trips to nearby pueblos and other diversions for their guests.

Santa Fe is a fascinating blend of Indian, Spanish, and Anglo influences, with a vibrant cultural life that includes art, drama, dance, and a lot of music. The Santa Fe Opera has become very well known, and its festival, along with a chamber music festival, is held during July and August. Grant Corner Inn is just two blocks from the city plaza and within walking distance of art galleries, shops, and the Repertory Theatre.

I am happy to welcome the Grant Corner Inn to the pages of *Country Inns and Back Roads* for the first time.

GRANT CORNER INN, 122 Grant Ave., Santa Fe, NM 87501; 505-983-6678. An 11-guestroom (private and shared baths) bed-and-breakfast inn in downtown Santa Fe. Breakfast and afternoon refreshments included in room rate. Picnic lunches can be arranged. Closed last 3 wks. in Jan. Wheelchair access. Within walking distance of shops, galleries, restaurants, and theater. Indian pueblos, music and art festivals, hiking, rafting, and skiing nearby. Children over 5 welcome. No pets. Louise Stewart and Pat Walter, Innkeepers. (See Index for rates.)

Directions: From Albuquerque on U.S. 25, go north on St. Francis, east on Alameda, north on Guadalupe, and east on Johnson.

THE LODGE ON THE DESERT
Tucson, Arizona (1976)

The slanting rays of the western sun, providing spectacular back-lighting for the great banks of clouds that seemed to skim the jagged peaks of the Santa Catalina Mountains, streamed through the casement window and lit up the interior of my spacious studio bedroom at the Lodge on the Desert.

Even though the afternoon temperature in September reached 85 degrees, I knew that later that evening I would want a fire in my fireplace to ease the chill of the cool desert night.

My bedroom was really most impressive, with three windows on two sides and a patio facing north. The two double beds had rich bedspreads that complemented the orange curtains, and an armful of freshly picked flowers lent an air of gaiety to the dark tones of the carved wooden tables and chests. The full-sized closet reminded me that many people come here to spend weeks at a time, enjoying the benefits of a friendly climate in both summer and winter, plus the many opportunities for outdoor recreation, as well as the pursuit of the arts.

Tucson is one of the most sophisticated cities in the Southwest, with many fine homes and attractive shops in the downtown area. The University of Arizona is an active cultural center with a continuing program of music, drama, and arts and crafts exhibitions.

"We are now into our second fifty years of family ownership. My father built the Lodge on the Desert outside Tucson in 1936," commented Schuyler Lininger, the *patron grande* of this resort-inn. "Now the city has grown up around us; fortunately, we have no tall buildings to disrupt our guests' view of the mountains, and yet we are set apart by the hedges around the property. However, many of our guests find nearness to the center of things in the city most desirable."

Here in the Southwest desert, during the outdoor weather, everybody gathers around the swimming pool, and here is where many conversations and lasting friendships start.

For cooler days, the Lodge has a very spacious and inviting living room with lots of books, which guests are free to take to their rooms, a chess game, a jigsaw puzzle, and many opportunities just to sit and relax.

The guest rooms of the inn have been designed after the manner of Pueblo Indian farmhouses, the beige adobe color frequently relieved by very colorful Mexican tiles.

Although the dining room features many dishes of the Southwest, I found there were also such favorites as Chateaubriand for two, roast rack of lamb, and several veal dishes. Schuyler explained that he and Helen have gone to great lengths to bring milk-fed Wisconsin veal to the table in different versions. Incidentally, one of the most popular features of the inn is breakfast served on the patios of the guest rooms in the beautiful early-morning sunshine.

I believe another guest succinctly summed up my feelings about the Lodge on the Desert while we were at the pool, taking advantage of that bright September sun to get a few more degrees of tan.

"What I like about it here," she said, "is the really endless variety of things that are going on in Tucson—the Art Center, the many different theaters, the new museum, the exhibition of Indian arts, the opera company, the ballet, the Tucson Symphony, the golf courses, the racetrack, and all kinds of sports events—it's so *civilized!*"

THE LODGE ON THE DESERT, 306 N. Alvernon Way, Tucson, AZ 85733; 602-325-3366. A 40-guestroom luxury inn within the city limits. American and European plans available in winter; European plan in summer. Continental breakfast included in European plan. Breakfast, lunch, and dinner served to travelers every day of the year. Wheelchair access. Near several historic, cultural, and recreational attractions. Swimming pool and lawn games on grounds. Tennis and golf 1 mi. Attended, leashed pets allowed. Schuyler and Helen Lininger, Innkeepers. (See Index for rates.)

Directions: Take Speedway exit from I-10. Travel about 5 mi. east to Alvernon Way, turn right (south) onto Alvernon (¾ mi.). Lodge is on left side between 5th St. and Broadway.

The date in parenthesis in the heading represents the first year the inn appeared in the pages of Country Inns and Back Roads.

RANCHO DE LOS CABALLEROS
Wickenburg, Arizona (1971)

Rancho de los Caballeros is a rather elegant ranch-inn. A continuous program of watering and irrigation makes it a green jewel in the desert. This is especially true of the 18-hole championship golf course. Many of the guest rooms and suites are built around a carefully planned cactus garden and oversized putting green and are decorated in Arizona desert colors with harmonizing hues of tan, yellow, and brown. Each accommodation, or "casita" as they are called in this part of the world, has a private patio and many of them have fireplaces.

A program of planned activities for younger people is one of the reasons this ranch experience is so popular with families. "We feel that it is a good balance," says innkeeper Rusty Gant, "because children of all ages have several activities every morning, and in the afternoon they can join their parents for more trail riding or tennis or a swim in the pool. At dinner the childrens' counselor gathers them all together, and they even have their own dining room. They are kept occupied until bedtime. This has proven to be an excellent idea for both children and their parents alike.

"The idea of a winter vacation on a guest ranch in Arizona never occurred to us," said a letter I received from a Michigan reader. "Wickenburg seemed like such a long way and we weren't quite sure what kind of people would be there. We certainly weren't horseback riders and we thought we might feel out of place. However, we were reading your book about how much you enjoyed the noon buffet around the pool at Rancho de los Caballeros and getting some horseback riding tips from one of the wranglers, and we began to think that maybe we would enjoy it too.

"The trip from Detroit to Phoenix was quite short and the ranch car met us at the airport. When I talked with Ann Giles on the telephone she assured me that we'd feel right at home and that we should bring our tennis rackets. She mentioned that golf clubs could be rented if we didn't want to carry them. We literally dragged our two early-teenage sons with us, and did their faces light up when almost as soon as we arrived they noticed other young people. I don't believe we saw them for the rest of the two weeks."

Rancho de los Caballeros . . . "the ranch of the gentlemen on horseback." The name alone has an unusually romantic, melodic sound, and its location in the high country is equally romantic. As my correspondent from Michigan said later on in her letter, "The mountains and the desert literally grow on you."

I love to sit on the terrace at sunset and watch the changing colors and dimensions of the Bradshaw Mountains far across the valley.

I've visited Rancho de los Caballeros many times since my initial visit in 1971 and have always had a marvelous time, so I am not at all surprised at the experience of my friends from Michigan.

On two different occasions during the last five years the annual meeting of the Country Inns and Back Roads Innkeepers' Association has been held at this ranch. These are men and women from all over North America as well as visitors from Britain and Europe who represent the highest ideals of innkeeping. We went back the second time because of all the services and provisions for entertainment and amusement.

As we were leaving, several innkeepers urged me to arrange for another meeting here again as soon as possible.

RANCHO DE LOS CABALLEROS, Wickenburg, AZ 85358; 602-684-5484. A 73-guestroom luxury ranch-resort, 60 mi. from Phoenix in the sunny, dry desert. American plan. Breakfast, lunch, dinner served to travelers daily. Open from mid-Oct. to early May. Wheelchair access. Swimming pool, horseback riding, hiking, skeet shooting, putting green, tennis, and 18-hole championship golf course on grounds. Special children's program. No pets. No credit cards. Dallas C. Gant, Jr., Innkeeper. (See Index for rates.)

Directions: Rtes. 60, 89, and 93 lead to Wickenburg. Ranch is 2 mi. west of town on Rte. 60 and 2 mi. south on Vulture Mine Road.

A number of inns have nearby airports where private airplanes may land. An airplane symbol at the end of the inn directions indicates that there is an airport nearby. Consult inn for further information.

TANQUE VERDE
Tucson, Arizona (1970)

The postmark on the letter was "Caldwell, New Jersey." It said in part: "We've been reading about your last visit to Tanque Verde Ranch, just outside of Tucson. It sounds very intriguing. My wife and I are enthusiastic about the prospect of a new vacation experience in the desert country. The idea of staying at a ranch that may have even survived Indian raids, and your description of steak over mesquite fires and bird watching, are most inviting. However, it is a long way for us to go, and neither of us has ever been astride a horse. We're both about fifty years old and we'd like a little more advice as to whether we should venture forth on this trip."

Until my first visit to Tanque Verde in 1969, horseback riding for me consisted of a couple short hauls on a Tennessee walking horse and one or two rides on the gentlest nag in my local livery stable. When I went out to Tanque Verde, I talked this over with the head wrangler, and he picked out a horse that he thought was the right size for my weight and had enough experience to guide me.

On that ride (the first of many during subsequent visits), I met a husband and wife from the Boston area, who were at a Western ranch for the first time and out on their first morning trail ride. We left the corral in single file and rode out into the desert. The entire experience was so exhilarating that by the time we got back to the ranch my Massachusetts neighbors were inquiring as to whether they could have more active horses and go for a longer ride the next day.

By the end of the week, these people had purchased some blue jeans, western shirts, cowboy hats, and boots, and knew all the horses by their first names.

Tanque Verde is a completely different type of country inn. There are many diversions, including both indoor and outdoor pools and an active tennis program. I spent one New Year's Eve there and had a great time with all the parents and children who had been there since Christmas.

In Tanque Verde's 100-year-old history as one of Arizona's pioneer guest cattle ranches, there are even stories of Indian raids. The ranch is set back in a semicircle of mountains, about a thirty-minute drive from downtown Tucson and the airport. The accommodations are in almost luxurious individual *casitas,* all of which have their own Spanish-style corner fireplaces. Everyone eats at long tables in the vaulted dining room, and there's nothing like the desert air to encourage big appetites.

One further point: Tanque Verde is open throughout the entire year, and during the summer there are many guests from Europe and Asia enjoying the full holiday in the desert. As innkeeper Bob Cote says, "We have so many guests speaking different languages, we could almost advertise that it's a good place for children to get some language tutoring."

This guest ranch was the first such accommodation to be included in *CIBR.* In subsequent years I have added a few others, both east and west. Tanque Verde, with genuine cordiality extended to all guests and its infectious informality, has served as a model for me.

TANQUE VERDE, 14301 E. Speedway, Tucson, AZ 85748; 602-296-6275. A 65-guestroom ranch-inn, 10 mi. from Tucson. American plan. Breakfast, lunch, and dinner served to travelers by reservation. Open year-round. Riding, indoor and outdoor pool, tennis, sauna, exercise room, and whirlpool bath on grounds. Robert Cote, Innkeeper. (See Index for rates.)

Directions: From U. S. 10, exit at Speedway Blvd. and travel east to dead end.

"European plan" means that rates for rooms and meals are separate. "American plan" means that meals are included in the cost of the room. "Modified American plan" means that breakfast and dinner are included in the cost of the room. The rates at some inns include a continental breakfast with the lodging.

THE BED AND BREAKFAST INN
San Francisco, California (1979)

Good, bad, or indifferent, every bed-and-breakfast inn or bed-and-breakfast home on the West Coast owes a debt of gratitude to the Bed and Breakfast Inn in San Francisco. For quite a few years it was the only one of its kind, and now I understand that there are over fifty in that city alone. It's a pity they did not all borrow the high standards and admirable objectives, as well as the idea, of the Bed and Breakfast Inn.

When it came to rewriting these pages on the Bed and Breakfast Inn, frankly, I was at a loss. I found that my early impressions of this inn, as I wrote about it in past editions, were complete in every respect.

However, I think this letter from Marily Kavanaugh explains why the inn has remained so popular in the face of so much competition.

"Bob and I feel that the two most important things for our guests are (1) a very special staff and (2) attention to details.

"There are other beautifully decorated inns in San Francisco but most are owned and operated by a group of investors. In our case, we give personal attention to all our guests. Telling guests how to get downtown, where to find the best pizza or handknit sweaters—this is where we really shine.

"Although we have a great staff, Bob and I feel it is our first job to go through the rooms every week. We notice everything that only an owner notices—desk blotters that need changing, magazines over two months old, plants ready for replacement, little pillows to be recovered, soap dishes with a chipped corner—the list goes on. I never feel this is the manager's job—it is the owner's job, and we do it very well.

"We continue to love the inn and the staff seems to love it, too."

Here are my impressions of the Bed and Breakfast Inn: the reception room, used as one of the breakfast areas, has a very light and airy feeling, enhanced by white wicker furniture, many flower arrangements, and light touches everywhere.

Some of the guest rooms are named after various parts of London. There's Covent Garden, Chelsea, Green Park, and Kensington Garden. The Mayfair Flat has a spiral staircase to a bedroom loft, a double tub, a kitchen, and a view of the Golden Gate Bridge.

Each room provides an entirely different experience. For example, many have completely different sets of sheets, pillowcases, and towels. There are all varieties of beds, including traditional shiny brass bedsteads. There are flowers everywhere, thermos jugs of ice-water, many books, baskets of fruit, electric clocks with an alarm, down pillows, and gorgeous coverlets and spreads. Five of the bedrooms have their own bathrooms, and the others share. Four rooms have the garden view. I saw old-fashioned British ceiling fans in some of the rooms.

The location of the Bed and Breakfast is another virtue. Charlton Court is a little dead-end street off Union, between Buchanan and Laguna. It's within easy walking distance of Fisherman's Wharf. In fact, San Francisco is such a "walking place" that it's convenient to everything. The nicest part of it is that when people get tired of walking, they can always take the cable cars!

THE BED AND BREAKFAST INN, Four Charlton Court, San Francisco, CA 94123; 415-921-9784. A 9-guestroom European-style pension in the Union Street district of San Francisco. Convenient to all of the Bay Area recreational, cultural, and gustatory attractions. Continental breakfast is the only meal offered. Open daily year-round. Not comfortable for children. No pets. No credit cards. Robert and Marily Kavanaugh, Innkeepers. (See Index for rates.)

Directions: Take the Van Ness Exit from Rte. 101 and proceed to Union Street. Charlton Court is a small courtyard street halfway between Laguna and Buchanan, off Union.

BENBOW INN
Garberville, California (1974)

The owners-innkeepers of the Benbow are Patsy and Chuck Watts, whom I have known for many years. The one outstanding quality that each of them has in such marvelous abundance is enthusiasm, and all of the improvements and additions to this truly unusual northern California inn have been undertaken by them with great joy and love.

"Ever since Day One," said Chuck, "we have been very happy and have had a really tremendous time. It's a continuing challenge and we've gotten a great deal accomplished, but I like the idea that the future is big with plans."

"We feel that we are a destination resort-inn, able to accommodate and provide amusement and diversion for all our guests of any age," chimed in Patsy. "We have acquired some fabulous antique pieces, most particularly a magnificent carved buffet for the dining room. We have added a beautiful carved mantel for the fireplace in the lobby and have installed an antique mantel and a fireplace in the lounge.

"We will be having our wine tasting in November, and this has now become a semi-annual affair, with many of the California boutique wineries represented."

I first visited the Benbow Inn in 1973 and was immediately intrigued not only with its location in the glorious redwood country of northern California, but also with its design, which shows definite influences of the Art Deco style of the early 1920s. There are also some touches of an English Tudor manor house found in the half-timbers, carved dark wood paneling, solid oak furniture, bookcases, hardwood floors, handsome oriental rugs, and truly massive fireplace in the main living room.

Some guest rooms are on the terrace and garden levels with private patios. With four-poster beds, antiques, and country fabrics, their decor is most attractive. Three of them have fireplaces and VCRs. Other guest rooms in the main inn had also been handsomely redecorated, and my own room, Number 313, was on the top floor and looked out over the gardens and a wonderful changing panorama of clouds.

The Benbow is, indeed, a destination resort-inn—in addition to swimming, it offers tennis on two tennis courts nearby, a good golf course within walking distance, hiking, and magnificent backroading. By the way, it's very accessible by public transportation since the Route 101 buses stop almost at the front door.

At Christmastime there's a twelve-foot tree with teddy bears playing drums hanging from every branch. Under the tree there are Patsy's very special antique, oversized toys. An antique sleigh is on the front porch filled with presents and wreaths. Holly and masses of decorations are all over the inn.

On Christmas Day there is a special two-seatings Christmas dinner and everyone has a wonderful time.

Incidentally, in the fall and all through the holidays, English tea and scones are served in the lobby. Chuck's mother, Marie, is the tea lady.

The Benbow also has a film library with over 300 classic films. These are shown every evening. On one of my visits I cheered and wept a little at James Cagney's great portrayal of George M. Cohan in *Yankee Doodle Dandy.*

Patsy, Chuck, and Truffles (their new Afghan hound, the most photographed canine in northern California) are having a wonderful time greeting guests, sharing their enthusiasm, and providing their own bubbling brand of warmth and hospitality. In short, they're model innkeepers. I'm glad they and the Benbow Inn found each other.

BENBOW INN, 445 Lake Benbow Dr., Garberville, CA 95440; 707-923-2124. A 55-guestroom English Tudor inn in the redwood country of northern California. On Rte. 101 near the Benbow State Park. European plan. Breakfast, lunch, and dinner served to travelers daily. Open mid-Apr. to Nov. 28; re-open Dec. 17 for holiday season. Swimming on grounds; golf, tennis adjacent. Hiking and magnificent backroading. Chuck, Patsy, and Muffin Watts, Innkeepers. (See Index for rates.)

Directions: From San Francisco follow Rte. 101 north 200 mi. and exit at Benbow.

BRITT HOUSE
San Diego, California (1981)

Lying abed in the morning in this exquisitely and lovingly furnished bedroom of the Britt House, I couldn't help thinking that Daun Martin, with her attention to important details, has placed her truly valued guests in an atmosphere of at least ninety years ago, with authentic furniture, wallpaper designs, lighting fixtures, and other significant features.

True, to begin with she has a most remarkable Victorian house as you can see from the Jan Lindstrom drawing. A marvelous stained glass window flanking the stairwell is a truly magnificent work. The preservation of the handcarved doorways and moldings and the interior make it an almost living museum.

My mind drifted back to my arrival on the previous afternoon when Daun had shown me to the Camphor Tree Room, a quiet, intimate bedroom done in forest green, teal, and peach, with a carved oak dresser and a matching headboard for the queen-sized bed. True to its name, it has a thrilling view of the eighty-year-old camphor tree surrounded by ferns and flowers, and also has its own balcony where breakfast can be taken. This is typical of other rooms, all of which are done with an abundance of lace curtains, velvet swags, beautiful woods, oversized couches, and marble-top dressers.

The Britt House's answer to "down the hall" bathrooms is to provide their guests with terry cloth bathrobes. It's wonderful to slip into one of these after a shower or a bath.

Daun's affection for animals has created an additional special feature at the Britt House. Not only are there some very nice kitty cats and a couple of amusing dogs on the premises, there is also a collection of stuffed animals of all kinds to be found in every bedroom. Usually they hold a welcoming note, personally addressed to each guest. Some of the animals are even taken out to dinner by guests. I know you won't believe this, but it's true. They sit them at the table, and everybody has lots of fun.

Britt House breakfasts are quite special. Freshly squeezed orange juice, eggs in a variety of styles, freshly baked yeast breads, sweet butter and honey, and European coffee, prepared filter-drip style, or tea are provided on the individual trays taken to each room. On Sunday morning, Daun's famous cinnamon twist bread is served with eggs over hash. There's a formal afternoon tea, too.

There are four bathrooms, two on each floor, and one has handsome twin antique bathtubs and bubble bath. The bathroom next to the billiard room offers a luxurious Finnish sauna that is available to all guests.

The Cottage, with its own private bath, just a few steps from the handsome camphor tree is decorated in cheerful blue and yellow, and has a romantically cozy bed-nook with a canopy, a full-sized bed, a kitchen, and a porch that faces the main house and the beautiful gardens.

These gardens have a remarkably tall hedge that protects the house, and provides excellent privacy. Regardless of what time of year I visit the Britt House, there always seems to be a profusion of flowers in bloom.

BRITT HOUSE, 406 Maple St., San Diego, CA 92103; 619-234-2926. A 10-guestroom bed-and-breakfast inn (private and shared baths) a short distance from Balboa Park with its world-famous zoo, Museum of Art, Man and Natural History. Reuben H. Fleet Space Theater, and the beaches, desert country, and Mexico (13 mi.). Breakfast only meal served (special dinners can be arranged with advance notice). Open all year. Sauna on grounds; jogging, biking, skating, bicycles nearby. No pets. Not particularly suitable for young children. Daun Martin and Robert Hostick, Innkeepers. (See Index for rates.)

Directions: Take Airport-Sassafrass turnoff coming south on Hwy. 5. Proceed on Kettner. Turn left on Laurel; left on Third; right on Nutmeg; right on Fourth St.; and come down one block to the corner of Fourth and Maple.

CARTER HOUSE
Eureka, California (1988)

When I first included the Carter House in my book *Bed and Breakfast, American Style,* I said it was "definitely a class act." I'm happy to say I haven't changed my mind.

Looking for all the world as if it had been standing on the hillside in Eureka for at least a hundred years, the house is actually an exact replica of a circa 1884 San Francisco house that was destroyed in the 1906 earthquake. Mark Carter discovered the plans for the house, which had been designed by the same architects who built the famous Carson Mansion, and he and a crew of three built the four-story structure in 1982. They followed the original plans, handcrafting the intricate wood wainscotings and moldings. Their work is really a marvel of craftsmanship in every detail.

Mark and his wife, Christi, are a warm and enthusiastic couple, and they've left nothing to chance in creating a most inviting atmosphere in this handsome Victorian inn. While retaining a period tone throughout the house, they have captured a light and airy feeling with whitewashed walls and large, undraped windows. Antique furnishings are complemented with polished oak floors, oriental rugs, marble fireplaces, green plants, and fresh-cut flowers. Mark also likes to exhibit the works of local artists, and he displays original contemporary paintings, ceramics, and baskets in the three main floor parlors.

There are wonderful views of Humboldt Bay and the marina as well as the remarkable Carson Mansion from the third-story guest rooms, which have high pitched ceilings. There are also guest rooms at street level, below the parlor, and a suite with a fireplace and jacuzzi on the second floor. They are all beautifully furnished with antiques, down comforters, fluffy pillows, and a flannel robe in the closets. Three rooms share a bath and the other four have their own private baths.

Breakfast at the Carter House is something quite special. The dining room table is laid with a crisp white tablecloth, beautiful Flow Blue china, crystal, and silver. The orange juice is freshly squeezed, the coffee is freshly roasted, and then there might be a honeydew and cantaloupe cup with a sauce of freshly diced mint leaves, Cointreau, and anise, or perhaps a poached pear in caramel sauce, or kiwi with puréed raspberries. There is almost always a just-baked fruit muffin and an egg Benedict or Florentine, and sometimes there is a smoked salmon platter. The *pièce de résistance* is Christi's melt-in-your-mouth apple-almond tart, constructed of paper-thin layers of phyllo pastry. This is just a sample, because Christi loves to cook, and she's always trying out new ideas.

They are now offering a one-entrée dinner for houseguests and, judging from what Mark tells me, it sounds very appetizing. The menu changes every day, depending on what is available locally, and fish and seafood are frequently featured. Some of their entrées have been fillet of red snapper with a mustard and basil sauce, grilled yellow-fin tuna, and fillet of beef with a peppercorn sauce. Fresh vegetables and a green salad accompany dinner, and a choice of two appetizers and two desserts is also available. The desserts, which are Christi's department, sound scrumptious—fresh lemon tart with lemon cream sauce or chocolate mousse paté with a Grand Marnier sauce.

The Carter House is on the fringe of Eureka's Old Town, where there are many beautifully restored turn-of-the-century buildings. This downtown restoration is one of the best I've seen and is not as commercial as many. It is right on the waterfront of Humboldt Bay.

Oh, one other thing. Mark has a 1958 Bentley, in which you may arrange to be transported to or from the airport. As I said, this is definitely a class act.

I'm very happy to welcome the Carter House to the pages of *Country Inns and Back Roads* for the first time.

CARTER HOUSE, 1033 Third St., Eureka, CA 95501; 707-445-1390 or 444-8062. A 7-guestroom (private and shared baths) Victorian mansion in a waterfront town in northern California, 200 mi. north of San Francisco. Breakfast and afternoon tea are included in room charge. Dinner is served daily to houseguests. Open all year. Scenic cruises in Humboldt Bay, scenic drives, golf, Carson Mansion, Clarke Museum, antiques and crafts shops, art galleries, and restaurants nearby. No pets. Mark and Christi Carter, Innkeepers. (See Index for rates.)

Directions: Take Hwy. 101 to Eureka. The inn is on the corner of L and Third Sts.

THE GREY WHALE INN
Fort Bragg, California (1980)

Ever since the first edition of this book in 1966, I have visited inns that were formerly gristmills, poorhouses, majestic mansions, carriage houses, stagecoach taverns, farmhouses, and log cabins. However, the Grey Whale is the first inn that began life as a hospital!

"The inn was built in 1915," explained John Bailey, who with his wife, Colette, acquired it in 1978. "It was the Redwood Coast Hospital before it was transformed into an inn in 1974."

John, Colette, and I were browsing through the fourteen guest rooms, twelve of which have private baths. Its early life as a hospital creates a distinct advantage for present-day inn guests, because the rooms are quite large, with many generous windows.

The Grey Whale features an unusual variety of textures and colors, ranging from the rich brown stain of the exterior boards to the brilliant colors of the interior carpeting and the wide selection of original contemporary paintings. The guest rooms have comforters with matching pillow covers, bright decorator sheets, and one has a working fireplace.

Each room contains a folder describing all of the sights and attractions of Fort Bragg and the Mendocino Coast, including the redwood forest, art galleries, the Botanical Gardens, the beautiful Pacific Ocean beaches, the Skunk Railroad, and a brief summary of some of the restaurants. (The Grey Whale offers bed and breakfast.)

When we passed through the second-floor dining room, Colette explained that she bakes all the breads and coffee cakes that are served on the continental breakfast. "These can be enjoyed right here, or the tray may be taken to the bedroom. Many guests like to eat breakfast in bed," she said.

Colette received two blue ribbons at the Mendocino County Fair and Apple Show—her apricot-prune coffee cake and the lemon-yogurt bread were winners, and St. Timothy's coffee cake won a third prize. John said, "Competition was keen, but no match for the specialties that we serve our guests at the Grey Whale Inn." These are now available in the Grey Whale Cookbook.

Motorists passing through Fort Bragg on Highway I just can't miss the Grey Whale, because it stands at the north end of town surrounded by a large grass and turf area with some very colorful plantings of marguerite, California poppies, amaryllis, African daisies, and geraniums.

"Whale watching is one of our great pastimes," said John. "The whale watch starts in mid-December and from then on through March there are programs planned at various points along the coast."

Along with the whale-watching programs, there is a whale festival that includes a whale art exhibit. Many nationally known marine artists will be coming to Fort Bragg again this year for the concurrent whale art exhibits at the Grey Whale Inn and the Wildlife Gallery in nearby Mendocino.

It was from John that I learned of the many activities and attractions in this section of northern California. "We have theater, crafts shows, scuba diving, fishing, hiking, and many museums," he reported. "We appeal to the art buff, the whale-watcher, the beachcomber, and anyone who wants to have some unhurried hours away from pressures."

THE GREY WHALE INN, 615 No. Main St., Fort Bragg, CA 95437; 707-964-0640. (California toll-free reservations: 800-382-7244.) A 14-guestroom inn located on Hwy. 1 at the north end of Fort Bragg. Continental breakfast included in room rates. (Only meal served.) Open every day in the year. Advance reservations important. Wheelchair access. Many natural, historic, and recreational attractions within a short distance. Beachcombing, scuba diving, fishing, and hiking nearby. Available by Greyhound Bus and Skunk Train. John and Colette Bailey, Innkeepers. (See Index for rates.)

Directions: From the south, follow Hwy. 101 to Cloverdale, take Rte. 128 west to Hwy. 1, and follow north to Fort Bragg. Alternate route: Exit Hwy. 101 at Willits, then west on Rte. 20 to Fort Bragg. Driving time from San Francisco, 4 hrs. Another alternative: Hwy. 1 along the coast. Driving time from San Francisco, 6 hrs.

HARBOR HOUSE
Elk, California (1975)

Here I was on the opposite side of the continent from New England, far away from my home in the Berkshires, but enjoying still another of my "second homes"—this time on the cliffs of the blue Pacific at Harbor House.

This is another good place to greet spring, because spring comes lustily and vigorously in this part of the world, and the sea in its many moods washes ashore gently or raucously, but the rhythm never ceases. I awaken in the morning to look through the trees to the great rock formations that seem to have been thrown almost helter-skelter from the end of the headlands. Helen and Dean Turner, the innkeepers, had thoughtfully provided a very comfortable chair in the window, with a perfect view of the sea stacks and tunnels, which, along with the arches, caves, and small islands, provide an unusual view from the inn.

This particular group of rock formations was at one time a staging area for the loading and the unloading of lumber schooners. Fortunately, the story of this community has been graphically presented in the unusual brochure of the inn, with dramatic photographs showing just the scenes that I have described.

The subtitle for Harbor House on the rustic sign on Route 1 is "By the Sea." Fewer words are more apt than these. Although the main entrance is on the highway, the immediate focus of all the attention is in the rear of the inn, which looks out over the Pacific, and almost every guest room has this view.

The main building of the inn was built in 1916 as an executive residence. The construction is entirely of virgin redwood from the nearby Albion Forest. In fact, it is an enlarged version of the "Home of Redwood" exhibit building of the 1915 Panama–Pacific International Exposition in San Francisco.

Guest rooms in the main building and adjacent cottages are individually heated and have private baths. Fireplaces and parlor stoves are stocked with wood, and some of the accommodations have sun decks.

I reflected that were it not for the dominance of the sea, the view from the *other* side of the house across the meadows and into the low coastal hills could be thought of as very beautiful.

Because Helen and Dean Turner have always had a great deal of involvement and interest in the arts, from time to time Harbor House presents programs by soloists and chamber music players. The living room with its wood paneling provides an ideal atmosphere. As Helen says, "So many artists live on the coast and an intimate concert in the living room is a wonderful way to hear them." Also, Helen tells me, "Sometimes these concerts are spontaneous and informal, as a talented guest sits down at the Steinway or picks up the guitar."

One reader wrote me, "Our dinner was the nice, slow, mellow kind I love and get so rarely. It was such pleasant, unhurried service. We were free to be alone together or speak to others if we wished, a wonderful blend of solitude and society.

"We got wonderful pictures of all the colorful flowers and scenery. . . . Beautiful as the pictures are, they do not capture what it was like to be there, or explain why I felt homesick when I had to leave."

HARBOR HOUSE, 5600 S. Hwy. #1, Box 369, Elk, CA 95432; 707-877-3203. A seaside inn with 5 guestrooms in the inn and 4 cottages, 16 mi. south of Mendocino, overlooking the Pacific. Modified American plan omits lunch. Breakfast and dinner served daily to houseguests. Open year-round. Ocean wading, abalone and shell hunting, fishing, and hiking on grounds. Golf, biking, boating, ocean white-water tours, deep-sea fishing, and canoeing nearby. Unsuitable for children or pets. No credit cards. Dean and Helen Turner, Innkeepers. (See Index for rates.)

Directions: Elk is approx. 3 hrs. from Golden Gate Bridge. Take Hwy. 101 to Cloverdale, then Hwy. 128 west to Hwy. 1. Continue on Hwy. 1 south 6 mi. to Harbor House.

A number of inns have nearby airports where private airplanes may land. An airplane symbol at the end of the inn directions indicates that there is an airport nearby. Consult inn for further information.

HERITAGE PARK BED & BREAKFAST INN
San Diego, California (1987)

"Yes, we call ourselves a bed and breakfast inn, but since we offer dinner to our guests, that makes us a full-service inn." Lori Chandler and I were enjoying a candlelight dinner in the unusually commodious Queen Anne room, with a waitress costumed in late Victorian fashion. This remarkably restored mansion is located in the seven-acre Victorian preserve of Old Town, San Diego. "Yes, it has won us a 'People in Preservation' Award," Lori proudly told me.

"It stood vacant here in the Park for two-and-a-half years collecting mold, dry-rot, and severe floor and roof damage," she said. "Then my mother, my two sisters, their husbands, and I saw the possibilities and we spent hundreds of hours in research. Fortunately, we found the original floor plan, which enabled us to restore the house very authentically."

Heritage Park is set in a very quiet enclave of painstakingly restored Victorian homes, surrounded with flowers and shrubs. The pleasant cobblestone street is for pedestrians, and cars are parked in the back.

"The mansion was built in 1889," Lori pointed out, "and has the typical Queen Anne characteristics, including a variety of chimneys, shingles, a two-story corner tower, and an encircling veranda. Featured in the *Golden Era* magazine in 1890, it was called an 'outstanding, beautiful home of southern California.'"

There are nine distinctive guest rooms, each furnished and decorated in a popular style of the late 19th century. Incidentally, the antiques and collectibles are offered for sale, and as Lori says, "You can keep your special occasion with you forever."

Our catered dinner, at which we were joined by Lori's mother, Mary, consisted of five courses, and I could have chosen from baked chicken marinated in herbs, lemon, and butter or roast leg of lamb; however, I opted for large shrimp served with feta cheese. There is also a simpler Victorian country supper. We were eating at the table in the bay alcove window in the Queen Anne room, a guest room, where normally a couple would have breakfast or dinner brought in.

The full breakfast includes omelets, quiches, soufflés, a fruit cup with fresh fruit, and Lori's very special award-winning Strawberry Jam Loaf.

"I hope you will share with your readers the joy that we feel about Old Town, San Diego," she said, as we walked out to the front veranda to enjoy dessert and coffee. "It was a mission at first, established in 1769. Old Town, San Diego, was officially classified as a State Historic Park and incorporated in 1968; there are tours available to visit the original buildings.

"I've done a lot of other things up to this time in my life," she said, sighing contentedly. "However, I think that my background in antique collecting, interior designing, entertaining, public relations, and teaching has finally come to one focal point, and I'm content to be an innkeeper indefinitely."

Lori has proudly written to me that Heritage Park is the first B&B in Southern California to be selected as the Small Business of the Month by the San Diego Chamber of Commerce.

HERITAGE PARK BED & BREAKFAST INN, 2470 Heritage Park Row, San Diego, CA 92110; 619-295-7088. A 9-guestroom (private and shared baths) restored Victorian mansion in the heart of Old Town, San Diego. A choice of catered dinners is offered. Breakfast included in tariff, as well as evening refreshments, and nightly showing of vintage films. Open year-round. Special festivities at Christmas. Wheelchair facilities. Balboa Park, the famous San Diego Zoo, and other cultural activities and entertainment in the San Diego area. No accommodations for children under 14. No pets. No smoking. Lori Chandler, Innkeeper. (See Index for rates.)

Directions: From Los Angeles follow I-5 south to Old Town Ave. off ramp; turn left on San Diego Ave., and right on Harney.

"European plan" means that rates for rooms and meals are separate. "American plan" means that meals are included in the cost of the room. "Modified American plan" means that breakfast and dinner are included in the cost of the room. The rates at some inns include a continental breakfast with the lodging.

THE INN
Rancho Santa Fe, California (1974)

I was seated on the patio of my little bungalow at the Inn at Rancho Santa Fe, catching one more hour of the fantastic March sunshine, hoping to return to New England that evening with a faint blush of sunburn or even suntan. It was wonderful and quiet except for the twittering of a few birds inhabiting the lush green shrubbery and eucalyptus trees found everywhere in this beautiful southern California community.

I had just completed a two-week tour of California from Mendocino to San Diego and had found a very quiet haven. The mood here is untrendy. Perhaps it is set by the Royce family, including owners Danny and his sister, Dorothy, who are very much in evidence, along with their assorted now grown-up offspring, also on the inn staff.

For example, Danny, who is a proud alumnus of Hamilton College in Clinton, New York, as was his father, Steve, was dressed in a tweed coat with a button-down shirt and tan chino trousers. I think that guests, whether from the East or West Coast feel very comfortable in this conservative and not-at-all-stuffy atmosphere. Somehow or other, gentlemen just naturally seem to feel more comfortable wearing coats and ties for dinner, and the smart shops and boutiques, a few paces away in the village, cater to the tastes and preferences of the female guests at the inn.

I have visited here in many different seasons, and find that the guests, some of whom stay for a week or two at a time, cut across the categories of age and preference. They are quite apt to be into tennis, golf, swimming, and the beach. They enjoy some of the excellent attractions in the area, including Balboa Park and the San Diego Zoo. It's an inn where one would spend many days without leaving the area. Guests can rest and read by the swimming pool or even join in a game of croquet on the front lawn.

The town of Rancho Santa Fe is one of the most attractively designed that I have ever visited. It has been well described as a "civilized planned community." The homes and estates have been created in perfect harmony with nature's generous endowment of climate and scenery. One of the dominating factors is the presence of the gigantic eucalyptus trees.

The "family" feeling is extended even further when guests learn that the stunning framed needlepoints, very much in evidence through the main lobby and living rooms of the Inn, have been done by Danny's mother. For example, there is one very large, extremely handsome piece showing a large eucalyptus tree. It has become the symbol of the Inn and is found on all the stationery. My favorite is a needlepoint clock on one wall of the cathedral-ceilinged living room.

Cottages are scattered among the towering trees, and there's recreation for everyone here, including the younger set. The Inn has membership in nearby private 18-hole golf courses, and there are three tennis courts and a croquet green on the grounds. The swimming pool has an outdoor terrace where luncheon and refreshments are available. Also, the Inn has a beach cottage at nearby Del Mar for use during the summer months.

One of the most useful and gratifying amenities at the Inn is a map showing many short motor trips to points fifty miles away, including Lake Elsinore to the north and Tijuana, Mexico, to the south. I am personally acquainted with the rolling ranch and orchard country to the east as far away as Julian. All of these trips make a stay at the Inn worth several extra days.

Readers who use this book as a travel guide will recognize that I have not confined myself to any one particular genre of inn. What I look for is some important common denominators, including a friendly warmth from the innkeepers and staff, as well as an ambience that makes every guest feel wanted and taken care of.

THE INN, P.O. Box 869, Rancho Santa Fe, CA 92067; 619-756-1131. A 75-guestroom resort-inn, 27 mi. north of San Diego Freeway #5 and 5 mi. inland from Solana Beach, Del Mar. European plan. Breakfast, lunch, and dinner served to travelers daily. Open year-round. Pool, tennis, and 6-wicket croquet course on grounds. Golf and ocean nearby. Daniel Royce, Innkeeper. (See Index for rates.)

Directions: From I-5, take Exit S8 and drive inland about 6 mi.

MADRONA MANOR
Healdsburg, California (1988)

Many Easterners visiting northern California for the first time are struck with the unusual number of Victorian homes and buildings. I was reminded of this once again during a short drive around downtown Healdsburg on my way to Madrona Manor. I turned in at the impressive white stone archway and drove up the long winding drive to the rambling front porch. I think one could circle the house for days and always find a new cubbyhole or corner or a hidden porch on each trip. I turned to look over the grounds and noticed that Madrona Manor sits on top of a knoll with flower gardens, sculptured hedges, numerous varieties of trees and bushes, and acres and acres of lawn.

I heard a step behind me and realized that the couple coming out the front door were the innkeepers of Madrona Manor, John and Carol Muir. "Oh, I see you are enjoying our view," John said. "As a matter of fact, while you're here you must go up to the third floor of the inn because it is even more impressive from there."

Like the Old Rittenhouse, Madrona Manor is furnished with beautiful Victorian antiques. There is a 100-year-old rosewood square piano in the music room, and throughout the house are massive pieces of carved walnut and mahogany furniture and oriental carpets. There are fourteen-foot-high ceilings and many fireplaces with brightly painted tiles.

"I love fireplaces," I told John. "How many of your guest rooms have them?" He thought for a moment. "We have nine rooms with fireplaces. Most guests like them very much and I'm always particularly happy when young people ask for a fireplace room."

The guest rooms have ten-foot-high canopied beds or carved headboards, huge armoires, chaise longues, dressing tables with bevel-edged mirrors, original light fixtures, and period wallpapers. "Five of our rooms have the antique furniture of the original owner, John Paxton, who was a San Francisco financier," Carol told me. "He built this house and also the Carriage House in 1881."

Later, when Carol and John were showing me the extensive grounds, including a great vegetable garden and fruit trees, I looked in at the Carriage House. John told me the massive carved rosewood front door had been imported from Nepal. In fact, the entire house is furnished with imported hand-carved rosewood. There are also two more buildings with guest rooms. All four buildings are listed on the National Register of Historic Places.

However, I think the big story at Madrona Manor is the food. Their big, efficient kitchen is a delight to behold, and includes a wood-burning oven, a mesquite grill, and a separate smokehouse. The Muir's son, Todd, is in command. The Muirs are obviously very proud of his talents as a chef. "Todd's cooking has attracted the attention of *Gourmet* magazine, and we have guests who drive all the way from San Francisco just for dinner," John told me. I'd certainly be happy to make the trip for the dinner I had, which included a wonderful crusty goat-cheese soufflé seasoned with rosemary and garlic, a perfect green salad, and mesquite-grilled monkfish that was absolutely delicious. The vegetables, fresh from the garden, were also perfect. I couldn't resist trying the Mexican flan with rose petals (delightful). There is a prix-fixe menu and an à la carte menu, and some further offerings are Muscovy duck leg stuffed with game paté, mesquite-grilled pork loin, cold poached Pacific salmon, and breast of chicken with mushrooms in Marsala sauce. Everything is given special and interesting treatment and is served with great aplomb.

Later that night, as I stood on the balcony of my room, looking out over the beautiful view, with Mount Saint Helena to the east, I thought a stay here in the Sonoma wine country at this beautiful inn is a very special experience.

We are happy to welcome Madrona Manor to the pages of *Country Inns and Back Roads* for the first time.

MADRONA MANOR (Romantik Hotels), 1001 Westside Rd., Box 818, Healdsburg, CA 95448; 707-433-4231. An 18-guestroom, 2-suite (private baths) Victorian mansion in the heart of Sonoma County wine country, 65 mi. north of San Francisco. Breakfast included in room rate. Dinner served daily; reservations recommended. Open year-round. Wheelchair access. Swimming pool on grounds. Golf, tennis, hiking, canoeing, fishing, winery tours nearby. Children and pets welcome by prearrangement. John and Carol Muir, Innkeepers. (See Index for rates.)

Directions: From San Francisco, follow Rte. 101 north to the 2nd Healdsburg exit. Continue north and turn left at Mill St. (first stoplight), which becomes Westside Rd.

MOUNTAIN HOME INN
Mill Valley, California (1987)

"Mount Tamalpais has been an international meeting place for many years. Transplanted Europeans, missing their tradition of hiking the Alps, came here, and there were Swiss, German, Austrian, English, Norwegian, Italian, Yugoslavian, and French tourists and hikers who mingled with the Bay Area residents, enjoying the wonderful mountain wilderness and trails."

Susan Cunningham and I were seated on the deck of the Mountain Home Inn, overlooking the truly gorgeous panoramic scenery that stretched out to include a view of the northern San Francisco Bay. "Actually, the inn was once accessible only by taking a train up the mountain to a small railroad stop and hiking the rest of the way up. Thank heavens, today our guests can drive all the way up to our front door. A wagon road wasn't built until 1884, and then the railway came a couple of years later. It was known as 'the crookedest railroad in the world,' with 22 trestles and 281 curves. It cost $1.00 from Mill Valley and only $1.40 from San Francisco for the round trip."

Susan left me for a moment to greet some new guests, and I thought of other places that I had visited with such tremendous views — Chateau Chevre d'Or overlooking the Mediterranean in southern France and the Snowbird Mountain Lodge in North Carolina. Views of the Bay, the Tiburon Peninsula, the East Bay Hills, and Mount Diablo can be enjoyed from each of the guest rooms, most of which have their own private balconies. Every one of the ten handsome guest rooms has an original design; some have jacuzzis, and there are also some with fireplaces. Built in three tiers, with hardwood floors, skylights, and a lobby dominated by four giant indoor redwood trees, the inn is decorated in the basic colors of beige and tan, which certainly blend well with the natural, rugged setting.

Susan returned with her eyes sparkling. "It took Ed and me four years to bring this building to the point where we felt we were ready to reopen it. Actually, it's the first luxury inn and restaurant on the mountain for many, many years. There used to be several of them, when people came up from San Francisco to enjoy the view and the hiking. At one time, I'm told, there was a Bavarian beer garden, where Germanic hikers, artists, and poets gathered to have a good time."

There are seemingly endless possibilities for hikes and drives through the mountain woods. Bird and sea-life sanctuaries are within easy driving distance, as are Stinson Beach and Point Reyes National Seashore. Horseback riding and tennis are also nearby.

Although the outdoorsy atmosphere is somewhat rustic, the menu at Mountain Home is quite sophisticated and extensive. The fish courses include mesquite-grilled fillet of ono fish, served with slivers of ginger root, and poached fresh fillet of salmon with sorrel sauce. The meat and poultry selections include roast fillet of pork, with calvados and apple brandy sauce, and medallions of milk-fed veal served in a cream sauce. A dining room and outside dining deck are reserved especially for overnight guests, and they may choose to have their complimentary continental breakfast outside on warm, sunny days. Lunch and dinner are served to other visitors in an upper-level dining room and deck.

Only a twenty-five-minute drive from San Francisco's financial district, there may be no other inn in the world that is so conveniently close to a major city and yet is so splendidly isolated from the everyday world.

MOUNTAIN HOME INN, 810 Panoramic Hwy., Mill Valley, CA 94941; 415-381-9000. A 10-guestroom (private baths) mountainside inn just 15 min. north of the Golden Gate Bridge. Breakfast and lunch served daily; dinner every night except Mon. Open year-round. Wheelchair access. Endless hiking possibilities with over 250 mi. of trails in Mt. Tamalpais State Park and adjacent lands. Near Muir Woods National Monument, Stinson Beach, Point Reyes National Seashore, horseback riding, and tennis. No pets. Susan and Ed Cunningham, Innkeepers. (See Index for rates.)

Directions: From the Golden Gate Bridge, exit right on Hwy. 1 at Mill Valley following all Mt. Tamalpais signs. After 3 mi. turn right on Panoramic Hwy. and go 3.25 mi. to the inn on the right side of the road.

THE PELICAN INN
Muir Beach, California (1988)

It was teatime at the Pelican Inn. Susan and Ed Cunningham and I were seated at a table in one corner of the dining room and would shortly be joined by the innkeeper, Barry Stock. Susan and Ed are the new owners of the Pelican as well as the owners of another *CIBR* inn a few miles away but much higher in the sky—the Mountain Home Inn.

The Pelican is about as close to being an English West Country inn as one could find. I could well imagine that I was seated in the Lobster Pot in Mousehole in Cornwall. The Pelican has an Inglenook fireplace with the inscription, "Fear knocked at the door, Faith answered; No one was there." There's a resemblance to the Royal Oak Inn in Yattendon, the place where I like to stay on the nights before my departures from England.

The waitress came in with a platter of most tempting snacks, including bangers, ribs, cheese, and soup. When I remarked on how tempting they all looked, Susan replied, "We've added many new items to our menu. Our luncheon menu now includes a plowman's lunch of hot rolls, cheddar or Stilton cheese, chutney, tomatoes, and whole small onions, as well as cottage pie, bangers and mash, and fish and chips." Ed added, "Dinners include beef Wellington, rack of lamb, and prime rib with Yorkshire pudding, as well as fresh fish dishes."

Susan and Ed were good friends with the original owner of the inn, my friend Charles Felix, an Englishman. Charles designed the inn, with its Tudor half-timbers and white exterior, and ran it most successfully for quite a few years. When he and his wife, Brenda, decided to go back to England, Susan and Ed were ecstatic at the prospect of becoming the new owners of the Pelican.

"Charles, of course, is a very hard act to follow," said Susan, "but I'm happy to say that one of our best moves was to make Barry Stock the innkeeper of the inn. He's from Devonshire, England, where he ran some establishments. It was in Exeter that he met his wife, Pamela, an American girl from Newport Beach, California. She lured him out here, and in the course of time they visited the Pelican and were smitten immediately. He was Charlie's right-hand man and managed the inn while he was away."

Almost on cue, Barry walked in and I had the pleasure of being introduced. He proved to have a very attractive English accent and soon all of us were enthusiastically conversing. When I asked him about Pamela, he said, "Her passion is the inn garden. She cultivates many different species of flowering plants, all of which could be found in an English garden."

Susan and Ed excused themselves to go back to their other inn, and Barry suggested that I might like to have a look around the inn.

"Susan and Ed have really done a masterful job of freshening up the inn," he said. "We painted, we repaired, we exchanged furniture that wasn't authentic to the period. We have several new Asian rugs with a 16th-century design, and we uncovered some beautiful wood floors, as you can see. I'm happy to say that we've received many compliments from guests who have been coming here for years, and this includes various members of Charles's family."

Our stroll took us abovestairs to the guest rooms, many of which have four-poster and half-tester beds. The Hogarth prints, which I admired on my first visit a number of years ago, were still in place.

"We now have a proper 'snug,' which is really an English term for a living room," Barry explained. "It's been furnished in 17th- and 18th-century English antiques and has a library and a fireplace. When we're not having a special party here, inn guests use it, and it is a popular place for them to curl up and read or to mingle with other guests."

Barry and I returned to the dining room, which was taking on a festive dinner air. The lights were reflected on the many carved chairs, beautiful old tables, and massive sideboards.

I'm delighted to re-include the Pelican Inn in the 1988 edition of this book.

THE PELICAN INN, Muir Beach, CA 94965; 415-383-6000 (for reservations, call between 9:30 and 4:30). A 6-guestroom (private baths) English inn on the northern California coast, 8 mi. from the Golden Gate Bridge. Breakfast included in tariff. Lunch and dinner open to the public. Open year-round. Wheelchair access to dining room. Swimming, beachcombing, backroading, walking, and all San Francisco attractions nearby. Ed and Susan Cunningham, Owners; Barry and Pamela Stock, Innkeepers. (See Index for rates.)

Directions: From Golden Gate Bridge follow Hwy. 101 north to Hwy. 1/Stinson Beach exit. Turn left at traffic lights and follow Hwy. 1/Stinson Beach Rd. 5 mi. to Muir Beach. (Do not go to Muir Woods.)

THE SANDPIPER INN AT-THE-BEACH
Carmel-by-the-Sea, California (1981)

It was a very stimulating morning at the Sandpiper because it had rained during the night in Carmel, and all of the flowers and bushes in the gardens in front of the inn were glistening with water, and birds were twittering merrily, going about from branch to branch. Inside, in the impressive cathedral living room, a good fire was burning and at the far end there were guests enjoying breakfast and reading the morning papers. In the reception area there was the pleasant hustle and bustle of departing guests promising to meet again next year.

Graeme and Irene Mackenzie, looking as bright and fresh as the morning, were moving from guest to guest making arrangements, expressing concern and hospitality in their clipped British accents. I happened to hear Graeme explaining what I took to be the inherent nature of Carmel to one of the guests.

"We who live here think that Carmel is a city of serendipity," he said. "We have houses and cottages with sunny balconies and courtyards, and I'm sure you've experienced the collection of small streets." I might add that Carmel's white beaches, narrow cypresses and magnificent seascapes are further rewards for the visitor.

"We're a kind of sleepy village," he continued. "There are no street lights, no sidewalks in residential districts, no street numbers, and, I guess most important, no neon signs."

I drifted over to another group where Irene was carrying on a lively conversation in French. She is quite at home with many other languages as well.

Each time I visit I'm impressed with the resemblance of this inn to an English country house hotel. Irene and Graeme fit beautifully into this ambience because they are both Scottish, so one might say that they blend right into the English and French antiques, oil paintings, flowered quilted bedspreads, wallpapered bathrooms, and freshly picked nosegays. Some of the bedrooms have wood-burning fireplaces, but there are no TVs or telephones in the rooms, ensuring peace and quiet. A recent innovation has been the addition of a third top sheet to each bed under the bedspread.

The inn itself is about seventy yards from the beach with sweeping views across Carmel Bay to Pebble Beach. The wide beach has white sand and is a marvelous place for sunning and picnicking. Both Irene and Graeme are very much interested in outdoor sports, including golf, tennis, and racquet ball, and are happy to introduce their houseguests to some of the clubs on the peninsula in which they have membership. There are also excellent back roads, as well as a tour of wineries in the area. The new Aquarium on Cannery Row is well worth a three-hour visit.

Later, after things had calmed down a bit and guests had gone off to play golf, walk the beach, or just sit in a quiet corner reading a book, I asked Graeme how an inn happened to be in this section of Carmel, where I had noted there were only private homes.

"The original guest house was built in 1930," he explained. "It came into existence before the very stringent zoning laws went into effect; hence our guests have the advantage of being in a very quiet section of the village and still only a few steps from the beach.

"We recently celebrated our tenth anniversary at Sandpiper, and both Irene and I find the greatest satisfaction in the number of returning guests each year."

THE SANDPIPER INN AT-THE-BEACH, 2408 Bayview Ave. at Martin St., Carmel-by-the-Sea, CA 93923; 408-624-6433. A 15-guestroom bed-and-breakfast inn and cottages near the Pacific Ocean. Breakfast only meal offered. Open all year. Carmel and Stuarts Cove beaches, Old Carmel Mission, Point Lobos State Park, 17-Mile Drive, and Big Sur State Park nearby. Ten-speed bicycles available; jogging and walking on beach. Arrangements can be made to play at nearby private golf and tennis clubs with pools and hot tubs. Children over 12 welcome. Please, no pets. Graeme and Irene Mackenzie, Innkeepers. (See Index for rates.)

Directions: From Hwy. 1 turn right at Ocean Ave., through Carmel Village, and turn left on Scenic Dr. (next to Ocean). Proceed to end of beach to Martin St. and turn left.

"European plan" means that rates for rooms and meals are separate. "American plan" means that meals are included in the cost of the room. "Modified American plan" means that breakfast and dinner are included in the cost of the room. The rates at some inns include a continental breakfast with the lodging.

THE SEAL BEACH INN AND GARDENS
Seal Beach, California (1981)

Like many other people, I am a natural born fan; such charismatic people as Frank Gifford, Casey Stengel, Leslie Howard, Marilyn Home, Martha Graham, and Marjorie Bettenhausen will find me in the front row, cheering with everything I've got.

I became a Marjorie Bettenhausen fan when I first visited the Seal Beach Inn, which at that time was little more than a motel from the 1920s. It had one very important thing going for it, however, and that was Marjorie's vision, talent, and enthusiasm.

Here are some observations from Marjorie herself about the inn: "It is a fairyland of brick courtyards, old ornate street lights, blue canopies, objets d'art, fountains, shuttered windows, window boxes, and vines. We are a family-run inn, a place of character, a thoughtfully designed place where guests are pampered and our service is friendly and caring.

"From the very start we saw the opportunity to create an inn that would have the ambience of inns that we have visited in southern France. We've been very fortunate since 1980, when you first visited, Norman, in having been discovered by many feature writers and also in having been on TV many times."

The French Mediterranean appearance is enhanced by the truly extraordinary gardens. All of the lodging rooms are named after flowers, including fuchsia, gardenia, and camellia. The full-time gardener keeps the flowers blooming even in winter with considerable aid from the mild year-round weather in this part of California. There are rare vines, climbing vines, flowering bushes, sweet-smelling bushes, deciduous trees, evergreen pear trees, and a wonderful variety of a cascading willowy tree that looks like a weeping willow, but really isn't. It stays green all year.

Lush plantings and antique newel posts are beside each guest room door, and in the rooms, lovely burgundy, rust, and peach comforters and dust ruffles set off the wrought-iron headboards. The bridal chamber, with its very own veranda beside the pool, is much in demand.

In addition, there are the Royal Villas, six of the most romantic, lavish suites imaginable. Marjorie says, "In all of California there are none that are more exquisite!"

The entrance to the inn from the street is through a three-sided square, around which the guest rooms are situated, and this is indeed a flower-filled courtyard, lit by street lamps that were rescued from the scrap pile at nearby Long Beach. There is a red English telephone booth in one corner, and a kiosk (that would be quite at home in Nice) has notices of all the nearby attractions. The library is an elegant guest salon with an impressive fireplace, books, and games. Breakfast is served in a small, çozy French-style tea room, presided over by a cheerful hostess.

Kay Trepp is responsible for the ambrosial breakfasts. Among her many accomplishments, she recently won first place for two entries in an important contest among other southern California innkeepers. When you visit the inn, ask about her "Chocolate Love Package."

Marjorie maintains that it takes many years to establish an inn par excellence and declares that "we finally are reaching the end of inn adolescence and moving into golden maturity. We want to be the best inn in the state, not just in beauty but in the warmth and love in which we serve."

So now it can easily be seen why I am a Marjorie Bettenhausen fan.

THE SEAL BEACH INN AND GARDENS (Romantik Hotels), 212 5th St., Seal Beach, CA 90740; 213-493-2416 or 213-430-3915. A 22-guestroom village inn located in a quiet residential area of an attractive town, 300 yds. from beach. Breakfast only meal served. Open all year. Near Disneyland, Knott's Berry Farm, Lion Country Safari, Catalina Island (20 mi. offshore), and California mountains and lakes 2 hrs. away. Long Beach Playhouse, Long Beach Music Center nearby. Swimming pool on grounds. Tennis, beach, biking, skating, golf nearby. No pets. Marjorie and Jack Bettenhausen, Innkeepers. (See Index for rates.)

Directions: From Los Angeles Airport take Hwy. 405 Freeway south to Seal Beach Blvd. exit. Turn left toward the beach, right on the Pacific Coast Hwy., left on 5th St. in Seal Beach, which is the first stoplight after main street. Inn is on the left, 2 blocks toward the beach on 5th St.

UNION STREET INN
San Francisco, California (1981)

"We are Edwardian, not Victorian."

Helen Stewart and I were having breakfast, seated in the sunny garden at the rear of the Union Street Inn. The fragrance of lilacs, camellias, and violets filled the air, and an occasional hummingbird darted from blossom to blossom. Some guests were enjoying breakfast on the spacious deck overlooking the garden, and there was the unmistakable aroma of fresh coffee and croissants. In this quiet retreat it was difficult to realize that we were in the heart of one of San Francisco's most attractive shopping and entertainment areas. "I say Edwardian," Helen continued, "because we're rather proud of the fact that in a city that has so much Victoriana, we are a bit different. The Edwardians, already into the 20th century, were less ostentatious than their elders. Their ornamentation was tempered by a new conservatism, and we like to feel that many of our decorations and furnishings are understatements."

Helen is a former San Francisco schoolteacher, who found herself involved in a mid-life career change. She restored and remodeled this handsome turn-of-the-century building, using tones and textures that are not only in the period, but also increase the feeling of hospitality.

The five bedrooms have such intriguing names as Wildrose, Holly, Golden Gate, and English Garden. Two have private bathrooms, and the others have running water in the rooms and share two bathrooms.

Two of the bedrooms have queen-sized beds with canopies, two have gleaming brass beds; all have really impressive, carefully chosen antiques. The brochure of the inn explains the different color schemes for each room. "If reservations are made sufficiently in advance, and the guests can anticipate a mood, these can all be coordinated." Helen made this comment with the faint suggestion of a twinkle.

My room had one of the queen-sized beds with very pleasant dark green wallpaper and matching draperies, which were most helpful in keeping the sun from intruding too early. The walls were adorned with two of the well-known Degas prints of ballet dancers. I thought they were quite appropriate, remembering King Edward's fondness for pretty women.

One end of the room had been turned into an alcove containing a rather elegantly decorated wash basin with mirrors and generous, fluffy towels. A very handsome antique mahogany dressing table had a three-way oval mirror. This is typical of the appointments of the other bedrooms, and I found many welcome living plants in all of the bedrooms.

Helen has converted the old carriage house at the bottom of the garden into a very fetching accommodation, with a large bay window overlooking the garden, and its own jacuzzi. The garden has been remodeled, and a Victorian-looking curved fence with a lovely old-fashioned gate has been added. It truly does resemble an English garden.

A glance at the comments from the guest book told me the story: "Happiness is staying here!" "What a refreshing change from typical hotel stays." "Like returning to visit an old 'friend.'" "We'll be back for a second honeymoon."

"How far are you from Fisherman's Wharf?" I asked, helping myself to another tasty croissant. "Oh, we're just minutes away," she said. "Our guests walk to Ghirardelli Square, the Cannery, and Pier 39. It's possible to take streetcars and cable cars to almost every point of interest in San Francisco."

UNION STREET HOTEL, 2229 Union St., San Francisco, CA 94123; 415-346-0424. A 5-guestroom (3 rooms share 2 baths) bed-and-breakfast inn. Convenient to all of the San Francisco attractions, including the cable car line. Breakfast only meal served. Open every day except Christmas and New Year's. Unable to accommodate children under 12. No pets. Helen Stewart, Innkeeper. (See Index for rates.)

Directions: Take the Van Ness exit from Rte. 101 to Union St.; turn left. The inn is between Fillmore and Steiner on the left side of the street.

VAGABOND HOUSE
Carmel-by-the-Sea, California (1976)

I had joined a group of other Vagabond House guests in the parlor, where we were all enjoying a continental breakfast. The conversation turned to the squirrels who were knocking on the windows and disporting themselves in the trees and the gardens. Owner Dennis Levett explained that they consume about thirty pounds of peanuts a week, and so saying, he opened up the window just enough to put some more peanuts on the outer ledge. "Every once in a while one gets inside," he said, "and then it's hilarious. Of course, they are very tame and they really do know how to find their way out again, but it's fun while it lasts."

I'll have to explain next that the breakfast we were enjoying was a *true* continental breakfast, with fresh pastries, cheese, hard-boiled eggs, and lots of coffee and tea. One of the guests remarked that it was like the continental breakfasts he had come to enjoy while traveling in Europe.

The Vagabond House is a delightful experience that begins when guests walk up the stone steps and enter an atmosphere that seems almost magical. There is a three-sided courtyard enhanced by many trees, including mock orange, magnolia, and live oaks. The plantings include camellias, primroses, tulips, and daffodils in great profusion, along with impatiens, rhododendrons, fuchsias, and many other varieties of flowers.

Accommodations are in eleven completely different cottage rooms or suites, many of which have their own woodburning fireplaces. The rooms are large and pleasingly furnished with Early American maple furniture, quilted bedspreads, and antique clocks; some have kitchens. Most rooms are supplied with coffeepots and fresh ground coffee for brewing.

Actually, reservations for three different inns may be arranged through the Vagabond House, and each provides a different kind of atmosphere. The Vagabond House itself is the best known and most popular of the three.

The other two are equally interesting in their own way. The San Antonio House, somewhat European in nature, is a smaller building in a very quiet residential section. Each large room has its own fireplace.

On the other hand, Lincoln Green, in another residential section of Carmel, is particularly suitable for children, with much more space for running about. The four little dwellings, called Maid Marian, Robin Hood, Little John, and Friar Tuck, offer a total of four suites, each with a living room and bedroom able to accommodate four people comfortably. In each living room is a stone fireplace and a sofa that turns into a bed.

Carmel is justly famous for its shopping and galleries, and a walk along Ocean Avenue will afford the chance to browse on the way down to the spectacular beachscape.

Another point of interest in the area is Point Lobos, just south of

Carmel. Its six-mile-long, unbroken coastline encompasses many spectacular views, as does the 17-Mile Drive. Incidentally, the main road south through Big Sur is now open, after being closed by mudslides.

Golf is one of the main reasons to come to this part of the world, and during the annual Bing Crosby tournament, many of the touring pros have reserved for years in advance at the Vagabond House.

VAGABOND HOUSE, Fourth & Dolores Streets, P.O. Box 2747, Carmel-by-the-Sea, CA 93921; 408-624-7738 or 408-624-7403. An 11-guest-room village inn serving a European continental breakfast to houseguests only. No other meals served. Open every day of the year. Bike renting, golf, natural beauty, enchanting shops nearby. Not ideal for children. Attended, leashed pets allowed. Dennis and Karen Levett, Owners; Honey Jones, Innkeeper. (See Index for rates.)

Directions: Turn off Hwy. 1 onto Ocean Ave.; turn right from Ocean Ave. onto Dolores, continue 2½ blocks. Parking provided for guests.

The date in parenthesis in the heading represents the first year the inn appeared in the pages of Country Inns and Back Roads.

VICTORIAN INN ON THE PARK
San Francisco, California (1988)

In spite of the proliferation of bed and breakfasts in San Francisco, I'm sure regular readers of this book have noted that for many years I've included only two—the Bed and Breakfast Inn and the Union Street Inn. However, Helen Stewart of the Union Street Inn convinced me that Lisa and William Benau were running just the kind of inn that belongs in *CIBR*.

Lisa and William are contemporary San Franciscans with a pleasant and easy informality that makes their guests feel very much at home. Lisa, who was a lawyer for several years, has forsaken that high-pressure world to take up innkeeping.

When I visited them in June, she was about to become a mother for the second time, and I'm happy to report that a new little innkeeper named Zachary made his appearance later that month. Three-year-old Cassandra thinks she will be a doctor rather than an innkeeper.

As we sat over breakfast in the sunny, oak-paneled dining room, Willie, as Lisa calls him, was explaining the location of the inn to the guests at the next table. "We're across from the panhandle of Golden Gate Park, and this section is popularly known as the Panhandle."

I asked Lisa how they found such a perfect example of Victoriana as this house, which is really quite a showplace. "My mother rescued it," Lisa said, as she poured me another cup of coffee. "I just happened to discover it through a chain of circumstances and when I saw it I could hardly wait to tell my mother—she was looking for a Victorian house to restore."

Shirley Weber, Lisa's mother, agreed that this was just what she was looking for, made an offer to the owner, "and everything fell into place," Lisa recalled. "Then the work began." In addition to the restoration experts and craftsmen who were called in to save and preserve original woodworking and decorations, Shirley and Lisa spent hours combing through salvage yards for old moldings, matching trims, old marble, claw-footed tubs, and the like.

"In other words," I interpolated, "you left no stone unturned in recreating a splendid Victorian mansion." "Exactly," Lisa smiled. "There are pictures in the parlor showing all the steps of our restoration. It has been declared a historic landmark."

I thought just walking in the large, beautiful mahogany front door with amber and crystal stained glass was exciting. The parlor is lovely with its eleven-foot-high ceiling, four tall, gracefully draped windows on a curved wall, and a classic hand-carved maple mantel over the white marble fireplace.

The choicest guest room is called the Belvedere Room, for the octagonal belvedere turret, which provides a balustraded porch where guests can enjoy a view of the park. From the outside the turret reminds me of a little gazebo perched on the roof. Willie told me there is only one other house with an open belvedere in San Francisco.

All of the guest rooms have something special about them and they are all decorated with taste and imagination, with comforters, down pillows, and flowers.

I enjoyed the continental breakfast with Lisa and Willie in front of the huge fireplace in the dining room, especially the cranberry bread Willie had baked. "I do a different bread every day," he said. "Sometimes it's bran muffins, sometimes zucchini bread. I get a kick out of it."

Now I'm glad to recommend a third B&B in San Francisco, and I'm happy to welcome the Victorian Inn on the Park to the pages of *Country Inns and Back Roads* for the first time.

VICTORIAN INN ON THE PARK, 301 Lyon St., San Francisco, CA 94117; 415-931-1830. A 12-guestroom (private baths) Victorian mansion overlooking Golden Gate Park and 1½ mi. from Civic Center. Continental breakfast included in room rate. Open year-round. Telephones and television available on request. Convenient to all of the cultural, historic, shopping, and sightseeing attractions of San Francisco. Children over 6 welcome. No pets. Shirley and Paul Weber, Owners; Lisa and William Benau, Innkeepers. (See Index for rates.)

Directions: From Hwy. 101, exit at Fell St. and continue past Divisadero St. to Lyon. The inn is on the right.

THE WINE COUNTRY INN
St. Helena, California (1978)

Three or four of us who were attending a meeting of the CIBR innkeepers were seated around the pool at the Wine Country Inn, enjoying the warm, welcome sunshine. "It looks a lot different than it did yesterday," said Jim Smith, who is the innkeeper of the inn. "We've had heavy rains and quite a little high water the last couple of days, but things have really calmed down now."

One of the innkeepers complimented Jim on what was then a new pool and jacuzzi. "Thank you very much," he responded. "I've never received as many compliments about the inn as I have this year and a lot of that has to do with the pool. It's become a popular area for socializing and swapping stories as to which winery tours to go on and which restaurants to enjoy."

It was a wonderful day in March. There were new leaves on the trees, the spring flowers were in profusion, wild geese were flying, and the small vineyards in the little valley just below the inn were starting to perk up. The natural wild mustard, lupines, poppies, and live oak trees blended with plantings of oleanders, petunias, and Chinese pistachios. This inn, which I saw almost the first day it was opened, has now taken on the patina that comes as buildings put on additional years.

The guest rooms are furnished almost entirely in antiques; some have intimate balconies and some have patios leading to the lawn. Many of the rooms have fireplaces, canopied beds, tufted bedspreads, and handmade quilts, along with a generous supply of magazines and books, and big, comfortable, fluffy pillows.

Visitors to the Napa Valley enjoy visits to the many wineries, as well as to mineral baths, geysers, a petrified forest, and several Robert Louis Stevenson memorial sites. There are also a number of antique shops in the area. Dotted with century-old stone bridges, pump houses, barns, and stone buildings, all of which are a delight to both painter and photographer, the manicured agricultural beauty of the valley contrasts with the rugged, tree-covered hills surrounding it.

In the many years since the Wine Country Inn was the first bed and breakfast inn in the Napa Valley there have been other inns created. However, I am convinced that it is still for me the most enjoyable experience in the valley. Patience and constant attention to details and maintenance have allowed the building, the trees, shrubs, and flowers to take on a real character of their own. It's hard to realize that it was actually built in 1975 as an inn. The architecture is batten board with a center section of stone and a mansard roof that is quite in keeping with the other winery architecture of this part of California.

On a more personal note I have to say that becoming acquainted with people like Ned and Marge Smith and their sons, Jim and Jeff, and watching the progress of such families over the years has always been a great source of satisfaction for me. Now, Jim's little three-year-old Michael has a baby sister, Kelly Elizabeth, who will be close to a year old by the time this book goes to press.

I think other innkeepers in California are fortunate to have such a model inn after which to fashion themselves. The care and consideration that have gone into the designing, and the result, prove that a country inn doesn't have to be old to be legendary.

It's the spirit that matters.

THE WINE COUNTRY INN, 1152 Lodi Lane, St. Helena, CA 94574; 707-963-7077. A 25-room country inn in the Napa wine valley of California, about 70 mi. from San Francisco. Continental breakfast served to houseguests; no other meals served. Open daily except Dec. 22-27. This inn is within driving distance of a great many wineries and also the Robert Louis Stevenson Museum. Swimming pool and spa on grounds. Golf and tennis nearby. No children. No pets. Jim Smith, Innkeeper. (See Index for rates.)

Directions: From San Francisco take the Oakland Bay Bridge to Hwy. 80. Travel north to the Napa cutoff. Stay on Hwy. 29 through the town of St. Helena, for 1¾ mi. north to Lodi Lane, then turn east ¼ mi. to inn.

CHANTICLEER INN
Ashland, Oregon (1988)

I settled back into one of the most comfortable upholstered chairs I've ever encountered and made a mental note of at least six books on the nearby shelves that I wanted to browse through. A sturdy little fire crackled cheerfully on the open-hearth fireplace, which I subsequently learned was constructed with stones from the nearby Rogue River. A beautiful arrangement of fresh flowers, some handsome books, and a basket of unshelled nuts were on the large round oak coffee table in front of me. The decorations and atmosphere of the room were most agreeable.

Innkeeper Jim Beaver sauntered in and sat down on the settee facing me. We started talking about what almost everybody talks about—the Oregon Shakespearean Festival, which is well over fifty years old now.

"It started as a modest little summer theater but now runs from mid-February through the end of October," he told me. "There are three theaters in the complex. One is the Elizabethan, with an outdoor stage patterned not after the famous Globe but the Fortune, a 16th-century London theater. The Festival won the Tony award for the best regional theater a couple of years ago. If you like theater, Ashland is heaven."

Nancy Beaver came in with a tea tray and some teatime goodies. "It's true that the festival with its many plays is certainly our biggest attraction, and it's only four blocks away," she said. "Off-season is really one of the best times to come to this part of Oregon. For one thing, the Shakespeare tickets are apt to be more available, and the fall weather is beautiful, with average daytime temperatures from sixty to seventy degrees." She passed me a cup of tea with two lumps.

Jim leaned forward. "There are many other attractions that bring visitors to Ashland. We've got great skiing, both downhill and cross-country, and we offer packages including a lesson, equipment, and transportation to and from the ski areas. There are good hiking trails in the mountains above town, white-water rafting on the Rogue and Klamath rivers, as well as sailing, water-skiing, windsurfing, and fishing in the nearby mountain lakes."

"Of course, you can always play croquet or bocce right here on our lawn," Nancy added. "Depending on the season, many guests just spend a great deal of the day relaxing and reading in our yard or on the porch, and during the winter they come in and do the same thing by the fire. But if they want more activity we have tennis courts nearby and a good golf course."

I had heard a great many compliments about the Chanticleer long before I arrived in Ashland. *Oregon Magazine* chose it as the best bed-and-breakfast inn in the state. The 1920s Craftsman bungalow-style architecture is a little deceptive from the front—the inn looks like a single-family dwelling, but having been built on a hill, it has three levels and is surprisingly spacious inside. The rooms are sunny and light, in pretty pastels with imported fabrics, antiques, brass bedsteads, comfortable chairs, fluffy comforters, and lots of fresh flowers and green plants. As Nancy pointed out, "Our queen-sized beds have firm mattresses; we have bedside reading lamps, roomy armoires, and closets; and each guest room has its own heating and cooling controls and direct-dial telephone."

I queried Nancy about what I'd heard was their exceptional breakfast, and she replied, "We're always searching for new ways of making what is frequently the dullest meal of the day something quite special. We have baked pears in custard sauce, sugared bacon, cinnamon scones, homemade blueberry-strawberry jam, veal sausage with apricot-ginger sauce, orange omelet soufflé with raspberry sauce, shirred eggs with Havarti cheese and dill, and steamed eggs on Canadian bacon with mousseline sauce." This epicurean repast can be enjoyed in the light and airy dining room or in your room.

The Chanticleer has been in my book *Bed and Breakfast, American Style* for many years. Now, for the first time, it gives me great pleasure to include it in *Country Inns and Back Roads*.

CHANTICLEER INN, 120 Gresham St., Ashland, OR 97520; 503-482-1919. A 7-guestroom (private baths) bed-and-breakfast inn overlooking Bear Creek valley and Cascade foothills. Open every day all year. A short walk from the Oregon Shakespearean Festival, Lithia Park, and many shops and restaurants. Rogue and Klamath rivers white-water rafting and Mt. Ashland's ski slopes nearby. Children over 5 welcome. No pets. Jim and Nancy Beaver, Innkeepers. (See Index for rates.)

Directions: Ashland is on Rte. 5, halfway between San Francisco and Portland. Gresham St. is in the center of town, running at right angles to the main street.

PARADISE RANCH INN
Grants Pass, Oregon (1988)

Once a working ranch, homesteaded in 1913, with cattle, horses, and other livestock, Paradise Ranch began taking guests many years ago. Nestled in the beautiful Rogue River Valley of southern Oregon, in the last few years it has become more of a resort-inn, with something for everyone. There are lighted, all-weather tennis courts and a resident pro, a heated swimming pool and spa, jogging and bicycle trails, several ponds stocked with rainbow trout and other fish, a lake with swans and ducks, a chip-and-putt green, horses and trails, and white-water rafting on the Rogue River. As if that weren't enough, there is also a recreation barn where any number of activities and special events take place.

Mattie and Oliver Raymond have been here for nineteen years and they run the ranch with the help of other family members, extending their friendly hospitality to their many guests. I find it particularly appealing as a wonderful place for families and children.

The white rambling ranch house, white fences, and neat outbuildings set against the backdrop of rolling, green meadows make a fetching picture, indeed. The guest rooms are all comfortably and individually furnished with flowered wallpaper, beamed ceilings, double and queen-sized beds, and, something I appreciate, extra pillows.

Mattie is justly proud of their chef, Billy Dunn, whom she describes as "one of the finest chefs in southern Oregon. He is classically trained and has worked at distinguished restaurants throughout this country. Actually, he was born here in Grants Pass, but ventured out into the world to learn cuisine. He emphasizes natural ingredients, and all of the breads and desserts are prepared daily in our kitchen." His menu is eclectic, with such dishes as chicken teriyaki, fresh fish in season, veal scaloppini à la Marsala, scampi Milanese, porterhouse steak smothered in onions and mushrooms, and a vegetarian plate. His hors d'oeuvres include escargot, sweet and sour chicken wings, and french-fried zucchini. The dining room has windows on three sides and overlooks the lake, with breathtaking views of the Cascade Mountains.

I noticed a little folder entitled "Fishing Guide" that has everything you need to know about fishing in the three stocked ponds. Prospective fishermen are cautioned about not fishing in the Garden Pond, which is reserved for their pet fish—they get fed, not caught. All the paraphernalia necessary for fishing can be obtained at the ranch. "We use barbless hooks," Ollie told me, "because the fish are so plentiful we feel it is not very sporting otherwise." You may catch a fish for your dinner if you like and Billy Dunn will cook it for you, in which case you pay for your dinner but not the fishing fee.

The game room of the barn has three pool tables, a beautiful Ping-

Pong table, and shuffleboard. There's also a piano, and on cool days, a cheery fire burns in the fireplace.

So, whether it's action in a white-water raft on the Rogue River or helping with a cattle roundup or simply relaxing under a tree, Paradise Ranch Inn offers an attractive vacation.

PARADISE RANCH INN, 7000 Monument Dr., Grants Pass, OR 97526; 503-479-4333. A 16-guestroom ranch-inn nestled in the beautiful mountains of the Rogue River Valley. Open year-round. Restaurant open to public; closed Mon. and Tues. Heated swimming pool, hot tub, lighted all-weather tennis courts, fishing, surrey rides, hayrides, trail rides, cattle roundup, square dancing, recreational center, and children-watching available on grounds. Spectacular Rogue River raft trips and all-day horseback riding, Shakespearean Festival, Crater Lake, and Oregon caves nearby. Children most welcome. Mattie and Ollie Raymond, Innkeepers. (See Index for rates.)

Directions: From the Bay Area follow Rte. 101 north to Crescent City and then Rte. 199 to Grants Pass; turn north on Rte. 5 and exit at Merlin. Go under Rte. 5, turn right on Monument Dr. for 2½ mi. Ranch is on left.

"*European plan*" *means that rates for rooms and meals are separate.* "*American plan*" *means that meals are included in the cost of the room.* "*Modified American plan*" *means that breakfast and dinner are included in the cost of the room. The rates at some inns include a continental breakfast with the lodging.*

STEAMBOAT INN
Steamboat, Oregon (1984)

I was on the Umpqua Highway (Route 138) on my way for a visit with Jim and Sharon Van Loan at the Steamboat Inn, a country inn that is a steelhead fisherman's dream.

This is the heartland of Oregon, and after a pleasant trip from Crescent City and Eureka, California, up Routes 101 and 199, I thrilled to the scenery on I-5 from Grants Pass to Roseburg.

Now, having left the Interstate and turning east, I was getting the feeling of what inland Oregon is really like. There were many cattle farms and fruit orchards gradually giving way to the beautiful upland country, and soon the road was running parallel to the North Umpqua River.

This idyllic trip along the river ended as I arrived at the Steamboat Inn and was immediately taken in tow by both Jim and Sharon, who are two very friendly people, quite suited to innkeeping.

I was shown to one of the eight rustic cabins, all of which are joined by a deck that extends out over the river, and soon I was enveloped in the euphoria created by the melodious, ever-present sounds of the water rushing by on its way to the Pacific Ocean.

I joined the other guests on the new back porch of the lodge in time to be well introduced by Jim and Sharon and to admire the art that lines the walls. After hors d'oeuvres we were all invited to sit down around the great table (actually, a huge pine slab) in the dining area and enjoy the main course. Sharon explained that a typical dinner includes several vegetables, homemade bread or pasta, and a selected entrée of the evening. Our main dish that evening, appropriately enough, was game hens with a fruited wild rice stuffing, which won the $5,000 grand prize in a Best-of-Country-Inns recipe contest in a recent national competition.

Guests for longer stays at Steamboat will not have the same main course at dinner twice. By the way, dinner is generally served a half hour after dark each night during the summer months and around seven during the winter.

Following dinner, I had a chance to talk with Jim and Sharon about how they came to be located here. "Originally, we came because of Jim's enthusiasm for fly-fishing. Also, Jim started attending a hotel management school as a result of his experiences with visiting inns in Japan," Sharon responded. "Then it occurred almost simultaneously to all of us that this would be a wonderful place to raise a family, and it seemed like a viable way of involving everyone and still being able to make financial progress."

Jim continued, "Although fly-fishing for steelhead is a big activity here about three months of the year, the rest of the time there are many nonfishing guests who arrive with the intention of remaining for one night and who extend their stay for two or three. It's an excellent place for families.

"Our new hideaway cottages feature a master bedroom with a king-sized bed, a bathroom with a soaking tub, a living room, kitchen facilities, a loft that can sleep two people, and a deck."

"Our guests enjoy the wonderful presence of the river," Sharon commented. "They can explore the waterfalls, swim in the creek, and return at night to put their feet up on the porch railing and read a good book. We also have frequent cooking classes that many of our guests enjoy. Information about classes is included in our brochure."

So we see the Steamboat Inn is a combination of a great many things, but the real, compelling attraction is the river—its sound, color, and ever changing textures.

STEAMBOAT INN, Steamboat, OR 97447; 503-496-3495 or 503-498-2411. An 8-guestroom rustic riverside inn in one of Oregon's most spectacular river canyon areas, 40 mi. west of Diamond Lake and 70 mi. east of Crater Lake. Open all year. Breakfast, lunch, and dinner served daily; breakfast is not included in the room rate. Dinner ½ hr. after sundown in summer, 7 p.m. in winter. Fishing, backpacking, and hiking in abundance. Sharon and Jim Van Loan, Innkeepers; Patricia Lee, Manager. (See Index for rates.)

Directions: From Roseburg drive 38 mi. east on Rte. 138.

A number of inns have nearby airports where private airplanes may land. An airplane symbol at the end of the inn directions indicates that there is an airport nearby. Consult inn for further information.

THE CAPTAIN WHIDBEY INN
Coupeville, Washington (1973)

I'm going to share with you the contents of my yearly letter from John Stone, the innkeeper of the Captain Whidbey Inn. I think it shows that country inns are continually adjusting and changing to meet the preferences and needs of their guests.

First, a word about the Captain Whidbey. It's an old-fashioned New England inn, way up in the northwest corner of the state of Washington. The New England part of it comes quite naturally because the original owners were Steve and Shirley Stone. Steve is a native of Nantucket Island, off the coast of Massachusetts in the East, and a good example of the old saying, "You can take the boy out of Nantucket, but you can't take Nantucket out of the boy"; the tweedy look, the unmistakable accent, and the corncob pipe are all there. John refers to his father as the "Innkeeper Emeritus."

The exterior of the inn, built in 1907, is of the distinctly regional peeled madrona logs, a shiny, red-hued wood, a large relative of the manzanita. The inn remains just about the same as it has always been, with highly polished log walls decorated with antiques and bric-a-brac.

The natural center of the inn is the living room, with a very big fireplace made of round stones. Here, everybody—houseguests and dinner guests alike—sits around talking and leafing through the dozens of magazines.

Some of the guest rooms are upstairs in the main house and an additional number of rustic lodges, called Lagoon Rooms, were built in the woods across the road from the main house a few years ago, and they overlook their own private lake. The guest rooms are tastefully furnished with antiques, and those in the main house have down comforters and feather beds. A nice area for general relaxing has been set aside for houseguests on the second floor with floor-to-ceiling bookshelves jampacked with books.

Now, to John's letter: "The gazebo we added last year by the lagoon, with a dining deck overlooking the Cove, enhances the inn as a great spot to have a wedding. The dining deck is ideal for lunch alfresco; guests can enjoy the warm sun, gentle breezes, and spectacular vistas with sailboats on the Cove and snowcapped mountains in the distance.

"I've been elected president of the Washington State Lodging Association for 1988, and they also named me Hotelier of the Year. I'm really honored.

"I have my Coast Guard license to carry passengers for hire on both power and sail vessels, and I've been taking guests on short cruises of Penn Cove on Saturdays and Sundays, similar to the sail you and I had on the *Wind Song*. Both the guests and I enjoy getting out on the water for a refreshing sail, and it gives me an hour or so to get to know at least six of our guests.

"My wife, Mendy, is in her third year teaching at the Oak Harbor Co-op Preschool. She also takes care of the fresh flowers inside and outside the inn. Our 8-year-old son, Andrew, continues the tradition of the Stones as a 'reading family.' Ian is 5½, and says he wants to be an innkeeper and sailor like his Dad."

The Captain Whidbey, located on the shore of Penn Cove, with the Cascades to the east, dominated by Mount Baker at more than 10,000 feet and Mount Olympus on the west at almost 8,000 feet, provides a most unusual and scenic country-inn adventure.

THE CAPTAIN WHIDBEY INN, 2072 W. Captain Whidbey Inn Rd., Coupeville, WA 98239; 206-678-4097. A 25-guestroom (4 cottages) (private and shared baths) country inn, on protected Penn Cove off Puget Sound, 50 mi. north of Seattle, 3 mi. north of Coupeville. European plan. Breakfast, lunch, and dinner served daily to travelers. Open year-round. Boating and fishing on grounds. Golf nearby. Pets allowed in cottages only. The Stone Family, Innkeepers. (See Index for rates.)

Directions: Whidbey Island is reached year-round from the south by the Columbia Beach–Mukilteo Ferry, and during the summer and on weekends by the Port Townsend–Keystone Ferry. From the north (Vancouver, B.C., and Bellingham), take the Deception Pass Bridge to Whidbey Island.

THE SHELBURNE INN
Seaview, Washington (1988)

"This little peninsula has the cleanest estuary in the country. We're kind of hidden away here, surrounded by waters and bays." David Campiche gestured out toward the wide expanse of sandy beach as he spoke. "There's an abundance of shellfish and oysters, salmon, sturgeon, and eight to ten varieties of whitefish. There are bird sanctuaries, state parks, big rock jetties with sea lions, and whale-watching, too." We had strolled out behind the inn and past some houses to the sand dunes bordering the beach. "This is one of the longest stretches of beach you'll find in the Pacific Northwest," he said. "It goes on for thirty miles."

I had driven down the coast with John Stone of the Captain Whidbey Inn in time for dinner in the Shoalwater Restaurant, which is actually part of the Shelburne Inn. I should explain that David Campiche and Laurie Anderson tend the inn, and their partners, Tony and Ann Kischner, run the restaurant. We had a dinner there that I can only describe as exquisite, starting with a smoked fish mousse served with a variety of assorted smoked seafoods. Then there were local escargots served with Oregon hazelnuts and butter. After that came a fillet of freshly caught sturgeon with a raspberry beurre blanc, followed by a green salad, which was followed by roast quail served with a marvelous sauce made from port wine, walnuts, and cream cheese. Among the dessert offerings was Ann's Cranberry-Swirl Cheesecake with Chocolate Cranberry Glaze, which placed first in a national contest. Tony Kischner is a most innovative restaurateur, and I'm not surprised that the restaurant has acquired national recognition, which, I guess, was started by the late James Beard when he wrote about the inn and the restaurant in his syndicated column.

Since the turn of the century there has been a Shelburne Inn in the tiny coastal town of Seaview. In those days wealthy Oregonians came by steamer and a narrow-gauge railway to spend their summers in the sleepy villages on Long Beach Peninsula, lazing on the pristine beach, fishing the bounteous waters, picking mushrooms, digging for clams, and clambering over the rocks around North Head Lighthouse, where the Columbia River empties into the Pacific Ocean.

In 1977, when David and Laurie found the Shelburne Inn, it was in a sad state. "There were cans in the rooms to collect the rainfall," David told me. He is a young, handsome fellow with a very relaxed, engaging manner. His bearded face is frequently wreathed in smiles. He speaks laughingly of the hard work of restoring and renovating an old building, but the etched and stained-glass windows, the tongue-and-groove wood paneling and open-beamed ceilings, brass chandeliers, and handsome antique-furnished rooms reveal how much thought and energy he and Laurie lavished on the inn. And still lavish.

The inn is listed on the National Register of Historic Places. Many of their antiques were collected during their travels in Europe and England; in fact, several of their stained-glass windows were rescued from an old church in Morcambe, England.

Despite their ten years of work, David says, "We're still working on it, and with our schedule we're about three years from having it right." I can't imagine how it could be any more "right" than it is, but they say they'll know when they have the rooms "just right."

Laurie, blond and blue-eyed, picked wallpapers and paint and lighting fixtures as well as the antique oak dressers and braided rugs and homespun quilts for the brass beds, and now she keeps the rooms bright with fresh flowers from their garden.

Some of their edible flowers adorned my breakfast plate the next morning, when I sat down at the big oval oak table in the pleasant lobby, where guests gather for breakfast and sociability. David and Laurie do great breakfasts. David makes his own sausage, while Laurie does all the baking.

A lovely old-fashioned inn, superb food, and friendly, hospitable hosts—I suggest you make your reservations now.

THE SHELBURNE INN, Pacific Hwy. 103 and 45th Pl., P.O. Box 250, Seaview, WA 98644; 206-642-2442. A 17-guestroom (private and shared baths) Victorian village hotel on Highway 103 on the Long Beach peninsula, 120 mi. northwest of Portland, Ore. Breakfast included in room rate. Shoalwater Restaurant open for lunch and dinner daily in the summer; check winter service. Reservations recommended. Gift shop and pub on premises. State parks, sandy beach, museums, fishing, and birdwatching nearby. No pets. David Campiche and Laurie Anderson, Innkeepers; Tony and Ann Kischner, Restaurateurs. (See Index for rates.)

Directions: Take U.S. 101 to the Long Beach Peninsula. In Seaview, take Rte. 103 a short distance. Inn is on the left. ⬤

OAK BAY BEACH HOTEL
Victoria, British Columbia (1979)

"Really, one of the most spectacular sights in this part of the world is the view of Victoria from the water at Christmas time!"

There were three of us enjoying the superb seaside view from the Tudor Dining Room at the Oak Bay Beach Hotel. There was Bruce Walker, the owner, whom I met at least twelve years ago on my first visit to this spectacularly beautiful part of the world, and his son, Kevin, who is the general manager of the hotel. Kevin's wife, Shawna Dee, had just excused herself to do a little shopping in the hotel gift shop.

"Actually, Christmas starts about the eighth of December for us," explained Kevin. "We start having buffet luncheons with special holiday season specialty items. The daily afternoon high tea also has some special holiday touches. These are in effect for the entire month.

"We have carolling in the lobby each night, featuring the Victoria Operatic Society, starting on the twentieth. That's when we serve roasted chestnuts and Christmas beverages."

"Our Christmas Eve gala buffet is really an extravaganza," Bruce offered. "Christmas dinner starts at 4:30 in the afternoon and there are two seatings.

"Everything continues up to and including the thirty-first, when we come to a smashing climax with our New Year's Eve dinner."

I understand that very few of you will actually be able to be at the Oak Bay Beach Hotel during the Christmas season; however, I'm sharing it with you to illustrate the real *esprit* which is present much of the time at Victoria's only seaside hotel.

For me, Victoria is the most English of all Canadian cities, and the Oak Bay Beach Hotel is like a visit to England's North Devon coast or Cornwall. Like the Mermaid in Rye, it also has the handsome Tudor-style half-timbers.

The English theme is carried out in the guest rooms, and in fact the third floor has the same white plaster and Tudor half-timber finish as the exterior of the building. The rooms and suites, all furnished with handsome antiques, have such names as Samuel Pepys, Prince Albert, and Queen Anne. The rooms in the back of the house overlook the Straits of Haro, with a view of Discovery Island and the San Juan Islands. Mount Baker rises ten thousand magnificent feet in the distance.

There are pleasant walks in the hotel's gardens and along the pathway down to the sea, as well as through the surrounding residential streets, with their attractive houses and the shops of Oak Bay Village. The Oak Bay golf course is a ten-minute walk away, and the hotel will arrange charter boat fishing. Killer whales, seals, and salmon are often spotted offshore.

"How does one see Victoria's Christmas lights from the water?" I asked. "That's very easy," Kevin replied. "We hold Christmas lights cruises on board our yacht, the *Mesouda*. It's a two-hour cruise, departing the inner harbor daily about 4:30. Not only that, but we're happy to provide hors d'oeuvres befitting the occasion. Our yacht has proven to be one of our most popular diversions during the summer. We have sunset dinner cruises in which guests are taken on a three-hour excursion around the beautiful Oak Bay waters and Victoria's inner harbor."

Now we could see Mount Baker in the distance dramatically lit by the sun's rays, and high tea was beginning to be served in the Tudor Dining Room. I started doing some mental figuring on how to be able to take a cruise on board the *Mesouda* myself.

OAK BAY BEACH HOTEL, 1175 Beach Dr., Victoria, B.C. Canada V8S 2N2; 604-598-4556. A 48-guestroom seaside inn located in one of the quiet suburbs of Victoria. European plan. Breakfast, lunch, and dinner served to travelers. Open every day in the year. A short distance from the spectacular scenery and recreational resources of British Columbia. Swimming on grounds. Daily yacht cruises. Golf, tennis, fishing, sailing, and Butchart Gardens nearby. No pets. Bruce R. Walker, Innkeeper. (See Index for rates.)

Directions: Take Johnson St. or Fort St. from downtown Victoria, east to Oak Bay Ave., which leads into Newport Ave. Turn left into Windsor Ave. to Beach Dr. Turn right and continue to 1175 Beach Dr. If arriving by air at Victoria Airport, I suggest you take public transportation to the center of the city and then take a taxi to the hotel.

SOOKE HARBOUR HOUSE
Sooke, British Columbia (1988)

Standing on the bluff at the top of the steps leading down to the shore, I looked out across the Strait of Juan de Fuca to the Olympic Mountain Peninsula and off to the east to East Sooke Park. Across the way was a very beautiful farm, toward which Sinclair Philip waved an arm. "Do you realize that farm is inhabited by a family of cougars? Seventy percent of the world's cougar population lives on Vancouver Island." I was amazed to hear that. Sinclair, a handsome, dark-haired young man with a neatly clipped beard, continued, "You can see deer on that farm and on our property, too. Harbor seals, sea lions, and otters are out there, and we frequently see gray and killer whales, too."

I had to admit this was a remarkable location for an inn, and Sinclair was certainly a walking encyclopedia on the infinite variety of animal and plant life that flourishes here on sea and land. I was looking down at a beautiful rock garden that terraced the slope, and there were many other gardens laced with little gravel paths surrounding the white clapboard inn buildings. They boasted masses of vegetables, herbs, fruits, and edible flowers. Some garden chairs were grouped on the terrace facing the water.

This is a very informal, contemporary place with an emphasis on the natural surroundings. There are lots of plants and flowers, magazines and books, and modern paintings and wall hangings. One of the two dining rooms is arranged as a sort of living/dining room with a comfortable sofa and rocking chairs grouped around a fireplace, and on the other side of the room the dining area is lined with windows overlooking the water.

Sinclair and his wife, Fredrica, with the help of friends and others, who are variously architects, artisans, and craftspeople, have created an environment that is aesthetically pleasing in every way. Many of the guest rooms have their own private gardens and porches, with double whirlpool baths placed to afford spectacular views of the ocean.

Every room has a special theme that is carried out in the decor; for instance, the Herb Garden Room is surrounded by herbs, and the hand-painted ceramic tiles in the bathroom depict various herbs. This is a split-level room with a fireplace and a private porch with a hot tub for two. (All of the rooms have fireplaces.) Stained-glass windows made with real underwater objects decorate the Underwater Garden Room.

Sinclair was telling me about the Indian Room. "This is the largest and most spectacular room we have, with a balcony extending the entire length of the room. There is a bathtub for two in front of the two-sided fireplace with a view of the ocean. It has multiple skylights, a vaulted ceiling, and is full of Indian artifacts and masks. Victor Newman, a very well-known Kwakiutl carver, helped decorate it."

Fredrica was born and raised in France, and she and Sinclair met at the University of Grenoble. This unusual and talented couple found Sooke Harbour House in 1979, and in the intervening years they have established an international reputation for their imaginative and creative cuisine. With the abundance of the sea just outside their kitchen door, the daily changing menu features such unusual items as sea urchin, octopus, sea cucumbers, abalone, and limpets. Their chefs concoct the delicacies that have aroused the admiration of food writers from around the world. Sinclair showed me a stack of clippings, including glowing accounts in the *New York Times,* the *Chicago Tribune,* the *Philadelphia Inquirer,* magazines in France and Germany, and many others. Besides their incredibly fresh fish and seafood specialties, they draw from their vast gardens and obtain local organically raised meats, like lamb, duck, suckling kid, squab, and young rabbit to round out their menu.

Watching the sun set over the ocean, I tried to think of someone who wouldn't love to stay here. I couldn't think of a soul.

I am delighted to welcome Sooke Harbour House to the pages of *Country Inns and Back Roads* for the first time.

SOOKE HARBOUR HOUSE, 1528 Whiffen Spit Rd., R.R. #4, Sooke, B.C., Canada VOS INO; 604-642-3421. A 13-guestroom (private baths) disarmingly informal country inn with a sophisticated cuisine on the west coast of Vancouver Island, 23 mi. west of Victoria. Full breakfast and light lunch included in room rate. Open year-round. Wheelchair access. Bicycles available on premises. Beachcombing, birdwatching, nature walks, Botanical Beach, kayaking, windsurfing, scuba diving, hiking in Pacific Rim park nearby. Children welcome. Well-behaved pets welcome. Smoking restricted in several rooms. Fredrica and Sinclair Philip, Innkeepers. (See Index for rates.)

Directions: From Victoria, take Hwy. 1 west to Hwy. 14. Continue on Hwy. 14 to Sooke. Turn left at Whiffen Spit Rd. (approx. 1 mi. past traffic light) and continue to inn.

Upper South

Eastern Time Zone

WEST

LEXINGTON
Beaumont Inn,
Inn at Pleasant Hill, *Harrodsburg*

KENTUCKY

TENNESSEE

■ **NASHVILLE**

Parish Patch Inn, *Normandy*

Hound Ears Lodge, *Blowing Rock*
Mast Farm Inn, *Valle Crucis*

Snowbird Mountain Lodge, *Robbinsville*   ■**ASHEVILLE**

Hemlock Inn, *Bryson City*

CHATTANOOGA

The Orchard Inn, *Saluda*

Auberge Provencale, *White Post*   The David Finney Inn, *New Castle*

DELAWARE

MARYLAND   WILMINGTON

Country Inn, *Berkeley Springs*

The Ashby Inn, *Paris*

Red Fox Tavern, *Middleburg*   The Inn at Buckeystown, *Buckeystown*

Wayside Inn, *Middletown*   Maryland Inn, *Annapolis*

Inn at Little Washington, *Washington*   WASHINGTON

VIRGINIA   Robert Morris Inn, *Oxford*

Morrison House, *Alexandria*

Jordan Hollow, *Stanley*

Graves' Mountain Lodge, *Syria*

Trillium House,   Prospect Hill, *Trevilians*

Nellysford   CHARLOTTESVILLE

Silver Thatch Inn, *Charlottesville*

General Lewis Inn, *Lewisburg*

Maple Hall, *Lexington*

verside Inn,   Gristmill Square, *Warm Springs*
ce Springs   Meadow Lane Lodge, *Warm Springs*

V I R G I N I A

The Fearrington House, *Pittsboro*

RALEIGH

NORTH CAROLINA

BEAUMONT INN
Harrodsburg, Kentucky (1979)

I love to visit Kentucky! There is a gentle quality to this landscape that matches the soft, unhurried accents of its people.

I paused for a moment in front of the Beaumont Inn, which dates well back into the days before the War Between the States, and tried to imagine what it was like when it began its career as a school for young ladies in 1845. Some years later it was Beaumont College, and in 1916 it was purchased by Mr. and Mrs. Glave Goddard and converted into the Beaumont Inn.

The ownership and management passed from Mrs. Goddard to her daughter, Mrs. Dedman, and then to Mrs. Dedman's two sons. Today, Bud Dedman is the owner, and his son, Chuck, following tradition, has become the fourth-generation innkeeper. To make it even more interesting, Chuck and his wife, Helen, have two children, one of whom, Dixon, although he is a very young lad, is already showing great promise as an innkeeper of the future.

Grasping the solid handle of the big front door, I stepped inside, and there was Chuck Dedman, who I always forget is such a tall man. As a matter of fact he has several brothers who are all well known for their height.

"I can see that you're looking around for Dixon," Chuck said. "He had to go on a very important errand for me, but he'll be back soon. Come on, I'll show you to your room."

I trotted along behind him, once again impressed by the number of rare items that have been collected and put in proper cases here at the inn. A group of antique fishing lures caught my eye, along with other Beaumont memorabilia, such as the collection of saltcellars — handsome small dishes that were used before the saltshaker came into being. Chuck's mother, Mary Elizabeth, had gathered together at least one hundred or more in a glass case.

"Oh yes, mother just loves things like that, and her history of the inn is always a best seller in our gift shop," he remarked.

The decorations and furniture in all the parlors and guest rooms reflect American history. The hallways on the main floor have several cabinets with beautiful old china and silverware, and the sitting rooms have elegant fireplaces and rose-patterned wallpaper.

In previous editions I have shared with the reader some of my enthusiasm for the bill of fare at the Beaumont. Probably topping everything is fried chicken and real Kentucky ham. Let me assure you that these taste nothing like any other food that bears the same name. The chicken almost falls off the bone and it's just about perfect, only exceeded perhaps by the tangy taste of real Kentucky ham, which is darker than some others you might have seen. These can be ordered at dinner in combination, and in spite of the fact that the menu has many other things I'll almost always end up with that combination.

The Beaumont is a wonderful place for an early spring vacation. There are three championship golf courses close by and some wonderful shopping. The food department of the gift shop at the inn features Beaumont Inn cornmeal batter mix, brown sugar syrup, green tomato relish, sweet pickle relish, chicken-cheese casserole, frozen fruit salad, and chopped country ham. These tempting foods are also served in the dining room. Let me recommend to one and all the cornmeal cakes that are served at breakfast. They have a taste like nothing else I have ever tried.

Chuck and I returned to the front hall and, sure enough, there was Dixon already greeting new guests and giving them some suggestions about things they might like to do.

It looked to me like it was going to be another splendid visit at the Beaumont Inn.

Incidentally, the cover on this edition is of the Beaumont Inn by moonlight, wonderfully captured by the artist Wooster Bard Fields.

BEAUMONT INN, Harrodsburg, KY 40330; 606-734-3381. A 29-guestroom country inn in the heart of Kentucky's historic bluegrass country. European plan. Lunch and dinner served to travelers; all three meals to houseguests. Lunch not available Mon. Open every day from mid-March to mid-Dec. Tennis, swimming pool, shuffleboard on grounds. Golf courses and a wide range of recreational and historic attractions nearby. No pets. The Dedman Family, Innkeepers. (See Index for rates.)

Directions: From Louisville, take Exit 48 from east I-64 and go south on Ky. 151 to U.S. 127 and on south to Harrodsburg. From Lexington, take U.S. 60 west, then west on Bluegrass Parkway to U.S. 127. From Nashville, take Exit I-65 to Bluegrass Parkway near Elizabethton, Ky., then east to U.S. 127.

THE INN AT PLEASANT HILL
Shakertown, Kentucky (1971)

Betty Morris and I were driving down the twisty road that leads to the Shaker Landing on the Kentucky River, just a few moments from the Inn at Pleasant Hill. Soon, a handsome paddlewheel river boat, the "Dixie Belle," came into view, and already there were people waiting to board her for the morning cruise.

This cruise, very popular with the inn guests, follows the seventy-five mile course of the river, bordered by impressive 315-foot limestone cliffs. Betty, who is manager of the Inn at Pleasant Hill, told me that a running history of the Kentucky River, including its importance to the economy of 100 years ago and the contributions made by the Shakers, is part of this cruise.

By an interesting coincidence, just as she pointed out the great railroad trestle that traverses the river, a freight train went by, right on cue.

The Inn at Pleasant Hill is located in a restored Shaker community in one of the most beautiful sections of central Kentucky. The Shakers were members of a religious sect, the United Society of Believers in Christ's Second Appearing. They were actually an offshoot of the Quakers. The founder was Mother Ann Lee, who brought her ideas to America late in the 18th century.

The Shakers held some advanced social ideas. They were hospitable to visitors and took in orphans and unwanted children. Their fundamental beliefs were in hard work and austere discipline that sought perfection.

This sense of perfection was extended into the design of their furniture, and many people learn about Shakers for the first time as a result of being attracted by the beauty and simplicity of the functional Shaker designs.

The Shakers lived in communal dedication to their religious beliefs of celibacy, renunciation of worldliness, common ownership of property, and public confession of sins, which culminated in the frenetic dances that gave them the name of Shakers.

There were five "families" at Pleasant Hill, established in 1805. By 1820 it was a prosperous colony of five hundred persons. "Family" had a particular meaning, since the Shakers did not believe in marriage. Men and women, they maintained, could live more happily as brothers and sisters helping one another, but living personally apart.

The Civil War, plus 19th-century industrialism and worldliness, seeped into Pleasant Hill, and the celibacy rules prevented the natural increase in their numbers. In 1910 they were dissolved.

The reception area of the inn is located in the Trustees' House, one of twenty-five or more restored buildings clustered along the single country road. To construct buildings of enduring strength, some with walls three or four feet thick, the Shakers quarried limestone from the river bluffs and hauled granite slabs a mile uphill from the river. Most of the buildings are a deep red brick or limestone.

The restaurant is on the first floor of the Trustees' House, and the guest rooms on the second and third floors are reached by two marvelous twin-spiraled staircases of matchless craftsmanship. There are many additional bedrooms on the second floor of restored Shaker buildings.

The experience of sleeping in a Shaker room is most refreshing. In my room were two single beds, each with its own trundle bed underneath. The Shaker rockers were classic, and the extra chairs were hung by pegs on the walls.

For the third time in fifteen years, the three-day international meeting of the CIBR Innkeepers' Association was held at Pleasant Hill in the fall of 1986. It was a resounding success.

THE INN AT PLEASANT HILL, Shakertown, KY. P.O. address: Rte. 4, Harrodsburg, KY 40330; 606-734-5411. A 63-guestroom country inn in a restored Shaker village on Rte. 68, 7 mi. northeast of Harrodsburg, 25 mi. southwest of Lexington. European plan. Breakfast, lunch, dinner served daily to travelers. No tipping. Open year-round. Suggest contacting inn about winter schedule. Closed Christmas Eve and Christmas Day. Ann Voris, Innkeeper. (See Index for rates.)

Directions: From Lexington take Rte. 68 south toward Harrodsburg. From Louisville, take I-64 to Lawrenceburg and Graeffenburg exit (not numbered). Follow Rte. 127 south to Harrodsburg and Rte. 68 northeast to Shakertown.

PARISH PATCH INN
Normandy, Tennessee (1986)

"Cortner Mill stayed with the same family from 1848 until the late 1950s. It was a working mill for that entire time. We've kept some of the original equipment right here, including the scale and some of the wonderful grain chutes."

Marty Ligon, the innkeeper at Parish Patch Inn, and I were seated on the porch at Cortner Mill in Normandy, Tennessee. Here above the dam, the waters of the Duck River seem so placid until they drop over the dam and gather momentum from their fall. Upstream on both banks the branches of the trees hang out over the water, and one branch has a rope swing, where one could swing out over the river, let go, and splash right into the water just like a lad in a Norman Rockwell painting. The sound of the water has a wonderful soporific effect. It's the kind of place to sit and read a book, maybe take a nap in one of the beautiful ladder-back rockers, or possibly even *write* a book.

The Mill, which also has its own accommodations, is actually part and parcel of Parish Patch Inn, the main house being just a few moments away. The combination of the two places provides a most interesting contrast in a country inn experience. The Mill has a pleasant rustic elegance, with four different guest rooms, including one bunk room with seven twin beds. I think the most impressive feature, of course, is the presence of the river and the dam.

The main house of the Parish Patch presents an entirely different aspect. This is a lovely board-and-batten structure with comfortable rooms, private baths, fireplaces, patios, rose gardens, and a swimming pool with an attractive poolhouse. Fresh-cut flowers and homemade pumpkin bread are some of the extra touches that make it enjoyable. The guest rooms are not at all rustic, unless you count the beautifully varnished overhead beams. All have splendid views of the rolling Tennessee countryside, and the outdoors is immediately available, in some cases, through a sliding door onto a balcony. There's a mixture of natural woods, with some excellent antique pieces and well-designed lamps and other necessities. All of the guest rooms have two double beds and a television.

Dinner is served in a very pleasant dining room, for houseguests only, by reservation. I asked Marty what kind of a menu is offered. "Well, we serve only one main dish," she replied, "and that could be meat loaf, fried chicken, chicken Cordon Bleu, roast beef, or stuffed pork chops. All of the breads, muffins, rolls, and coffee cakes are homemade right here. Mildred Kimbro is the cook, along with her daughter, Kay, and she is happy to take suggestions."

Provisions are made for people traveling with children, with some outdoor swings, slides, bars, and other equipment. The house itself overlooks great cornfields on two sides, and the whole immediate area is surrounded by an old-fashioned Tennessee split-rail fence.

I'd like to suggest that readers making reservations at the Parish Patch Inn talk over their preferences with Marty or Phyllis Crosslin, the manager, because there are a number of options.

Everything at both locations is beautifully maintained and cared for, and yet within just a few moments' walk you're in the beautiful Tennessee countryside.

PARISH PATCH INN, Normandy, TN 37360; 615-857-3441. A 10-guestroom elegant inn in the verdant Tennessee countryside. European plan. Evening meals are served to houseguests only with advance reservation. Open all year. Closed Christmas Day. Wheelchair access. Swimming pool on grounds. Fishing, boating, canoeing, picnicking, bicycling, bird watching and backroading nearby. Personal checks accepted. Marty Ligon, Innkeeper; Phyllis Crosslin, Manager. (See Index for rates.)

Directions: From Shelbyville continue south on 41-A for 7.2 mi. and look for a left turn at the sign for Normandy. Turn left onto Dement Rd. and follow signs to inn. From I-24, take Exit 97 (Beechgrove-Shelbyville-Hwy. 64 Exit). Take Hwy. 64 west to Wartrace. In Wartrace do not cross RR tracks. Take Hwy. 269 east. Pass shops and turn left at yellow light, up hill. Inn is 4 mi. from Wartrace.

A number of inns have nearby airports where private airplanes may land. An airplane symbol at the end of the inn directions indicates that there is an airport nearby. Consult inn for further information.

THE FEARRINGTON HOUSE
Pittsboro, North Carolina (1988)

In the 17th and 18th centuries, many English immigrants to America settled in North Carolina. That's why I was interested to learn that R. B. Fitch, a native North Carolinian, went back to England for inspiration in the design of the Fearrington House. When I saw the arrangement of attractive, low buildings with their roofs pitched at different levels, grouped around the courtyard, with the pump in the middle and all the little gardens, I immediately thought of the Bell Inn in Buckinghamshire, England.

And sure enough, R.B., as he prefers being called, told me that a visit to the Bell Inn provided him and his wife with their inspiration for the courtyard.

"Jenny and I have made several trips to England, collecting old furniture and antiques and original art. The old pine flooring, for instance, came from an 1850 London workhouse."

Included in the group of inn buildings is the sun room, where afternoon tea is available, and the garden house, which is a living room where guests can get together.

Jenny, R.B.'s wife, has created fourteen superb guest rooms, mostly suites, every one of which is completely different from the others. I thought I could hear the pristine strains of a Mozart quartet as R.B. was showing me the guest rooms, and I asked him where that heavenly sound was coming from. "We have a wonderful sound system in all the rooms, including speakers in the bathroom. It's a great way to brush your teeth," he laughed. He's got heated towel racks in the bathrooms too.

"Each room has been designed to take advantage of the wonderful vistas," R.B. told me. There are open fields, woods, gardens, nearby Bynum Ridge, and a country village to be seen from the many windows of the different rooms.

The village is a story in itself. R.B. has turned a farmstead of over 600 acres into a tiny rural community where the homes of about 400 inhabitants nestle unobtrusively in the surrounding forest. The village center was once a cluster of old farm buildings.

Now, the old milking barn is a pottery with a resident potter, another farm building is now an excellent, well-stocked market and general store, and there is even a post office in the old blacksmith shop. The restaurant, a lovely white-columned farmhouse, is in the old Fearrington home, built in 1926.

Food, I discovered, was of paramount importance in their plans. They wanted to bring back Southern cooking at its finest, and the menu offers such interesting items as Carolina crab cakes with tomato and corn relish, Chatham County goat cheese salad, corn chowder with hickory-smoked duck sausage, crayfish fritters and creole butter, and grilled Carolina quail with savory cabbage and a ginger sherry sauce.

There are many other more usual dishes, but everything is cooked and served with a special flair and accompanied by buttermilk biscuits and homemade breads. I couldn't make up my mind between the lemon meringue pie and a hazelnut meringue with chocolate ice cream and fresh raspberry sauce. They were both incredible.

I asked R.B. what his philosophy had been in creating this very interesting and outstanding settlement. "We've tried to blend it into the rolling countryside so that it looks like it's been around for a long time. The 650 acres that make up the village were in the Fearrington family for over 200 years, and when we bought it in 1974 our commitment was to preserve its heritage and beauty."

About all I would add is that I can't think of another inn with the same level of luxury and elegance, in a more beautiful setting.

We are happy to welcome the Fearrington House to the pages of *Country Inns and Back Roads* for the first time.

THE FEARRINGTON HOUSE, Fearrington Village Center, Pittsboro, NC 27312; 919-542-2121 or 967-7770. A 14-guestroom (mostly suites) luxury inn and village in rolling farm country 8 mi. south of Chapel Hill, the home of the Univ. of No. Carolina. Breakfast included in room rate. Picnics available. Restaurant is open for dinner Tues. thru Sat. and Sun. brunch. Sun. and Mon. eves. reservations recommended. Open year-round. Swimming pool, croquet lawn, crafts shops, country walks on premises. Cultural, social, and athletic events at Univ. of No. Carolina; also Duke Univ. and No. Carolina State Univ. nearby. Children over 12 welcome. Nearby kennels available for pets. No smoking in guest and dining rooms. Jenny and R.B. Fitch, Owners. (See Index for rates.)

Directions: The Fearrington House is located halfway between Chapel Hill and Pittsboro on U.S. 15/501.

HEMLOCK INN
Bryson City, North Carolina (1973)

"What's it really like at the Hemlock Inn?" I've been joyously answering that question for a great many years as a result of some really inspiring visits with Ella Jo and John Shell. This time, however, I'm going to share with you a letter I received from Mr. and Mrs. J. Brooks Brown, which apparently was mostly written by Helen Brown. I think it puts us right into the picture at the Hemlock Inn.

"We have stayed fifteen times at the Hemlock Inn and would like to share with you some observations about it. My husband, Brooks, and I, who are in our mid-sixties, travel by car from our home in Jacksonville, Florida, in just one day's time for that delicious 6:00 p.m. casual, family-style dinner. . . .

"How great it is to sit around the large Lazy Susan tables with guests who seem to be in concert with our same needs—not all seeming to need the entertainment of radio, TV, golfing, swimming, guided hiking or walking tours, but, instead, much-needed rest and freedom from pressing responsibilities. There is the freedom to converse without competitive conversation, to spend one's day in quietness together in those beautiful surroundings—most particularly for us in long walks or hikes down at the historic Deep Creek region. This can be a short or long hike.

"At each Hemlock stay we find renewal in having had our day started by John's loving prayer of grace in the lodge; new expressions of love for each other in tranquil, quiet, beautiful wild-flowered surroundings; discussing and working out a few problems of our own or those of friends; making plans for grandchildren, family, or friends, or in stopping by the wonderful melodious stream to picnic or just to enjoy.

"You might say that we have the freedom here to catch up on the 'loose ends of life' at our own pace and to celebrate life during this getaway week at a slower tempo. . . .

"Another uniqueness about Hemlock is the freedom of choice of accommodations. There are all kinds of guest rooms, including some in cottages with even room for our grandchildren. Of course, all of them have private baths.

"We have played the shuffleboard that you have described and noticed that many guests enjoy a good game of ping-pong, the outdoor porch rockers, quiet reading or game playing in the cheerful book-filled mountain-view room or in front of the large stone fireplace. Many couples, singles, or families hop in their cars and manage to take untold trips to interesting 'nobs' or 'overlooks,' or hike on the scenic trails. Ella Jo says that there are over 700 miles of maintained trails in the Great Smokies.

"So, I might end by saying, if you have survived this long letter so far, Brooks and I leave Hemlock with renewed vigor, memories for our memory bank, healed spirits to continue to meet a busy life, and, as John Shell says, 'a grateful reverence for those God-given things we certainly have in abundance.'"

Thank you, Brooks and Helen Brown. I've taken a few editing liberties with your splendid letter, and I am delighted to share your feelings for the Hemlock Inn. Perhaps we'll meet there sometime in the near future.

HEMLOCK INN, Bryson City, NC 28713; 704-488-2885. A 25-guestroom Smoky Mountain inn, 4 mi. from Bryson City and 60 mi. from Asheville. Modified American plan omits lunch. Breakfast and dinner served to travelers by reservation only. Sunday dinner served at noontime. Open late April to early Nov. Wheelchair access. Near Fontana Dam, Cherokee, and Pisgah National Forest. Shuffleboard, skittles, ping-pong, hiking trails on grounds. Tubing, rafting, and tennis nearby. No pets. No credit cards. Ella Jo and John Shell, Innkeepers. (See Index for rates.)

Directions: From Hwy. 74 take the Hyatt Creek Rd.–Ela exit. Bear right until you reach Rte. 19. Turn left on Rte. 19 for approx. 1 mi., and turn right at inn sign. Take county road to top of mountain.

HOUND EARS LODGE
Blowing Rock, North Carolina (1971)

There are very few sights more inspiring to the golfer in me than to look over the golf course on a pleasant June morning from the balcony of Hound Ears Lodge. In the foreground is a lake fed by a small mountain stream that winds its way through the valley. This lake also serves as a hazard for the final hole and a very good 9-iron shot to the green is necessary to stay out of trouble.

The fairways that stretch out in the distance toward Grandfather Mountain are being watered by great fountains sent forth by the automatic watering system. When this is completed and the mist burns off, there is revealed a ring of mountains around the entire area. However, in the meantime, the greenskeepers are busy sweeping off the moisture that has accumulated overnight and the head greenskeeper can be seen tootling about in his golf cart, making sure that everything is ready for another day's play.

I had arrived at Hound Ears early in June, just at the time when the special golf packages, in effect since April, were being replaced by the regular social season. It was a good opportunity for me to have a pleasant visit with David Blust, the assistant manager at Hound Ears, who actually started as a bellboy a number of years ago. It's hard to imagine a more enthusiastic devotee of not only Hound Ears, but of golf and of North Carolina. We enjoyed a few moments of listening to Gene Fleri, who plays piano in the pleasant lounge before dinner and in the dining room during dinner. It is said that he can play any song that anyone can name.

Hound Ears is a golf- and ski-oriented country inn, but is somewhat different in atmosphere than the other *CIBR* inns in North Carolina. It is a luxurious, modified American plan resort-inn and the rates reflect the additional services and elegance. In the many, many years that I have been revisiting Hound Ears I've always found a very gratifying number of *CIBR* guests.

Among the many amenities offered are turn-down service each evening, the *Charlotte Observer* at the door every morning, fresh towels supplied to the rooms while guests enjoy dinner, and a careful monitoring of guests at the main gate by courteous custodians. Advance reservations are to be preferred; however, occasionally there are some guest rooms available.

The property surrounding Hound Ears has been purchased by home-owners who have built attractive, luxurious vacation homes, and who are very much involved in the future and welfare of the entire resort complex.

A great many of the guests are from Florida, and during the warm weather they escape to this very high mountain area to enjoy all of the relative coolness, as well as the golf.

During the winter, in addition to being near several downhill ski areas aided by snowmaking, Hound Ears also has its own beginners' and intermediate slopes, providing enjoyment for those of us who are looking for a less vigorous downhill experience.

The staff at Hound Ears is made up for the most part of students from nearby Appalachia College in Boone. These are very pleasant, alert young people who have grown up in the area, for whom Hound Ears is a source of pride.

The furnishings, appointments, interiors, and exteriors are carefully harmonized. For example, my room was done in complementary shades of brown and yellow. All of the buildings are set among the rhododendrons and evergreens, and in many places huge handsome boulders were allowed to remain where they rested. The road was built around them, curving and twisting and climbing.

Nearby Grandfather Mountain is a place where the Scottish clan gathering is held during the second week in July. Scotsmen gather from all over the globe to take part in athletic competitions, dances, and piping. There are also a number of other cultural and recreational events.

HOUND EARS LODGE AND CLUB, P.O. Box 188, Blowing Rock, NC 28605; 704-963-4321. A luxurious 25-guestroom resort-inn on Rte. 105, 6 mi. from Boone. Near natural attractions. American plan. Meals served to houseguests only. Open year-round. Tennis, 18-hole golf course, swimming, and skiing on grounds. David Blust, Innkeeper. (See Index for rates.)

Directions: From Winston-Salem, follow Rte. 421 west to Boone, then travel south on Rte. 105 to inn. From Asheville, follow Rte. I-40 east to Marion then Rte. 221 north to Linville and Rte. 105 north to inn. From Bristol, Va., and I-81, follow Rte. 58 east to Damascus, Va., then Rte. 91 to Mountain City, Tenn., and Rte. 421 to Boone, and Rte. 104 south to inn (5 mi.)

MAST FARM INN
Valle Crucis, North Carolina (1988)

"People in this part of North Carolina are very fond of just sittin' and talkin'." Francis and Sibyl Pressly and I were engaged in one of the most popular activities at the Mast Farm Inn—porch-rocking. They were telling me about the outbuildings around the rambling old farmhouse, which is on the National Register of Historic Places as "one of the most complete and best-presented groups of 19th-century farm buildings in western North Carolina." The Mast Farm had grown from the tiny log cabin built in 1812 by David Mast.

"The building with the bell tower is the old smokehouse," Francis continued. "Then there's the spring house. Then if you move on around, you come to the old woodshed and the apple house, or ice house, which has foot-thick walls, and we still use it for storing our potatoes and apples."

"Are any of the other buildings used for anything now?" I wondered.

"Oh, sure, we do some woodworking and keep our tools in the old woodshed," Francis replied.

"There's a nest of wrens who are using the old wash house," Sibyl added. "It was considered to be a very innovative wash house because it was built right over a stream and it had lattice work above, so the cool breezes could blow through. There are still two big old iron pots in there."

"Actually," Francis said, "we've restored these buildings to show what an old mountain farmstead was like. We have really made every effort to remain faithful to the past in this entire restoration."

I would say that Francis and Sibyl have succeeded admirably in their objectives. The main house, its long porch stretching around the side with rocking chairs and swings, must look very much as it did in the early 1900s, when it was first turned into an inn. A stay at the inn feels very much like a step back in time, with no telephones or television to shatter the peaceful country atmosphere.

Both originally from North Carolina, Francis and Sibyl had been living in Washington, D.C., where Francis was an administrator with the National 4-H Council, and Sibyl a physical therapist in geriatrics.

In the few years since they began renovating the farmhouse, they have shored up foundations, buttressed walls and floors, painted, papered, brought in craftsmen for woodworking, and done all those things that are necessary to bring a neglected and derelict old house back to its former dignity and beauty.

Today, the rooms fairly sparkle with turn-of-the-century antique furnishings and mountain crafts. There are fresh flowers everywhere and as one of their guests told me, "The inn is squeaky clean from one end to the other, and the room appointments seem to have been chosen not for their country atmosphere, but to make the guests comfortable."

I can see that the Presslys are very good at putting their guests at ease. They are very welcoming and make a point of introducing everyone. When it comes to meals, Sibyl says, "We serve our guests the kind of food that we enjoy."

They describe it as "country cooking with a gourmet flair." That means vegetables and fruit from their garden down by the river. The menu is prix fixe and dinner might be an appetizer, sautéed mountain trout, vegetable strudel, corn pudding, garden vegetables, salad, fresh-baked rolls and cornbread. Dessert could be a fruit cobbler with ice cream, hot fudge cake, fudge nut cake, sour cream apple pie, or Shaker lemon pie.

But as I started to say, we were sitting out on the porch, rocking, and Sibyl and Francis were telling me about how they'd happened to come here. As I looked out over the beautiful mountain valley, I could see just what it was about these North Carolina hills that had attracted them so much.

We are happy to welcome Mast Farm Inn to the pages of *Country Inns and Back Roads* for the first time.

MAST FARM INN, P.O. Box 704, Valle Crucis, NC 28691; 704-963-5857. A 10-guestroom (private and shared baths) farmhouse inn set in a beautiful mountain valley between Boone and Banner Elk in western North Carolina. Modified American plan includes breakfast and dinner. Dinner served to the public Tues. thru Sun. lunch. Reservations necessary. Open Jan. to mid-Mar.; May 1 to Nov. 1. Fishing, canoeing, golf, hiking, skiing, country walks, crafts, and country fairs nearby. Children over 12 welcome. No pets. No smoking. Sibyl and Francis Pressly, Innkeepers. (See Index for rates.)

Directions: The Boone/Banner Elk area is accessible from any direction. Watch for Valle Crucis on NC 105. Mast Farm Inn is 3 mi. from Rte. 105 on Rte. SR 1112.

THE ORCHARD INN
Saluda, North Carolina (1985)

I had finished every last bit of the succulent chicken Madras and now I was trying to stretch out a scrumptious blackberry cobbler so it would last as long as possible. I peered through the window, where nature had just put on a marvelous sunset, high in the North Carolina mountains. A pinpoint of light in the valley far below caught my eye.

Ken Hough joined me for a moment, having completed the busiest part of his evening in the kitchen as chef. "Have you ever wondered who lives down there where we can see that light?" I asked. Ken, among a number of other careers, has been headmaster of a college preparatory school in Charleston and also an operatic tenor. He smiled broadly at my question and replied, "It's funny you should mention that because I've often wondered the same thing. Of course, we could never find it in the daytime and the chances are we could never find it by night either."

The inn is midway between Hendersonville and Tryon and, like some other North Carolina inns, has a truly spectacular view. I was very flattered a few years ago when Ken and his wife, Ann, who has a marvelous feeling for interior design, reprinted some things I had said about them in the 1985 edition of this book: "Because I spend so much time in an automobile, I have invented a little game of my own. I call it 'Inn Word Association.' I think of an inn, then think of words that I associate most readily with it.

"In the case of the Orchard Inn there are many words that come to my mind—flowers, original paintings, music, sculpture, a breathtaking view, cordiality, intellectual curiosity, good conversation, mountain tranquility, and the changing tones and colors as they are affected by the mists off the mountains at various times of the day.

"The Orchard Inn combines country farmhouse warmth with many touches of southern plantation elegance. It has oriental rugs, original artwork, baskets, quilts, and Flow Blue china. Ann has exercised splendid taste in decorating the ten guest rooms with antiques, including some with iron and brass beds and hand-woven rag rugs."

This inn has one of the most interesting second-floor hallways I have ever seen. Several bookshelves are loaded with books and magazines, including very old but readable ones. There are all kinds of unusual curios, dolls, children's toys, a dollhouse, and contemporary drawings, watercolors, and prints from the French Impressionists.

A year ago *Gourmet* magazine writer Mimi Elder wrote about her dinner at the inn, extolling Ken's culinary arts. The article, "A Corner of Carolina," opened with a lovely photograph of the old iron triangle used to call the guests to meals. The dining room is in the wonderful, long, glassed-in porch overlooking the rolling peaks of the Warrior Mountain Range. It's really quite magical after dusk has fallen—every table is candlelit, and the strains of Schumann, Mozart, and Scarlatti float out into the gathering night.

Ann joined us at the table and mentioned that Ken's cooking school was most successful this past winter. "We're going to continue it. Surprisingly enough, mostly men came—their wives came along to sit by the fire and knit and we all had fun as well as good cooking." If the reader is interested in learning more about not only the cooking school but other special weekends that are offered throughout the year, just drop the inn a line.

Ken and Ann excused themselves and once again I was left looking out into the darkness at that one single pinpoint of light. I wondered if perhaps they, too, might be looking up at the lights of the inn.

THE ORCHARD INN, Box 725, Saluda, NC 28773; 704-749-5471. A 10-guestroom (private baths) mountaintop (2,500 ft.) inn a short distance from Tryon in western North Carolina. Breakfast included with room rate. Dinner available. Open year-round. Antiquing, hiking, wildflower collecting, birdwatching, and superb country roads abound. No pets. No credit cards. Ann and Ken Hough, Innkeepers. (See Index for rates.)

Directions: From Atlanta, take I-85 north to I-26. Continue north to Exit 28 and Hwy. 176. Inn is on Hwy. 176, 2 mi. off I-26. From Asheville, take I-26 south.

SNOWBIRD MOUNTAIN LODGE
Robbinsville, North Carolina (1973)

Bob and Connie Rhudy and I were seated where everyone sits at Snowbird Mountain Lodge—on the terrace that almost hangs over Lake Santeetlah, at least 1,000 feet below. Gazing over the railing we could see a tiny automobile on the thin, winding sliver of road climbing the adjacent mountain. Directly in front of us, almost close enough to touch, were at least fifteen majestic peaks with heights from 4,000 to 5,000 feet.

Since my first visit to Snowbird quite a few years ago, I have always associated it with the increasing number of birds that make this area their habitat. I understand that some guests can identify as many as 110 different species. In the last couple of years wildflower walks have become extremely popular.

Connie and Bob were especially enthusiastic about the nature hikes led by several knowledgeable guides in the past two years. "They have become enormously popular," Connie said. "There are wildflower, bird, and plant hikes, and our guides are acknowledged authorities in their fields. They are each here at different times during the spring and summer, and we have many reservations for next spring's adventures already."

Rustic Snowbird Mountain Lodge, built of chestnut logs and native stone, harmonizes beautifully with its mountain setting. Two huge stone fireplaces add beauty and warmth. (There is also steam heat for the cooler months.)

The main lounge is paneled in butternut, the dining room in cherry, and guest rooms are paneled in a variety of native woods with custom-made furniture to match. The comfortable beds have bright bedspreads.

The Rhudys have two excellent assistant innkeepers in their daughter, Becky, who is now enrolled at the University of North Carolina, and their son, Bobby, who will complete his senior year at Furman University in June. Bobby plays the piano in the evenings for their guests. All of the Rhudys have combined to make this mountaintop lodge a veritable haven for guests who enjoy the many outdoor activities in the area.

Boxed lunches are provided in lieu of lunch at the lodge, if guests prefer. Snowbird is on the full American plan.

"Last year we did something for the first time that we're going to continue," explained Bob. "We decided to add one final weekend to our season and call it 'Fall Finale at Snowbird.' Fresh hot coffee starts the Friday afternoon and then after the evening meal, which will have fresh mountain trout and homemade coconut cream pie, we'll gather in front of a roaring fire to enjoy music from some of our local musicians. After breakfast on Saturday morning, a packed lunch will be available for anyone wishing to explore the Joyce Kilmer–Slickrock Wilderness Area. Following a dinner of Rock Cornish game hens we'll retire to our sitting room for another evening of reading, games, and swapping stories of the day's activities. The weekend closes on Sunday morning with a delicious breakfast of country sausage and blueberry pancakes."

Sounds like a wonderful way to wind up the autumn.

SNOWBIRD MOUNTAIN LODGE, Joyce Kilmer Forest Rd., Robbinsville, NC 28771; 704-479-3433. A 22-guestroom inn on top of the Great Smokies, 12 mi. from Robbinsville. American plan (room and 3 meals). Open from end of April to early Nov. Lunch and dinner served to travelers by reservation only. Shuffleboard, table tennis, archery, croquet, horseshoes, badminton on grounds. Swimming, fishing, hiking, backroading nearby. Guided walks for nature lovers by reservation. Not suitable for children under 12. No pets. The Rhudy Family, Innkeepers. (See Index for rates.)

Directions: The inn is located at the western tip of No. Carolina, 10 mi. west of Robbinsville. Approaching from the northeast or south take U.S. 19 and 129; from the northwest take U.S. 129, then follow signs to Joyce Kilmer Memorial Forest.

A number of inns have nearby airports where private airplanes may land. An airplane symbol at the end of the inn directions indicates that there is an airport nearby. Consult inn for further information.

THE ASHBY INN
Paris, Virginia (1988)

It's been my privilege to meet many interesting, cultured, and witty innkeepers in the years I've been writing this book, and I'd have to place John and Roma Sherman in the top ten percent of that group. Roma, who is a transplant from the English Midlands, ran an advertising agency in Washington, D.C., before she took up innkeeping. John, an ex-journalist, spent thirteen years on Capitol Hill advising and writing speeches for some of the country's top political leaders. Since leaving Congress, his clients are strictly corporate presidents. And he amuses himself and his patrons with a witty and original monthly newsletter, which will give you a chuckle if you get on his list.

Sitting with them in their English-style pub (really the original kitchen with walnut beams and a stone fireplace), it was fun to listen to their stories. "It took us five years of looking to find this place," Roma said. "But when I saw it, I knew this was it. John was out of town, and I told him if he didn't cancel his fishing trip and come and see it, I was going to buy it without him. The next day at dawn we headed for Paris—and bought the inn."

Later, when I was touring the house with John and we were looking out the window of an upstairs guest room, he said, "This is what stopped us—that view right there." It was indeed a lovely view of a green hillside and fields, beautiful trees, white fences, hedges, and flowers. "There are Black Angus cattle over there, and we often have flights of Canada geese. You can even catch a glimpse of wild turkeys or white-tailed deer now and then."

The Ashby Inn, a white clapboard Colonial house built in 1829, sits on a wide, quiet street in the little village of Paris. John and Roma have done a meticulous renovation of the house, preserving its pristine Colonial personality with authentic antique furnishings.

"A friend who is a real 'restorationist' helped us choose Colonial paint colors and hand-stenciled the borders on the floors," John told me. Those floors, of course, are of wide pine-board. The guest rooms are all different, with a painted headboard in one and a cannonball bed in another. There are Windsor rocking chairs, antique blanket chests and wardrobes, quilts, candlewick spreads, dried herb wreaths, and 110-year-old rag rugs ("which wear better than new ones," John says).

A pleasant sitting room with a fireplace is well stocked with books, magazines, and newspapers, and there are four dining rooms, as well as a lovely patio for outside dining.

But, as their brochure states, "the heart of the Ashby Inn is its kitchen. The menu is limited, thoughtful, and guided more by tradition than trend—Roma Sherman brings to the menu regional specialties from her native England like beef and mushroom pie, fish stews, and Stilton cheese."

However, John's newsletter betrays a more adventurous bent in cuisine: "The most unusual of chef Paul Shell's selections is a pan-blackened breast of chicken. . . . Paul coats the breast with butter, fresh thyme, and black pepper, keeps it cold, then tosses it in a very hot cast iron skillet."

Roma said that their cozy taproom was a regular gathering place for the "locals." When she mentioned they were mainly breeders, owners, trainers, jockeys, and other riders, who stop in after a race or a hunt, I remembered that we were in the middle of hunt country, where they do things like "ride to hounds," play polo, and have point-to-point races.

When I asked John what he felt was distinctive about their inn, he said, "We have a spectacular view of the foothills of the Blue Ridge . . . we grow our own vegetables and herbs . . . we serve a lot of game when the leaves begin to turn."

We are pleased to welcome the Ashby Inn to the pages of *Country Inns and Back Roads* for the first time.

THE ASHBY INN, Rte. 1, Box 2/A, Paris, VA 22130; 703-592-3900. A 6-guestroom (private and shared baths) 1829 Colonial inn in a tiny village just west of Middleburg, approx. 1 hr. from Washington, D.C. Breakfast included in room rate. Dinner served daily; reservations recommended. Picnic lunches available. Open year-round. Air conditioning in rooms. Croquet lawn on premises. Horse shows, races, stable tours, hiking, country walks, state parks, antiquing, backroading, fishing, and floating on the Shenandoah River. Well-behaved children over 10. No pets. John and Roma Sherman, Innkeepers. (See Index for rates.)

Directions: From Washington, D.C., take Rte. 50 west through Middleburg and Upperville. After Rte. 50 becomes 4 lanes, continue 1 mi. to Rte. 759, and turn left to Paris.

GRAVES' MOUNTAIN LODGE
Syria, Virginia (1972)

Of all of the thousands of inn and hotel brochures that I have seen, none is more handsome, better designed, or more informative than "Mountain Hospitality," the booklet that describes literally five generations of innkeeping at Graves' Mountain Lodge.

For over 130 years, five generations of the Graves family have been innkeepers in the shadow of the Blue Ridge Mountains near Syria, Virginia. In the early 1850s, Paschal Graves opened an "ordinary," or inn, along the Blue Ridge Turnpike on land now part of the Shenandoah National Park. The ordinary was a natural stopping point for travelers making the seventy mile journey between Gordonsville and New Market. Here horses were changed to make the climb over the mountains, and farmers on foot herded their livestock to market along the turnpike or hauled wagonloads of bark and carts of apples, corn, and chestnuts.

Around 1857 the Graves family moved to their present location and for 100 years "took in" travelers and vacationers in their rambling farmhouse. Today's innkeeper is Jim Graves, and he can recall as a boy growing up the fun and work of having visitors arrive. Their cook fried chicken, baked hams and fresh fruit pies and cakes. Dinner was served family-style and people came from all around to have chicken. As he said, "When we had a lot of guests in the summer, our family moved out of the bedrooms and slept on the porch. We didn't mind because vacationers usually brought children for us to play with. We became friends with many of them and later some came back to work on the farm."

A lot of very exciting things have happened since Jim was a young boy. He met and married Rachel Lynn Norman, who shared his enthusiasm. Even during their courting days they drew sketches and developed ideas about a rustic but modern mountain resort. They discovered that they had the same pedigree; they are both descendants of Captain Thomas Graves, who sailed to Jamestown in 1608. Rachel's family stems from Thomas Graves' oldest son, born in England, and Jim's family is descended from a younger son, born in Virginia. Twelve generations later their marriage united two branches of a 375-year family tree. By the way, this tree is pictured in "Mountain Hospitality."

One of the most colorful figures connected with Graves' Mountain Lodge was Jim's father, "Mr. Jack," who was still on the scene during my first visit many years ago. It was a common sight to see him come to dinner fresh from his farm chores, but in clean overalls, to be on hand to meet all of the guests.

As I leafed through the pages of the booklet, I realized that very little has changed since the original concept of Graves' Mountain Lodge four generations ago. The new lodge is a unique collection of old and new buildings, each with a history all of its own. Over the years I have described the outbuildings that also serve as guest quarters. In recent years two additional buildings with tastefully furnished motel-type bedrooms enjoy a fantastic view of the great valley filled with cattle, sheep, farmland, and acres and acres of peach and apple trees.

What about the food at Graves' Mountain Lodge? Well, here is Rachel Graves telling me about Sunday night supper at Graves' Mountain Lodge. "Sunday night dinner will be country ham, cold fried chicken, country-fried potatoes and onions, green beans, baked tomatoes, corn pudding, coleslaw, maybe one or two other vegetables, and probably spiced peaches or apples. Usually on Sunday night we have hot fudge cake for dessert.

"Tonight, we will have between 250 and 300 people. Last Sunday, we had about 700 people."

The original Graves family, including Mr. Jack, I'm sure, would be glad to know that everybody is served family-style inside the lodge and on the porch.

Although the lodge is operated on the American plan—three meals a day with lodging—those who want to stop by for a meal can call for a reservation and are always welcome.

GRAVES' MOUNTAIN LODGE, Syria, VA 22743; 703-923-4231. A 41-guestroom secluded, rustic resort-inn, including cottages and 2 motel units, on Rte. 670, off Rte. 321, 10 mi. north of Madison, Va., 38 mi. N.W. of Charlottesville, Va. American plan. Breakfast, lunch, dinner served to travelers by reservation only. Closed Dec. 1 to late Mar. Swimming, tennis, horseback riding, hunting, fishing, a special nature walk, rock hunting, and hiking on grounds. Golf nearby. Jim and Rachel Graves, Innkeepers. (See Index for rates.)

Directions: Coming south from Wash. D.C., take I-66 to Gainsville. Follow Rte. 29 south to Madison, turn right onto Rte. 231 west, go 7 mi. to Banco, turn left onto Rte. 670 and follow 670 for 4½ mi. to lodge.

THE INN AT GRISTMILL SQUARE
Warm Springs, Virginia (1977)

Bruce McWilliams was explaining the workings of the waterwheel at Gristmill Square:

"The waterwheel is known as an 'overshot wheel,' " he said. "It is driven by the weight of the water flowing into the buckets at the top of the wheel. It was manufactured in 1900 by the Fitz Waterwheel Company in Hanover, Pennsylvania, and operates from this little brook. There's been a mill on this site continuously since 1771, although the present mill building was erected in 1900."

Gristmill Square is built around a three-sided square, formed by an old mill, a blacksmith's shop, and a hardware store. Guest rooms were created in the old hardware store and there are three country stores in the former blacksmith's shop. Most of the guest rooms are furnished with antiques and old prints, although some are done in a more contemporary style.

There are other bedrooms available in period buildings adjacent to the inn or across the village street from Gristmill Square. Both the Virginian Room and the Miss Jenny Payne Room, two rooms in the Steel House, have four-poster beds and fireplaces.

The Waterwheel Restaurant has been artfully fashioned from the grain mill, which was operated by the waterwheel. The heavenly aroma of the grain, the beige patina of the walls, and the geometric patterns created by the beams and posts make a most unusual setting for a candlelight dinner.

The menu features roast duckling with apricots, pan-fried trout with black walnuts, veal à l'orange, and broiled mountain trout.

The McWilliams family has also provided additional amenities for guests who enjoy longer stays. The Bath and Tennis Club has a swimming pool and tennis courts that are playable for most of the year, and there is a sauna in the Steel House. In one of the golfing capitals of the world, the famous Cascades and Lower Cascades golf courses are a short drive away. The Warm Springs Pools are within walking distance.

There is horseback and carriage riding nearby as well as exceptional trout fishing, downhill and cross-country skiing, and some of the most beautiful backroading and hill-walking to be found west of Scotland.

Adding to the cultural attractions of the area are the Garth Newel chamber music concerts, performed on summer weekends.

Bath County is located in the west-central portion of Virginia. The 540-square-mile area is within one day's drive of half the population of the northeastern United States. The elevations range from 4,477 feet above sea level to 1,140 feet, where the Cowpasture River flows into Allegheny County. Visitors began coming to the springs of Bath County as early as 1750 and it's been increasing in popularity every year since.

THE INN AT GRISTMILL SQUARE, P.O. Box 359, Warm Springs, VA 24484; 703-839-2231. A 14-guestroom unusual restoration with a restaurant and many resort attractions in a small country town in the Allegheny Mtns., 19 mi. no. of Covington. European plan. Restaurant open for dinner daily Tues.-Sun., and Sun. lunch. Lunch served May 1 to Nov. 1, Tues.-Sun. Restaurant closed Mon. Suggest calling for details. Tennis courts, swimming pool, and sauna on grounds. Golf at nearby Cascades or Lower Cascades. Skiing at Snowshoe, West Va., about an hr. away. Skating, riding, hiking, fishing, hunting, antiquing, and backroading nearby. Children welcome. The McWilliams Family, Innkeepers. (See Index for rates.)

Directions: From Staunton, Va., follow Rte. 254 to Buffalo Gap; Rte. 42 to Millboro Spring; Rte. 39 to Warm Springs. From Lexington, take Rte. 39 to Warm Springs. From Roanoke, take Rte. 220 to Warm Springs. From Lewisburg, W Va., take I-64 to Covington; Rte. 220 north to Warm Springs. From northern W. Va. travel south to Rte. 39 east to Warm Springs. The inn is on Rte. 645. From Rte. 220 going north, turn left on Rte. 645 in Warm Springs. From Rte. 39W turn left on Rte. 692 and left again on Rte. 645 at Warm Springs. ✈

The date in parenthesis in the heading represents the first year the inn appeared in the pages of Country Inns and Back Roads.

THE INN AT LITTLE WASHINGTON
Washington, Virginia (1988)

This inn is remarkable for several reasons, the foremost probably being the chef and co-owner, Patrick O'Connell, who has gained an international reputation for his innovative cuisine. Another reason is the luxurious and intriguing ambience, which reminded me very much, on a smaller scale, of Chewton Glen, a posh country house hotel in Hampshire, England. Also, the Inn at Little Washington is a member of Relais et Chateaux, one of the very few inns in the United States to be accepted in that prestigious French organization.

Lest you think this sounds too grand and overwhelming, let me hasten to assure you that Patrick and co-owner Reinhardt Lynch couldn't be more relaxed and gracious hosts. They've come a long way from the days back in 1978 when they first opened the restaurant in a former garage/country store. At first, there were just the two of them and a fourteen-year-old kitchen boy. "We had a long telephone cord, and I took reservations at the stove while I stirred the sauces," Patrick recalls.

Today, ten years later, they have a staff of forty, a beautiful restaurant, and ten exquisitely decorated guest rooms, along with a reputation that draws all sorts of luminaries from "big" Washington, sixty-seven miles distant, and many visitors from the West Coast and Europe.

This is a very sophisticated inn in a very pastoral setting. The village of Washington has one stoplight, a post office, a church, a cafe, and a wonderful general store, and is surrounded by the rolling foothills of the Blue Ridge Mountains. The central square was laid out by George Washington in 1749. If you were to take an early morning stroll, you might see a deer in the fields, where wild roses bloom.

It's a different world when you step past the four-pillared porch and into the entrance hall, with its two-story-high ceiling, which has a remarkable stained-glass effect. The feeling is Victorian, with beautiful antique furnishings, imported English fabrics and papers after the style of the William Morris movement, and *faux bois*—woodwork specially painted to simulate a grain.

Tables in the restaurant have long skirts and several overcloths. Basket lamps covered in peach taffeta hang over each table, and the partitions dividing different areas are topped by lace panels, which add a rather quaint, old-fashioned touch.

As one might expect, the staff is polished and deft, and the food is superb. Some of Patrick's specialties are sweetbreads with crab, capers, and lemon; smoked goose breast and black-eyed peas vinaigrette; shiitake mushrooms with vermicelli; and shrimp flavored with juniper berries in a mustard and dill sauce. Two desserts that caught my eye were the "Strawberry Intensifier," a concoction of strawberry sorbet, strawberry ice cream, wild strawberries, and strawberry sauce; and a grapefruit-pecan-chocolate tart—a dark chocolate and nut crust covering a creamy custard with just a tang of grapefruit.

Breakfast in the Garden Room is a total delight. Windows and french doors on all sides look out on a lovely enclosed garden and a little finch twitters merrily in his cage.

Guest rooms are decorated in various styles, from Chinese to Italianate. There are huge beds, beautifully draped windows, deep window seats with cushions, chaise longues, and all sorts of interesting antique pieces. There are two suites with upstairs bedrooms. The bathrooms are done in brass and marble.

If it's the "lap of luxury" you're looking for, this must be the place. But make your reservations early!

I'm happy to welcome the Inn at Little Washington to the pages of *Country Inns and Back Roads* for the first time.

THE INN AT LITTLE WASHINGTON, Middle and Main Sts., Box 300, Washington, VA 22747; 703-675-3800. A 10-guestroom luxurious inn and restaurant in the foothills of the Blue Ridge Mountains, 67 mi. west of Washington, D.C. Continental breakfast included in tariff; dinner reservations guaranteed for overnight guests. Dinner is served Wed. thru Sun. Open year-round. Blue Ridge Mountains, Shenandoah National Park, antiques shops, country walks, backroading nearby. No children under 10. No pets. Patrick O'Connell and Reinhardt Lynch, Innkeepers. (See Index for rates.)

Directions: From Washington, D.C., take I-66 to Rte. 211. Continue to Washington, Va.

JORDAN HOLLOW FARM INN
Stanley, Virginia (1985)

I'm not sure of the protocol, but I think I'm godfather to a colt. It all happened on a visit to Jordan Hollow Farm, when a foal was born and Marley Beers named him "Norman" — I have his most recent photo, and he's a beauty.

"He'll have to earn his keep," she said, "because we are a working horse farm. We raise German Holsteiner and thoroughbreds, as well as keeping pleasure horses for our guests. However, it's not necessary to be a horse rider to enjoy yourself here. Many of our guests who have never ridden in their lives and have come for the wonderful Shenandoah Valley mountain experience begin to feel at home with these beautiful animals, and we have persuaded them to try one of our beginners' rides. We never take out more than five or six people at a time and we have both English and Western saddles. There are some very quiet trail horses that are trustworthy for beginners and we have advanced horses for experienced riders.

"In most other places there is a walking trail ride and everyone goes in a long line. You see the scenery but you don't really have too much of an equestrian experience. We do things differently because we want everybody to enjoy as many experiences as possible."

Marley and her Dutch husband, Jetze (pronounced Yet-sah), purchased this former Colonial horse farm several years ago and began creating an inn for the enjoyment of their guests. Jetze speaks several different languages, and both of them have traveled widely and are sophisticated hosts. They met in Africa.

This African influence is mirrored in one of the three dining rooms with decorations from Africa. In many ways, they seemed quite in place with the rest of this wonderful atmosphere that is so removed from the hubbub of the city.

One of the engaging features of the inn is the pub, called the "Watering Trough." Jetze has built an adjoining fountain and gardens with umbrella tables and chairs. On the night of my visit I sat up rather late with the innkeepers and another couple from Washington. I asked the gentleman what he enjoyed most about being here, and he said, "Just the peace and quiet and opportunity to read, take walks, and enjoy good food and good company."

This convivial atmosphere continues at dinner. Marley is the cook and describes the food as "country French" style, with plenty of fresh fruits and vegetables, and homemade breads and desserts. She particularly recommends their roast quail and rib eye steaks.

The guest rooms are all furnished with comfortable, cozy country-inn furniture, with different types of beds and other pieces in each room, as well as dried flower arrangements, calico comforters, and wonderful, thick, fluffy towels.

The latest news is that Norman now has a full brother named Simpson, who promises to be just as big but even more handsome. Norman has shed his baby coat and is now a beautiful dark gray with flecks of white. He stands fifteen hands. I have a framed photograph of him in my study.

On a guest's birthday, along with a birthday cake, Marley and Jetze have revived the old Virginia custom of buttering that person's nose, thus "helping him to slide through the next year without difficulty." I guess I'll have to return to Jordan Hollow on Norman's and Simpson's birthdays and butter their noses!

JORDAN HOLLOW FARM INN, Rte. 2, Box 375, Stanley, VA 22851; 703-778-2285 or 2209. A 20-guestroom restored Colonial horse farm 6 mi. south of Luray in the northern Shenandoah Valley of Virginia. Open year round. Breakfast, lunch, and dinner served daily to houseguests. Restaurant open to public Wed. thru Sun. The horse center is on the property with a wide variety of horses and lessons from beginner thru advanced. Scenic trail rides are planned for various levels of skill. Swimming, volleyball, ping-pong, board games, walking, and xc skiing on the premises. Hiking, canoeing, fishing, skiing, golf, tennis, auctions, museums, antiques, crafts shops nearby. Sorry, no pets; boarding kennel nearby. Marley and Jetze Beers, Innkeepers. (See Index for rates.)

Directions: The inn is located 6 mi. south of Luray, Va.; 12 mi. from the Skyline Drive; and 19 mi. from I-81 at New Market. Go south from Luray 6 mi. on Rte. 340; turn left on Rte. 624; left on Rte. 689; and right on Rte. 626.

L'AUBERGE PROVENÇALE
White Post, Virginia (1988)

Swinging gently in the hanging wooden swing on the wide front porch, Celeste Borel and I had been talking about how she and Alain, her husband, had found this beautiful 1753 stone farmhouse and had opened a country inn. During a lull in the conversation, I heard a flock of geese honk their way across the sky and watched as they settled on a pond in the nearby field. Crickets chirped, and far off in a pasture cattle lowed.

As reluctant as I was to leave this tranquil and bucolic scene, the aromas wafting from the kitchen, where Alain was practicing his art, were too much for me, and I eagerly followed Celeste into one of the three cozy dining rooms, where other guests were just sitting down to tables set with snowy white linen, overlaid with blue cloths, sparkling crystal, and gleaming silver. It was a very pleasant dining room with a fireplace, polished wood floors, and walls lined with French paintings and prints, including a Picasso.

"How do you happen to have a picture of the Pope's palace and the bridge of Avignon on your menu?" I asked Celeste.

"Alain was born and raised in Avignon," she replied. "He started working in his grandfather's restaurant there when he was thirteen, and he has been in the restaurant business ever since." Later, when I saw all of the articles that have been written about L'Auberge Provençale and Alain's cuisine, I realized he has become quite famous as a French chef. They frequently have diners who have driven from Washington, D.C., ninety minutes away.

Alain showed me the huge herb and vegetable garden. "We also have two cherry trees, a purple plum, a peach, a pear, and an apple tree, as well as raspberry bushes."

Alain calls his menu "cuisine moderne—classic Provençale French combined with *nouvelle,* but in substantial portions." Some of his starters include sautéed sweetbreads with port, capers, and pine nuts; duck *foie gras* with pears and turmeric; and a Provençale rabbit soup. Entrées could be roast squab with fresh peaches, cloves, and cinnamon basil served with wild rice; Moroccan-style medallions of lamb; veal with pomegranate wine and green peppercorns; and several other choices. There are wonderful desserts, such as chocolate genoise with white chocolate mousse and mocha sauce and homemade ice cream in an almond tulip cup.

Guest rooms in the main house and in an adjacent cottage are attractively and comfortably furnished with antique and wicker pieces and pleasingly decorated in soft colors, flowered and white eyelet spreads, paintings, and fresh flowers. There are four-poster beds and white iron beds, and two of the rooms in the main house have fireplaces.

The next morning as I sat on the porch at breakfast, savoring one of Alain's perfect omelets and watching as the landscape emerged from the lifting mists, I pondered on what an interesting set of circumstances we had here.

Deep in the farming country of the Shenandoah Valley, in the tiny early American village of White Post—so named because George Washington as a young surveyor had erected a white post there—Celeste and Alain Borel have created a French country inn and restaurant. This combination has drawn guests from far and wide; one guest even arrived by helicopter, setting down in their back yard.

"There's an airstrip across the road," Celeste told me, "and the man who owns it has been kind enough to let single-engine planes land there. Then, Billy Thompson, who restores antique autos in town, will pick up and deliver them in one of his classic cars, if they so desire." That's what I mean about an interesting set of circumstances.

I am happy to welcome L'Auberge Provençale to the pages of *Country Inns and Back Roads* for the first time.

L'AUBERGE PROVENÇALE, Rte. 340, P.O. Box 119, White Post, VA 22633; 703-837-1375. A 6-guestroom (private baths) French country inn and restaurant in Clarke County in the Shenandoah Valley, 90 min. west of Wash., D.C. Breakfast included in room rate. Picnic lunches by arrangement. Dinner served daily except Thurs. Open year-round. Antiques and country shops, Burwell-Morgan Mill, Blandy Farm, White Post antique car restoration, point-to-point horse races, Skyline Drive, and magnificent backroading nearby. Well-behaved children over 10 welcome. No pets. Celeste and Alain Borel, Innkeepers. (See Index for rates.)

Directions: From Wash., D.C., take Rte. 50 to Rte. 340, where there is a 3-way traffic light. Turn left and continue 1 mi. to inn.

MAPLE HALL
Lexington, Virginia (1987)

It is always somewhat in the nature of a homecoming for me to return to Lexington, Virginia. I lived in nearby Lynchburg for five years and made many trips through the beautiful Blue Ridge Mountains to follow the fortunes of the Virginia Military Institute and Washington and Lee sports teams. There are many lovely old buildings on both of those college campuses, and even the downtown business buildings have a weathered and attractive appearance. Lexington has a gentle quality of the past, and indeed is a most historic place, at the same time keeping pace with the present and the future. There is an informal walking tour of downtown Lexington, which will reveal many unexpected architectural delights.

Susan and Peter Meredith and the many members of their family have been developing Historic Inns of Lexington for the past few years. It began with the Alexander-Withrow House, which I first visited many years ago, and continued with the McCampbell Inn. Both of these offer bed and breakfast, and are conveniently located in the business district. These two have now been joined by a most imposing old plantation called Maple Hall, a few miles north of Lexington.

This lovely old red brick mansion with its handsome white columns has always been admired by all who pass by it. The small red brick house next door may have been the original plantation house. This is now the guest house, offering three guest rooms, a living room, and kitchen.

The guest rooms in the main house are of generous size and appropriately furnished. There are fireplaces and modern conveniences.

Don Fredenburg, who is the manager of all three of the Historic Inns of Lexington, told me that Maple Hall was built on 257 acres around 1850. "It is of the typical mansion-plantation architecture that characterized the South during the pre–Civil War days," he said.

At the time of my visit, the dining room was open for dinners on Wednesday through Saturday and for a very impressive Sunday brunch. "Our guests from the Alexander-Withrow and the McCampbell also enjoy dinner here."

Dinner is served either in the quiet, impressive dining room or in the glass-enclosed patio off the garden. I had chosen fresh salmon fillets from a menu that included four or more other main items.

"Peter has built a pier on the pond at Maple Hall and stocked it with fish," Don continued. "There are also several miles of hiking trails cut through the fifty-six acres of woods and pastures so that guests can take a leisurely stroll or perhaps even do some running.

"Lexington is certainly a growing place," he remarked. "For one thing, the Virginia Horse Center has opened and the first show was a big success. Over forty events are scheduled for 1988. A number of dignitaries from Texas and Virginia were also in Lexington in September to commemorate Sam Houston's birthplace across the road from Maple Hall."

Readers who want to stop at Maple Hall may check in directly at Maple Hall, while guests at the Alexander-Withrow and the McCampbell Inn should check in at the main reception desk at the McCampbell Inn in the center of Lexington.

The Merediths have always been great builders and designers and restorers, and I'm happy to say that Maple Hall is a credit to their craft and enthusiasm. Located as it is in such a beautiful area of the Blue Ridge Mountains, I'm sure that it is going to provide a real Southern country-inn flavor for inn devotees and business travelers.

MAPLE HALL (Historic Inns of Lexington), 11 No. Main St., Lexington, VA 24450; 703-463-2044. A 16-guestroom (private baths) mansion-inn, just 7 mi. north of Lexington. Hearty continental breakfast included with room rate. Dinner served Wed. thru Sat.; Sun. brunch. Open all year. Ideal for back-road wanderers or business travelers on I-81 and I-84. Lexington has many activities both summer and winter besides those at Virginia Military Institute and Washington and Lee University. The Blue Ridge Parkway is just a few miles away. Golf, hiking, Appalachian Trail, and canoeing also available. No pets. Mr. and Mrs. Peter Meredith and sons, Owners; Don Fredenburg, Innkeeper. (See Index for rates.)

Directions: Maple Hall is 7 mi. north of Lexington on Rte. 11. From I-81 take Exit 53.

MEADOW LANE LODGE
Warm Springs, Virginia (1978)

I was wandering about in the great barn at Meadow Lane Lodge, located in Bath County, Virginia, a few minutes from the famous Cascades Golf Course in Warm Springs. Here, sheep and goats graze and gambol. Chickens, ducks, guinea fowl, geese, and turkeys inhabit the old horse stalls in the large stable and freely wander in the areas around them. Cats and kittens mingle, as do the farm dogs. No one hurts anyone and there is respect everywhere.

A few moments earlier I had reluctantly gotten up from a wonderful breakfast featuring a special recipe for scrambled eggs blended with some aromatic herbs, prepared by innkeeper Philip Hirsh. Although Phip, as he is called, is a retired executive, he still takes great pride in occasionally doing the Meadow Lane breakfast.

In the beautiful Allegheny Mountains, Meadow Lane Lodge is an integral part of the Hirsh estate, comprised of 1,600 acres of woods, fields, and streams. In such an atmosphere, tranquility and relaxation are almost guaranteed.

Two suites and three double bedrooms are available in the main house, while Craig's Cottage, named for a Hirsh grandson, will accommodate two to four people. The cottage boasts a big stone fireplace in a lovely high ceilinged bedroom with a large picture window looking over the meadows and mountains.

Cathy Hirsh led me off to one corner, saying, "Yesterday, Phip and I took a couple of hours off, and with two of the dogs went up into the woods to walk around the horse exercise track, which was hewn out of the forest by Phip's father. We saw lady-slippers in bloom and lots of trillium and dwarf iris. Then we drove along the Jackson River to the trout ponds and the spring where the wild azalea and dogwood are flowering, and the watercress is a great patch of vivid green. Our river is one of Virginia's designated scenic rivers and two miles of it flow right through the farm.

"On cool spring and fall mornings and evenings, the two fireplaces in the living rooms of the lodge are always in use. I'm sure you noticed that the upstairs rooms have screened-in porches with delightful views and breezes. Later on, our large front porch with its wicker furniture will be a scene for lots of relaxing and chatting with other inn guests."

Additional accommodations are offered in the center of the village of Warm Springs in the Francisco Cottage, which has been restored and furnished in the manner of the log house originally erected on the site, circa 1820. This cottage offers a very pleasantly furnished living room, porch, bedroom, kitchen, and bath, and an impressive view of the hillsides.

Cathy and Philip are excited about the newest addition to Meadow Lane. "It has been designed like an old Pennsylvania barn with an overhang and beautiful stonework at one end," Cathy told me. "There are two guest rooms with baths, plus a vaulted-ceiling living room with a big picture window. The building looks old and fits in beautifully with the rest of the farm."

They report that their new six-wicket English croquet court is very popular with guests, and Meadow Lane Lodge is now a member of the U.S. Croquet Association.

MEADOW LANE LODGE, Star Route A, Box 110, Warm Springs, VA 24484; 703-839-5959. A 10-guestroom lodge-inn on a portion of a large estate about 10 min. from the center of Warm Springs and near the famous Cascades Golf Course. Guestrooms are in the main house and a cottage on the grounds and also in Francisco Cottage in Warm Springs. A full breakfast is the only meal served. Open Apr. 1 thru Jan. 31. Minimum stay in the lodge is 2 nights; in Francisco Cottage, 3 nights. Dinners are available at nearby restaurants. Tennis court, swimming, horseback riding, and excellent fishing on grounds. Also, miles of hiking and walking trails. Golf, skeet and trap shooting nearby. Children over 6 welcome. Small dogs accepted with prior approval. Philip and Cathy Hirsh, Innkeepers. (See Index for rates.)

Directions: From Staunton, Va., follow Rte. 254 west to Buffalo Gap; Rte. 42 south to Millboro Spring; Rte. 39 west to Warm Springs. From Lexington, take Rte. 39 west. From Roanoke, take Rte. 220 north to Warm Springs and Rte. 39 west to Meadow Lane Lodge.

MORRISON HOUSE
Alexandria, Virginia (1987)

Although this book is about "country inns," over the years I have received requests for my recommendations of places in cities. About twelve years ago, I included the Algonquin Hotel in New York City as a discreet "country inn in the city," and since then, I have recommended a few others.

Similarly, Morrison House in Old Town, Alexandria, about twenty minutes from downtown D.C., is not a country inn on a back road, but it is the answer to having quiet, elegant lodgings in an atmosphere that is quite reminiscent of Knightsbridge, London. Further, if you have business or pleasure in the nearby nation's capital it is a most rewarding experience to return to Old Town, with its rows of 18th- and 19th-century houses, diverting shops, and safe walking at night.

The new four-story, Federal-style building is red brick with black shutters, with a main entrance reached by twin curved staircases encircling a fountain and rising to a portico supported by Greek columns.

Seated in the small courtyard in front of the hotel, I was enjoying the freshness of the early morning air and thinking back over the events of my first visit on the previous evening. When I pulled up in front of the entrance, my automobile door was opened by a properly attired butler—not a bellboy, but a butler. I learned that this gentleman is a very important part of the service offered at Morrison House. He was relaxed, efficient, not pompous, extremely accommodating, and a veritable fountain of information about where to go in the D.C. area and how to get there. In the meantime, my car had been whisked away to the hotel's underground parking garage.

Off the first-floor reception area was a pleasantly elegant guest lounge with camelback sofas, Chippendale chairs, and loveseats upholstered in satin brocade. Gracefully draped floor-to-ceiling windows looked out over a quiet street.

If all of this talk of butlers and European elegance seems a little stiff, let me assure you that it is quite relaxed, and designed to provide a very pleasant stay.

This is also true of the guest rooms, which have mahogany four-poster and canopied beds, made up in the European style with triple sheets. The bathrooms are done in Italian marble, and there are terrycloth robes and little reminders to the effect that should a traveler have forgotten such things as a toothbrush, comb, shaving cream, and so forth, the same can be obtained by calling the reception area.

All of the additional thoughtfulness and amenities reflected in this hotel are the result of the extremely broad travel experiences of owners Mr. and Mrs. Robert Morrison. I had a very enjoyable chat with them about various European and British hotels that we both have enjoyed, and, not surprisingly, one mutual favorite was La Residence du Bois in Paris, included in the European edition of this book.

As might be expected, part of the Morrison adventure is the restaurant with the intriguing name of Le Chardon d'Or (the Golden Thistle). There are two menus for both lunch and dinner: à la carte and fixed-price. The à la carte prices are more expensive than those of many country inns, but very much in line with other restaurants in the D.C. area. French contemporary cuisine is the order of the day, served by formally clad waiters.

I must congratulate the Morrison House on being awarded membership in Prestige Hotels, an elite group of independent European hotels.

MORRISON HOUSE, 116 S. Alfred St., Alexandria, VA 22314; 800-367-0800 or 703-838-8000. A 47-guestroom elegant, luxury hotel in a historic section of Alexandria, 20 min. from D.C. Restaurant open for breakfast, lunch, and dinner; Sunday brunch. Open year-round. Conveniently located to visit all of the D.C. area historic, recreational, and cultural attractions. Attractive weekend rates. Mr. and Mrs. Robert Morrison, Owners; Thor Halvorsen, General Manager. (See Index for rates.)

Directions: From National Airport, drive south on Geo. Washington Pkwy. to King St. Turn right and continue for 2 blks. and turn left on S. Alfred St. The hotel is on the left at midblock. From the Beltway/U.S. 495, take Exit U.S. 1 north to Prince St. Turn right and continue for 1 blk. to S. Alfred St. Hotel is on right side.

PROSPECT HILL
Trevilians, Virginia (1979)

As often as I have visited Prospect Hill, a restored plantation home outside Charlottesville, Virginia, I am always delighted by the wealth of information Bill Sheehan has compiled about the history of the inn.

Although the Roger Thompson family owned it in 1732, its real progress began when William Overton purchased the property and increased it to over 1,500 acres in 1840. He enlarged the original house by adding two wings and a spiral staircase.

As Bill says, "During the War Between the States the son of the owner returned to find everything in a completely rundown condition and of course the slaves were gone. I don't believe that he really ever recovered from this catastrophe."

Today, guest rooms of a late-18th-century nature are in the main house and in three of the outbuildings formerly occupied by slaves and servants of the plantation. These include Uncle Guy's House, with rooms both upstairs and down, the Overseer's Cottage, with a suite, and the Boys' Cabin.

Further restoration and renovation have been going on industriously during the last two years. "The last building that we are renovating," Bill told me, "is the old Carriage House, which was built sometime in the 1840s. We have added four magnificent Palladian windows to the open archways on each end of the house to keep the original flavor of the building's use as a carriage house. We have converted the old tool room into a sitting room and modern whirlpool bath. The upper floor of the Carriage House is called the Groom's Quarters and was originally used for that purpose. It was a place for the grooms and drivers of visiting guests at Prospect Hill to spend the night.

"Perhaps equally exciting is Mammy Katie's Kitchen, which was built around 1720 and named after the slave, Mammy Katie, who was one of the few slaves who remained on the plantation after the Civil War. She probably helped raise young William Overton. The kitchen building has the original fireplace, exposed beams, and ceiling joists dating to the 1720s. We, however, in our tradition of having 18th-century bedrooms and 20th-century bathrooms, added a small deck behind the kitchen for breakfast in the morning, a large bedroom with a picture window with a beautiful view across our pasture. It also has a modern whirlpool bath. We've put several of these in our rooms wherever possible.

"We are also updating Uncle Guy's House. This is the building that we first renovated back in 1977 and we have extended the bathrooms.

"Prospect Hill retains its original character of an 18th-century plantation while having all the modern amenities for our guests."

Dinner is served Wednesday through Saturday by reservation and the menu has some very French touches because Bill and his wife, Mireille, travel widely in France and the cuisine is patterned after their experiences. Bill is in charge of the kitchen and he explains the entire dinner to all of the guests at the one seating per evening. His introduction always starts with "Welcome to our home, Prospect Hill."

This part of Virginia really offers a most impressive historical experience, particularly with Monticello, Jefferson's home, and the reproduction of the Michie Tavern nearby. There are numerous historical markers in the area, and Charlottesville itself has the impressive campus of the University of Virginia and its wonderful Georgian buildings. All of this is set in the greening countryside with the Blue Ridge Mountains just a short drive away.

PROSPECT HILL, Route 613, Trevilians, VA 23093; 703-967-0844. A 10-guestroom country inn on a historic plantation 15 mi. east of Charlottesville, Va., 90 mi. southwest of Washington, D.C. Bed and breakfast-in-bed Sun. thru Tues. Modified American plan with full breakfast-in-bed and full dinner Wed. thru Sat. Dinner served Wed. thru Sat. by reservation. Dining room closed Sun., Mon., and Tues. Breakfast always served to houseguests. Swimming pool. Near Monticello, Ashlawn (Pres. Monroe's home), Univ. of Virginia, Castle Hill, and Skyline Drive. Children welcome. No pets. Bill and Mireille Sheehan, Innkeepers. (See Index for rates.)

Directions: From Washington, D.C.: Beltway to I-66 west to Warrenton. Follow Rte. 29 south to Culpeper, then Rte. 15 south thru Orange and Gordonsville to Zion Crossroads. Turn left on Rte. 250 east 1 mi. to Rte. 613. Turn left 3 mi. to inn on left. From Charlottesville or Richmond: take I-64 to Exit 27; Rte. 15 south ½ mi. to Zion Crossroads; turn left on Rte. 250 east 1 mi. to Rte. 613. Turn left 3 mi. to inn on left.

THE RED FOX INN AND TAVERN
Middleburg, Virginia (1979)

While I strolled with the chef through the immaculate kitchen at the Red Fox, he proudly announced, "We make all our own breads and desserts. We also make all our own sauces and soups, and bone our own meats. We are very adaptable in our cuisine, with some nouveau, some Italian, and some classic French things. We use only sweet butter. You won't find preservatives or coloring in any of our food."

There are not many country inns in North America that have remained in the same building for more than 200 years; however, the Red Fox in Middleburg, Virginia, which started as a simple way station when the road to the west was known as "Ashby's Gap Turnpike," has passed the midway point of its third century and is an integral part of American history.

Joseph Chinn was the first proprietor and the inn became known as Chinn's Ordinary. His first cousin was George Washington, who was engaged by Lord Fairfax to survey the area around the tavern, which in turn became known as Chinn's Crossroads.

It's probably true that soldiers from both the American and British lines stopped at this local tavern during the war for American independence. During the War Between the States, Confederate General Jeb Stuart needed lodging for the night and chose the large rooms above the tavern. It was in these rooms that Colonel John Mosby and his Raiders had a celebrated meeting with Stuart, and it was downstairs in the tavern where many of the wounded received care. Among modern-day celebrities who have visited the Red Fox is President John F. Kennedy, who held a rare press conference in the pine-paneled Jeb Stuart Room.

The main entrance leads directly into one of the two low-ceilinged dining rooms where the thirty-inch-thick walls are appropriately decorated with paintings and period pewter and copper. There are seven dining rooms in all. Cheery fires are always lit during the chilly months. A secluded terrace at the rear of the inn underneath the trees has an intimate outdoor feeling and is very popular during the clement weather.

More casual dining is available in Mosby's Tavern, where oak paneling, old pine floors, and stenciled ceilings contribute to the relaxed atmosphere.

Guest rooms in the Red Fox Inn and Tavern are carefully furnished in the 18th-century manner with period antiques and four-postered beds, most with canopies. Some of the rooms have original fireplaces, and all have private baths, direct-dial telephones, and central air conditioning. Fresh flowers, current issues of local country magazines, thick, cotton bathrobes, besides sweets and a *Washington Post* each morning, are some of the extras that make an overnight stay enjoyable.

In keeping with the tradition of naming rooms for famous local personalities, one is called the "Duffy Room" in memory of a colorful fox-hunting and steeplechasing personality, Louis Duffy.

Just a stone's throw from the Red Fox is the Stray Fox Inn, built as a private dwelling long before the Civil War. Guest rooms are carefully furnished with fabrics, furniture, wallcoverings and accessories in the 18th-century style. Stenciled floors and walls, hooked rugs and original wooden mantelpieces preserve the traditional character of the building. The McConnell House, the very latest addition, provides five more guest rooms.

An interesting gallery specializing in 19th-century animal and sporting art has been opened in the old stables of the Stray Fox, and various oil paintings and watercolors, oriental rugs, and bronzes of that period are also featured.

THE RED FOX INN AND TAVERN, Middleburg, VA 22117; 703-687-6301. A 19-guestroom historic village inn (13 of the rooms in the Stray Fox) near the Blue Ridge Mountains, approx. 40 mi. from Washington, D.C. European plan. Breakfast, lunch, and dinner served to travelers. Open every day of the year. Wheelchair access. Near Manassas Battlefield, Oatlands, and Oak Hill (President Monroe's White House), Upperville Horse Show, Foxcroft School, and Nat'l Beagle Trials. Spectator sports such as polo and steeplechasing available nearby. No activities for small children. Sorry, no pets. The Reuter Family, Innkeepers. (See Index for rates.)

Directions: From Washington D.C., exit the Beltway (495) at Rte. 66 west, to Rte. 50 west. Follow Rte. 50 west for 22 mi. to Middleburg. From Winchester and the Shenandoah valley, take Rte. 81 and exit at Winchester onto Rte. 50 east for 30 mi. to Middleburg.

SILVER THATCH INN
Charlottesville, Virginia (1986)

The visiting innkeepers from *CIBR* had finished a tour of the guest rooms at the Silver Thatch, and we were seated under a beautiful Siberian elm tree in a little courtyard formed by a new building with four additional bedrooms. Cathy Hirsh from Meadow Lane Lodge clapped her hands and said, "Come on everybody, lunch is ready and it is really scrumptious." So we filed over the red brick walk, remarking on how happy the birds sounded and what a beautiful day in May it was.

It was Bill Sheehan, the innkeeper at Prospect Hill in nearby Trevilians, Virginia, who first suggested that I visit the Silver Thatch.

"It is really exceptional," he declared, "and Tim and Shelley Dwight are doing wonderful things at dinner as well."

Phil Hirsh from Meadow Lane Lodge also backed up Bill Sheehan's praise, so when I arrived to meet the Dwights and see the inn I was already prepared for something special. I certainly wasn't disappointed. The inn is a Colonial structure of much charm, dating back to 1780. I learned, with some amusement, that the original construction was performed by Hessian soldiers who were taken prisoner during the battle at Saratoga, New York, and marched south to Charlottesville. The original two-story log cabin section of the building is now called the Hessian Room. Of course, there have been several additions through the years, including a recent one by the Dwights themselves.

The addition of the new guest wing, which was constructed in the same Colonial architectural style, now brings the total of guest rooms to eight, all with their own private baths and decorated with Colonial antiques and folk art and antique beds and country quilts, dressers, and armoires.

Tim, as maitre d', greets guests, and Shelley enjoys her cooking duties. The three dining rooms are elegantly appointed with white tablecloths, sparkling glassware, and soft candlelight. The menu, featuring Continental cuisine with emphasis on Southern specialties, changes every month. For instance, in October, there was Autumn Chicken, chicken breasts with apple brandy and fresh pears in a light cream sauce; Tangier Island duckling with peaches and cinnamon; red fish Provençal, sautéed with mushrooms, tomatoes, and olives in a white wine sauce; filet mignon with a bleu cheese demi-glacé sauce; and veal Virginia, veal medallions in a brandied cream sauce with crabmeat and capers.

Tim and Shelley have found that being fifteen minutes from the Blue Ridge Mountains means that spring and fall are particularly busy times.

The nearby attractions are exceptional. The inn is located just eight miles from downtown Charlottesville and minutes away from the University of Virginia, the Skyline Drive, and the Blue Ridge Parkway. Thomas

Jefferson's Monticello and James Monroe's Ash Lawn provide an interesting experience, as does a visit to Michie Tavern. The area also has fox hunting and steeplechase events.

Tim tells me that their swimming pool and tennis courts get quite a workout during the summer, while in the winter, after a day skiing or browsing in the many antique shops, everyone's favorite spot is in front of the fireplace in the cozy lounge.

Although we were having a special light lunch that day, Wendy Gibson from the Robert Morris Inn in Oxford, Maryland, was exclaiming over the dinner menu for that evening. "Just look at this," she said, "they are having Raspberry Chicken or roast duckling served with peach brandy sauce and black walnut pasta—that's pasta cooked with sautéed chicken strips, walnuts, and apples in a teriyaki ginger sauce. I think we ought to stay for dinner, too."

SILVER THATCH INN, Off Rte. 29 at 3001 Hollymead Rd., Charlottesville, VA 22901; 804-978-4686. An 8-guestroom country inn on the outskirts of Charlottesville, 15 min. from the Blue Ridge Mtns. Lodgings include breakfast served to guests only. Dinner is served Tues. thru Sat. evenings. Open year-round. Swimming and tennis on premises. Golf, horseback riding, hiking, skiing, biking, jogging, and wonderful back roads are all available nearby. Convenient to visit Monticello, Ash Lawn, and the University of Virginia. Not readily adaptable to children under 10. Tim and Shelley Dwight, Innkeepers. (See Index for rates.)

Directions: The inn is 2 hrs. south of Washington, just off Va. Rte. 29. Turn east 1 mi. south of the airport road intersection onto Rte. 1520 and proceed ½ mi. to inn.

TRILLIUM HOUSE
Wintergreen, Nellysford, Virginia (1985)

First, I'd better explain Wintergreen. This is a ten-thousand-acre residential community-cum-four-season resort on the slopes of the Blue Ridge Mountains, three hours southwest of Washington, D.C., and an hour from Charlottesville. Tucked away in the mountains is an 18-hole golf course, an extensive tennis compound, a sixteen-acre lake, landscaped swimming pools, an equestrian center, and ten ski slopes.

The Wintergreen gate is just one mile from the Reeds Gap exit of the Blue Ridge Parkway.

Now, Trillium House. A rambling cedar building with dormers and pitched roofs, this country inn at Wintergreen is named after one of the many species of wildflowers that grow in abundance in these mountains.

Rustic, but quite modern, the Trillium House makes an excellent first impression. After stopping at the gate, Trillium guests receive from the courteous gatekeepers a pass and directions upward through various clusters of condominiums to Trillium, on one of the highest points at Wintergreen. It happens to be directly across the road from the Wintergarden, a brand-new recreation complex with both indoor and outdoor swimming pools, exercise rooms, and a very attractive restaurant looking out on a splendid view of the Blue Ridge Mountains. It is just a short walk to one of the many ski lifts. Strange as it may seem to some northerners, this part of Virginia has first-rate cross-country and downhill skiing.

I stepped through the double entrance doors at ground level into the "great room" with a 22-foot cathedral ceiling and Jefferson sunburst window. A massive chimney with a woodburning stove dominates the room. Across the back of this room and up a short flight of steps stretches a balcony with a most impressive library, and on the other side of the fireplace is a big-screen TV-watching room and gathering place.

Hallways stretch out from both sides of this room, along which are guest rooms and suites, many of them containing heirlooms that Ed and Betty Dinwiddie have brought from their former homes.

The dining-room windows put the guest on almost intimate terms with the 17th fairway and green, and watching the chipmunks and squirrels and birds around the feeders provides entertainment at breakfast.

I would describe Trillium House as being basically informal. It is, after all, an area where one would come to enjoy all of the great outdoors, from walking and hiking to golf, tennis, and swimming. Gentlemen are comfortable with or without jackets at dinner, and Ed and Betty have a way of immediately making everyone feel at home.

Speaking of dinner, it is available on Friday and Saturday nights with advance reservations. Betty did all the cooking the first couple of years, but now they have Ellen English, whom they call their "super chef" and associate innkeeper. "Our dinner guests tend to come again and again to enjoy stuffed tenderloin of beef and Ellen's various chicken, veal, and seafood creations."

If by some chance you are arriving unannounced, it's necessary to have the gatekeeper phone ahead to Trillium House so that you can be introduced.

The Trillium House country inn experience is much greater than I can describe in one edition. The entire area—the beauty of the mountains, the vistas, and the splendid facilities are almost beyond my descriptive powers.

TRILLIUM HOUSE, Wintergreen, P.O. Box 280, Nellysford, VA 22958; 804-325-9126. A 12-guestroom country inn within the resort complex of Wintergreen. Breakfast included in room rate. Dinner served Fri. and Sat. on request. Open year-round. Please call for reservations at times other than the dinner hour. Extensive four-season recreation available, including golf, tennis, swimming (indoor and outdoor pool), and downhill skiing, hiking, bird watching, and horseback riding. Ed and Betty Dinwiddie, Innkeepers. (See Index for rates.)

Directions: From points north and east take the Crozet/Rte. 250 exit from I-64. Go west on Rte. 250 to Rte. 6 and turn left. Follow Rte. 151 south to Rte. 664; turn right on 664 to Wintergreen entrance. From Blue Ridge Parkway, exit at Reeds Gap, going east on Rte. 664.

THE COUNTRY INN
Berkeley Springs, West Virginia (1975)

"Let me tell you about our West Virginia springhouse water, which is from right here in Berkeley Springs and is shipped as far away as Miami, Florida!"

Once again I was having lunch in the Garden Room at the Country Inn with Jack and Adele Barker, whom I have been visiting for more than half of the twenty-two years that I've been writing this book.

Although it was a very warm midsummer's day, the atmosphere in the Garden Room was really springtime. It has a translucent ceiling, and its many, many growing plants, red and white tablecloths, strings of tiny white lights, and flags from all countries create a very festive air.

Jack continued, "There is a TV station in Miami that did a test on bottled water, and our water came out number one. It's just plain good spring water, and we're happy that it satisfies the folks in Miami."

I had landed earlier that morning at the Washington airport and made the relatively short trip through the countryside to this eastern panhandle of West Virginia well in time for lunch.

The first thing we did was to tour Country Inn West, the new building I wrote about in the previous edition. Each floor has a different decorative color scheme, and there is an elevator and rooms for the handicapped. Guest rooms in the new building are larger, with more sumptuous bathrooms, and provide an interesting contrast to the rooms in the older building, with their brass beds and individual furnishings.

The hallways throughout both of the buildings of the Country Inn are hung with prints, reflecting Jack's interest in paintings and art. In fact, one entire living room has been set aside to display these well-chosen works of art for sale to the guests. There are reproductions of Italian, Flemish, French, and English masters, as well as American primitives. In particular, there are excellent and reasonably priced reproductions of turn-of-the-century French theatrical posters.

Jack was particularly enthusiastic about the completed spa, where it is now possible "to take the mineral waters," for which this section of West Virginia is famous, right at the inn.

The talk at lunch turned to the theme of dinner menus and events that have been developed over the past few years. There is a Hawaiian night, a Mexican fiesta night, a French night, and a Greek night, with appropriate ethnic specialties. "The Hawaiian night is the most popular," Adele said. "We have a professional Hawaiian band, entertainment, with dancers in grass skirts, and every guest receives a Hawaiian lei, and they wear their bright shirts. It's very festive and very popular during the winter months."

The regular menu at the inn has such country items as ham, smothered chicken, duckling with orange sauce, and homemade hot breads. Desserts on the luncheon menu include chocolate mousse cake, black cherry cake, whiskey cake, pecan pie, coconut cream pie, and cheesecake.

Almost since the very start I've seen continuing changes and improvements at the Country Inn, and since 1972 there has always been something "in the works." "The completion of our Renaissance Spa provides the use of relaxing Swedish techniques and deep muscle massage," Jack commented. "And we expect that our facial massage and make-up analysis will be equally attractive to our guests."

Another very nice custom that many guests will appreciate is the Sunday church service conducted by the staff in the meeting room.

This section of West Virginia, identified as the Potomac Highlands, offers boating and fishing as well as many, many antique shops and excellent backroading in every season. Guests come in the winter to enjoy the quiet peacefulness, and now, with the opening of Country Inn West and the new spa and massage facilities, more and more people will be able to enjoy this truly country-inn hospitality.

THE COUNTRY INN, Berkeley Springs, WV 25411; 304-258-2210. A 72-guestroom (some shared baths) resort inn on Rte. 522, 34 mi. from Winchester, Va., and 100 mi. from Washington, D.C., or Baltimore, Md. European plan. Breakfast, lunch, and dinner served to travelers. Open every day of the year. Wheelchair access. Berkeley Springs Spa adjoins the inn. Hunting, fishing, hiking, canoeing, antiquing, championship golf nearby. Jack and Adele Barker, Innkeepers; Bill North, General Manager. (See Index for rates.)

Directions: Take I-70 to Hancock, Md. Inn is 6 mi. south on Rte. 522.

GENERAL LEWIS INN
Lewisburg, West Virginia (1973)

I had just returned from a walking tour of Lewisburg with its 19th-century residences and generous sprinkling of historic markers. I paused for just a moment at the bottom of the crescent-shaped drive that leads to the inn to read a marker that said, "Confederate troops under General Henry Heth on May 23, 1862, were repulsed by Colonel George Crook's Brigade."

As I settled into one of the rocking chairs on the long, shaded veranda, Mary Hock Morgan came out and joined me. "Well, what do you think of our little town?" she asked. I readily admitted that, as always, I was still completely captivated by Lewisburg.

"It was established in 1782 and is the third oldest town in the state," she said proudly. "It was named for General Andrew Lewis, who defeated the Indians at the first battle in the American Revolution in 1774.

"The old part of the inn, where the dining room is located, was built in 1798 as a private dwelling. My mother and father purchased the house in 1928 and hired a well-known architect, Walter Martens, who designed the West Virginia Governor's Mansion, to add on the section that embraces the lobby and the matching west wing. Care was taken to capture the feel of the early period, including the use of hand-hewn beams from the slave quarters in the dining room and lobby areas. Work was completed in 1929. It took my parents many years to collect all of these antiques, including the four-poster canopy bed you are going to sleep in tonight."

We were joined by innkeeper Rodney Fisher. "I usually seat the dinner guests in the evening," he told me, "and I try to learn a little about them. It's also a good time to tell them a little about the General Lewis and its history, and about the town of Lewisburg and other country inns that might be on their route."

The General Lewis Inn is like a permanent flashback to old West Virginia. It is furnished almost entirely in antiques. There is a sizable collection of old kitchen utensils, spinning wheels, churns, and other tools used many years ago, as well as an unusual collection of chinaware and old prints. The parlor has a friendly fireplace flanked by some of the many different types of rocking chairs that are scattered throughout the inn. The atmosphere is made even more cozy by the low-beamed ceilings.

The inn is surrounded by broad lawns, and in the rear there are fragrant flower gardens, tall swaying trees, and even a small rock garden.

The menu has many things that I associate with country cooking— pork chops with fried apples, pan-fried chicken, apple butter, country ham, and home-baked rolls and biscuits, to name a few. The entrée selection includes new specialties such as chicken Randolph, coquille St. Jacques, and a lean, smoky pork barbecue. The dessert menu includes many new mouthwatering items.

Rodney told me they have added four tables with umbrellas to their garden area. "This has given us a delightful and very popular outdoor dining area. Weather permitting, we serve lunch there every day. It is really a hit with the local ladies."

Dusk had fallen while we were talking, and the gaslights that illuminate the tree-lined streets began to dot the late twilight. Our talk turned to some of the famous golf courses here in the Greenbrier area, and we discussed some circle tours of the mountains that would include the fabulous scenery and a generous glimpse of rural West Virginia.

I have a letter from a recent guest who writes, "We returned to the General Lewis for our first anniversary, and our second stay was every bit as romantic and wonderful as the first . . ."

Small wonder that some call it "almost heaven."

GENERAL LEWIS INN, Lewisburg, WV 24901; 304-645-2600. A 30-guestroom (private baths) antique-laden village inn on Rte. 60, 90 mi. from Roanoke, Va. European plan. Breakfast, lunch, and dinner served daily. Dinner reservations necessary. Dining room closed Christmas Day. Famous golf courses nearby. Mary Hock Morgan, Proprietor; Rodney Fisher, Innkeeper. (See Index for rates.)

Directions: Take Lewisburg exit from I-64. Follow Rte. 219 south to first traffic light. Turn left on Rte. 60, two blocks to inn.

RIVERSIDE INN
Pence Springs, West Virginia (1977)

I happen to be very fond of roast duckling. I've had this succulent dish, I'm sure, in more than half of the country inns in this book. On this particular occasion I was having fruit-stuffed duckling prepared for two at the Riverside Inn. Ashby Berkley, complete with a long leather vest over a dashing white shirt with billowing sleeves, set the plate in front of me and twirled his mustache. "I know how you feel about duckling," he said. "So, I'm anxious to see what you say about this."

The menu at the Riverside Inn might include Colonial meat pies, mountain rainbow trout, fresh seafood pie in a cheese pastry, baked glazed chicken, lamb chops, and steak. The famous scalded English slaw, a hot cabbage salad with bacon-vinegar dressing, is now traditional. The English mulled cider served before each meal is made from fresh cider pressed especially at the nearby Morgan Orchard.

As odd as it may seem, Ashby Berkley has created at the Riverside Inn the ambience of 17th-century Jamestown, Virginia, and I dare say that the impressive log building is probably a great deal more substantial than the accommodations the Jamestown settlers enjoyed.

The Riverside Inn has the intimacy of a Colonial roadside tavern where travel-weary guests once refreshed themselves with the tablefare of their hosts. It is located on the bank of the Greenbrier River, whose placid waters ran amock a year ago and unfortunately completely wiped out the inn's foundation, floors, kitchen, porches, cottages, grounds, and in fact almost everything. "We were closed eight months, but did reopen on July 4, and everything is normal once again," Ashby told me.

I asked him whether or not he had been tempted to move away from this valley where he had gown up. "Oh, I wouldn't think of leaving this beautiful place," he said. "I know I am prejudiced, but it is the perfect place for anyone who appreciates being close to nature. We are the fourth most rural state in the nation and are eighty percent forested. It is almost like an undiscovered island set down in the middle of the busy East Coast, and all you have to do to commune with nature is to open the doors and windows and let it come in.

"It's difficult to concentrate with the sun streaming through the brilliant fall foliage hanging over the green of the valley, alive with birds and all the river life. Each season here is so uniquely different. Spring is like living in a wildflower garden. The lush, green, quiet summer can shut out the world. Fall is a parade of color and splendor that I have never seen matched anywhere, and the majesty of our untamed mountains—stripped of their blanket of leaves during winter—is not unlike the mystery and strength of the ocean, a force bigger than man. I think you can see why I stay here."

The two of us sat for awhile staring at the rugged massive fireplace, and the light from the fire flickered on the tops of the massive oak tables, which were set off by the pewter underplates and the pistol-handled knives.

In response to a question, Ashby explained that at the moment there are no lodgings available; however, there will be some very interesting additions and changes in 1989.

I must confess that all the time that Ashby and I were talking I was enjoying one of the most delicious roast ducklings that it has ever been my pleasure to eat. Augmented as it was by orange, baked and glazed carrots, bourbon sweet potatoes, and stuffed acorn squash, I couldn't help but think a little guiltily that the settlers of early Jamestown could not have fared one-tenth as well.

RIVERSIDE INN, Rte. 3, Pence Springs, WV 24962; 304-445-7469. A country restaurant on the Greenbrier River on Rte. 3 in the beautiful West Va. mountains, between Hinton and Alderson; 12 mi. from Lake Bluestone. No lodgings until 1989. Dinner served 5 to 9 p.m. Mon. thru Sat. from May 31 to Labor Day; open Wed. thru Sat., April 15 to May 31 and Labor Day to Oct. 31; open Fri. and Sat., Nov., Dec. Closed Christmas and Jan. to April 15. Lunch served by special reservation only. Skiing, boating, hiking, swimming, spelunking, white-water canoeing nearby. O. Ashby and Kelley Berkley, Innkeepers. (See Index for rates.)

Directions: From the east, take Alta exit off I-64, follow Rte. 12S to Alderson, then 8 mi. on Rte. 3W to Pence Springs. From the west, from W. Va. Tpke. follow Rte. 3 from Beckley through Hinton to Pence Springs. The inn is located in Pence Springs on Rte. 3 between Hinton and Alderson.

THE INN AT BUCKEYSTOWN
Buckeystown, Maryland (1987)

This elegant Victorian inn immediately appealed to me because one of its themes is "clowns." I've always been very attached to clowns and have, in fact, played two of Shakespeare's most famous clowns on stage, Feste in *Twelfth Night* and Touchstone in *As You Like It*.

There are enough clowns and pictures of clowns and clown dolls and clown posters to satisfy the most avid of clown enthusiasts. Some are reproductions of famous paintings, including the famous Rouault clown, and there are clowns laughing, crying, playing instruments, clown dolls on each of the beds, books on clowns, and a wonderful collection of china clown dolls in a case on the second floor, where there is also a little shop with clown dolls for sale, along with candies, jams, and other craft items, some of which are directly connected with the Inn at Buckeystown. Because innkeepers Dan Pelz and Marty Martinez are true collectors, there are many other collectibles, having to do with American Indians, glassware, early California art, postcards, and Victorian posters.

However, I think the main theme at this inn is hospitality, and this is best personified by the evening meal. A different set menu is offered each night of the week. Wednesday, the night I was there, happened to be "Ethnic Night," and since this was the third Wednesday of the month we had Basque chicken. Other dishes in the ethnic category for Wednesdays include Mexican, German, Country French, and Curry. Dinner is served family style around a big table at seven o'clock each night, with no smoking in the dining room. Everyone sits down together, and thanks to Dan and Marty, all of the guests soon become well acquainted. As Dan says, "It is in the tradition of the late 18th and early 19th century in this part of Maryland." He added, "Our guests prefer to dress a little for dinner and men wear coats and ties."

Another extremely hospitable feature is a perfectly wonderful wrap-around front porch with rocking chairs and other comfortable furniture. Stepping off the porch, you'll find yourself on broad grassy acres, which are part of the parklike surroundings, with many varieties of trees and bushes.

The guest rooms are all authentically furnished in beautiful Victorian style, with such modern comforts as electric blankets and air conditioners.

St. John's Cottage has added a new ambience to the inn. Marty and Dan converted a small 1884 church into a romantic getaway. It has cathedral ceilings, stained-glass windows, a fireplace, a great bathroom, two bedrooms, and a well-appointed living room with paintings and many fascinating books.

Buckeystown is within an hour of Washington, D.C., Baltimore, and

Gettysburg, and within a half-hour of New Market (the antiques capital of Maryland), Harper's Ferry, and Leesburg. Dan points out that the area is a paradise for architecture buffs, historians, antiquers, and outdoors people. Nearby Frederick is a beautifully restored historic town with many sites of interest, beautiful shops, and all city conveniences.

I would be remiss if I failed to mention that the other innkeepers besides Dan and Marty are a Maine coon cat named Joshua, Priscilla, an arrogant Persian, and innkeeper Becki, who is at the heart of the inn.

THE INN AT BUCKEYSTOWN, Buckeystown, MD 21717; 301-874-5755. An 8-guestroom (private and shared baths) inn in a historic village. Rates include dinner and breakfast. Open year-round. Minimum stay of 2 days required on all holidays and on weekends from Oct. 1 to Jan. 1, and from Apr. 1 to July 1. Conveniently located to enjoy all of the historic and cultural attractions of the region. No facilities for children under 16. No pets. Dan Pelz, Marty Martinez, Owners; Rebecca Shipman, Innkeeper. (See Index for rates.)

Directions: Buckeystown lies 4 mi. to the south of the Buckeystown exit off I-270 in Frederick, and 5 mi. to the south of the Buckeystown exit off I-70 in Frederick. Inn is located on Maryland Rte. 85.

A number of inns have nearby airports where private airplanes may land. An airplane symbol at the end of the inn directions indicates that there is an airport nearby. Consult inn for further information.

MARYLAND INN
Annapolis, Maryland (1970)

This time I was approaching Annapolis from the south and east, coming along U.S. 50 over the thrilling expanse of the Bay Bridge, with its two suspended roadways over the Chesapeake. There were a number of freighters in the shadowy mist making their way up through the bay, and several sailboats were running before the wind.

I turned off at the sign for the Naval Academy and followed Maryland Route 450, continuing on between the Naval Academy and St. John's College. Then, using the steeple of St. Ann's Church as a heaven-pointing guide, I made a right turn and came into Church Circle and the Maryland Inn. The discreet sign at the front door indicated that Charlie Byrd was appearing in the King of France Tavern. Some folk singers were scheduled for later on.

I couldn't help but think that Thomas Hyde, who built the original inn and advertised it as "an elegant brick house in the dry and healthy part of the city . . . one of the finest houses in the State for a House of Entertainment," would be quite pleased with the many different aspects of the Maryland Inn today.

I'm certain that the guest rooms far exceed any of Mr. Hyde's wildest dreams. I have been visiting the Maryland Inn since the late 1960s, and I've seen all of the rooms undergo an impressive restoration of both furnishings and decor.

The modern equivalent of innkeeper Hyde is Paul Pearson, who has recently added four other historic inns to his first love, the Maryland Inn. All are 18th-century buildings, tastefully restored and furnished. They include one of the most remarkable of all the restoration projects in Annapolis—the 1747 Reynolds Tavern. When asked if Washington slept at any of his inns, Paul declares that there is no truth to any such rumor. Indeed, it seems clear that Washington's greater contributions to his country were made during his waking hours, many of which were spent in and about the family of inns that surround the famous Maryland State Capitol, where Washington resigned his commission in the Continental Army and where the first meeting of patriots leading to the drafting of the United States Constitution took place just over 200 years ago. To walk among these lovely buildings is to savor the same atmosphere experienced by George Washington and other men and women who were forming the destinies of our country. Reservations for these inns can be made through the Maryland Inn.

Over a cup of tea in the Treaty of Paris dining room, I asked innkeeper Peg Bednarsky, a dear friend of many years, about the menus of the restaurants in the inn. "Well, as you know we're located right on Chesapeake Bay, so we have eight to ten fish offerings every day, including red snapper, grouper, trout, swordfish, mako shark, cohoe salmon, pompano, monkfish, flounder, and rockfish. We musn't forget the famous crab bisque, the popovers, and cornsticks." I agreed with that, as I took another delicious bite of a cornstick.

Mr. Hyde, there's lots of toe-tapping excitement at your Maryland Inn these days.

MARYLAND INN (Historic Inns of Annapolis), Church Circle, Annapolis, MD 21401; 301-263-2641. (U. S. reservations: 800-847-8882; within Md.: 800-638-8902.) A 44-guestroom village inn in a history-laden town, 20 mi. from Baltimore and Washington. Near the U. S. Naval Academy and Chesapeake Bay. Breakfast, lunch, and dinner served to travelers daily. Open year-round. Music nightly in the King of France Tavern. Tours can be arranged to historic and scenic points of interest. Paul Pearson, Proprietor; Peg Bednarsky, Innkeeper. (See Index for rates.)

Directions: From Baltimore, take Rte. 2 south to first directional turnoff Washington/Annapolis. From Washington, take Rte. 50 east to Annapolis Naval Academy/Rowe Blvd. exit.

"European plan" means that rates for rooms and meals are separate. "American plan" means that meals are included in the cost of the room. "Modified American plan" means that breakfast and dinner are included in the cost of the room. The rates at some inns include a continental breakfast with the lodging.

ROBERT MORRIS INN
Oxford, Maryland

The Robert Morris is on the eastern shore of Maryland beside the Tred Avon River. One of the ways to reach it is via the famous Cape May-Lewes ferry, which i've been riding ever since my first visit. Oxford is, surprisingly enough, still one of the most unspoiled villages in North America. It has several pre-Revolutionary and Federalist houses that are remarkably well preserved. Incidentally, you can get a copy of "This and That About Olde Oxford, Maryland" by Howard B. Gerhardt at the front desk of the inn. It's an extremely well-written informal history of Oxford.

The news from the inn is that the Sandaway Lodge has been completely done over in a country-romantic theme with handmade pine, pencil-post king-sized beds, love seats, and country furnishings. One bathroom has an antique chandelier over the bathtub. Two of these rooms are for nonsmokers, which now gives the inn a total of six rooms set aside for nonsmokers.

The decorations in the main house have always attracted attention and the murals in the dining room depict some scenes from other places in North America, including Natural Bridge, Virginia, and Boston Harbor. The guest rooms in the main house are decorated in a casual motif with country rugs and coverlets and a variety of interesting knickknacks on the walls, among which are the tops of china serving dishes of many different designs.

The inn's location in the Chesapeake Bay area means that there is considerable emphasis on seafood at lunch and dinner—crabcakes, baked seafood au gratin, lobster pie, seafood pot pie, and fresh fish with a Robert

Morris special sauce. There are, of course, other poultry and meat offerings as well.

The inn starts taking reservations on the tenth of January for the current year, and accommodations should be reserved as early as possible, even for midweek stays.

A letter from Wendy told me how she and Ken sent some Robert Morris crabcakes to author James Michener in Sitka, Alaska, when he was working on a book there. "We heard that he was homesick for the Eastern Shore and our crabcakes. They made it via Federal Express in under forty-eight hours."

The Gibsons are extremely "family oriented" people. During a part of 1987, Ken, Wendy, and their two sons, Kent, 16, and Ben, 14, traveled to *CIBR* inns in North America and Britain.

I had the opportunity to talk to Ken and Wendy briefly at the international meeting of the CIBR Innkeepers' Association, held at Rancho de los Caballeros in 1987. They are still vibrating from the exceptional time all four of them had on their "year off." Ken had great praise for his brother, Jay, who ran the entire inn during the time that Ken and Wendy were away. You will notice that he is listed as the innkeeper below, while Ken and Wendy are designated owners.

They wound up their trip with an excursion to Alaska on the Inside Passage. They also visited several *CIBR* inns in the Northwest.

ROBERT MORRIS INN, Oxford, MD 21654; 301-226-5111. A 33-guest-room waterside inn and lodge (mostly private baths) in a secluded Colonial community on the Tred Avon, 10 mi. from Easton, Md. (Some rooms with private porches and some nonsmoking rooms; two cottages only available for children.) European plan. Breakfast, lunch, and dinner served to travelers and guests daily. Open year-round except Christmas Day and Feb. 1 till mid-Mar. Wheelchair access. Tennis, golf, seasonal river swimming, sailing, fishing, and bicycles nearby. Recommended for children over 10. No pets. Wendy and Ken Gibson, Owners; Jay Gibson, Innkeeper. (See Index for rates.)

Directions: From Delaware Memorial Bridge, follow Rte. 13 south to Rte. 301 and proceed south to Rte. 50, then east on Rte. 50 to Easton. From Chesapeake Bay Bridge, follow Rte. 50-301 to Rte. 50 and proceed east to Easton. From Chesapeake Bay Bridge Tunnel, follow Rte. 13 north to Rte. 50 and proceed west to Easton. From Easton, follow Rte. 322 to Rte. 333 to Oxford and inn. ✉

THE DAVID FINNEY INN
New Castle, Delaware (1986)

In April 1985, I was literally the first guest ever to sign the David Finney Inn guestbook! On my second trip, innkeeper Judy Piser pointed out that fact to me: "You were our very first overnight guest!"

First, a word about the town, whose historical and architectural treasures are a well-kept secret. The earliest settlement began around 1638, shortly after the Swedish government established a new-world foothold in nearby Wilmington. The early colonists were not only Swedish but also Finnish and Dutch adventurers in search of readily available farmland. Ships' ballast and building bricks from Holland have been found in excavations. Such colorful personalities as Peter Stuyvesant also figured prominently in the early history. He purchased about thirty miles of land along the west bank of the Delaware River and established Fort Casimir, which also became the name of the town. When the English arrived, they renamed it New Castle.

Aside from this fascinating continuing history, the real charm of New Castle lies in the fact that in the historic part of the town the architecture and building design remains almost totally pre-1800. As trite as it may sound, a walk across the village green is indeed an experience akin to stepping back in time. This green is dominated by the Immanuel Church and its grounds, where there are graves of men who in earlier days helped to build the United States of America. There are many other beautifully harmonizing residences and buildings of varying architectural styles that blend in extremely well.

The inn property is part of a 1650s Dutch land grant. The building dates back to 1685, with major additions in every century since. It has been a large, luxurious home, hosting some of America's most important people. At least three signers of the Declaration of Independence knew it well.

Furnished with antiques, it is an exceptionally fine restoration/renovation, featuring four two-room suites and thirteen double rooms, all with private baths. Breakfast, lunch, and dinner are served in the restaurant, and there is courtyard dining in season. Entertainment is offered in the tavern, where the nautical theme is heightened with museum-quality model ships.

The evening menu, which changes daily, includes charcoal-grilled swordfish steak with teriyaki butter, and grilled breast of duck with water chestnuts, snow peas, and ginger sauce. It's a little hard to pin the cuisine down because it reflects not only the area, but a continental theme as well. A continental breakfast is complimentary and tea is served to houseguests in the afternoon.

Five museums in the town display life as it was lived in the Dutch and

English Colonial periods with guides to explain every detail. It is a delightful experience to walk along the Strand and other streets lined with antique homes, or to visit the marketplace and the village green.

Among the seasonal events and festivals in historic New Castle are "A Day in Old New Castle" on the third Saturday in May, which includes a tour of private homes, gardens, and public buildings; "May Market," the first weekend in May; "Separation Day," the first Saturday in June, celebrating the separation of Delaware from England. There are also numerous other art and antique shows and a Christmas candlelight tour.

There is history aplenty in New Castle, and fortunately for the enthusiastic country-inn-goer, the town and area are splendidly served by the David Finney Inn. What a pleasure for me to have been the first guest!

THE DAVID FINNEY INN, P.O. Box 207, 216 Delaware St., New Castle, DE 19720; 302-322-6367. A 21-guestroom (private baths) meticulously restored 18th-century inn in a historic riverfront village, 35 mi. south of Phila. Continental breakfast included in tariff. Breakfast, lunch, and dinner served every day of the year. Many historic, recreational, and cultural attractions in New Castle or nearby. Convenient off-street parking available. No entertainment facilities for children under 10. No pets. Tom and Louise Hagy, Proprietors; Judy Piser, Innkeeper. (See Index for rates.)

Directions: Coming south on the New Jersey Tpke., take the first exit after crossing the Delaware River Bridge and turn south on Rte. 9, which goes directly into New Castle. The inn is located in the historic section of Old New Castle. ✒

SOUTH CAROLINA

36 Meeting Street, *Charleston*

CHARLESTON

Guilds Inn, *Mt. Pleasant*

GEORGIA

Greyfield Inn, *Cumberland Island*

■ JACKSONVILLE

FLORIDA

■ ORLANDO

Chalet Suzanne,
Lake Wales ●

MIAMI

Lower
South

Eastern Time Zone

CUMBERLAND ISLAND

Cumberland Island is the southernmost and largest of a chain of barrier islands that starts at Cape Hatteras and extends to the Florida-Georgia border. It is eighteen miles long and three miles wide at its widest point. There are 26 varieties of wild animals and 323 species of birds identified. The island has one road, Grand Avenue, a dirt and shell affair, which traverses the length of the island through the live oak.

In recent years the National Park Service acquired a great portion of the island and has taken the necessary action to forever maintain it as a nature preserve.

Marshland fringes much of Cumberland's shores, protecting them from the current and the tide. Its principal inhabitants are the ubiquitous fiddler crabs and long-legged wading birds. The live oak avenues create an atmosphere akin to a cathedral.

The eighteen-mile beach is the most striking feature of the island and one can walk for hours in delicious solitude except for the sanderlings that scurry out of the clutching fingers of the waves, and the pelicans skimming the water. Shells abound and it's impossible to come back empty-handed.

The dunes, which are carefully protected, provide still another intriguing atmosphere. At the edge of the forest there is a group of lakes, which have their own particular wildlife. Egrets and herons fish these waters as well as ducks who stop off as they travel north and south.

Besides the wildlife there is a rich history of the island that covers pre-Columbian times as well as occupation by the Spaniards, the British, and later on some enterprising men from the new American republic. In the early 1800s there were a few plantations on the island, but after the War Between the States the island was dominated by the presence of the Carnegie family who raised an impressive mansion of brick and stone at Dungeness with formal gardens, swimming pool and stables. Unfortunately, it burned in 1959.

GREYFIELD INN
Cumberland Island, Georgia (1982)

This is the story of Grandma Ferguson, who is the granddaughter of Thomas Carnegie (brother of Andrew), and the Ferguson family—including her grandsons, Andy and Mitty—and of the flora and fauna of one of the last remaining impressive nature preserves on the East Coast. It is only a part of the story of Greyfield Inn, located on Cumberland Island, off the southern coast of Georgia.

I paid my first visit to this gorgeous, haunting part of the world in 1975. I had the pleasure then of spending part of a day with Lucy Ferguson, known to everyone as "Grandma." It was Grandma who first introduced me to Cumberland Island, with its eighteen-mile stretch of beach, fascinating dunes, and secret ponds. She also showed me the ruins of Dungeness, built by her grandparents, which unfortunately burned in 1959.

Once again, as on my first visit, I was on the ferry boat, *R.W. Ferguson,* and Captain Mitty Ferguson was updating me on Greyfield Inn. We left Fernandina Beach at 3:00 p.m. and were making the hour-and-a-quarter run up the passage between the island and mainland to the Greyfield dock.

"Of course, everything is much the same as it was when you were here the first time," he said, keeping a guiding hand on the wheel. "The Fergusons, including Grandmother, are still very much in the picture, so that we are a family team dividing the chores. We also have some excellent staff, including a wonderful naturalist/guide. Our guests rave about her tours, which explore many aspects of this magnificent island."

By this time the ferry was within sight of the Greyfield dock, and I could see once again the gleaming, three-story mansion through the mysterious grove of live oaks. Andy waved to us, and soon, with the other guests, I was bundled into the jeep and driven to the impressive front entrance of the inn with its majestic steps and broad veranda. As soon as I stepped inside, it all returned to me: the paintings, the oriental rugs, the mahogany furniture, the silver on the sideboard, the great fireplaces, and the great collection of books. Andy showed me to my corner room and then joined me in front of the fire for a cup of late afternoon tea.

I joined the other guests at dinner in the candlelit dining room and the conversation dealt with the wonders of the unspoiled beach, where the magnificent loggerhead sea turtles lay their eggs, and where guests sometimes can see the young hatching. The shore birds and the marine life are there, as are deer, wild horses, wild turkeys, and the dense live oak forest.

The newest acquisition is a gazebo that stands in the meadow between the primary and secondary dunes—a great spot in which to get out of the sun at midday, to watch the sun rise and set, or just to lie about reading and watching the shore birds.

There were several guests who had been at Greyfield for many days who were saying, "It takes a day just to find out what is here, and at least two days more to explore it."

Several of the guests had seen a recent issue of *Audubon Magazine* with the article by John Mitchell on Cumberland Island and Greyfield Inn.

It was wonderful to be back at Greyfield once again.

Do not plan on visiting the Greyfield Inn if you have only one night, and be certain to check with the inn about the ferry schedules. Incidentally, the 1735 House in Fernandina Beach is an excellent overnight stop before taking the afternoon boat to the island. The Greyfield Inn is the only public overnight accommodation on Cumberland Island.

GREYFIELD INN, Cumberland Island, GA (mailing address: Fernandina Beach, FL 32034); 904-261-6408. A 9-guestroom (private baths) mansion on an island off the coast of southern Georgia. Accessible from Fernandina Beach, Fla., or on a Natl. Park Service ferry from St. Mary's, Ga. Check with inn on ferry times. Rates include full breakfast and dinner, as well as either box lunch or informal noon meal. Open every day in the year by reservation only. Beachcombing, swimming, fishing, clam digging, photography, birdwatching, bicycles, walking and driving tours, natural history tour. No pets. The Ferguson Family, Innkeepers. (See Index for rates.)

Directions: The R.W. Ferguson leaves from the public dock at Fernandina Beach, Fla., at either 3 or 5 p.m., depending upon the day of the week (check with inn). Also check with inn on National Park Service ferry schedule from St. Mary's, Ga. Autos are left on the mainland. Island also accessible by small plane or helicopter. ◤

GUILDS INN
Mount Pleasant, South Carolina (1988)

I think there's something about a bow tie that indicates a wonderful lack of stuffiness on the part of the wearer. Both Guilds (pronounced "Guiles") Hollowell and his son, Gervais, wear bow ties and are as warm, enthusiastic, and friendly a pair of innkeepers as you'd ever want to meet. Wife and mother Joyce is very much part of the picture, too. This is one of those Southern families that radiate good humor and fun. Perhaps because I lived in Virginia for a few years, I have always felt close to Southerners, and I had the added pleasure of being on the scene when Gervais was given the news that he was going to be a father. Such a burst of excitement, with shaking of hands and clapping on backs and much laughter and congratulations!

Guilds and Joyce and their five sons spent months restoring and remodeling their inn which began its life as a grocery store in 1888. They also created a restaurant called Supper at Seven. Now, Gervais, who is a newlywed, manages the inn and sees to the comfort of their guests. He is a very gracious host and a virtual fount of information.

Although Guilds Inn is not furnished with genuine antiques, you'd never know it. The furnishings are particularly fine reproductions of antique furniture; in fact, Gervais showed me several pieces that have been meticulously copied from the DuPont collection at the Winterthur Museum, and they are most impressive. There are beautiful highboys, lowboys, secretaries, breakfronts, and many other handsome pieces that were made by the Kindel Furniture Company. I was interested to learn that the Hollowells own a furniture store down the street, where some of these pieces can be purchased.

The village of Mount Pleasant was originally settled by farmers and also served as a summer retreat for many Charlestonians in the late 19th century.

The entrance to the inn is through a picket fence at one side of the building and across a pretty lawn and garden. Joyce has done a handsome job of decoration, with rich colors in fabrics, carpets, and walls. There are many original paintings and engravings. Each of the six guest rooms has been carefully and attractively furnished with queen-sized or twin beds and some of the other pieces I mentioned. One room has a Connecticut tall-post bed of cherry with a handmade fishnet canopy. All rooms have whirlpool baths and telephones, along with turn-down service and the morning newspaper.

It's a "make-your-own" breakfast in the butler's pantry in the Morning Room, which is well stocked with juice, fresh fruit, muffins and pastries, cereal, sausage or ham biscuits, and, of course, coffee or tea. The sunny Morning Room is a pleasant gathering place for breakfast and conversation.

"We want to allow our guests to experience the more leisurely and gentle pace of village life," Guilds told me, "and we've tried to carry that over into our restaurant. Our chef prepares many of the timeless recipes from Mount Pleasant's early days." Their Supper at Seven restaurant has a single seating with a fixed menu of four courses. Some of their regional specialties are fillet of beef on fried eggplant, seafood chowder, local channel bass in puff pastry, Caesar salad, tomato cups with fresh corn, low country squash pie, fresh figs filled with white chocolate mousse, and bourbon chocolate pecan pie. I understand they have a wide reputation for their fine cuisine, and many guests make the short trip over the bridge from downtown Charleston to enjoy a leisurely dinner. There is also a small cafe in the front of the building that is a popular place for lunch.

Being so close to Charleston and yet away from "the madding crowd" makes the Guilds Inn an especially desirable stopping place. After a strenuous day spent taking in all the historic sights of Charleston or attending such famous events as the Spoleto Festival, it would be a blessing to be able to retreat to this peaceful and quiet inn.

We are happy to welcome Guilds Inn to the pages of *Country Inns and Back Roads* for the first time.

GUILDS INN, 101 Pitt St., Mt. Pleasant, SC 29464; 803-881-0510. A 6-guestroom small inn and restaurant in a quiet, residential neighborhood across the bridge from Charleston. Breakfast included in room rate. Dinner served Tues. thru Sat., by reservation only. Open year-round. All of the cultural and historic attractions of Charleston nearby. Joyce and Guilds Hollowell, Owners; Gervais Hollowell, Innkeeper. (See Index for rates.)

Directions: Take Rte. 17 or 701 in Charleston, and cross the bridge into Mt. Pleasant, taking Whilden St. south to Venning St. Turn right on Venning and go 1 block to Pitt St.

36 MEETING STREET
Charleston, South Carolina (1988)

Charleston is one of America's wonderful old cities where architecture and art have joined hands, creating an ambience that's impossible to duplicate. Travelers who want to see some of the beautiful 18th- and 19th-century houses are often frustrated because public tours are limited to just a few days a year.

Not so at 36 Meeting Street, where my friends Suzanne and David Redd have opened their home as a bed and breakfast, and you can look at the interior of this 1740 "single house" and all the wonderful antique furnishings and portraits to your heart's content. At the same time you'll enjoy all the hospitality and fun the Redds radiate.

If you asked him, I'm sure David would play a piece for you on the exquisite harpsichord in the drawing room. "We looked for a harpsichord for five years before we found this one," David told me, as he sat down to play. "This is a handmade replica of an 18th-century French harpsichord, the original of which is on display in the museum at Yale University." Whereupon, he launched into a brilliant rendition of a work by Mouret.

He is a native Charlestonian and a professional organist. He is Minister of Music at the oldest Baptist church in the South, the beautiful First Baptist Church of Charleston, designed by Robert Mills, who also designed the Washington Monument. David also plays the carillon and organ for the Citadel Military College in Charleston.

You may be wondering what I meant by "single house." Suzanne informed me that in the 1700s many houses were built only one room wide, and in Charleston they're called single houses. In New Orleans, they're called shotgun houses. An addition in 1860 joined the 1740 kitchen house to the main house.

Suzanne explained that Charleston single houses were typically open on the water side with a porch or piazza so that the sea breezes could blow through the house, and so that privacy could be maintained on the front of the house.

The drawing room mantel has the "fretwork" signature of Thomas Elfe, a renowned Charleston cabinetmaker active between 1747 and 1775. The original structure has remained the same over the years.

Actually, 36 Meeting Street is included in the official tours of historic houses in Charleston, and David and Suzanne show their house to hundreds of people at those times.

As you can imagine, the entire house is furnished beautifully and authentically with a mixture of French and English antiques. All of the three guest rooms are suites, with canopied beds and handmade quilts. One room has one of the best preserved 1740 cooking fireplaces in the city. Another room has a screened piazza where guests can enjoy their breakfast while looking out over the beautiful, wide, tree-lined boulevard.

Accompanied by flowers and the morning newspaper, breakfast makings are provided in the kitchenette of each suite and feature homemade sweet breads and fresh fruit.

Another spot where guests can take their breakfast might be the pretty garden where there are little tables among the camellias, azaleas, geraniums, and tea olive. The gentle Charleston climate encourages the profusion of flowers, along with magnolia and holly trees, which are everywhere.

Old Charleston is a place of balustrades, cupolas, dormers, scrollwork, cobblestones, old street lamps, beautiful old trees, gorgeous mellowed brick walls, overhanging galleries, and a gazebo in the park.

With all of the interesting events that go on throughout the year, especially the Spoleto Festival in May and June, I would advise early reservations at 36 Meeting Street.

I am happy to welcome 36 Meeting Street to the pages of *Country Inns and Back Roads* for the first time.

36 MEETING STREET, 36 Meeting St., Charleston, SC 29401; 803-722-1034. A 3-suite 18th-century bed-and-breakfast home in Charleston's historic district, 2 blocks from the famous Battery. Ingredients for a continental breakfast included in room rate. Open year-round. The Dock St. Theatre, historic sites, shops, restaurants, and many attractions within walking distance. Children welcome. No pets. David and Suzanne Redd, Innkeepers. (See Index for rates.)

Directions: On east side of Meeting St., south of Tradd St., and 2 blocks north of So. Battery St.

CHALET SUZANNE
Lake Wales, Florida (1973)

After my first visit to Chalet Suzanne a number of years ago, I wondered if it really did happen or was it like the musical *Brigadoon,* in which the fictional Scottish village returns for one day every 100 years. This is a reaction I frequently get from guests who visit this unusual country inn in central Florida. Sometimes they can hardly believe it.

However, there is no doubt that Chalet Suzanne is a real place. The bridges, steeples, cupolas, minarets, peaked roofs, flat roofs, castle towers, domes, treasures, antiques, and pagodas are all there. It's a world of pastels in Bavarian, Swiss, Oriental, French, English, Turkish, Chinese, and every other style you can think of, and the nice part of it is that the guest rooms are all comfortably furnished in this wonderful Arabian Nights atmosphere.

It was all started in the early 1930s by Bertha Hinshaw, and now her son, Carl, and his wife, Vita, are continuing with their own touches—the newest of which is a spectacular new covered walkway to the dining area, graced by a beautifully carved window with Tiffany angel roundels from All Angels Episcopal Church in New York City.

To the people who live in Florida, Chalet Suzanne is best known for its exceptional food. In fact, it was recently awarded the "Golden Spoon" for the nineteenth consecutive year of being listed among the top twelve restaurants in Florida. *Mobil Guide* has given it four stars and it has the *Travel-Holiday Magazine* award for fine dining.

Dinner is served in the wonderful around-the-world ambience of the dining room, with Persian tile tables, Venetian glass lamps, clocks, statuary, stained glass windows, an old piano, and an eclectic collection of goblets and stemware—no two tables are set alike. By the way, there is a very intriguing little table for two set in the front window, which is reserved for honeymooners, if possible.

Most of the guests visiting Chalet Suzanne for the first time order the well-known chicken Suzanne, beautifully browned and glazed. It is prepared by Carl, who, in addition to being the "chief pilot" of the airfield (oh, I forgot to mention the airfield), is also the "principal stirrer" in the soup factory, and in addition to everything else is the chef at the inn.

Dinner also can include the original baked grapefruit centered with a sautéed chicken liver, the famed Chalet Suzanne romaine soup, hearts of artichoke salad, petite peas in cream and butter, a grilled tomato slice, deliciously hot homemade rolls, a mint ice, and tiny crêpes Suzanne.

The remark "It's almost like a Disney movie" is frequently heard at Chalet Suzanne, and I guess it's more than a coincidence that Disney World and many other famous attractions, including the beautiful Cypress Gardens waterskiing shows, are just a short distance away.

Oh yes, there is a 2,450-foot airstrip at Chalet Suzanne and it comes out of Carl Hinshaw's lifelong love of flying. The flying tradition continues because Carl and Tina's son, Eric, is also a pilot.

Never ones to rest on their laurels, Vita tells me they've been hard at work, tending the lush landscaping and gardens, restocking the lily pond with goldfish and waterlilies, adding a new fountain, and building a new flower conservatory and greenhouse.

They are busy bees, indeed, making sure their guests have a wonderful time at Chalet Suzanne.

CHALET SUZANNE, P.O. Drawer AC, Lake Wales, FL 33859; 813-676-6011. A 30-guestroom phantasmagoric country inn and gourmet restaurant, 4 mi. north of Lake Wales, between Cypress Gardens and the Bok Singing Tower near Disney World. European plan. Dining room open from 8 a.m. to 9:30 p.m. Closed Mon. from June to Nov. Wheelchair access. Pool on grounds. Golf, tennis nearby. Lots of opportunity for good jogging. Not inexpensive. The Hinshaw Family, Innkeepers. (See Index for rates.)

Directions: From Interstate 4 turn south on U.S. 27 toward Lake Wales. From Sunshine State Pkwy., exit at Yeehaw Junction and head west on Rte. 60 to U.S. 27 (60 mi.). Proceed north on U.S. 27 at Lake Wales. Inn is 4 mi. north of Lake Wales on 17A. ✈

"European plan" means that rates for rooms and meals are separate. "American plan" means that meals are included in the cost of the room. "Modified American plan" means that breakfast and dinner are included in the cost of the room. The rates at some inns include a continental breakfast with the lodging.

ONTARIO

The Opinicon, *Elgin*

● The Briars, *Jackson's Pt.*

TORONTO

LAKE ONTARIO

Oban Inn,
Niagara-on-the-Lake

■ NIAGARA FALLS

ST. LAWRENCE RIVER

QUEBEC

CANADA
U.S.A.

ERIE

QUEBEC ■

L'Auberge du Roy, *Deschambault* ●

MAINE

Handfield Inn,
● *St. Marc-sur-le-Richelieu*

BANGOR
■

■ MONTREAL

● Hovey Manor, *North Hatley*

PORTLAND
■

BOSTON
■

Eastern Time Zone

GULF OF ST. LAWRENCE

NEW

RUNSWICK

Shaw's Hotel, *Brackley Beach*

P. E. I.

CAPE BRETON I.

SYDNEY ■

Inverary Inn, *Baddeck*

MONCTON ■

Marshlands, *Sackville* ●

NOVA SCOTIA

■ HALIFAX

IS

Marathon Hotel, *Grand Manan Island*

ATLANTIC

■ ANNAPOLIS ROYAL

● Milford House, *South Milford*

YARMOUTH ■

OCEAN

Eastern and Maritime Canada

Atlantic Time Zone

MARATHON INN
Grand Manan Island, New Brunswick (1976)

Grand Manan is a quiet, unspoiled island of great natural beauty fifteen miles long and four miles wide—a paradise for naturalists, bird watchers, photographers, artists, divers, and rock hounds. The best way to experience the island is by walking.

As the ferry from Black's Harbour approached the wharf at North Head on Grand Manan Island, I could readily see that this was a place where men made their living from the sea. There were fishing boats, seining weirs, and weathered docks on tall stilts; a necessity because of the very high tides in the Bay of Fundy. I could see the Marathon Inn at the top of the hill—a gleaming, three-story building with a mansard roof.

On this particular trip Jim Leslie had suggested in a very mysterious way that something unusual and exciting had been going on at the inn on at least two occasions during the year, and said that he would fill me in when we had a chance to chat.

The owner-innkeepers of the inn are Jim and Judy Leslie, and Jim's mother, Fern. The Leslies are all Canadians. Fern is from Saskatchewan, and both Judy and Jim were brought up in Toronto.

The first thing I did on arrival was to take a plunge in the heated swimming pool and arrange for a game of tennis. Jim joined me about an hour before dinner on the front porch overlooking the harbor.

"Our guests often like to take advantage of the chance to go deep-sea fishing for herring, pollock, and haddock with the island fishermen. There are also boating trips to Gannet Rock, Machias Seal Island, and Tent Island. Children seem to have a wonderful time here, and that is very gratifying.

"We have some excellent spring programs that are available to our guests at a slight additional charge," Jim said. "There are three four-day birdwatching tours in May and June conducted by Mary Majka. Also in June we have a special photographic workshop conducted by Freeman Patterson and a watercolor seminar by John Austen. We also have a super dark room.

"During the fall months we have a program called 'Ocean Search' that enables our guests to learn more about the great whales off the island and also to go out on the sea in boats. Our naturalist shows slides several evenings during the week with special emphasis on those great mammals during that time."

Finally, I could contain myself no longer. "What is this mystery you're talking about?" Jim smiled broadly and replied, "That's exactly what it is: an old-fashioned 'whodunit' mystery, in which our guests can hunt down clues and suspects. We supply them with a complete kit of clues when they arrive on Fridays. Before the weekend is out we've had a 'crime' with suspects and detectives, and finally we solve the mystery by figuring out who the culprit was.

"We've done these for the past few years and they are a huge success. We're already booked for some additional weekends this year, as well. You don't have to be a fan of Miss Marple or Sherlock Holmes, but it helps to get into the swing of things. Everybody has a terrific time. Tell your readers that they will have to telephone in advance to make a reservation."

So, I have now solved part of the mystery; however, I made a reservation on the spot for one of the "whodunit" weekends at the Marathon Inn. Doesn't the idea sound intriguing?

MARATHON INN, North Head at Grand Manan, New Brunswick, Canada E0G 2M0; 506-662-8144. A 38-guestroom resort-inn on Grand Manan Island in the Bay of Fundy, 40 mi. from St. John in New Brunswick. Modified American and European plans. Closed in winter months. Breakfast and dinner served to travelers daily. Heated swimming pool, tennis courts on grounds. Beachcombing, bird watching, swimming, fishing, hiking, diving, bicycles, golf nearby. Whale watching in season. Pets allowed on ground floor annex. Jim, Judy, and Fern Leslie, Innkeepers. (See Index for rates.)

Directions: Grand Manan Island is reached by ferry from Black's Harbour, just off Rte. 1, midway between Calais, Maine, and St. John, New Brunswick. Check inn for schedule.

MARSHLANDS INN
Sackville, New Brunswick (1975)

Every year I hear from a great many readers who have driven across Maine into New Brunswick to reach Nova Scotia and Prince Edward Island by the land route.

Almost all of these letters make some reference to the Marshlands Inn, just a few miles from the Nova Scotia border and the Prince Edward Island ferry. I'd like to reach back into the past to 1975 and share a portion of a letter from a honeymooning couple.

"Our itinerary from Calais, Maine, took us to the Marathon Inn off the coast of New Brunswick and then to the Marshlands Inn for a late lunch. The setting, decor, and food exceeded our expectations. We never expected to find such a sophisticated inn so far north.

"While paying our bill we found a copy of *Country Inns and Back Roads,* perused the table of contents, and noted your entry regarding the Marshlands. We found that we were in complete agreement with your comments and enjoyed your personal observations."

What was true in 1975 is for the most part still true these many years later. There has been one change recently at the Marshlands Inn. My dear friends Herb and Alice Read have sold the inn to Mary and John Blakely. Mary worked for four years at Marshlands as a hostess. She and John both come from England, where Mary's family had an English-style country inn in the Derbyshire hills. The Blakelys have been busy creating some very pleasant guest rooms in the carriage house, which they named Stonehaven. They tell me the rooms have oak floors and are furnished in antiques, "no reproductions, but the baths are modern."

In a conversation that I had with Mary, she filled me in on some of the new offerings being prepared by their French chef.

"Our chef calls the appetizer the entrée and the main dish, dinner," Mary told me. "He does traditional French cuisine as well as a little bit of nouvelle. One of his specialties is sauces.

"We have many new things on the menu, including cultivated mussels from Prince Edward Island or Nova Scotia. We serve them in wine or in stock, depending on the preference of the guest. We also have an excellent Caesar salad. We have specials three or four days a week, with appetizers and entrées. Incidentally, our chef does a halibut mousse with a pink peppercorn sauce and also a smoked cod mousse made with red peppers. We also have a Middle Eastern dish called cous-cous. This is a lamb dish with semolina.

"Of course, we still have the same dishes for which the Marshlands has gained such a fine reputation, including Atlantic and Miramichi salmon. Many of our guests ask for fiddlehead greens almost as soon as they check in."

The first thing that a newly arrived guest sees when entering Marshlands is the graceful, curving staircase, a carved settee, and many ancestral portraits. There are two high-ceilinged parlors for houseguests and diners waiting to be shown to their tables.

The guest rooms are almost all furnished in antiques and Persian rugs, and runners muffle footsteps in all the halls. Each guest room has a four poster bed and is decorated in a different color scheme and period wallpaper. My favorite room is on the third floor under the eaves, where there is a bow-shaped window with a sitting alcove, a leather-topped writing desk, a marble reading lamp, and a high dresser with a pedestal mirror.

One of the enduring traditions at Marshlands is the delicious hot chocolate, served every evening around ten o'clock. It's a time when guests who may have been otherwise occupied find themselves congregating and talking over the day's experiences.

Let me reassure my honeymooning couple from 1975 that the Marshlands Inn is all that it was during their visit and perhaps a great deal more.

MARSHLANDS INN, Box 1440, Sackville, N.B., Canada E0A 3C0; 506-536-0170. A 25-guestroom (mostly private baths) village inn near Tantramar Marshes and Fundy Tides. European plan. Breakfast, lunch, and dinner served to travelers daily. Open from Feb. thru late Nov. Golf, xc skiing, curling, hiking, and swimming nearby. John and Mary Blakely, Innkeepers. (See Index for rates.)

Directions: Follow Trans-Canada Highway to Sackville, then Rte. 6 for 1 mi. to center of town.

INVERARY INN
Baddeck, Cape Breton, Nova Scotia (1972)

We were all gathered in the living room at Inverary for our annual meeting of all the *CIBR* inns in the Canadian Maritimes. There was a very cheerful fire burning against the chill created by a late October rainstorm. Surrounding us were the trappings that I had seen so often in Scottish inns, such as Tartan drapes, family portraits, and books and magazines of interest to people of Scottish heritage. There were not one, but two, grandfather clocks and very comfortable chairs and settees, where the innkeepers were gathered to exchange ideas and tell stories. It was wonderful to see them here again.

In between the rain showers we had taken walks down along the shore of Lake Bras d'Or, past the heated outdoor swimming pool, the new lakeside tennis courts, and the new house of Scott MacAulay and his wife, Terri. Their son, Matthew Scott MacAulay, became one year old on last All Saints Day. His grandfather and grandmother are Danny and Isobel MacAulay, the innkeepers of the Inverary Inn.

Our tour also took us past the waterside seafood restaurant set among the pine trees, where lobster, fresh fish chowder, and other Nova Scotia seafood are offered. The restaurant has a most attractive view of a boatyard, and some of the fishing boats and sailboats can easily be seen while enjoying one of the those delicious Nova Scotia lobsters. A pontoon boat, moored next to the Fish House, takes inn guests out in the evening, and Dan MacAulay is the skipper.

Our walk also included a visit to the wee chapel on the grounds of the inn. "It was the gift of one of our guests," Isobel said. "For everyone it has become a haven of quiet and peaceful serenity. I'm sure to visit here almost every day myself."

But she had other news for us. "Our plan to be open the year around has been a great success," she exclaimed. "We feel that this is going to be a wonderful place particularly for people in the Maritimes to come for a 'getaway weekend.' This is especially true because of the addition of our indoor swimming pool and health club." All of the innkeepers present cheered and congratulated her for such an interesting innovation. Unless I am poorly informed, this is one of the few inns in Nova Scotia to be open twelve months of the year.

The Inverary Inn has several types of accommodations; some are in the main house and others are in adjoining outbuildings and cottages. The newer lodging rooms are principally used to accommodate bus tours. With this in mind, *CIBR* travelers should indicate that they are from *CIBR* when they call to make reservations, and at that time specify the kind of accommodation they prefer. The main house and the Old Barn have the more traditional kinds of rooms.

A letter I received from a couple from Gaithersburg, Maryland, read, in part: "Recently my wife and I enjoyed a portion of our honeymoon at the Inverary Inn. The thing that captured our admiration was the stunning ambience and the warmth and friendliness we experienced from every staff member. We carried away from the Inverary Inn two hearts full of fond memories."

INVERARY INN, Box 190, Baddeck, Cape Breton, N.S., Canada B0E 1B0; 902-295-2674. A 50-guestroom resort-inn on the Cabot Trail, 52 mi. from Sydney, N.S., on the shore of Lake Bras d'Or. European plan. Breakfast and dinner served to travelers daily. Lunch available from June thru Oct. Open year-round. Heated outdoor pool, indoor pool, health club, tennis courts, bicycles, and children's playground on grounds. Boating and small golf course nearby. Isobel MacAulay, Innkeeper. (See Index for rates.)

Directions: Follow Trans-Canada Hwy. to Canso Causeway to Baddeck.

MILFORD HOUSE
South Milford, Nova Scotia (1974)

The time was 7:30 a.m. I awakened to the sound of the lake water lapping against the shore, and looked out of the window of my cabin to see an errant canoeist drifting by in the middle of the lake. I bounded out of bed, in and out of the shower, and dressed rapidly so as not to miss a single moment of my time at this "almost-wilderness" resort-inn in southern Nova Scotia.

My accommodations, like all the others, were in a tidy, rustic cabin where there were two bedrooms and a large combination sitting and dining room with windows overlooking still another view of the lake. There are over two dozen of these cottages situated well apart along the wooded shores of two lakes, within walking distance of the main lodge. Each cottage has its own lakeside dock, two to five bedrooms, a living room with a fireplace, electricity, and a bathroom with a tub or a shower. Some of them are insulated and contain housekeeping facilities ideal for a cross-country skiing holiday or just a secluded winter vacation. There were fresh flowers in my cabin and although the furnishings were plain, everything was absolutely spic and span. All the cottages are provided with maid service, ice, wood, and kindling, delivered daily.

I walked down to the end of the lane and up the woods road toward the main lodge for breakfast, happening to meet another guest bound in the same direction. "Oh, I think it's a wonderful place here," she said. "We left the windows open and just loved listening to the loons. My husband and I are going to stay and take a canoe trip."

We continued on up to the main lodge with its comfortable living room, large dining room, library and games room. Milford House guests take their breakfasts and dinners at the main lodge, where there are vegetables from the garden, roasts, fresh fish, native blueberries, raspberries, and ample home-baked breads and pastries. Breakfast consisted of bacon, eggs, pancakes, homemade muffins, and coffee—and, especially, lots of conversation with other guests.

Returning guests are most enthusiastic about the Milford House chef, who has made several interesting changes in the menu. Margaret told me that his reputation has also increased their dinner business considerably.

For a number of years, even before my first visit in 1973, the Milford House has been expertly managed by Margaret and Bud Miller. It was their daughter Wendy who gave me my first tour, and about whom I have written continuously over the years. For the benefit of Wendy's many friends, she finished her officers' training course and is now an instructor in the Canadian Armed Forces. I do miss seeing that twelve-year-old young lady who showed me around not so very many years ago.

The Millers' other daughter Linda visits in August, too, with her three children, who are becoming well known at the inn. Linda designed and hooked a wall hanging of the Milford Inn with symbolic figures around the outside of the oval picture. It has truly been a conversation piece. Margaret told me that she was planning to have some Christmas cards made of it.

What has made the Milford House attractive to many repeating guests is the fact that the area is virtually unspoiled; however, it is easily traversable by canoe.

When I left, the remaining guests stood on the porch waving. And when I passed the big tree at the corner, true to the Milford House tradition, I didn't look back. A lovely, old-fashioned custom.

MILFORD HOUSE, South Milford, R.R. 4, Annapolis Royal, N.S., Canada BOS 1AO; 902-532-2617. A rustic resort-inn with 27 cabins on 600 acres of woodlands and lakes, 90 mi. from Yarmouth, N.S., near Kejimkujik National Park. Modified American plan. Breakfast and dinner served daily with picnic lunches available. Open from June 15 to Sept. 15; fall and winter by special reservation. Tennis, fishing, croquet, canoeing, birdwatching, and swimming on grounds. Deep-sea fishing and golf nearby. Warren and Margaret Miller, Innkeepers. (See Index for rates.)

Directions: From Yarmouth follow Rte. 1 to traffic lights in Annapolis Royal. Turn right and continue on Rte. 8, 15 mi. to inn. The Blue Nose Ferry from Bar Harbor to Yarmouth N.S., arrives in time for guests to make dinner at the Milford House.

THE BRIARS
Jackson's Point, Ontario (1980)

There's an unusually large full-color map of the Briars and Lake Simcoe, prepared by innkeeper John Sibbald, in addition to some very informative literature, which you can obtain by writing the Briars.

I'll go into details about this map in just a moment, but first let me tell you about the Briars, a lush 200-acre estate on the south shore of Lake Simcoe, about forty-five miles north of Toronto. Guests are accommodated in cottages clustered by the lake or in handsome guest rooms in the Manor and its new wings. The inn is set in expanses of deep green lawns surrounded by sculpted hedges and giant pines. A peaceful river meanders through the golf course, and little streams wander under wooden bridges in the scenic woods and fields. I would term the Briars a distinctive Canadian resort that blends its rich past with modern facilities to offer an attractive holiday for guests with family or friends.

In the more than twenty years that I've been traveling in North America, I've come to the conclusion that while Canadians and Americans have lived side by side for many years and both speak the same language, there are still some subtle differences. For one thing, Canadians are basically more conservative than Americans. In this respect they are more like the English. I found that they prefer some of the more quiet things of life, such as good walking, quiet fireside reading, and a little less flamboyant approach to life in general.

And now to the map. In one corner it details a most interesting history since 1819, and traces ownership through more than 170 years to the present Sibbald family.

Actually, the Briars takes in so much territory and so many activities that it really requires this map to give a good overview. It shows the relationship of the Briars to the Red Barn and Peacock House, the gardens, the tennis courts, the wilderness, and of course the 18-hole golf course, the lake, and the village of Jackson's Point.

It shows the location of all of the many lakeside cottages and the golf clubhouse, as well as Saint George's Church, which I visited for the first time with John Sibbald a number of years ago, and the route of a great circle tour around Lake Simcoe with many points of interest.

With this map in hand it's easy for the guest to locate the many recreational possibilities at the Briars. In winter the property becomes a snowy paradise for walking and cross-country skiing, skating, tobogganing, and snowshoeing. When the temperature falls there is a beautiful indoor pool, sauna, whirlpool, and exercise room.

In summer, there are two outdoor pools, all of the lake's recreational advantages, the golf course, lighted tennis courts, lawn sports, and wooded walking trails. There's fishing, sailing, and windsurfing every day of the year on Lake Simcoe.

Early on, one of the things that intrigued me greatly about the Briars was the fact that the Canadian novelist Mazo de la Roche lived in this area, which undoubtedly supplied her with the atmosphere later portrayed in her famous *Whiteoaks of Jalna* books. She was a guest in one of the cottages at the Briars during the last five summers of her life.

I pored over this map for at least an hour, discovering things that I had never known before about the Briars and Lake Simcoe.

On the wall in the reception area there is a quote from Stephen Leacock, who had a longtime association with the Briars. "There is a wild grandeur in those highlands of Scotland, and the majestic solitude where the midnight sun flashes upon the ice peaks of Alaska. But to my thinking, none of these will stand comparison to the smiling beauty of the waters, shores, and bays of Lake Simcoe and its sister lake, Couchiching."

THE BRIARS, Jackson's Point, Ontario, LOE 1L0 Canada; 416-722-3271. A resort-inn on the shores of Lake Simcoe, approx. 45 mi. north of Toronto. Open every day. Breakfast, lunch, and dinner served to non-residents. Summer activities include 18-hole golf course, two outdoor swimming pools, indoor swimming pool, whirlpool, sauna, lakeshore swimming, 5 all-weather tennis courts, and many lawn sports. Winter sports include xc skiing, skating, tobogganing, snowmobiling, ice-fishing, and curling. There is a children's program during the summer and Christmas holidays. Excellent for families in all seasons. John and Barbara Sibbald, Innkeepers. (See Index for rates.)

Directions: Jackson's Point is located near Sutton, Ontario. From Hwy. 401, via Hwy. 404/Woodbine. Continue to Sutton and then Jackson's Point, ½ mi. east on Hedge Rd.

THE OBAN INN
Niagara-on-the-Lake, Ontario (1977)

"January, February, and March are wonderful times to be here in Niagara-on-the-Lake."

We were passing through the reception area, and innkeeper Gary Burroughs deftly drew an Oban Inn brochure from the rack and pointed out that there were two photographs of the inn, one in summer, showing the flowers and lawns, and the other in winter, with ample snow and a beautifully decorated Christmas tree.

"The village and shops are still here, but this is before our famous Shaw Festival brings crowds, and summer folks come in, and the feeling here at the inn is slower and more relaxed and such great fun. As you know, we do not salt our roads; instead they are rolled after each snowstorm, so once again there's a lovely sort of country-village feeling during the wintertime. Also I want to point out that the really exceptional Niagara Historical Society and Museum is open and it provides both Canadians and Americans with an extensive and interesting background of the area. We have a wonderful collection of beautiful old homes, along with English-style shops, that make our village one of the most pleasant places to walk on a brisk winter's day."

Well, it was far from winter during my last visit, and Gary and I were touring the golf course that almost surrounds the inn on two sides. When we got to a point where there is a little lighthouse, he pointed out that we could see the lights of Toronto in the distance, across the corner of the lake, and on the other side, almost close enough to throw a dollar across the river, is Fort Niagara on the American side. "It was originally a French fort and it was right here that there were some skirmishes between the Canadians and the Americans during the War of 1812. That's the mouth of the Niagara River out there," he pointed out.

I can well understand why I get letters from guests who enjoyed their stay, not only in Niagara-on-the-Lake, but also at the Oban itself. There is a wonderful, distinctively Canadian feeling to this inn, and while literally thousands of Americans visit the town and the inn each year, that wonderful Canadian feeling continues undisturbed.

For example, in the inn there is a pub with a magnificent oil painting of George Bernard Shaw, along with photographs of stars of theater and cinema who have appeared at the Shaw Festival during past years. The luncheon fare is typical of what I've enjoyed at pubs in England many times. Real English porridge is served at breakfast.

The dining room overlooking the lake is considerably enhanced by the care and attention given to the flowers by Gary's mother, and here is still another Canadian quality reflected in the inn—the love of flowers.

The dinner menu also reveals the Oban's mix of the old world and the new. For example, among the appetizers is a homemade paté, a tradition in England and on the Continent. The main menu items have the ring of the English countryside: roast prime ribs of beef with Yorkshire pudding and calves' sweetbreads with bacon served on toast. The patrons of the inn include businessmen from the town, as well as a few Canadian-American visitors. In the evening, there are informal, jolly sing-alongs around the piano in the corner, as well as quiet entertainment.

Our swing around the golf course was coming to an end, but we were being treated to a really sensational sunset. Here, in mid-July, nightfall takes its time about coming, and even well after nine o'clock there were sailboats returning from the lake or the river. Gary even found a golf ball. It was obvious that this generous and sensitive man really loves the town and loves the inn, and it was such a pleasure to be with him. "I think it's dinnertime now and I know Sarah will be waiting. Are you ready?"

You bet I was.

THE OBAN INN, 160 Front St., Box 94, Niagara-on-the-Lake, Ontario, Canada LOS IJO; 416-468-2165. A 23-guestroom village inn on a quiet street in one of Canada's historic villages, approx. 12 mi. from Niagara Falls, N.Y., on the shores of Lake Ontario. All plans available. Breakfast, lunch, dinner served daily to travelers. Open every day of the year. Near Ft. George and Ft. Niagara, and the Shaw Festival. Golf, xc skiing, sailing, fishing, tennis nearby. Owner-controlled pets welcome. Gary Burroughs, Innkeeper. (See Index for rates.)

Directions: Exit Hwy. 55 at St. Catharines from the Queen Elizabeth Hwy. Follow signs to Niagara-on-the-Lake.

The date in parenthesis in the heading represents the first year the inn appeared in the pages of Country Inns and Back Roads.

THE OPINICON
Chaffey's Locks, Elgin, Ontario (1981)

Ever since I was a boy I've been hearing about those wonderful, almost inaccessible, fishing and hunting resorts in Canada that are always situated on sylvan lakes and surrounded by primeval forests. Friends of my father would disappear a couple of times each year and return with tales of fish that practically leapt into the boat and game in Paul Bunyan dimensions. There were stories about highly voluble guides and idyllic days spent in the forest and on the water, followed by trenchermen's meals, very often including the day's catch.

In the summer of 1980 I found such a Canadian retreat with all of the virtues listed above, plus many more that make it a wonderful place for a rusticated vacation.

The Opinicon resort-inn is situated on a lovely wooded hill overlooking Opinicon Lake, and surrounded by seventeen acres of well-groomed lawns, giant oaks, a large flower garden, and quiet spots in the woods or on the lake from which to observe nature. Accommodations are in the main building, an old-fashioned, two-storied, yellow clapboard residence with completely modernized rooms, many opening onto a porch or balcony. In the woods, set back from the lakeshore, are a series of cottages accommodating from two to eight persons each.

The cheerful dining room offers three sumptuous meals a day under the American plan, and I understand they've had the same chef for many years. Guests' freshly caught fish can be cooked and served at any meal, and the dining room is conducted like many old resort-inns that have now disappeared. I sat at the same table and had the same waitress for all my meals. She and the other waitresses were friendly young ladies from the area.

Innkeeper Al Cross, whose Bay State accent I recognized immediately, is from Newton, Massachusetts. His wife Janice's family has been running this resort-inn for many generations. Al is a somewhat rumpled type of man who is always on the go, greeting guests, taking care of their needs, and keeping the staff members on their toes.

With over 200 lakes in the area, the Opinicon is known for its great fishing. It appeared to me that about fifty percent of the guests in residence during my visit were interested in this sport, for which boats and experienced local guides can be arranged. The inn provides basket lunches, if desired.

On the other hand, many people enjoy the great variety of recreational activities available, including boating, lake and pool swimming, tennis, croquet, shuffleboard, horseshoes, ping-pong, volleyball, and for the occasional inclement days, a good lending library. There's also an honest-to-gosh country store.

One of the most interesting things to do is to take the short walk to Chaffey's Locks, which are a part of the Rideau Canal System. This system was opened in 1832 to connect Kingston with Ottawa, thus avoiding the rapids of the St. Lawrence. It is still a navigable waterway, and the locks, models of stone engineering construction, are operated by hand by two gatekeepers.

The Opinicon is a great place to take the entire family for a real Canadian woods holiday. Rates have been structured in such a way that it is within the financial means of the average North American family, especially when you think of hungry kids eating three meals a day.

THE OPINICON, Chaffey's Locks, RR 1, Elgin, Ontario, Canada KOG 1CO; 613-359-5233. An 18-guestroom resort-inn on Opinicon Lake, part of the Rideau Canal System of eastern Ontario; accommodations also available in rustic cottages. Full American and modified American plan. Open early April to late November. Fishing, boating, tennis, heated swimming pool, shuffleboard, bicycles on grounds, golf course nearby. Excellent for children of all ages. No credit cards. Personal checks accepted. Albert and Janice Cross, Innkeepers. (See Index for rates.)

Directions: From south: Interstate 81 to 1000 Island Bridge to Ontario Rte. 401 west. Turn off Exit No. 645 at Rte. 32 (right), go north to Rte. 15, turning right (north). Follow to 2 miles beyond Elgin (bypassed). Turn left on Chaffey's Locks Rd. From east: Rte. 401 west to Exit No. 696 (Brockville), turn north (right) on Rte. 42, follow Rte. 42 to Crosby, turn south (left) on Rte. 15 for 2 miles and turn right on Chaffey's Locks Rd.

A number of inns have nearby airports where private airplanes may land. An airplane symbol at the end of the inn directions indicates that there is an airport nearby. Consult inn for further information.

SHAW'S HOTEL
Brackley Beach, Prince Edward Island (1975)

I'm certain a great many of our readers enjoyed the Public Television presentation of *Anne of Green Gables,* an adaptation of Lucy Montgomery's splendid novel about a girl growing into young womanhood on Prince Edward Island. If you missed it, be sure to catch the reruns. Anne may never have actually existed, but her spirit is there, as well as an attractive, typical gabled house that she *might* have lived in.

Prince Edward Island is one of the great surprises of North America. For one thing, ocean water temperatures along the wide P.E.I. beaches average sixty-eight to seventy degrees in summer and the sun is excellent for tanning. It has one of Canada's finest national parks, stretching twenty-five miles along the Gulf of St. Lawrence. There are wild seascapes, breathtaking views, and an atmosphere of hospitality, because this has been a resort area for more than a century.

During the summer months there is an excellent theatre at the Confederation Centre of the Arts of Charlottetown, offering a choice of musicals that play to capacity houses almost every night.

Prince Edward Island is very popular in July and August, so reserve well in advance and be sure to obtain ferry information.

I first visited P.E.I. and Shaw's Hotel in 1974 and never thought that I could be this far north and find ocean water so wonderfully warm and enjoyable.

I had taken the ferry from Caribou, Nova Scotia, that morning. There is another ferry from Cape Tormentine, New Brunswick. It is possible to stay at the Marshlands Inn in Sackville and take the ferry over the next morning. I had driven down from the Inverary Inn on Cape Breton in northern Nova Scotia, so the Caribou crossing was more convenient.

I found that Shaw's was part of an original pioneer farm started in 1793; had become a hotel in 1860; and today, still has many of the characteristics of an operating farm.

Some of the accommodations are single and double rooms in the main building, a Victorian house with a brilliant red mansard third story. There are also individual cottages, accommodating from two to eight people. This is most convenient for families who return every summer. The cottages are spaced far enough apart to insure privacy. Five of them have their own fireplaces.

Shaw's Hotel is surrounded by many trees and broad meadows. The view from the dining room might include a sailboat bobbing along on the bay. There is a good mix of both Canadian and American guests, and Robbie Shaw says that there are always a few people from California, Washington, New York, and Alberta.

One of the most attractive features about Shaw's Hotel is the fact that it is only a short distance through the woods to the beach. All of this summertime outdoor activity, including swimming, sailing on the bay, deep-sea tuna fishing, golf, tennis, bicycling, walking, and horseback riding, contribute to very big appetites, so the main dishes include fresh salmon, lobster, mackerel, cod, and halibut. Dinners are fun because everyone is eager for a hearty meal, and enthusiasm is high after a day of recreation.

Children are particularly happy in this atmosphere. Robbie Shaw said he has had as many as twenty to thirty children at one time at the height of the season. "There is always plenty of elbow room," he said. "We don't have any trouble keeping the parents of the children amused either. Besides the beach, there are riding horses nearby, and it is fun to ride along the beach and on the bridle paths. I have been doing it all my life. My father, who passed away in 1985, always loved the children."

SHAW'S HOTEL, Brackley Beach, Prince Edward Island, Canada C0A 2H0; 902-672-2022. A 24-guestroom and 10 guest cottages (some shared baths) country hotel within walking distance of Brackley Beach, 15 mi. from Charlottetown. American plan. Breakfast and dinner served to travelers daily. Open from June to Sept. Tennis, golf, bicycles, riding, sailing, beach and summer theater nearby. Pets allowed in cottages only. Robbie Shaw, Innkeeper. (See Index for rates.)

Directions: Prince Edward Island is reached by ferry from either Cape Tormentine, New Brunswick (near Moncton), or Caribou, Nova Scotia. In both cases, after arriving on P.E.I., follow Rte. 1 to Charlottetown, then Rte. 15 to Brackley Beach. P.E.I. is also reached by Eastern Provincial Airway, VIA Rail Canada, and Air Canada.

HANDFIELD INN (Auberge Handfield)
St. Marc-sur-le-Richelieu, Quebec (1983)

The Richelieu River, part of the waterway that carries boats to the Saint Lawrence and down to the tip of Florida, was blue and sparkling in the summer sun. I was relaxing on the grassy banks directly in front of the newest group of traditional Quebec houses, which had been redecorated and furnished by Conrad and Huguette Handfield and named Maison LaFlamme. The marina in front of Auberge Handfield ("auberge" is really the French word for inn) had several visiting boats, and there were people sitting around the swimming pool enjoying animated conversations in both French and English.

In thinking about the new accommodations, I realized that the inn would become, with the tennis courts to be added very shortly, a resort-inn, since there were a great many things to do on the grounds or nearby.

Guest rooms in the main inn are furnished in the old Quebec style but with touches of modern comfort, including tile bathrooms and controlled heating. Many of them have rough wooden walls and casement windows overlooking broad fields. Huguette told me that most of these guest rooms are decorated either with antiques or furniture made by local craftsmen. Maison LaFlamme's guest rooms have a water view.

A summer visit here is really not complete without attendance at the summer theater presentation in a very cleverly converted ferry boat. The plays are all French comedies and have been commissioned by Huguette especially for performances at Auberge Handfield.

However, let's get back to the "country inn" aspects of Auberge Handfield. Certainly one of them would be the cuisine. As Conrad said, "There are two menus—one is traditional French cuisine and the other is nouvelle cuisine. So you see our guests can really have a choice for whatever may be their preference." I won't take the time here to list the main dishes except to say that I like French cuisine in any form, particularly the wonderful pastries on display for dessert.

The main dining room is very cozy and warm, and tables are on the sunny, converted, glassed-in porch. The natural wood contributes to a feeling of comfort and warmth. An interesting point is that the dining room is open all afternoon, so that guests can always get something to eat. It's open from breakfast until ten o'clock each night.

Auberge Handfield is essentially French and it is not necessary to travel very far from any place in the United States or Canada to enjoy as French an experience as you would have in any village in France. The language is French, the villagers greet you in French, and the stores are French. They will help you out if you are in any difficulty. Essentially, it's a wonderful French experience.

I should also mention that "sugaring-off" parties are held from

March until the end of April and are very popular with inn guests. They are held in a rustic sugar shack in a maple grove just a few miles from the inn. I have enjoyed them myself very much.

The Handfield Inn is a great many things: it is a venerable mansion that has seen a century and a half of history; an enjoyable French restaurant; a four-season resort; and perhaps best of all, it is an opportunity to visit a French-Canadian village that has remained relatively free from the invasion of developers. Its ancient stone houses and nearby shops remain untouched, and its farms still raise good vegetables and poultry.

HANDFIELD INN (Auberge Handfield), St. Marc-sur-le-Richelieu, Quebec, JOL 2EO, Canada; 514-584-2226. A 45-guestroom (some shared baths) French-Canadian country inn about 25 mi. from Montreal. Different plans available. Please consult with inn in advance. Open year-round. Breakfast, lunch, and dinner served daily to travelers. Ladies are expected to wear a skirt or dress and gentlemen a coat at dinner. All summer and winter active sports easily available. Many handcrafts, antique, and historical tours in the area. No pets. M. and Mme. Conrad Handfield, Innkeepers. (See Index for rates.)

Directions: From Champlain, Victoria, or the Jacques Cartier bridges, take Hwy. 3 to Sorel, turn right at Hwy. 20. From the east end of Montreal, go through the Hyppolite LaFontaine Tunnel. Rte. 20 passes through St. Julie, St. Bruno, and Beloeil. Leave Hwy. 20 at Exit 112, turning left on Rte. 223 north. Handfield is 7 mi. distant.

The date in parenthesis in the heading represents the first year the inn appeared in the pages of Country Inns and Back Roads.

HOVEY MANOR
North Hatley, Quebec (1973)

The entire six pages of an article on Hovey Manor which appeared in *Sel & Poivre,* Quebec's leading food magazine, were in French, and even if my French is a bit sketchy I could see that there were many, many compliments for some of the wonderful dishes prepared by Belgian chef Marc de Canck.

A letter from Steve and Kathy Stafford at Hovey Manor indicated that they were both very pleased that the magazine was in agreement with them regarding Marc's talent. "Marc loves Hovey Manor and he will be here for many years to come. By the way, we have received new dinnerware from Europe with our own logo."

Hovey Manor is a traditional inn with all the resort facilities for a complete vacation experience. In the summer there are canoes, paddle boats, fishing, and tennis on the grounds.

Windsurfing has proved to be very popular with the guests, and lessons are available for everyone from kids to grandmothers. It's a fine, exhilarating exercise and offers a good escape without taking too much time. Sailboats and water skiing are also available at reasonable rates. By the way, there are ten golf courses within a half-hour's ride, and there is summer stock at the Piggery Theatre and concerts at the Mount Orford Arts Center nearby.

There seems to be something special going on at all times during the summer—beach barbecues, a lake cruise to Ripplecove Inn at Ayer's Cliff where you can have lunch if you like, chamber music concerts, poetry readings with wine and cheese, and various other events.

Festival Lac Massawippi runs from mid-July to mid-August, and the Abenaki Room at Hovey Manor will be the site of one of Festival Lac Massawippi's art exhibits, featuring the works of Eastern Township artists.

Nine new bedrooms and an expansion of the dining room have been completed. As Steve describes them, "The bedrooms are quite deluxe, many with fireplaces, private balconies, four-poster beds, and whirlpool baths, which are particularly attractive to cross-country and alpine skiers." Steve hastened to add that Hovey's atmosphere will not change.

The new guest rooms are furnished with a combination of antiques, antique reproductions, and works of local cabinetmakers, as well as artwork by Eastern Township artists.

I mentioned skiing, and actually Hovey has 150 kilometers of groomed cross-country ski trails right from its door, and also a ski package offering inn-to-inn skiing, where the inn transfers the cars and the baggage. Ski instruction is also available. Downhill skiers enjoy an interchangeable ticket, valid at four big mountains in the area, all with extensive snowmaking equipment. There's a great après-ski atmosphere in Hovey's historic Tap Room, where, on selected evenings, the chefs broil steaks and fresh salmon over the live charcoal hearth.

The two-language menu is quite European, and chef Marc de Canck emphasizes contemporary cuisine featuring beautiful presentation and ligther sauces. Desserts are sinfully good—or bad—depending on your viewpoint.

HOVEY MANOR, North Hatley, Quebec, Canada JOB 2CO; 819-842-2421. A 36-guestroom resort inn (12 with woodburning fireplaces) on Lake Massawippi, ½ hr. from U.S./Canada border. Modified American and European plans. Breakfast, lunch, dinner served every day. Open all year. Wheelchair access. Lighted tennis court, two beaches, sailing, canoeing, paddleboats, water skiing, windsurfing, fishing, xc skiing, and sleigh rides on grounds. Downhill skiing, horseback riding, racquet sports, and golf (10 courses) nearby; also many scenic and cultural attractions nearby. Sorry, no pets. Stephen and Kathryn Stafford, Innkeepers. (See Index for rates.)

Directions: Take Vermont I-91 to Vermont/Quebec border and follow Rte. 55 to No. Hatley Exit 29. Follow Rte. 108E for 5 mi. to T junction at Lake Massawippi in North Hatley. Turn right for ¾ mi. to Hovey Manor sign and private drive on left.

L'AUBERGE DU ROY
Deschambault, Quebec (1987)

Let's assume that you are planning a trip to Quebec—a delightful experience. In addition to stopping outside of Montreal at Auberge Handfield, described in the previous pages, let me suggest another French country experience near Quebec City.

If I thought Auberge Handfield was a French adventure, then L'Auberge du Roy turned out to be even more so. It is owned and kept by two very vivacious and obliging French-Canadians, Isabelle and Jean-Claude Lisita. Jean-Claude is the chef and is most voluble in one language only: French. Isabelle is the hostess and fortunately is conversant in English.

Upon my arrival, Isabelle showed me to my room on the second floor and at the same time gave me a tour of all the other guest rooms as well. Everything—the floors, the windowsills, the beds, the closets, just every possible surface—was immaculately clean.

L'Auberge du Roy is totally French-Canadian. Among the decorations in the dining room, for example, are hanging plants, painted plates decorating the wall, and a bottle of wine on the table which is both a suggestion and a decoration. There were many, many little figurines on tables and mantelpieces. The rugs, paintings, and prints were unmistakably French.

Also, there was an aroma from the kitchen that spelled nothing else but French cuisine. I had an opportunity to talk with Isabelle and Jean-Claude about this, and learned that he had been a French chef for many years in nearby Quebec City. It was their dream to own an *auberge* in the countryside.

After discussing the menu, I decided on a special duckling dish, cooked with black olives. I must admit that I was tempted by the salmon with lemon and also the medallions of beef. I'm very fond of sauces, and I guess I had come to the right place. The dessert menu featured a chocolate mousse made with brandy, as well as a sugar tart named after Isabelle—I think I can understand why.

The Lisitas acquired this property a few years ago at a time when it was very run-down, and they have put much into making it an engaging country inn.

Within a few steps of the inn is a stream with a wonderfully melodious waterfall, which can be heard from the guest rooms and the front porch. The lawn extends to the grassy bank, where the brook ripples across the dam and drops down into a little pool below, continuing a short distance to the Saint Lawrence River. It is delightfully quiet and cool.

I had a very good time and a happy stay at L'Auberge du Roy. I think Isabelle and Jean-Claude viewed my halting French with good humor, and

I made the acquaintance of a bilingual neighbor, Maurice Angers, who explained some of the things that I needed for this book in greater detail.

In closing, may I say that I haven't yet found an inn to my taste that also serves dinner in Quebec City, but L'Auberge du Roy is close enough so that the traveler will have all the advantages of visiting that historic city, and at the same time, an opportunity to return to the countryside for peace and quiet.

L'AUBERGE DU ROY, 106 Rue St.-Laurent, Deschambault, Quebec G0A 1S0; 418-286-6958. A 6-guestroom (private and shared baths) French-Canadian countryside inn, just a few miles from Quebec City. Breakfast, lunch, and dinner served every day. From Oct. 1 to May 1 the inn is closed on Mon.; the remainder of the year the inn is open 7 days a week. Tennis court and swimming pool on grounds. Many historic and scenic attractions nearby. No amusements for children under 12. Isabelle and Jean-Claude Lisita, Innkeepers. (See Index for rates.)

Directions: From the north, take Hwy. 40 up the north side of the St. Lawrence River to Quebec City. Exit at Deschambault. From the south, use Exit 156 (Villeroy), off Rte. 20. Then follow Rte. 265 to Deschaillons, and Rte. 132 to the Deschambault-Lotbinière ferry.

The date in parenthesis in the heading represents the first year the inn appeared in the pages of Country Inns and Back Roads.

NEVIS AND SAINT KITTS

Nevis and Saint Kitts are two islands that lie in the northern part of the Leeward Islands in the eastern Caribbean. After quite a few years of association with Britain, they attained a full independence in 1983, and the Federation of Saint Kitts and Nevis is now a country of its own, with a population of 44,000, of which 35,000 live on Saint Kitts and 9,000 on Nevis.

A travel-writer colleague of mine, Jennifer Cecil, suggested Nevis to me when I said that I thought I was ready for my first Caribbean vacation in at least twelve years. This idea was further strengthened for me when I learned that two longtime friends of mine from the Berkshires, Dr. Frank Paddock and his wife, Sis, had been coming to Nevis for many, many years. A great deal of what I am sharing with you in this section has been greatly enhanced by their having generously shared with me their enthusiasm for both of these lovely islands.

Although the land is beautiful, the sea and the surroundings are gorgeous, I think it is the Nevisians and the Saint Kittitians who make this a really fulfilling experience.

There are some interesting differences and similarities between the two islands. Saint Kitts is much larger, has a greater population, and is really much more sophisticated than Nevis. This is partly attributable to the fact that the cruise ships can come in to Basseterre and their passengers may walk around the downtown shops. Also, it's possible to fly from New York or Miami directly to Saint Kitts on the jumbo jets. The longer runways and larger airport on Saint Kitts make the country directly available from almost anywhere in the world.

On the other hand, I learned that the Nevisians are quite happy with the state of affairs that makes it necessary to reach Nevis either by ferry from Saint Kitts or by smaller airlines from Antigua. Taxis are available at both airports and also at the ferry landings.

The two islands lie in the tropics. Air temperature ranges from a minimum of 74° F. to a maximum of 84° F., with an average of 79° F. The average water temperature is 80° F., average annual rainfall is 55 inches, and the average duration of sunshine per day is more than 8 hours. These islands are warm, and the climate is very pleasant and healthy, with extremes tempered by the breezes from the northeastern trade winds. Usually dry and mild weather is experienced during the period from November to April; the period from May through October is warmer with higher rainfall.

A passport is required except for holders of proofs of identity issued to nationals of Canada and the United States visiting for a period of less than six months.

The currency used is the East Caribbean dollar (EC $). Currency may be exchanged at any bank, and at the time this went to press the rate of exchange for the U.S. dollar was approximately EC $2.68 to U.S. $1. I did not find that credit cards were widely accepted. Inns accept personal checks.

Various car-rental firms offer different makes and types of cars. A refundable deposit is frequently necessary. I personally rented a Mini-Moke from Mr. Johnson while I was on Nevis and would recommend it to anybody. It is a sort of overgrown golf cart with a canvas top and no sides. They're really fun.

Before driving any vehicle, including motorcycles, a local temporary driver's license must be obtained from the traffic department either in Basseterre or Charlestown in Nevis. Driving on both islands is on the left side of the road. The British ways are given up very slowly.

As far as entertainment and sports are concerned there is an 18-hole international championship golf course on Saint Kitts, available to all visitors.

Most inns on both islands have their own tennis courts, or arrangements can be made to use nearby courts. These are generally hard surfaced.

Swimming may be enjoyed at several white sand and black volcanic sand beaches on both the Caribbean and Atlantic sides of the islands. Of course, there are wonderful facilities for scuba diving, snorkeling, deep-sea fishing, sailing, cruising, and surfing. Arrangements can be made through each inn.

Horseback riding and hiking tours are also available, and tours by a horse-drawn carriage are a lot of fun.

There are several restaurants on both islands.

There are duty-free shopping facilities, and available goods range from perfumes to textiles and high-fashion clothing to porcelain, crystal, and jewelry.

Locally produced batik and tie-dyed clothing, fabrics, and hangings are among the local handicrafts, which also include a wide range of articles made of coconut shell or fiber, as well as straw goods, basketware, and ceramics.

The main vacation or holiday season runs from mid-December to mid-April. This is when there are more visitors. However, there is no rainy season and the islands are at their best during the summer, when the inns offer accommodations at reduced tariffs.

Light summer clothing, preferably in cotton or cotton mixtures rather than nylon, is recommended. Dress is informal at most inns.

Electricity is basically 230 volts AC; however, transformers may be supplied by inns and some have direct 110 voltage.

The water is safe, even the tap water.

I'm further indebted to Sis Paddock for presenting me with a copy of an excellent book by Joyce Gordon: Nevis: Queen of Caribees, *which should be read by all visitors to Nevis before, during, or after their trip. It's available from stores on both islands.*

Because the economy of the islands was supported in early times by the sugar plantations, a great many so-called Great Houses were built, most of which have been abandoned by what came to be impoverished owners. Some of these houses, along with their sugar factories, still remain, and it is possible to walk through them and get a very strong impression of what life was like in those halcyon days. Many of the inns I visited had at one time been a part of these sugar plantations.

There are two disparate figures in history forever connected with Nevis. One is Alexander Hamilton, who was born on the island in 1757. A very impressive museum has been built on the foundations of his birthplace and is maintained by the Nevis Historical and Conservation Society.

The other figure is Horatio Nelson, whose first encounter with Nevis would make a very good movie. I'll leave that for the reader to discover in Joyce Gordon's book. However, the woman to whom he proposed and who subsequently became his wife lived here. This was long before he became such a heroic figure in British Naval history.

I visited an excellent small museum devoted to Nelson memorabilia, and it contains every possible category of artifact from china, pottery, paintings, and tinted prints to all kinds of published books—novels, fiction and non-fiction—dealing with this man, who later became the hero of Trafalgar and subsequently the subject of much controversy.

This museum, called Morning Star, is the private collection of Mr. Abrahams and is open to visitors most mornings. March, 1987, marked the 200th wedding anniversary of Lord Horatio Nelson to Frances "Fanny" Nisbet, and the wedding was re-created for all to see and participate in. Some of the events included a sail-in of large ships from various islands around Nevis, authentic costumes, historical drama, and an actual wedding ceremony, held at Montpelier Plantation, the original site of the wedding. It was followed by a gala ball.

A full information kit may be obtained from the Saint Kitts-Nevis Tourist Board, 414 East 75th St., New York, NY 10021, 212-535-1234.

NISBET PLANTATION INN
Nevis, West Indies (1987)

I left Frank and Sis Paddock playing tennis with some of their island friends, and wandered down the truly impressive aisle of palms, which leads from the lovely old stone main building of Nisbet Plantation to the shore of the Atlantic. I could see a number of beach chairs already in place. Inn guests were adding to their generous tans or, perhaps for first timers like me, getting a faint tinge of red.

Each side of this spacious aisle had very pleasant little bungalows or cottages, usually designed with two suites in each. They are all very neat and tidy, with screened-in porches and very attractive plantings and exterior design. Guests stay in these buildings and congregate and take their meals at the main house.

The private beach has a bar and restaurant, serving breakfast and lunch daily, and an off-shore reef protects the swimming area and provides good snorkeling. Equipment is available.

I wandered back up to the tennis game, which was just ending, and was introduced to several more guests, of whom there seemed to be an equal number of Britons and Americans. Of course, we chatted about Nevis and how relatively undiscovered it really is and how much they were enjoying their holiday.

The main building, which includes the dining room, is a very handsome structure with a screened-in veranda, which wraps around three sides. The chintz-covered furniture, along with the many plants, photographs of Nevis, and a bookshelf that also has many classical recordings, lends an air of hominess to the entire scene.

The adjoining beach and the many waterside activities make Nisbet Plantation Inn a popular vacation getaway.

NISBET PLANTATION INN, Nevis, West Indies. U.S. reservations: 218-722-5059. A 33-guestroom (private baths) oceanside resort inn. Modified American plan includes breakfast and dinner. Open year-round, but sometimes closed for 1 month midsummer. Swimming, snorkeling. tennis, croquet, fishing, boating, water-skiing, horseback riding, guided mountain climbing on premises or nearby. Not recommended for children under 12. George G. Barnum, Jr., Managing Director; Michael Mudd, Resident Manager. (Call directly for rates.)

Directions: See general travel information on Nevis. Nisbet Plantation is a short taxi ride from the New Castle Airport.

CRONEY'S OLD MANOR ESTATE
Nevis, West Indies (1987)

Each of the inns of Nevis and Saint Kitts has some memorable feature. Here at Croney's (as it is known locally), I learned that the special feature was the cuisine.

I had been assured and reassured many times by my dinner companion (arranged through the courtesy of owner Vicki Knorr), a college professor from the Northeast, that the food here was little short of superb. "I have been coming here for many years and I have never had anything but the most fabulous meals," he declared.

Later, Vicki came out of the kitchen, where she does all the cooking, and we had a chance to talk about some of her favorite dishes.

"One of our appetizers, which our guests love, is sautéed shrimp, dipped in coconut. We have a set meal every night, and frequently we serve a baked half lobster, filled with a conch dressing and basted in butter. Everyone likes this."

She warmed to her subject. "Curried chicken we do with many condiments. We import our lamb from the States rather than New Zealand, but it is the seasonings that make it unusual. We use a lot of rosemary. We also stuff a leg of lamb with a very good spicy dressing."

Croney's is a restored sugar plantation dating back to a 1690 land grant, on the slopes of Mount Nevis, 800 feet above sea level on the tradewind side of the island. The garden, which utilizes the stone hearth kitchens of the plantation, is a lovely outdoor facility for lunches and is the scene on each Friday evening of the steak and lobster buffet with dancing to a steel band.

The *National Geographic* magazine mentioned it as being the best and longest-lived inn of all the Nevis plantations. One of the really intriguing features is the fact that a lot of the machinery connected with the original plantation has been left in place. This is the mid-19th century mechanized machinery, and it has the look of modern mechanical sculpture.

There are ten guest rooms, all with verandas and colorful quilts, and some with sitting rooms.

There is a fresh-water swimming pool surrounded by tropical foliage. The Cooperage Dining Room, a room where the coopers once made barrels for the sugar mill, provides another attractive ambience.

As I was leaving, Vicki pointed out that the temperature, year-round, ranges between 69 and 82 degrees Fahrenheit, which calls for a light blanket at night and definitely suggests a sweater for bare shoulders after dark.

CRONEY'S OLD MANOR ESTATE, P.O. Box 70, Charlestown, Nevis, West Indies, Leeward Islands; 809-469-5445. U.S. reservations: 800-223-9815. A 10-guestroom former Nevisian sugar estate. American plan. Open year-round, but check if planning to come in midsummer. Swimming pool on grounds. Free beach and town transportation. Horseback riding, sailing, snorkeling and more sports available. Not suitable for children under 12. No credit cards. Vicki and Gregg Knorr, Owner-Managers. (Call directly for rates.)

Directions: See general directions to Nevis and St. Kitts. Take taxi from airstrip and make arrangements to rent a car for a longer stay.

HERMITAGE
Nevis, West Indies (1987)

On this typical February morning in Nevis, which reminded me very much of June temperatures in the Berkshires, I was on the road that circles the island on my way toward a daytime visit to the Hermitage. I had enjoyed dinner there the previous evening with owners Maureen and Richard Lupinacci, along with Frank and Sis Paddock and Pam Barry. It had been one of those idyllic Nevisian evenings, with great food and lots of laughter.

Now I turned off onto a narrow road that was nothing more than two concrete tracks, with grass growing up between and brushing the bottom of the car. I was going ever upward toward Mount Nevis.

The night before I had learned that the main house of the Hermitage is one of the oldest on Nevis, and is featured in a book of Caribbean architecture. The photographs of the Hermitage in the book have some details that are quite impressive. This has been Maureen and Richard's home for some years, and relatively recently they turned it into an inn. They have roots in Quakertown, Pennsylvania, and Richard is with the bank in nearby Charlestown.

Alexander Hamilton Museum

There are three guest rooms in the main house and other guest rooms in outbuildings connected with the original plantation. Each guest room in the cottages has a gallery overlooking the swimming pool and a working kitchen, so it's possible to stay at the Hermitage on the European plan.

The wood walls of the dining room are adorned with some beautiful English china, patterned in light blue flower patterns, and paintings of native Nevisians. The living room has a very high peaked ceiling, and is decorated with a combination of antiques, prints of British soldiers in uniform, and maps.

There is a set meal every night—a three-course dinner with an emphasis on such Caribbean fish as red snapper, grouper, and parrot fish. I enjoyed their baked chicken with rice and papaya. Fish baked in banana leaves is another popular dish.

Incidentally, both Maureen and Richard are very much involved in restoration and preservation projects on Nevis, and are an excellent resource in helping the guests experience the Nevis of the past and present.

HERMITAGE, Nevis, West Indies; 809-469-5477. An 11-guestroom former plantation, now a comfortable Nevisian country inn. Modified American, or European plan on a weekly basis. Open year-round. Swimming pool on grounds. All of the activities of Nevis are nearby. Transportation to the beach can be arranged. Children over 6 can be accommodated in apartments en famille. *No credit cards. Richard and Maureen Lupinacci, Owners. (Call directly for rates.)*

Directions: See the main directions to both St. Kitts and Nevis. Consult with the inn about transport from the airstrip.

GOLDEN ROCK ESTATE
Nevis, West Indies (1987)

There were quite a few of us going home that morning: Ernie and Jane, Bill and Brucie, Shirley and Henry, and me. Tessa would stay on for another four or five days, and John and Nancy would leave the next day. However, we all made arrangements with Pam Barry, the innkeeper at Golden Rock, to return again in February of next year.

I believe, as is the case with other guests, we were all drawn together by the courtyard at Golden Rock, one side of which is formed by the mellowed old stone walls of a sugar plantation and the other by a bordering garden. The third side is open to the sea and faces east to the Atlantic.

It was here in the courtyard that we gathered for breakfast and lingered on for long chats, lots of laughter, and frequently arranged outings on Nevis. The courtyard also was the setting for lunch each day, although we did have the option of a picnic lunch that could be anything from hamburgers to broiled lobster at the inn's hut on a nearby beach, which was reached conveniently by car or by the Golden Rock bus. On one night a week the scene changed completely, when a Caribbean string band held forth, led by a clever flutist, and we were wafted away on the wings of the music.

My accommodations were similar to the others—a large bedroom, ample enough for two people to share without any difficulty at all. Like the others, it had its own terrace overlooking the Atlantic. From mine, I could watch the morning and afternoon games of tennis, while others shared the view of the swimming pool. There are also two- and three-bedroom villas for families or friends traveling together.

Like most of the other inns I visited on Nevis and Saint Kitts, Golden Rock is a former sugar plantation, and the gray stone main building has a lounge and reception area as well as a dining room. It is situated above the ocean in the foothill area of Mount Nevis.

There is an eleven-acre stretch of sandy beach owned by Golden Rock on the wild and surfy windward side of the island. There you can put on your mask and fins and experience some of the best in shore snorkeling that Nevis has to offer.

Now, as we gathered for one final breakfast and talked about returning, I learned that for some it would be the third or fourth trip. I can imagine that along about the first of December I'll start to figure out ways to return to Golden Rock again.

GOLDEN ROCK ESTATE, Nevis, West Indies; 809-469-5346. U. S. reservations: 800-223-5186 (Northeast), 800-223-5581 (nationwide). A 12-guestroom (private baths) inn with additional larger accommodations for families or couples traveling together. Modified American plan includes breakfast and dinner. Open year-round. Swimming, tennis, beach, sports available on premises. Numerous opportunities for visiting historic sites such as the Alexander Hamilton birthplace, Fig Tree Church, and others nearby. Arrangements can be made to rent Mini-Moke automobiles. Pam Barry, Innkeeper. (Call directly for rates.)

Directions: To reach Nevis consult earlier section.

MONTPELIER PLANTATION INN
Nevis, West Indies (1987)

While the guests at Golden Rock Plantation were predominantly American and the mix at Nisbet Plantation Inn was about equally divided between Britons and Americans, the percentages at Montpelier slightly favored the British guests.

Perhaps this can be partially attributed to the fact that proprietors James and Celia Milnes Gaskell are themselves quite British, and the ambience of this resort inn, with its beautiful English furniture and oil portraits of ancestors, is decidedly Albionesque.

When you phone or write for information and reservations, be sure to ask for a copy of the mimeographed general information on Montpelier; a more informative précis of what to expect I have seldom read. As well as mentioning the hillside location overlooking the sea, the "fast-playing hard (tennis) court in lovely surroundings," and the many other amenities, it includes what it does *not* have, such as no telephones in the guest rooms, no dress code, no tennis pro. A very handsome four-color brochure has some lovely views of the stone buildings and gorgeous gardens, as well as the swimming pool and the private beach nearby.

Some of the guest rooms, in individual cottages, have an ocean view and the others have an inviting view of Mount Nevis. Since the general outlook is to the west, guests can sit on their private patios and watch the sun go down. It's fun to wander around Montpelier, with its stone terraces and gardens.

In its description of the cuisine at Montpelier, the general information mentions fresh lobster and conch, "imaginative use of local produce," and that Montpelier keeps its own pigs and sheep. "The outside dining terrace gives views past floodlit palm trees to the ocean two miles away and to the lights of Saint Kitts, twelve miles distant."

James Gaskell summed up Montpelier for me: "It is known to a few perceptive travel writers and agents, and to a number of guests who hope that it will retain its personal nature, its consistently good food, and its happiness. They need not worry."

MONTPELIER PLANTATION INN, Nevis, West Indies; 809-469-5462. U.S. reservations: 203-438-3793. A 16-guestroom resort-inn on a hillside overlooking the sea, with mountain views. All rooms have two double beds and showers. Modified American plan includes breakfast and dinner. Lunch, if desired, additional. Private beach house on Pinney's Beach with transportation provided. Tennis, swimming pool, water sports, hiking, ocean beach available on premises or nearby. Not recommended for children under 12, especially in winter season. No credit cards. James and Celia Milnes Gaskell, Owners. (Call directly for rates.)

Directions: See general directions for transportation to the island of Nevis. Take a taxi from the airstrip to Montpelier, although arrangements can be made to rent a car in Charlestown en route. It is necessary to stop at the police station to get a Nevis driving license.

RAWLINS PLANTATION
Saint Kitts, West Indies (1987)

Philip Walwyn and I were strolling about the grounds and gardens of the Rawlins Plantation, which is family owned and managed and has the atmosphere of an English country house.

"The first Walwyn came to Nevis in 1677," he told me. "Later, the family moved to Saint Kitts, and in 1790 became owners of the plantation. The original house burned down some years ago, and the new buildings designed by us in 1970 have been carefully blended into the ruins of the old plantation works.

"This boiling house that you see here is a hundred years old and was used to manufacture fancy molasses, but is now a cool courtyard, where we dine every day.

"We are about 350 feet above sea level and Mount Misery, behind us, rises to nearly 4,000 feet. That island you see off the coast is Statia."

Earlier, I had picked up my rented car at Basseterre, the principal town on Saint Kitts, where the big jets land. I had driven out to the far end of the island and turned into the sugar cane fields, where the waving stalks were half again as high as my automobile. I parked my car on the grass, and a gentleman with faded blue shorts and a blue shirt appeared almost instantly and introduced himself as Philip Walwyn, the proprietor.

As we continued our pleasant walk, he pointed out the eight cottage accommodations, including a windmill, originally built in the 17th century to provide power to grind sugar cane. It has been converted into a suite, complete with a bathroom and sitting room. There are also guest rooms in the plantation house. These are all light and airy and attractively furnished.

"I would say that we offer peace, unpolluted air, beautiful surroundings, relaxation, and excellent food, most of which is homegrown. We have a set meal every evening at 8:00 p.m., and we have provisions for special diets. Our cuisine is not really French, and the local meats and vegetables are prepared in more of a western style.

"I'd say that Saint Kitts, and particularly Rawlins, is not for the person who is looking for the 'bright lights.' There's plenty to do; the rain forest and the craters are accessible to those who enjoy vigorous walking, and we have a pool fed from our own spring in the mountain. There are two golf courses near Basseterre, and we have our own 75-foot catamaran. By the way, the five-minute drive to the beach is provided without charge."

As we walked back to my car, I heard Philip use that wonderful expression that seems to be so typical of English hoteliers and innkeepers, "Do tell your readers about Rawlins Plantation here on Saint Kitts; we're a small inn so we can look after people very well."

RAWLINS PLANTATION, Box 340, St. Kitts, West Indies; 809-465-6221. U.S. reservations: 617-367-8959. Modified American plan includes breakfast and dinner, afternoon tea, and laundry service. In season minimum stay 4 days. Open year-round. Swimming pool, grass tennis courts, and lawn sports on grounds. Golf, tennis, walking and hiking, beach and water sports nearby. Open year-round. No credit cards. Philip and Frances Walwyn, Owners. (Call directly for rates.)

Directions: See the general directions for reaching St. Kitts by air. Arrangements can be made with Rawlins Plantation for either a taxi or a car rental.

Index

The rates listed here represent a general range of rates for two people for one night at each inn and should not be considered firm quotations. Breakfast may or may not be included, and tax and gratuities are usually not included. The rates cover both high and low seasons. It is well to inquire as to the availability of various plans and packages.

Rates are approximate for 2 people for 1 night
*B&B or other rates available

AP means 3 meals included
MAP means lunch and dinner included

*B&B or other rates available

Rates are approximate for 2 people for 1 night

AP means 3 meals included

MAP means lunch and dinner included
*B&B or other rates available

Rates are approximate for 2 people for 1 night
*B&B or other rates available

AP means 3 meals included
*B&B or other rates available

MAP means lunch and dinner included
*B&B or other rates available
**Weekly AP rate available